D0083459

FLORIDA STATE
UNIVERSITY LIBRARIES

JUL 11 1995

TALLAHASSEE, FLORIDA

Turning Point

Turning Point

The Gulf War and U.S. Military Strategy

Edited by

L. Benjamin Ederington
and
Michael J. Mazarr

Westview Press
BOULDER • SAN FRANCISCO • OXFORD

UA
23
T85
1994

All rights reserved. No part of this publication may be reproduced or transmitted in any form or by any means, electronic or mechanical, including photocopy, recording, or any information storage and retrieval system, without permission in writing from the publisher.

Copyright © 1994 by Westview Press, Inc.

Published in 1994 in the United States of America by Westview Press, Inc., 5500 Central Avenue, Boulder, Colorado 80301-2877, and in the United Kingdom by Westview Press, 36 Lonsdale Road, Summertown, Oxford OX2 7EW

Library of Congress Cataloging-in-Publication Data
Turning point : the Gulf War and U.S. military strategy / edited by L.
Benjamin Ederington and Michael J. Mazarr.
    p.   cm.
Includes bibliographical references and index.
ISBN 0-8133-2292-8
1. United States—Military policy. 2. Military art and science—
United States. 3. Persian Gulf War, 1991. I. Ederington,
Benjamin. II. Mazarr, Michael J.
UA23.T85   1995   94-25303
355'.033573'09049—dc20   CIP

Printed and Bound in the United States of America

⊗   The paper used in this publication meets the requirements
      of the American National Standard for Permanence of Paper
      for Printed Library Materials Z39.48-1984.

10   9   8   7   6   5   4   3   2   1

Contents

Part III: Elements of Future Military Strategic Thought

Part IV: Summing Up

Preface

Why another book on the Persian Gulf War, four years after its sudden conclusion? The simple answer is that this is not primarily a book about the Gulf War itself. It offers a wide-ranging look at the future of U.S. defense policy and military strategy that takes the Gulf War as its point of departure.

Our goal in this project was straightforward: to gather the best authorities on foreign and defense policy and obtain from them their most trenchant thoughts on what the future holds. Thus we were lucky enough to recruit two of the most farsighted strategic thinkers writing today—Edward Luttwak and Martin van Creveld; four of the very best American political scientists—Robert Jervis, Joseph Nye, Richard Rosecrance, and Thomas Schelling; perhaps the West's most eminent military historian, John Keegan; four top U.S. military analysts in Kenneth Allard, Eliot Cohen, John Cushman, and Jeffrey Record; and three first-rate regional experts (and experienced military men) in Edward Atkeson, Larry Budge, and Thomas McNaugher.

In some cases, these writers provided us with shorthand versions of their most important recent arguments. Thus Edward Luttwak summarizes his case for the shift from an era of geopolitics to one of geoeconomics; Richard Rosecrance restates his vision of a new "concert of powers," and Joseph Nye his model of "soft power"; Eliot Cohen reprises his concluding thoughts in the Gulf War air power survey; and Martin van Creveld recalls his case for a transformation in the nature of warfare. In other chapters, as in those by Thomas Schelling and Robert Jervis, the authors apply decades of thought on a particular problem—deterrence—to the current era in new and illuminating ways.

One key characteristic of any successful anthology is that the various chapters talk to one another. This can be done explicitly, with cross-references and mutual quotation. But it is often more revealing—and less obtrusive—when done implicitly, when chapters quietly argue with one another or modify each other's conclusions by elaborating upon reasoning offered elsewhere.

We have tried to ensure such intellectual cross-fertilization. Thus Eliot Cohen, Edward Luttwak, Jeffrey Record, and Martin van Creveld all have somewhat different things to say about the utility of airpower. Luttwak and Richard Rosecrance discuss the nature of U.S. power-projection strat-

ix

egies, and Record builds on their proposals in his chapter. John Cushman takes the theme of multilateralism developed in the early chapters and shows its complexities and challenges in military command-and-control arrangements. Martin van Creveld points to a future dominated by low-intensity conflict; Robert Jervis examines the difficulty in applying traditional deterrence to such wars.

In addition to communicating on specific issues, the chapters that follow share a number of broad themes. One deals with the increasing prominence of economic, as opposed to military or "geopolitical," concerns at the heart of international politics. Another suggests the impossibility of a new *pax Americana*—but notes the overriding importance of continued U.S. leadership in a multilateral era. A third theme deals with the change in U.S. military strategy from global containment of a single foe to rapid and decisive interventions in regional conflicts. And the attentive reader will discover other, less obvious threads running throughout the book as well.

Finally, as the mix of authors suggests, we aimed in this volume to promote a discussion between military strategists and political scientists. At this period of strategic flux, such a dialogue is more important than ever. Vast changes in international politics carry dramatic significance for the future of warfare; startling evolutions in the character of war may in turn affect the shape of world politics. Now more than ever, military analysts and political scientists must grasp the implications of each others' work. Our hope is that this volume can contribute in some small way to that process.

Michael J. Mazarr
Washington, D.C.

Notes on the Contributors

Dr. Edward N. Luttwak is a senior fellow and director of the Geoeconomics Program at the Center for Strategic and International Studies in Washington, D.C. He is the author of eight books on military history and strategy, including *Strategy: the Logic of War and Peace* (Harvard University Press, 1987), *On the Meaning of Victory* (Simon & Schuster, 1986), and *The Pentagon and the Art of War* (Simon & Schuster, 1985). Dr. Luttwak received his Ph.D. from Johns Hopkins University.

Dr. Richard Rosecrance is professor of Political Science and director of the Center for International Relations at the University of California at Los Angeles. Before joining the faculty at UCLA, he was the Carpenter Professor of International and Comparative Politics at Cornell University. His most recent works have included *America's Economic Resurgence: A Bold New Strategy* (Harper and Row, 1990) and, as coeditor, *Beyond Realism: Domestic Factors and Grand Strategy* (Cornell University Press, 1993). Dr. Rosecrance received his B.A. from Swarthmore College and his Ph.D. from Harvard.

Dr. Joseph S. Nye, Jr. was recently selected to serve as chair of the National Intelligence Council. Previously, Dr. Nye had been director of the Center for International Affairs at Harvard and continues to hold the university's Clarence Dillon Professorship of International Affairs. His extensive writings on international relations theory include *Understanding International Conflicts* (HarperCollins, 1993), *Bound to Lead: The Changing Nature of American Power* (HarperCollins, 1990), and *Power and Interdependence* (with Robert Keohane, HarperCollins, 1977). A Rhodes scholar, Dr. Nye received his B.A. from Princeton and his Ph.D. in Government from Harvard.

Dr. Eliot A. Cohen recently completed directing the U.S. Air Force's official analysis of the Gulf War, the *Gulf War Air Power Survey*. He is currently director of Strategic Studies at the Paul H. Nitze School of Advanced International Studies at Johns Hopkins University. Dr. Cohen previously taught at the Naval War College and Harvard University. He is the author of several books, including *Citizens and Soldiers* (Cornell

University Press, 1985) and *Military Misfortunes* (with John Gooch, Free Press, 1990). Dr. Cohen earned both his A.B. and his Ph.D. from Harvard.

Mr. John Keegan is currently senior defense and military correspondent at *The Daily Telegraph* in London. A career military historian and journalist, Mr. Keegan studied at Balliol College, Oxford, and was a senior lecturer in the War Studies Department at Sandhurst. He is the author of numerous books on military history, including his edited volume, *Churchill's Generals* (G. Weidenfeld, 1991), *The Second World War* (Viking Press, 1990), *The Price of Admiralty* (Viking Press, 1989), and his classic work, *The Face of Battle* (Penguin Books, 1976).

Lieutenant General John H. Cushman, U.S. Army (Ret.) During his thirty-eight-year career in the U.S. Army, General Cushman, a graduate of the U.S. Military Academy at West Point, commanded the 101st Airborne Division and the I Corps Group that defended the western sector of Korea's demilitarized zone. Since his retirement, he has been an affiliate of the Program on Information Policy Research at Harvard and is the author of several of its publications, including *The Korea Command and Other Cases* (1986), *Issues in Mideast Coalition Command* (1991), and *Lessons of the Desert Storm End Game* (in progress).

Dr. Thomas C. Schelling is currently Distinguished Professor of Economics and Public Affairs at the University of Maryland. After graduating with a B.A. in Economics from the University of California at Berkeley and a Ph.D. in Economics from Harvard, Dr. Schelling taught at Yale and Harvard Universities before joining Harvard's John F. Kennedy School of Government in 1969. He is the author of numerous works on military strategy and arms control, including *Choice and Consequence* (Harvard University Press, 1984), *The Strategy of Conflict* (Harvard University Press, 1960), and his classic work on nuclear strategy, *Arms and Influence* (Yale University Press, 1966).

Dr. Robert Jervis currently holds the Adlai E. Stevenson Chair of International Affairs at the Institute of War and Peace Studies of Columbia University. Before joining the faculty at Columbia, Dr. Jervis taught at Harvard and the University of California at Los Angeles. He received his B.A. from Oberlin College and his Ph.D. in International Relations from the University of California at Berkeley. Among his numerous works on nuclear strategy are *The Meaning of the Nuclear Revolution* (Cornell University Press, 1989), *Psychology of Deterrence* (Johns Hopkins University Press, 1985), and *Perception and Misperception in International Politics* (Princeton, 1976).

Mr. Jeffrey Record is the author of *Hollow Victory: A Contrary View of the Gulf War* (Brassey's, 1993). During the past twenty years, he has served as a legislative assistant to Senator Sam Nunn, as a columnist for the *Baltimore Sun,* and as a defense analyst at the Brookings Institution, the

BDM Corporation, and the Hudson Institute. Mr. Record's previous publications include *Revising U.S. Military Strategy* (Brassey's, 1984) and *Beyond Military Reform* (Brassey's, 1988).

Colonel C. Kenneth Allard is currently Senior Military Fellow at the Institute for National Strategic Studies, National Defense University and an adjunct professor in the National Security Studies Program at Georgetown University. He holds a master's degree from Harvard University and a doctorate from the Fletcher School of Law & Diplomacy, Tufts University. He has served on the faculty of the United States Military Academy at West Point, as special assistant to the Army Chief of Staff, and as Dean of Students at the National War College. His book, *Command, Control and the Common Defense,* (Yale University Press, 1990) won the 1991 National Security Book Award (Furniss Prize).

Major General Larry D. Budge, U.S. Army (Ret.) After thirty-one years as an active duty U.S. Army officer, Budge retired with the rank of major general. A graduate of the U.S. Military Academy at West Point and a Rhodes Scholar, General Budge received an M.A. in Philosophy, Politics, and Economics from Oxford University. During his military career, Budge served on the staff of the National Intelligence Council and as a brigade commander and, subsequently, as a division chief of staff with the U.S. Army in Europe.

Major General Edward B. Atkeson, U.S. Army (Ret.) is a senior associate at the Center for Strategic and International Studies and a senior fellow at the Institute of Land Warfare. During his military career, he served on the staff of the director of central intelligence as national intelligence officer for general purpose forces and was deputy chief of staff for intelligence with the U.S. Army in Europe. A graduate of the U.S. Military Academy and the Army War College, General Atkeson holds an M.B.A. from Syracuse University and was a fellow at the Center for International Affairs at Harvard University. He is the author of *The Final Argument of Kings: Reflections on the Art of War* (Hero Books, 1988)

Dr. Thomas L. McNaugher is a senior fellow in the Foreign Policy Studies Program at the Brookings Institution. He received a B.S. degree from the U.S. Military Academy and M.P.A. and Ph.D. degrees from Harvard University. Before joining Brookings, Dr. McNaugher was a policy analyst at the Rand Corporation and an active duty U.S. Army officer. His several books include *Arms and Oil: U.S. Military Strategy and the Persian Gulf* (Brookings, 1985) and *New Weapons, Old Politics: America's Military Procurement Muddle* (Brookings, 1989).

Dr. Martin van Creveld is currently professor of History at Hebrew University in Jerusalem. He received his Ph.D. from the London School of Economics and was a fellow of War Studies at Kings College, Cambridge. Author of more than six books on military history, Dr. van Creveld's most recent works have included *The Transformation of War* (Free Press, 1991), *Technology and War* (Free Press, 1989), and *Command in War* (Harvard University Press, 1985).

PART ONE

The Context for Military Strategy

1

The Global Setting of U.S. Military Power

Edward N. Luttwak

Certainly in the short term, possibly for a long time, the global setting of U.S. military power will continue to be shaped by its own achievement, or precisely by the perceptions left behind by the events and outcome of the 1991 Gulf War.

In general terms, those perceptions strongly reinforce the ability of the United States to deter acts of aggression that unambiguously affect oft-declared U.S. interests. The United States, to be sure, was undoubtedly a superpower even before January 1991—indeed by then it was the world's only superpower. But until the early results of the bombardment of Iraq became apparent, it was *not* generally appreciated that the United States could swiftly and very powerfully punish acts of aggression *without* having to mobilize and deploy a vast multiservice array of forces. To be sure, there was just such a mobilization and deployment after the Iraqi invasion of Kuwait. But once the air offensive started, it became clear that the United States could have acted much more swiftly by using airpower alone. By contrast, the failure to overthrow the Ba'ath regime or dislodge Saddam Hussein from power undercut the deterrent effect of the ground components of Desert Storm.

Even before the Gulf War, the United States could undoubtedly deter some potential aggressors because of its overall military capabilities. But because of the time, cost, and political exposure required to deploy an expeditionary force of Desert Shield proportions, potential aggressors of considerable strength (regionally) could calculate—as Saddam Hussein obviously did—that the United States would be unwilling to deploy an expeditionary force against them. On that basis, they could remain un-deterred by the theoretical potential of U.S. military power as a whole.

But in the wake of the Gulf War, potential aggressors must contend with the demonstrated capabilities of U.S. airpower alone, whose use against them does *not* entail the time, cost, and political exposure of any very large, multiservice, expeditionary deployment.

In other words, Desert Shield demonstrated both the vast capabilities and acute limitations of the United States as an expeditionary military power, that is, the long delay till full deployment, the vast cost, the potential for casualties, and the resulting tenuousness of the domestic political consensus. By contrast, the air dimension of Desert Storm demonstrated the ability of the United States to act swiftly and very effectively, with none of the above limitations. Thus, more precisely, as of the eve of combat, Desert Shield by itself had showed to a potential aggressor of considerable strength that the United States could not deploy enough forces to reliably defend, let alone counterattack, for months on end and would only do so (given the requisite cost and risks) if the most valuable direct interests were at stake. Desert Shield thus weakened U.S. deterrence vis-à-vis strong potential aggressors if their aims did *not* plainly threaten the most valuable U.S. interests. The air dimension of Desert Storm by contrast, had the opposite effect of greatly reinforcing U.S. deterrence, by showing to potential aggressors that their ground strength could be made irrelevant while their vulnerabilities to air attack could be fully and swiftly exploited, at low cost and low risk.

In addition, the Desert Shield experience has left behind another lesson for potential aggressors, one that is certainly unfortunate from the U.S. point of view. If any potential aggressors are *not* deterred by what happened to Iraq for whatever reason—notably including their failure to appreciate the capabilities of U.S. strategic airpower—they might well deduce from Iraq's experience that aggression must be supplemented by preclusive actions to inhibit or at least delay U.S. expeditionary deployments into the theater—and by preemptive attacks to disrupt these deployments in their early, fragile phases, to the degree that they cannot be prevented. (The denial by fire of the Sarajevo airport by Serb forces may be an early example.)

Finally, it must be recognized that even in its enhanced post-Desert Storm state, U.S. deterrence is still inevitably subject to many limitations. Most notably, it can only reasonably be expected to deter acts of aggression that are (1) unambiguous, that is, not plausibly deniable; (2) on a significant scale; (3) vulnerable to air action only, or whose protagonists are so vulnerable; and (4) aimed at very important U.S. interests or close allies or that otherwise affect values that can plausibly be depicted as very important U.S. interests in themselves.

These are substantial limitations. As of this writing they have allowed the prolonged continuation of Serbian military action in Bosnia-Hercegovina. (The only evidence that suggests the possibility that the leaders of the Serbian government did modify their conduct for fear of a U.S. military response are the steps it has taken to keep its involvement plausibly deniable; ostensibly, the fighting is carried out not by government units but by local volunteers.)

The Downfall of Geopolitics

It is now becoming evident that the collapse of the Soviet Union has caused an even wider collapse of the entire phenomenon that may very loosely be described as "Geopolitics," that is, the exercise of military-diplomatic strength in pursuit of territorial security or territorial expansion and of influence over other states, or to resist such influence. More precisely, geopolitics as here defined[1] has become provincialized, what was till very recently the chief concern of the major states in the central arena of world affairs now persists only in the peripheral and backward parts of the world where territorial struggles continue. By contrast, the greatest states in the central arena of world affairs are preoccupied by a new struggle for economic leverage and industrial supremacy, here defined as "geoeconomics."

In the Middle East, in the Balkans, on the Indian subcontinent and other such unfortunate parts of the world, territorial (and ethnic/territorial) struggles continue as they have throughout history. In those zones of conflict, military strength remains as important as ever. And so does diplomacy in its classic form, still serving as it always has to convert even the most marginally plausible uses of military strength into an actual source of influence—whether to threaten adversaries or to reassure weaker allies.

But in the central arena of world affairs, where Americans, Europeans, Japanese, and other peoples both collaborate and compete, the situation has changed drastically. War between them has become almost unthinkable, while external dangers of attack are either remote or localized now that the Soviet Union is no longer a threat and no longer arms and supports aggressive smaller allies such as Cuba, Vietnam, and Syria. Hence, both military strength and classic diplomacy have quite suddenly lost most of their traditional importance within this arena.

But the millennium of brotherly love has yet not arrived. First, the major states in the central arena of world affairs—and certainly the United States—still have geopolitical contentions with the more aggressive and politically backward of the peripheral states that have been left behind by the geoeconomic transformation. Second, the condition of the former Soviet Union and of China is not sufficiently stable to ensure the durability of their very new commitment to the path of geoeconomics; a reversion to geopolitics remains a definite possibility.

Moreover, even between the major states the millennium has not yet arrived. The internal solidarity of peoples still derives from a common national identity that excludes other peoples. To say "American" is to speak of something that is meaningful only because there are non-Americans. In many cases, it is still a cultural identity that defines the "we" as against the "them." To be French or Italian or even Brazilian is a much more specific cultural "we" than the multicultural American "we." In the case of Japan and Korea, this exclusive identity is still widely imagined to be racial, although it is enough to see a Japanese crowd, ranging in color from pink-white to olive green to expose the fantasy. But whatever the nature or justification of such national identities, world politics is still dominated by states (or the association of states that is now the European Union) that are based on a "we" that excludes a larger "them."

States are of course *territorial* entities, marked off against each other by borders, jealously claimed, and still often closely guarded. In fact borders have now been extended more than ever before to include 200-mile "economic zones" into the sea, while fiscal borders go even beyond them, as each state seeks to tax multinational corporations and multinational incomes at the expense of all other states.

Therefore, even when there is no thought of any military confrontation, even when they cooperate every day both bilaterally and in dozens of international organizations, the very nature of states is relentlessly adversarial.

But states and governments are not merely adversarial by nature, and they do not merely reflect, as a mirror might, underlying national identities. Consciously or not, their everyday actions and declarations meant to protect, promote, or advance "national interests" also tend to stimulate, encourage, accommodate, harness, and exploit adversarial popular sentiments that define an "us" against a hostile "them." In the backwaters of world politics where territorial conflicts continue, wars or threats of war provide an ample outlet for hostile sentiments. But when it comes to the central arena of world affairs, where Americans, Europeans, and Japanese collaborate and contend, it is chiefly by economic means that adversarial attitudes are now expressed.

The Rise of Geoeconomics

This new version of the ancient rivalry of states I have called geoeconomics.[2] In it, investment capital for industry provided or guided by the state is the equivalent of firepower; product development subsidized by the state is the equivalent of weapon innovation; and market penetration supported by the state replaces military bases and garrisons on foreign soil as well as diplomatic influence. The very same things—investment, research and development, and marketing—are also done every day by private enterprises for purely business reasons. But when the state intervenes to encourage, help, or direct those very same activities, it is no longer plain economics that is going on, but rather geoeconomics.

The geoeconomic arsenal includes other weapons old and new. Tariffs can be merely taxes, imposed with no other aim in mind than to raise revenue; likewise, quota limits and outright import prohibitions may be meant only to cope with an acute shortage of hard currency. But when the purpose of such trade barriers is to protect domestic industry and allow it to grow, it is again geoeconomics that we face—current equivalents of the defended frontiers and fortified lines of war.

There are also hidden trade barriers, the geoeconomic equivalents of the ambush. These include the deliberate framing of health and safety or any other regulations on labeling, packaging, or recycling characteristics to covertly keep out imports. Prohibitive tariffs or simply import bans can do that more straightforwardly, but most countries have signed the General Agreement on Tariffs and Trade (GATT), which prohibits the imposition of tariffs at will. Thus some countries will resort to regulatory trickery to camouflage trade barriers. In the case of Japan, for example, until the 1980s foreign cars were *individually* inspected for compliance with Japanese safety rules. Importers were forced to pay an inspection fee for each car and to wait until customs officials completed their inspections, car by car. Had the U.S. government adopted the same rule, it alone might have stopped the great flood of Japanese automobile imports.

But what most resembles the ambush are the customs-house conspiracies that circumvent the GATT rule against arbitrary tariffs and quotas. During the early 1980s, for example, the French government decided that its domestic electronics industry could learn to produce VCRs. But with the Japanese already in mass production, French industry clearly needed to gain time. The solution was to issue a routine administrative decree that required all VCRs imported from overseas to pass customs inspection at Bayeux, a very small town in Normandy, with a badly understaffed customs house. As Japanese VCR exports to France collapsed, the Japanese government duly complained—but not too much; it could not run the risk of a comparison.

Imports of new high-technology products that threaten domestic industries can sometimes be defeated and not merely delayed by employing the device of compulsory "standards." In telecommunications and broadcasting, for example, frequencies are allocated by the state for each separate purpose. If new foreign products threaten local industry, the relevant state authority can stop all imports by announcing that it must first set standards. Then it can secretly consult with local industry so as to deliberately set standards that will exclude imported products. At that point, the announcement of the new standards is held up until local industry has tooled up and fully prepared for mass production. When the market is finally opened, the locals can start to sell—while foreign exporters are just starting to reconfigure their products.

Arbitrary standards can keep out exports even when there is nothing new to regulate. For example, Japanese standards require that plywood be made of tropical hardwoods. The result has been to protect Japan's plywood industry from U.S. and Scandinavian competitors that rely on cheaper softwood raw materials. (And there is a side effect: the destruction of tropical rain forests.)

Trade barriers can sometimes be used to assist the growth of export industries. Countries that have scarce natural resources can impose export taxes on raw materials but not on worked products to encourage the growth of local processing. Most African countries, for example, no longer allow the export of raw logs, but only of wood already cut into planks and studs. Saudi Arabia and other oil producers achieve the same effect by selling crude oil at high prices while offering refined products and more especially petrochemicals at low prices.

But in geoeconomics, as in war, the offensive weapons are more important. Of these, research and development force-fed with government support and the taxpayers' money is perhaps the most important. Just as in war the artillery conquers territory by fire, which the infantry can then occupy, the aim is to conquer the industrial territory of the future by achieving a decisive technological superiority. Japan's new "Real World" computing program is only one of the many such efforts now under way in the central arena of geoeconomics. The European Union and the United States both sponsor their own microelectronics and computing programs, as well as many smaller ones.

In 1990, for example, the U.S. Advanced Battery Consortium was established to develop a more efficient power source for electric cars than lead-acid batteries. With $130 million from the U.S. Department of Energy and another $130 million jointly provided by General Motors, Ford, and Chrysler, the Consortium's purpose is to fund R&D projects. The collaboration of all three U.S. automobile companies means that this is not merely a business undertaking but a U.S. geoeconomic offensive against the Japanese automobile industry, fittingly carried out by a typically Japanese-style government-plus-industry consortium.

State-encouraged research and development is crucial, but production may also need assistance. Airbus Industrie thus receives operating subsidies, and so do many other favored private companies and entire industries. Often there is no need for overt payments; government purchasing on generous terms achieves the same effect. Japan, for example, had no computer industry to speak of in 1960 when the Ministry of International Trade and Industry (MITI) launched a five-year program for the national production of computers.[3] The first steps were the imposition of stiff tariffs, the funding of computer research, and the offer of low-interest loans for buyers. (IBM had already established a factory in Japan, but its computers were not considered "national" enough; only the customers of its Japanese competitors could receive credit on favorable terms.)

Next, MITI offered to allow IBM's U.S. and British competitors to sell on the Japanese market if they agreed to form joint ventures with Japanese companies and agreed to share their technology with them. When IBM's System 360 made the joint-venture Japanese computers obsolete, MITI's response was the Super High Performance Electronic Computer Program, which pooled the resources of government and industry laboratories in an effort to catch up. In the meantime, the government helped the weak local industry by purchasing its products even though they were both inferior and more costly than IBM's. And so it continued, until two decades later Fujitsu emerged as the equal of a greatly weakened IBM.

The final offensive weapon is "predatory finance." Export sales of aircraft, for example, can be secured against stronger competitors by offering loans at below-market interest rates. The United States has its Export-Import Bank to provide loan guarantees, and all major trading countries have their equivalents. Thus, foreigners can routinely expect to pay lower interest rates for their credit purchases than local borrowers, but the accusation of predatory finance is reserved for cases in which interest rates are suddenly reduced in the course of a fought-over sale.

The present relevance of all of the above is that the persistence of geoeconomic rivalries reflects the existence of national attitudes that interfere with geopolitical collaborations against third parties and even imply the theoretical possibility of a reversion to geopolitical hostility.

New Elite Goals

In traditional geopolitics, the goals were to secure and extend the physical control of territory and to gain diplomatic influence over foreign governments. The corresponding geoeconomic goal is not to achieve the highest possible standard of living for a country's population, but rather to acquire or protect desirable roles in the world economy. Who will develop the next generation of jet airliners, computers, biotechnology products, advanced materials, financial services, and all other high-value output in industries large and small? Will the designers, technologists, managers, and financiers be Americans, Europeans, or East Asians? The winners will have those highly rewarding and controlling roles, while the losers will only have the retail business and assembly lines—if their home markets are large enough or if fully assembled imports are kept out by trade barriers. We have already seen that when transplants replace domestic production, the local employment of manual and semiskilled labor may continue, but finance and all higher management is transferred back to the country of origin.

Geoeconomics is therefore a very appropriate projection on the world scene of typically meritocratic and professional ambitions, just as war and diplomacy reflected typically aristocratic ambitions, offering lots of desirable roles for military officers and diplomats who were aristocrats, or acted as if they were aristocrats, or at least relished aristocratic satisfactions. The meritocracy of technologists and managers is not much less modest. They do not desire bemedaled uniforms or the diplomat's ceremonies, but they also want to be *in command* on the world scene as the makers of technology and not mere producers under license; as the developers of products, not mere assemblers; as industrialists, not mere importers.

But not all states are equally inclined or equally capable of participating in the new struggle. Quite a few already have economically activist policies and bureaucracies or are seeking to acquire them (Japan is their model). If they can advance rapidly in skills and education, they may succeed at the new game even if their total economy is small; modern technology offers ever more diverse avenues for industry, including some specialized enough not to require production on any huge scale. Thus, small but well-educated populations can be much more successful in geoeconomics, as in plain business, than they could ever be in world politics, where size always counts and may alone be decisive.

Be they large or small, most third-world states, however, are cursed with bureaucracies too ineffective to engage in geoeconomic activities. In quite a few, and almost everywhere in Africa, any government funding for any purpose simply becomes another opportunity for wholesale thievery, while every regulation is corruptly circumvented (for example, raw logs are still exported by bribing customs officials to classify them as planks). Within Europe, the members of the European Union were originally variously inclined, from always state-minded France to newly free-market United Kingdom—but as a group they now seem set to collectively pursue geoeconomic goals.

As for the United States, it tends to engage in much geoeconomic practice while loudly rejecting its principles. Listening to their speeches, one might think that many U.S. political leaders are genuinely unaware of the fact that the two largest U.S. export industries are agriculture and aerospace—both subject to much state intervention and both the recipients of much generous assistance.

Just as there is no successful warfare without effective armed forces, there can be no successful geoeconomic action without economic bureaucrats both effective and honest. But even in advanced countries where bureaucrats are honest and even efficient, especially in advanced countries, actually their central role in any geoeconomic action is bound to distort it, for consciously or otherwise they will manipulate what is being done for their own purposes. Perfectly honest, well-meaning bureaucrats who happen to serve in economic ministries or departments of commerce and industry can be expected to pursue the normal ambition of bureaucrats—to serve the state well and to gain recognition and power in the process—by furthering their own geoeconomic schemes of industrial defense or industrial conquest. Equally honest bureaucrats who happen to be in foreign affairs ministries may pursue their own equally normal ambitions by furthering schemes of tariff reduction and international economic cooperation. But in the states that are in the central arena of world affairs, where war and classic diplomacy have so greatly declined in importance, the bureaucratic balance is now tilted.

For European and Japanese bureaucrats especially, but increasingly for U.S. bureaucrats as well, geoeconomics offers the only possible substitute for the military and diplomatic roles of the past. Only by invoking geoeconomic imperatives can they claim authority over mere business leaders and the citizenry at large. Those who were ambitious enough to seek career advancement in the great institutions of the state will not want to devote their lives to such petty warfare and diplomacy as will continue in backward regions of the world even in a fully achieved geoeconomic era. Well before that point is reached, most first-world bureaucrats and their bureaucracies will eagerly embrace geoeconomics because without it, mere commerce alone would reign on the main stage of international life. With it, the authority of state bureaucrats can be asserted anew, not in the name of strategy and security as in the past, but rather to protect "vital economic interests" by means of geoeconomic defenses, offensives, diplomacy, and intelligence.[4]

In the train of history, the last wagons—the poorest countries with the most inefficient and corrupt state bureaucracies—cannot *yet* wage wars. Their armies are incapable of operating much beyond their frontiers, being fit only to rob and oppress their own citizens at home. For the same reason, those states cannot yet act geoeconomically either, or indeed do anything at all to their own economies than would be better than doing nothing at all.

The wagons in the middle—countries with partly developed economies and state bureaucracies of like quality, some poorer such as India and Pakistan and some richer such as Turkey or Iraq—are all capable of war against each other and are usually much too absorbed in territorial conflicts to seriously pursue geoeconomic policies. Often their governments do try to develop industry, but except in the case of military industries, their efforts are usually weak and inconsistent. And those that are free of warlike entanglements, such as Brazil, for example, attempt geoeconomic action at their peril, for neither their economies nor their bureaucracies are up to the task.

The wagons at the head of history's train—the United States, the countries of Europe, Japan, and others like them—are all materially capable of waging war effectively, but their social atmosphere is allergic to it. Certainly their populations and governing elites are now convinced that they cannot usefully fight one another with fire and arms, virtually for any reason. Yet their states are still organized for warlike rivalry, and so they seem set to pursue its same purposes by geoeconomic means.

To be sure, rulers and states have always pursued economic goals and have never lacked for economic quarrels. More than two thousand years ago, Rome and Carthage fought over Mediterranean trade as well as for security against each other and for glory—and commercial wars were hardly a novelty even then.

In the past, however, the outdoing of others in commerce and industry was often overshadowed by the more pressing priorities of war and diplomacy. Then, commerce and its needs were utterly subordinated, as profitable trade links were cut by warring armies and as wars were fought alongside trading rivals against trading partners. Thus, in 1914, France went to war against its chief trading partner, Germany, in alliance with the United Kingdom, its chief rival in the colonial trades. Certainly if security needs dictated an alliance against a common enemy while, by contrast there was a head-to-head competition in commerce or industry with that very ally, the preservation of the alliance had absolute priority, for its aim was survival, not merely prosperity.

That indeed is how all the commercial quarrels between the United States and Western Europe—over frozen chickens, microchips, beef, and others—and between the United States and Japan—over everything from textiles in the 1960s to supercomputers in the 1990s—were so easily contained during the decades of the Cold War. As soon as a trade dispute became noisy enough to attract the attention of the political leaders on both sides, it was promptly suppressed, often by paying off the loudest complainers. What could not be risked was the damage that unchecked trade quarrels could do to political relations, which would in turn threaten alliance solidarity before a menacing Soviet Union.

Now, however, as the importance of military threats and military alliances continues to wane for the countries in the peaceful central arena of world affairs, economic priorities are no longer suppressed, but can instead emerge and become dominant. Trade quarrels may still be contained by the fear of their purely economic consequences, but not by strategic considerations. And if the internal cohesion of nations and countries must still be preserved by a unifying external threat, that threat must now be economic, or rather geoeconomic.

The New Vectors of Conflict

All is unthreatening but far from quiet on the eastern front. We are reminded once again that the equilibrium of all things existent results from the clash of opposing forces as new antagonisms have arisen to replace the East-West antagonism now decayed. When we see the great number of lesser contentions that have emerged within the former extent of the Warsaw Pact, from Germany to Vladivostok, both inside the former Soviet Union itself, and then in turn inside its separate republics, as well as in the former non-Pact Yugoslavia, we must accept that something suspiciously similar to a "law of the conservation of conflict" is in effect. The unknown future can thus be framed by a single question with several possible answers: If the sum total of human hostility cannot diminish, but only change its vectors, what new vectors of conflict will assure its future constancy?

Will the Soviet-Western antagonism be wholly replaced by the rivalry of the nationalities large and small within the former Soviet sphere and beyond it? Or, if that is insufficient, will the global equilibrium require North-South confrontations as well? Acute demographic pressures, cultural collisions, and economic resentments certainly irritate relations between Latin America and the United States, between North Africa and Western Europe, and between Central Asians and Eastern Slavs. But one may doubt if a clash of opposing forces can arise between the materially dominant North and the less competent, very fragmented South. Will a far better alternative emerge from the conjoint discovery of a common enemy of all humanity in the ecological destructions and disruptions of our days? Or will the global equilibrium be sustained by the *internalization* of hostility within the former grand alliance of the Free World, with old and new animosities fracturing the grand coalition of Americans, East Asians, and Europeans that arose in response to the growth of Soviet power? And finally, there is the simplest of solutions, a revival of un-friendly Russian power, perhaps caused by a stereotypical regression to tyranny on the part of disenchanted reformers.

What is the future of war? Are we simply to accept the despairing commonplace that attributes war to "human nature"? Life is action, and action will evoke reaction, but life need not forever include every particular form of action. The human nature theory of the perpetuity of war thus begs the question of why war should continue when all manner of other unfortunate proclivities have not, including cannibalism, slavery, and dueling.[5] Unfortunately, these analogies are not persuasive because their referents are conditioned by economic and social factors that certainly impinged on them, but need not impinge on war. Nor are those analogies as reassuring as some seem to believe; cannibalism and the rest endured on the remote peripheries for a very long time after their disappearance from more advanced parts of the world. Slavery, for example, was already falling into desuetude in the later Roman Empire, yet was not everywhere legally abolished until the 1960s (Mauritania was the last holdout) and may even be said to have experienced a sinister revival in the heart of Europe during the Second World War. By that calendar, war could still live on for a millennium in more backward settings, even if we were to conclude that it will not occur again among more advanced countries.

The more plausible approach of some students of conflict relies on the inductive method to predict the future of war. Without resting on dubious analogies with unpleasant practices no longer current, their method only compares like with like, classifying the internal and external conditions under which states have fought wars and then assessing the scope of war's future prevalence accordingly. By far their most important finding is that under modern conditions democracy may have become war-inhibiting, which it was definitely not at its Greek inception. For example, a very recent examination of belligerent powers between 1816 and 1976 reveals that states of democratic governance have often fought nondemocratic states and that the latter have often fought one another, whereas states definable as democratic have only fought each other very rarely.[6] In a recent article, the virtual absence of war among democracies is described as "perhaps the strongest non-trivial or non-tautological statement that can be made about international relations."[7]

If that assessment of the past indeed predicts the future, then the scope of possible wars is greatly reduced. The democratic state is no longer rare; democracy prevails in the Americas as well as in Europe and Oceania, and it is not absent from Asia, which includes India, by far the most populous of democracies. But several objections have been raised to challenge the validity of the finding that democracies do not fight one another, including the implications of the small size of the sample for studied periods when democracy was still a very unusual form of government.[8]

In a more general sense, however, the proposition that democracies do not fight one another is confirmed by the empirical evidence—still proceeding inductively—and can gain deductive support from the converse of some positive theories of war. We might accept the common notion, for example, that many wars break out because prewar crisis communications among the future belligerents have broken down or have been willfully interrupted, thus preventing the peaceful resolution of the precipitating disputes. The converse of this theory is that the open communications that occur within democratic states automatically ensure their intercommunication also, thereby perpetuating at least implicit negotiations that can allow the crisis to be peacefully resolved.

Another commonplace theory is that many wars happen because their expected costs and benefits are assessed optimistically by elites who regard war as socially enhancing and who systematically underestimate costs, in part because they expect to be sheltered from the privations of war, if not its dangers. The converse of this social theory of war—a version of the militarism thesis—is that in the democratic state the costs and benefits of war are assessed by the entire society. Because the nonelite majority has no privileged claim on its putative benefits while being fully exposed to its possible costs, war will more often be judged undesirable.

There are still other positive theories of war whose converse is relevant to the argument. If we leave them aside, however, and simply accept the proposition that democratic states do not fight one another, we would still have to anticipate an abundance of future wars among the large number of states that are not democratic and between the latter and democracies.

The Internalization of Conflict

The easy prediction that war does have a future, and quite possibly a larger future than its recent past, is made downright redundant by the proliferation of armed struggles already caused by the "internalization" of conflict.[9] Once upon a time, all the conflictuality contained within the Warsaw Pact and Yugoslavia, too, was externalized in the East-West struggle of the Cold War.

Now, by contrast, it is expressed by ethnic quarrels and outright wars once suppressed by that greater confrontation: in Yugoslavia—with Croat/Serb, Serb/Muslim-Bosnian, and Croat/Muslim-Bosnian fighting already under way, and Serb/Kossova Albanian fighting very probable; in Georgia—with Georgian (Kartveli)/Ossetian and Georgian/Abkhaz fighting under way, and Georgian/Adhjar fighting probable; in Moldavia—with Romanian/Gagauz and Romanian/Russian fighting under way; between Armenia and Azerbaijan; and between Azeris and Armenians inside Armenia.

Even without fighting under way or at all probable, other quarrels also fall under the rubric of the internalization of conflict, including the separation of Slovakia from Bohemia and Moravia and the separatist pressures in both Italy and the United Kingdom. And, of course, if Russia (that is, the Russian Federation) is weakened, the potential for separatisms large and small (and possibly violent) is very great, for Russia itself contains more than 80 non-Russian ethnicities of some cultural significance, some very small but others of several million. In what follows, the figures placed in parentheses (which give populations in millions or fractions of millions) are, however, based on territory and not ethnicity because 1989 ethnic census data is not yet available.

The Russian Federation as now constituted contains the following:

1. Five autonomous provinces: Adighe (0.4) and Karachai-Cherkess (0.4) in the North Caucasus; Gorno-Altai (0.2) in western Siberia; Khakass in eastern Siberia (0.5); and Jewish (0.02) in the far east. Of these, only the Muslim Adighe and Circassians (Cherkess) could sustain separatisms by joining other Muslim separatists nearby.

2. Ten autonomous regions: Nenets (0.05) in the northern region; Khanty-Mansi (1.2) and Yamal-Nenets (0.4) in western Siberia; KomiPermyak (0.02) in the Urals; Dolgan-Nenets (0.06), Evenki (0.02), Ust-Orda Buryat (0.13), and Aga-Buryat (0.08) in eastern Siberia; and Koryak (0.04) and Chukchi (0.16) in the far east. Of these, the Nenets have a vigorously nascent native/ecological movement similar to Inuit feeling in Canada and Alaska as well as Native American movements in the United States. The (Mongol-like) Buryats could easily be drawn into the Buryat Autonomous Region, (A.R.) as will be discussed below.

3. Sixteen autonomous republics:

   • Karelian (0.8m) and Komi (1.3) in the northern region. The Karelians are virtually Finns, and although it is not clear how many ethnic "Karelians" inhabit the Karelian A.R., successful Finland attracts even pure Russians from St. Petersburg.

   • Mari (0.75), Mordvinian (0.9), and Chuvash (1.3) in the Volga-Vyatka region. Kalmyk (0.3) and Tatar (3.6) in the Volga region. The Buddhist Kalmyk have a small but vibrant diaspora in New Jersey and a spiritual leader in the Dalai Lama; on the other hand, they are ethnically and religiously isolated in the heart of the Russian Federation. The marginally Muslim Tatars have strong national sentiments and a large diaspora, with a strong presence in Moscow.

   • Dagestan (1.8), Kabardino-Balkar (0.8), North Ossetian (0.6), and Chechen-Ingush (1.3) in northern Caucasus. These predominantly Muslim nationalities are already drifting toward outright separatism, which is likely to flourish (with the Ossetians inside the Federation uniting with the Ossetians in Georgia if at all possible).

- Bashkir (3.9) and Udmurt (1.6) in the Urals. The Bashkirs have a nascent national movement as well as substantial numbers (more than a great many U.N. member states).
- Buryat (1.0) and Tuva (0.3) in eastern Siberia. The Buryats could be drawn into the orbit of an independent Mongolia. The Tuvans were once independent, but only as a Soviet "front" operation.
- Yakut in the far east. It is not clear how large the native population is in Yakutia (pop. 1 million). They are analogous to the Inuit of nearby Alaska and increasingly share with them a strong native and ecological sentiment.

One could continue in this vein to examine other separatist tendencies and other potential struggles that the internalization of conflict might unleash, but the point has been made—the scope for post–Cold War ethnic wars is very great.

North-South Tensions . . .
and Proliferation

Will the great antagonism between the Soviet Union and the Western alliance be replaced by a clash of North-South opposing forces? The demographic pressures, cultural collisions, and economic resentments that are already manifest in the overall relations between Latin America and the United States, North Africa and Western Europe, and between Russians and Central Asians lend some plausibility to this straightforward equilibrium solution that would simply rotate the fault line of conflict by 90 degrees. And because for all Europeans—Russians included—the adjacent South is largely Islamic, the 90-degree solution is that much more plausible, given the exasperated rejection of Western cultural influences by not a few Muslims and the violent extremism of some. In Western Europe, on the other hand, the Islamic visibility of North African and South Asian migrants is evoking hostile reactions and even seems to be reviving ancient fears of the Saracen in France and Italy.

No such serious cultural strife complicates North-South contentions between the Americas over illegal migrants, illegal narcotics, and the impeccably legal burden of indebtment. Yet even the least weighty of these contentions, the flow of illegal narcotics, can provoke surprisingly intense reactions. Former U.S. secretary of the treasury Donald Regan has suggested the repudiation of our own currency, in the large denominations supposedly fashionable in Bogotá, at only ten days' notice; such is the frenetic urge to punish the cocaine suppliers, or rather those of them who would inexplicably fail to convert all their banknotes in time, that the cruel dispossession of nameless dollar-holders in harsh and bankless parts of the world is overlooked. Also advanced in earnest was the suggestion that all aircraft originating from Latin America should be shot down if they fail to comply with both flight plans and radio instructions from the ground. That procedure may or may not achieve the interception of nar-cotics, but it would no doubt effect a marvelous improvement in the standards of navigation and English comprehension of Latin American pilots. Finally, some members of Congress have called for the most direct remedy of all, the bombardment of coca-growing areas in Latin America—nonnuclear bombardment one presumes. At least one Latin American official has noted that if bombardment is the solution, it would surely be more efficient to bomb the rather concentrated consuming districts in the United States rather than the diffused producing districts in his own coun-try. In the meantime, Latin Americans are regaled with the spectacle of expensive helicopters and expensive U.S. drug enforcement officials de-scending on the meager coca fields of penniless migrant families, there to solemnly cut down their only crop while providing no alternative suste-nance.

Much bitterness is caused by the revealed priorities of such efforts. While the United States manifests such an intense interest in the growing of coca, it shows no interest whatever in the growing of coffee, whose unprecedentedly low prices have been ruining the middling class of coffee farmers that has long sustained political moderation in several Latin Amer-ican countries. Much more broadly, of course, the United States is seen as indifferent, or nearly so, to the economic travails still widespread in Latin America. The ensuing resentment can only be amplified by the readiness of the United States to proffer monies and equipment to deal with what remains, after all, a marginal phenomenon for the region as a whole.

To be sure, North-South contentions in the Americas are nothing when compared to the problems that have surfaced elsewhere along the great divide. Europeans looking south now confront the sinister novelty of the chemical agents, ballistic missiles, and nuclear ventures of North Africa and the Middle East. True, the demolition of Iraq's arsenal—both con-ventional and otherwise—is apt to discourage emulation; missiles and chemical agents proved useless to Saddam Hussein in dissuasion and war-fare alike. And it is also true that the emerging capacities for long-range mass destruction present only a very small threat as yet. Nevertheless, the military arsenals of the countries of the Mediterranean's southern shore from Morocco to Syria are already setting a new floor on the possible scope of European disarmament. Even before Saddam Hussein launched his range-extended Scuds against Israel as well as Saudi Arabia, there was real concern over the missile threat from the south in Spain, Italy, and Greece. Now, in the aftermath of the Gulf War, few Europeans would accept a situation in which a totally denuclearized and largely demilitar-ized Europe would coexist with heavily armed powers to the south, several already equipped with missiles that can reach them.

Moreover, even embryonic capacities for mass destruction add a sharp edge to the accumulating cultural tensions between a Europe, liberal and pluralist as never before, and a South, wherein the militancy of Islamic defensiveness leads to daily expressions of intolerance. A vicious circle is at work; the increasing rigidity of Islamic practice, itself a reaction to the infiltration of Western habits, tastes, and values, is increasing the incompatibility of Islam with the requirements of modernization. That must lead to an ideological crisis of the first order, which might as easily eventuate in outward explosions as in secularizing implosions. In the meantime, the chimera of pan-Islamic solidarity is no longer as frightening as it once was. From August 1990, Saddam Hussein tried to mobilize support throughout the lands of Islam to shield him from the consequences of his invasion of Kuwait. Expressions of popular solidarity duly came forth in abundance, from neighboring Jordan and far off Malaysia, from Maghreb in the far west to Yemen in the deep south and from Muslim minorities in both Israel and India as well as in the former Soviet Union. Had a pan-Islamic vote been held, Saddam Hussein would have been the easy winner, because anti-Western sentiments are indeed strong. But virtually all Islamic governments are dictatorships, and all but a handful chose to ignore mass opinion. Hence, the coalition was scarcely damaged by Saddam Hussein's appeals. Even Pakistan remained in the anti-Iraqi alliance in spite of the expressed views of the most senior military leaders as well as of the solidly anti-American "street."

The military establishments of southern Europe have already officially defined the "Southern Threat" as their chief preoccupation; yet when all motives and means of conflict are listed and summed up, one still remains with some irritating interpenetrations and some isolated threats, not with a North-South confrontation of opposing forces. Leaving aside the inconceivable notion of an inter-American conflict and the remotely hypothetical prospect of a North-South confrontation within a fragmented Soviet Union, one cannot seriously anticipate the emergence of cohesive arrays of opposing forces even in the case of Europe and its own South. And it may be doubted whether such a confrontation could come to pass within the horizon of useful speculation, given the political disunity that begins on the southern shores of the Mediterranean and the material imbalance between that North and that South in all the potential sources of military power.

True, much has been said in recent years of the diffusion of military power in the global South, and its implications are certainly not to be minimized in particular contexts. Yet the record of the Gulf War confirms what was already learned in the lesser wars of recent years: The availability of military equipment for the countries of the South is greater than their ability to provide trained operators for such equipment; the availability of trained operators is greater than their ability to provide satisfactory maintenance; the availability of properly functioning and adequately maintained units is greater than their ability to provide competent tactical leadership for them; and the availability of forces properly functioning, adequately maintained, and competently led is greater than their ability to provide effective operational command for such forces. Hence, the military yield of acquired equipment can be very low.

Although in many parts of the South the strength in place is already sufficient to inhibit lighthearted expeditionary adventures, it is utterly insufficient to threaten the North in turn. The exception, of course, is the encapsulated threat of bombardment missiles aimed beforehand at fixed targets, which require only routine maintenance in the interim. That particular danger may yet evoke an exceptional response, but it is unlikely to be a sufficient basis for a militarized North-South confrontation.

The Scope of Future Wars

We have already concluded that there is no barrier of democratic governance to the many wars that nondemocratic states might fight with one another, while additional wars are possible between democratic and nondemocratic states. One such war has already been fought against Iraq, and it is easy enough to list plausible scenarios of other possible wars—while recalling that the exercise is almost bound to be futile because expected wars are likely to be avoided by deterrence or conciliation. It is the unexpected wars that actually happen.

Thus, North Korea may yet attack South Korea, and while a war meant to forcibly unify the peninsula should continue to be reliably deterred—because the advantage of surprise cannot carry Northern forces all the way to Pusan—a limited offensive meant only to wreck the Seoul capital area is another matter. That is not a danger wholly far-fetched, because the dynamic growth of the South has long undermined the legitimacy of Kim Il Sung's regime. The sheer proximity of forward-deployed North Korean forces to the Seoul conurbation means that its preclusive defense cannot be assured with high confidence. And because such a war would be motivated by the perceived necessity for the survival of the regime—rather than any hope of gain—it is not easily deterred. Assuming strict rationality on his part, Kim Il Sung's successor can only be deterred by a combination of defense and retaliation that the South estimated would be as simultaneously capable of containing damage to the South and inflicting damage on the North in degrees sufficient to leave the North relatively worse off after a spoiling attack.

Nor can a Syrian-Israeli war be totally ruled out. In spite of the seemingly repetitive nature of Arab-Israeli warfare, its scope has been progressively circumscribed over the years. In 1948 and 1949, the armies of Egypt, Lebanon, Syria, and Transjordan all sent invasion forces to engage in the first Arab-Israeli war. By 1967, Lebanon was no longer capable of participating, leaving the fighting to Egypt, Jordan, and Syria. By 1973, Jordan could not fight on the requisite scale, and only Egypt and Syria cooperated in the surprise attack that started the October war. By 1982, when it was Israel that started the fighting, Egypt was no longer capable of waging war with Israel (with which it then had a peace treaty), and only Syria remained in the fight. Now that Iraq can no longer be a contender either, Jordan cannot risk war with Israel without its support, so

Syria would have to fight alone. Because the Syrian regime cannot expect to prevail against Israel in any conceivable circumstances, it, too, can only resort to war out of sheer desperation.

Further wars can as easily be imagined between Hungary and Romania (over Transylvania) or—on the "western" side of the former dividing line of conflict—between Greece and Turkey. But to list hypothetical wars remains a futile exercise, and only the survival of the phenomenon is predictable. The continued possibility of U.S. interventions of one kind or another must be predicted also, but their locales and purposes have become quite unpredictable.

And that, above all, is the great change brought about by the end of the Cold War for the formulation of U.S. global strategy and the defense policy that provides its means.

The End of the "Garrison Era" in U.S. Defense Policy

Once the Cold War was militarized after the outbreak of the Korean War in June 1950, the global military strategy of the United States rapidly acquired the basic form it was to retain for decades even as its nuclear content first waxed and then waned.

That was strategy based on two large, fixed garrisons of ground and tactical air forces, one in Western Europe centered on Germany and the other in northeast Asia centered on Korea, which also had a strictly secondary "expeditionary" adjunct. Never so weak as to be mere "trip-wires," never so strong as to be considered self-sufficient to provide a reliable forward defense, the two garrisons required both the upkeep of varying reinforcement capabilities and the complement of strategic-nuclear "extended deterrence."[10] The garrison strategy also required a further complement: enough naval strength to secure the sea lanes across the Atlantic and Pacific against both Soviet submarine interdiction and against the antishipping strength of Soviet long-range naval bombers based on land.

As it happens, the U.S. Navy was always much too strong institutionally to allow itself to be confined to the narrow sea-control role that the garrison strategy required—which notably did not justify the very large aircraft carriers that the U.S. Navy especially favored.[11] Nor was the Marine Corps—another institution of exceptional political strength—satisfied with the flanking role it had in the garrison strategy, which relied primarily on armored and mechanized forces. Instead of adapting to the garrison strategy, both the U.S. Navy and the Marine Corps actually continued to focus on its secondary expeditionary adjunct, successfully diverting vast resources for the purpose while claiming more or less persuasively that their essentially expeditionary forces could also be of use to assist the garrisons.

Thus while the U.S. Army and Air Force developed their weapons and forces to serve the garrison strategy, the U.S. Navy and Marine Corps designed their forces primarily for expeditionary purposes, regardless of their lower priority in U.S. defense policy for much of the time.

After decades of continuity, the retreat of the Soviet Union from Central Europe and its subsequent collapse—along with the extreme implausibility of any Russian aggression in Europe or northeast Asia—have fundamentally altered the basic determinants of U.S. military strategy, mandating equally basic changes in U.S. defense policy.

Fixed garrisons based on "heavy" ground forces with *tactical* air as well as naval and strategic-nuclear complements were highly appropriate to counter geographically fixed threats. They are not appropriate to cope with unpredictable threats that can emerge in unpredictable locations.

To be sure, Russian strategic-nuclear capabilities remain in being; there are also Russian land forces that remain deployable. The turmoil that has overtaken the former Soviet Union also presents wholly new dangers, if not willful threats, some associated with a still possible reversion to a centralizing dictatorship and others associated with the opposite possibility of an outright disintegration on national, or rather ethnic, lines within the Russian Federation itself. But the possibility of deliberate Russian "threats" (already very low as of now) can only wane in coming years, simply because an economy less and less centralized can hardly sustain even the present reduced array of Russian forces, let alone provide for their growth.

As for the possible dangers that now emanate from the former Soviet Union in its disintegration, most hardly admit military responses. The greatest danger of all is obviously the unauthorized or accidental launch of an intercontinental ballistic missile, or several of them. The eventual remedy might be a "thin" system of ballistic missile defense, but the only near-term precaution would be to assist the Kremlin in providing supplies for the KGB nuclear guard detachments and their families (in their scattered locations, their logistics must be increasingly precarious). Even that, of course, cannot ensure the continued discipline of the KGB nuclear guard detachments nor their ability to actually safeguard nuclear weapons from disaffected military units or local insurgents. That is why even before August 2, 1990, it was perfectly clear that the *salient* threats that could be planned against were likely to arise within the vast North African–West Asian "zone of conflict" centered on the Persian Gulf but extending from the Atlantic coast of Morocco to the Bay of Bengal.

It follows that in shaping U.S. strategy for the post–Cold War era, the relative priority assigned to *globally deployable* expeditionary forces should now greatly increase, obviously at the expense of the "heavy" ground forces and shorter-range tactical air forces that were essential for former garrison strategy. It only remains for U.S. defense policy to acknowledge the change and reallocate resources accordingly.

What was not at all clear until the Gulf War, however, was whether forces that were globally deployable could in fact cope with the sometimes very heavily armed opponents likely to be encountered in the North African-West Asian zone of conflict. That light ground forces could do little offensively against large armored/mechanized forces of even minimal competence (and not much defensively in open, trafficable terrain) was understood and accepted. That U.S. naval forces could secure the sea lanes and blockade opponents was also taken for granted (though the relevance of blockade as an instrument of war obviously depends on the nature of the opponent). What was strongly debated, however, was the crucial question of how much could be expected from airpower strategically applied, and that is the question that was answered quite unambiguously over the skies of Iraq in 1991.

Notes

1. This is indeed a loose usage; the term properly defines a geographically based theory of state behavior.

2. That is, the logic of conflict in the grammar of commerce; see Edward N. Luttwak, "Geopolitics to Geoeconomics," *The National Interest,* no. 20 (Summer 1990): 17–23.

3. Kenneth Flamm, *Targeting the Computer: Government Support and International Competition* (Washington, D.C.: The Brookings Institution, 1987).

4. By the summer of 1990, both the Central Intelligence Agency and the National Security Agency were conducting in-house studies of their potential role as suppliers of commercial intelligence. Nothing is more natural than the attempt of bureaucrats to find new justifications to keep their bureaucracies well funded, but of course official intelligence on business decisions, price negotiations, and so on is only of value if there is an official user who can benefit from it, such as an activist MITI-type agency of government.

5. See, most recently, John Mueller, *Retreat from Doomsday: The Obsolesence of Major War* (New York: Basic Books, 1989). The section that follows echoes the writings of Samuel P. Huntington, most recently his brief summary: "No Exit: The Errors of Endism," *The National Interest,* no. 17 (Fall 1989): 3–11.

6. Ze'ev Maoz and Nasrin Abdolai, "Regime Types and International Conflict, 1816–1976," *Journal of Conflict Resolution,* 33 (March 1989): 3–35, as cited by Huntington, "No Exit."

7. Ibid., 6, citing Professor Bruce Russett.

8. Ibid., 7.

9. Bipolar conditions amplified some conflicts but supressed others (such as Greece/Turkey and Hungary/Romania).

10. The deterrence of direct nuclear attack against the United States itself was, in fact, always a lesser-included case of the far more demanding "extended deterrence" that extended over the allies of Europe and northeast Asia.

11. As opposed to the smaller carriers required for sea control.

2

Post–Cold War U.S. National Interests and Priorities

RICHARD ROSECRANCE

What Are the Future Interests of the United States?

U.S. interests in the future will be as concerned with gaining economic cooperation from other nations as they will with opposing others' military power. The United States will also be concerned with political and social evolutions in other countries because its interests would be served by promoting democratic trends elsewhere when it can do so without incurring unacceptable economic and political costs.

The United States can focus primarily on the means of gaining economic cooperation for two reasons: (1) It presently has no strong likely or potential major power enemy, and (2) it is as concerned with economic outcomes as it is with military outcomes. Further, economic conditions are likely to change more rapidly than military ones, as has been the case in the past quarter century.

Military and Power Interests: The Northern Hemisphere

In the 1890s, Admiral Alfred Thayer Mahan concluded that the dominant sea power possessed a fundamental advantage in world politics over nations that were landlocked or did not possess command of the seas. Countries without sea power would be vulnerable to blockade and unable to develop a worldwide empire.[1]

A decade later, English geographer Halford Mackinder rejected these notions. He believed that a country with a strong industrial and resource base and a network of railways to move its goods and forces to many locations would have superiority over any sea power. It would not need to acquire an empire to assert its dominance. Great Britain, for example, could not move the better part of its forces on land and would not always be able to enforce a continental balance of power; as Lord Salisbury admitted, "We are fish." According to Mackinder, England would therefore be strongly affected by industrial and communications development on great continents that it could not penetrate from the sea. The landmass of the future (as industrialization, resources, and new communications lines were developed) was to be Eurasia, which Mackinder called the "World Island," and the center of the World Island was Russia, or the "Heartland." Mackinder's dictum was who controlled the Heartland and its resources would ultimately control the World Island and whoever controlled the World Island would ultimately control the world.[2]

A third view was offered by Nicholas J. Spykman, the Yale geopolitician. Writing at the close of the Second World War, Spykman reasoned that both Mahan and Mackinder were wrong. Sea power was no longer dominant, and the Heartland of Eurasia was less important than the "Rimlands"—an arc extending from the United Kingdom and Western Europe through the Middle East, South Asia, and then up to Japan. Spykman believed that whoever controlled the Rimland would have greater advantages than the possessor of the barren and arid Heartland.

Today each of these conceptions looks antiquated, though Spykman's is probably closest to the mark. In fact, it appears that the United States has an essentially Northern interest to protect, because it is northern economies, technologies, supplies of capital, and trained labor that can shift the balance of power in world politics. In particular terms, the rim of the Northern Hemisphere, comprising as it does Japan, North America, the former Soviet Union, and Europe, is most critical to the United States. This has become even more true as North America moves to include part of the south under the aegis of the North American Free Trade Area (NAFTA) and Europe moves east as the European Union (EU) enlarges. A power that managed to aggrandize three of these four regions of the Northern Hemisphere would have an enormous, almost unstoppable advantage in world politics, at least for the next twenty years. In present terms, such a grouping would represent 50 to 61 percent of world gross national product.[3] Even if new International Monetary Fund (IMF) purchasing power parity measures of GNP are employed, the outcome is not dramatically changed.[4]

Some worry about the emergence of the cultural factor in world politics, such as might lead to a clash between civilizations.[5] Although it would be premature to dismiss such concerns, two reasons exist for not regarding them as potent threats at this time. First, economic factors have turned out, even in the Arab world, to be more decisive determinants of political alignments than cultural ones. Japan's joining of the democratic developed world has turned an Asian state into an essential member of the Western group of nations. Somewhat similar transitions are already in process for South Korea, Taiwan, Singapore, Thailand, Malaysia, and Indonesia. Even Vietnam is likely to develop close relations with Western economies. China will follow.

Second, if cultural associations were to become more important in the Middle East or the mainland of Asia, the economic strength of Islamic fundamentalism, even if buttressed by Confucian support, would still not constitute a significant challenge.[6]

Military and Power Interests: Elsewhere

Given the essentially Northern distribution of world power, the United States should not be greatly involved in areas where important economic and strategic interests are not at stake. The Somalian rescue operation was tolerable because it could be performed within acceptable costs, and for a time it garnered considerable international support. The Gulf War, though a diversion from the standpoint of Northern interests, was again acceptable because it did not involve excessive and continuing costs. If one neglects research and development costs of the weapons systems employed, the United States probably made money and improved (temporarily) its balance of payments as a result of the Gulf War. In addition to costs, one needs to stress here that U.S. involvement in other contexts (for example, in Eastern Europe or in territories of the former Soviet Union) must be conditional upon local support and also on the agreement of neighboring major powers—Germany, France, and Britain. An intervention in Bosnia that lacked financial backing from Germany and Japan would be questionable, and without the support of Russia and contingents from the United Kingdom and France, it would be a disaster. For these reasons, intervention in southern Sudan or Angola seems highly undesirable. The United States will always be quite sensitive to developments occurring in Latin America, but these can probably be dealt with much more effectively by economic penalties and inducements than through the threat or use of force, as traditionally practiced. Intervention in Haiti would also have to be conditioned on a strict calculus of costs and limited in time.

Economic Interests

We have two fundamental economic interests: (1) to create an open world economy and (2) to create a prosperous world economy. If both these objectives are gained, the likelihood of war declines. This is because economic means can achieve—satisfactorily and without bloodshed—what might otherwise be sought militarily—the control of markets, resources, technology, and capital. An economically open and prosperous world does not stimulate aggression as a means of redressing an unfavorable economic position. The incentives that led to aggression by Japan (markets and raw materials) and to a lesser extent by Germany (*Lebensraum* and the resources of Eastern Europe) in the Second World War would then become irrelevant.

An Open World Economy. It is important to realize that a world economy can be generally open without achieving perfect goods, capital, or labor mobility. In the past, openness has largely been measured by low barriers to the movement of merchandise trade among nations. Capital mobility and labor mobility were not then regarded to be extremely important. Today and for the immediate future at least, goods mobility could well decline as tariffs or administrative restrictions upon trade increase. Note the effects of the creation of a more restrictive European Union (under the Maastricht accord) as well as the trade-diverting effects contingent upon the formation of NAFTA. On the other hand, economies will still be open if capital mobility can substitute for a decreased movement of goods. If foreign direct investment can leap over the newly erected tariff barrier and produce within the tariff zone what formerly would have been exports, the same economic result is achieved. In this respect, capital mobility helps to substitute for the diminished flow (in terms of exports and imports) of goods. No one has suggested that capital controls would be applied to these new trading zones. Thus, the result will still accord with economic openness. A further point is that the mobility of labor can partly substitute for an immobility of capital. If capital does not move to areas of labor abundance, then labor may seek to move to areas of capital abundance. There are, of course, political objections to this movement, particularly under recessionary conditions in the migrant's new host country. Nonetheless, the welfare economics objective of a gradual equalization of the returns to capital can be partly achieved in this way. Nothing at present, in other words, suggests a breakdown of the openness of the world economy, despite what has been written about the supposedly retrograde effects of creating new trading blocs.[7]

A Prosperous World Economy. One can scarcely overstress the need to create a growing and equalized prosperity in the world economy. In simple game theory terms, a static world economy creates a constant-sum game in which the product shares can only be redivided and not increased, which is an invitation to constant competition over relative gains. An increasing-sum game, on the other hand, does not automatically produce relativistic competition. If each player can improve his or her position by increasing the size of the pie, conflict is reduced among them. It is perhaps not surprising that when the size of the pie was fixed or declining, some nations sought to improve their relative shares as they did during the Great Depression (1929–1939). Economic growth in this sense substitutes for the need for extra territory and reduces the incentive to expand. If, like some economic experts, the nations of the world were to conclude that smaller countries actually solve the public goods problem of creating economic growth more easily than large ones do, the trend toward territorial aggression might actually be reversed.[8]

This is not to say that aggression is usually economic in its genesis or that political or ethnic incentives do not play an important role. They do. However, it would be useful to furnish sufficiently attractive economic rewards to major players so that they would be willing to settle for having a voice within the councils of nations and in the decisions of the Group of Seven (the United States, Japan, Germany, Great Britain, France, Italy, and Canada) instead of insisting upon an exit from the system.[9] To make economic rewards effective, it is important to cultivate a small discounting of future gains so that nations are willing to wait for promised returns. This may be easier in some domestic contexts than in others. It is also important to have some international regulative machinery available to punish those who are discontent with their returns and who demand an immediate territorial or military payoff. Overall, however, it is important to remember that the pursuit of economic growth does not suffer from Prisoner's Dilemma incentives in world politics; gains for one power are consistent with and indeed are more likely to be attained in the context of similar gains for others.[10] It is very difficult for one economy to grow in an open world economy if others' markets are not also growing.

How Can Those Interests Be Achieved?

Diminishing Antagonism

The end of the Cold War heralded a period of healing among the major powers, but seldom have such rapprochements been accomplished smoothly and successfully. The most signal success, perhaps, was the reintegration of France into the European Concert system (in which it was joined by Great Britain, Austria, Russia, and Prussia) after the defeat of Napoleon in 1815. But the world failed to reintegrate the Weimar Republic of Germany into the League of Nations or to get it to accept the discriminatory principles of the Versailles Peace. After the collapse of the Anglo-Japanese alliance, Japan also staked out a separate and divisive role in international politics.[11] Because of the outbreak of the Cold War at the end of the Second World War, no attempt was made to co-opt the Soviet Union into a Western system of security and economic relations. Today the world has a fourth chance to reconcile erstwhile enemies. The most important issue is whether we shall succeed in regard to Russia and other republics of the former Soviet Union. The United States should reward those Russian leaders who are moving their country forward. Ideally, the U.S. military relationship with Moscow could be shifted onto a plane not too different from its military relationship with France. This would mean that precise net assessment calculations would no longer be the sole measure of stability (as they are not between the U.S. and Canada and the U.S. and the United Kingdom). The Russians might be technically vulnerable, but that would not disrupt the favorable economic and political accord between them and the United States.[12] This means that, just as in its relations with closer allies, the United States has to think about the political problems that Russian leaders face and how best to help them solve them. This obviously suggests the availability to Russia of Western capital and markets as well as managerial and economic know-how. If the United States succeeds in co-opting (not just Yeltsin but other) democratic leaders in Russia, it will build a political base that will stand it in good stead. Foreign direct investment will be very important to Russian development and reform once the ruble has been stabilized.

But economic factors are only one—and perhaps not the most important—variable in the United States' long-term relations with the new Russia. Equally or more significant will be an understanding of Russian national interests in Europe, the Far East, and the Balkans. A special consultative relationship with the Russian leaders will be extremely important in avoiding conflicts of interest in Eastern Europe. The United States will have to understand that they must be able to sell military equipment abroad—it is one of their few major means of gaining foreign exchange. It also should consider undertaking long-term contracts to buy oil, natural gas, and minerals from them. Under appropriate circumstances and when the Common Agricultural Policy subsidies for agriculture in the European Union (EU) have been drastically reduced, the United States should encourage the export of grain from a reorganized Russian agricultural sector to the European Union, reinstating the traditional nineteenth-century trading relationship. More significantly, it should not cavil at Russian leadership in the Commonwealth of Independent States (CIS) or at Russian concerns about the fate of its ethnic minority population in the Baltics and other independent republics. The United States should make sure that its policy on Bosnia has Russian assent, if not active cooperation. This probably means slightly downplaying its ties with Kazakhstan, Belarus, and the Ukraine, however important they may be in other (strategic) terms. Because the United States will not be defending Kiev from the Russians, it may be better to recognize a new nuclear power there than to press for a policy of nonproliferation, no matter what the cost. Finally, the United States should heighten the position and status of the new Russian regime. From the eighteenth century to 1989, Russia was a great power. In time, it will be one again. In the interim, it must be taken seriously by the world community and the other great powers and given the treatment that it has always been accorded.

If the United States succeeds in drawing Russia closer to the democratic community, it will greatly reduce past foreign policy costs of containing such a huge nation in strategic and conventional terms. US$30 billion of critical foreign assistance now may be more effective than ten times as much spent on strategic and conventional deterrence later on.

Promoting Cooperation

It is a well-worn chestnut of international theory that major powers have to cooperate to maintain a balance against any putative aggressor. Many still believe that this was the typical nineteenth-century strategy. In fact, the balance of power was typically invoked only at the last minute, and its effect was generally to bring on war rather than to deter it.[13] Such an ineffective policy can hardly be tolerated today. In fact, it is now more appropriate to use the *real* nineteenth-century strategy, which actually consisted, as far as possible, in co-opting those who were thinking of disturbing the peace. In this way, Louis Napoleon's France was temporarily pacified after 1860, and Bismarck's Germany became a satisfied power after 1871. Russia was brought to the bar and co-opted in 1878, without war. It was only in 1914 and 1939 that co-optative mechanisms failed; as a result, the balance of power had to be enforced militarily.

Today, war is virtually unthinkable between the United States and Europe or the United States and Japan. Although the situation pertaining to the former Soviet Union is more complex, it is also not likely to call for the use of military force in the next decade or so, and hopefully it never will. It is important to bear in mind here that none of these national groupings could possibly achieve rational economic interests as a result of war.

This is particularly true as nations have come to recognize that land, natural resources, and fixed capital are no longer the objects of national ambition. Territorial aggression was a rationally defensible activity so long as the acquisition of territory might dynamically transform a nation's relative power. In the seventeenth and eighteenth centuries, this was the case. In the nineteenth century, fixed industrial capital and resources (like iron ore and coal) became equally important. With the exception of fixed capital (which might be destroyed), they could be acquired in a war of aggression. Germany sought to improve its stock in 1914, and both Germany and Japan were bent on gaining natural resources from 1939 to 1941.

Today the situation has greatly changed. Additional land, particularly if it contains a hostile population, is not necessarily an asset. Fixed capital would almost certainly be destroyed even in a major conventional conflict. Mobile capital, as the Iraqis found when they seized Kuwait City, can vanish in an instant. Natural resources, with the possible (and temporary) exception of oil, are no longer as critical as they once were. Europe and Japan don't have any oil and still have prospered because they have been able to buy it at cheap prices on world markets. Possession of large oil reserves has not prevented either the former Soviet Union or the United States from encountering economic difficulty. It is quite interesting that the country without physical resources—Japan—is leading the pack in world economic politics.[14] Its only resource is labor—human capital—and this enables it to compete effectively with every other nation.

What then should a nation hope to gain from conquering another? It can acquire a stock of labor but cannot guarantee that it can be employed productively. And labor may migrate away as many Vietnamese have done, undermining the economy of the home nation while invigorating that of the new host.

More important still, it is not just that aggression increasingly fails to serve an economic purpose but that such purposes can be served much better through peaceful trade. The truth is that war has become inefficient economically; peace is much more effective. Therefore, a key policy of the United States in the years to come must be to grease the mechanism of trade and capital flows. The most important economic assets cannot be seized; they can only be acquired through patient and persuasive inducement. Susan Strange has recognized that the successful countries of the twenty-first century will be those that can *induce* (not seize) capital, technology, and labor supplies to enter their economies.[15] Thus, an extremely important U.S. strategic interest is to maintain a favorable economic climate at home, toward which both foreign and domestic capital, technology, and talented work forces will naturally gravitate. If such flows take place, the U.S. economy will have ample investment and an increasingly sophisticated range of exports, which will lead to both high productivity and a higher rate of economic growth than had been experienced in the past twenty years.

The need to diminish antagonism with other northern nations primarily refers to the U.S. relationship with Russia. The need to promote cooperation applies to the U.S. relationship with Japan and Europe. This does *not* mean that the United States should not compete even more vigorously than before with its great allies. It also does not mean that the terms of the economic relationship with these two groups should not be altered to U.S. advantage. The United States has borne (with considerable economic consequences) the main burden of the task of containing communism for the past two generations. Its allies should now treat it more fairly and equally in economic terms. As they previously gained free-rider benefits, now the United States should be an occasional free rider. In essence, then, cooperation with other major national groupings should involve maintaining an open and prosperous world economy, gradually equilibrating any persistent economic imbalances. War is not likely in the relationships of democratic states,[16] and in any event there is no valuable good or objective that now can be more profitably attained by war than by peace.[17]

New Mechanisms

A New Concert of Powers

How much exertion do these goals require of the United States of America? In the past, the United States largely solved the collective goods cooperation problem for its allies by undertaking to pay the major costs of security itself. In its own economic interest, however, the United States can no longer afford to play the role of a benign hegemon. Thus, it faces two new features of the domestic and international balance. First, the United States must cut its defense budget and pay less internationally if it is to revivify its economy. (This does not, however, necessarily entail cutting commitments abroad). Second, because of the pattern of opposition and support in world politics, the United States has less need for a large defense budget. Combining these two (partly countervailing) features, it can probably remain just as involved in the world as it has been for the past fifty years, but at much less cost. It can have relatively extended and inexpensive commitments.

All of this is possible because there is now an inchoate world concert of powers in international politics. Although the balance of power has been hailed as the main regulatory device for the past two centuries (a device that found new expression in bipolar nuclear deterrence during the 1950s), the concert system is both cheaper and more effective. If it can endure, it has the advantage of sharing the burdens among four or five major world powers or groupings. In the early nineteenth century, the European Concert of Nations solved the intervention task by delegating one of its members to perform this function in different regions of the world. At least between 1815 and 1830, European powers were agreed on the need to prevent another major war; they could restrain partisan ambitions among themselves and offer a joint response to local security threats. No action would be taken unless the consent of the major members was obtained. In today's concert, Japan, Europe, the United States, and Russia must agree if action is to be taken to police local disputes.

Continuing U.S. Leadership

The major difficulty confronting a concert of nations, of course, is that its actions may well be limited to the least common denominator of policy agreement among its major members. We know from cooperation theory that members of an economic cartel may well violate their obligations to reduce output. The Organization of Petroleum Exporting Countries (OPEC) functions relatively effectively because Saudi Arabia has the production capacity to increase suddenly its own production of oil, thereby reducing the price and punishing deviators. The Concert of Europe did not function as well because the nation that might have exercised similar leadership, Great Britain, frequently isolated itself from continental disputes or did not play an effective role in them. Its participation was episodic. In the same manner, it is unlikely that a world concert can function if the United States does not play a strong and continuing role as *primus interpares*, first among equals, within it. Unless the United States takes a lead, little will be done. Japan and the European Union are preoccupied by internal problems, and only Britain and France (within Europe) seem to retain policy vigor and autonomy. Russia is also confronting internal difficulties and is not likely to take the lead in foreign policy questions. As a result, the United States usually attempts to sell its position to its most vigorous allies (the United Kingdom and France) and then seeks to hammer out a wider coalition agreement including Germany, Japan, and ultimately Russia. In any event, the United States, possessing superior military assets, has to take a strong line because the United Kingdom and France, whatever their individual plans, cannot usually accomplish military intervention on their own. Without the United States' agreement and participation, little if anything could be done by such a concert.

Will the Concert Hold Together?

In the past, concerts failed as the issues creating them dwindled in significance. After the revolutions of 1848, regimes were thoroughly challenged and faced a likely loss of power. They were much more concerned about maintaining their own domestic rule than preventing war internationally. The cooperative consensus underpinning the European Concert eroded as a result. Thus, the primary question for the next ten years is whether there will be similar erosion or breakup of the present world concert. Some contend that this erosion is already occurring and that the absence of any powerful external foe dissipates concert energies and resolve. Coalitions, it is said, only work when there is an enemy. When the enemy disappears or is co-opted, coalitions lose their raison d'etre.

Whatever may have been true in the past, however, there is reason today for continuing cooperation of the major world powers. This is for economic as well as political and security reasons. They need access to each others' resources, markets, capital, and technology. No economy functions effectively today in isolation; to be shut out of other countries' markets exacts huge costs, to be denied industrial alliances with other countries' firms is devastating, and to be denied access to other countries' capital is disastrous. At the very least, Europe and the United States will have to stick together. Foreign direct investment among them will greatly increase as both Maastricht and NAFTA come into effect. The economic stake of each in the prosperity and success of others' economies will increase.[18] Russia also clearly needs access to capital and markets overseas. Japan cannot be cut off from them. Thus, the economic interests of the major world powers underscore and are largely coterminous with their security interests. The vital criterion of economic growth in an open world economy produces a greater consensus in international politics and in the concert mechanism.

U.S. Military Tasks and Forces

Assuming that there are no major tensions between the four units of the Northern Rim—Japan, North America, Russia, and Europe—the United States will need to deploy forces that can provide an early warning for intervention by the world concert. This means a continuing need for airlift and sealift capabilities and for afloat support in or near areas of local conflict. It may mean a better status of forces arrangement in Egypt, for example, once the Arab-Israeli negotiations have made progress so that the United States can assist the parties in reducing their arms. It is possible that U.S. forces could be brought nearer to CIS trouble spots if Poland, the Czech Republic, or Hungary were to move closer to or actually join NATO. But since it will not actually be the U.S. objective to intervene between the autonomous republics of the former Soviet Union, these forces would only serve purposes of political reassurance and stability. Here the enlargement of the European Union could well be more important than the military actions of the United States. After Poland, the Czech Republic, and Hungary join the EU, the Baltic states will be the next candidates to consider. Their early admission to Europe would provide a kind of political deterrence to a Moscow perhaps overly tempted to raise questions about the Russian minorities in those countries.

There may be regions where a further spread of nuclear weapons is inevitable, as it has become in the Middle East and southern Asia. As mentioned earlier, we have probably spent too much of our political capital trying to persuade the Ukraine to give up its (Soviet) nuclear weapons. We are neither going to defend Kiev nor give it strategic guarantees. We must ask ourselves what alternatives the Ukrainians have to ensure their security.

This is not true in northeast Asia, on the other hand; more than titular North Korean weapons capabilities would not be accepted by Japan and might lead it to go nuclear as well. Continuing the stationing of U.S. forces in Japan and Korea, Washington guarantees U.S. protection for both South Korea and Japan against such threats. It also makes the peaceful unification of Korea more likely. U.S. forces in Germany also obviate German fears that might in other circumstances produce a national nuclear force, which would destabilize the relationship with Eastern Europe as well as Moscow.

It should be noted here that forces redeployed to CONUS (the continental United States) lose all political deterrent capability. In 1914, Germany would not have permitted Austria to fight a Serbia in which large continents of Russian troops were based. Germany would not have attacked France if a U.K. force had been previously stationed on the Marne. U.S. forces stationed abroad do not have to be large, and perhaps they can be smaller even than current estimates. But they need to signal U.S. willingness to respond. CONUS forces do not do that and certainly would not perform that function for sensitive Germans and Japanese.[19]

The Concert and U.S. Security Interests

Some will claim that there is a theoretical inconsistency between U.S. membership in a concert of powers (which might decide to intervene anywhere—in Africa, Asia, or Eastern Europe) and U.S. interests that I have argued are largely confined to relationships with the four major groupings of the Northern Rim. First, this inconsistency is only theoretical. In practical terms, the concert will not intervene if the United States does not want to. Second, if the intervention in third areas is inexpensive, there is no disadvantage. If the intervention is expensive but if the United States is not expected to bear a large burden of the costs, again there is no difficulty. All these activities, however, would put an extra strain upon our base structure overseas, and that might have to be developed or enlarged. Certainly mobile conventional contingents will be at a premium in the future. Over time, this would suggest greater concentration upon general-purpose forces and less upon strategic contingents. There will, of course, be pressures to modify the ABM (antiballistic missile) treaty to permit a limited BMD (ballistic missile defense) buildup to cope with small attacks from new nuclear powers. Any substantial BMD deployment, however, would encroach upon Russian deterrent capabilities and certainly should wait upon Moscow's agreement.

Conclusion

If one can make a comparison between the Cold War world and the world at present, one key conclusion is that the United States used to rely heavily upon strategic nuclear forces based in CONUS. Today, it must place even more emphasis upon conventional forces and forces based overseas. Second, during the Cold War, the United States attached almost no importance to improving its economy and certainly did not condition its own defense contributions on the strength of its economic base. It procured them willy-nilly. Today, the health of the U.S. economy must be a primary consideration. Third, while bipolar nuclear deterrence was a successful policy during the Cold War era, it had very large opportunity costs. Today, effective concert mechanisms—that is, agreements among the great powers—could reduce those costs considerably. Fourth, the United States sought to regulate the international system through containment, opposition, and the balance of power. It did not believe that potential opponents could be co-opted to our point of view. Co-optation using economic resources and blandishments is now a far more efficient regulator of the system than the threat of military force, which, however, may still have to be used as a last resort. This is not only because national objectives have become more economic in character but also because we have no major enemies at the present time. New powers like China are much more likely to respond to a policy of integration into the system than to one that excludes or opposes them. China is becoming a trading state, and about 50 percent of its GNP now derives from the private sector.[20] The United States should encourage that sector and strengthen its influence in Beijing. This cannot be done, for instance, by denying Most Favored Nation status to China.

In the most general terms, the United States previously relied upon a huge production of military hardware to exert influence in world politics. It then put less emphasis upon the diplomacy of coalition building. But leadership does not necessarily depend upon a vast weight of production; it relates as much to subtlety and timing of diplomatic initiatives and to the responsiveness of the nations to whom they are addressed. In a world without enemies, the United States can keep the concert functioning through diplomatic as much as military leadership. Others are likely to respond more favorably than they were. As world politics turns to economics as a major desideratum and measure of influence, the improvement of the U.S. economy will also strengthen our position. Paul Kennedy believed that U.S. defense expenditures and commitments abroad were roughly proportional to one another; any cut in expenditures was likely to involve a symmetrical cut in commitments.[21] Events of the past few years, however, suggest that this is no longer true. The United States can continue to honor commitments and exert leadership without spending the vast sums of the Cold War era.

Notes

1. See Alfred Thayer Mahan, *The Influence of Seapower upon History* (New York: Sagamore Press, 1957).
2. Halford Mackinder, "The Geographical Pivot of History," *Geographical Journal* (April 1904).
3. GNP of Great Powers, 1987, as percent of world total and in trillions of U.S. $:

	% of World Total	Trillions of US $
United States	24.8	$4.526
USSR	13.2	2.410
Japan	13.1	2.387
NATO Europe	24.3	4.442
Total North Rim	75.4	13.742
World Total	100.0	18.226

Source: Ruth L. Sivard, *World Military and Social Expenditures 1991* (Washington, D.C.: World Priorities, Inc., 1991).

4. Recent estimates of purchasing power parity measures of GNP by the IMF in trillions of US $:

	Purchasing Power	International Currency
United States	5.61	5.61
Japan	2.37	3.36
China	1.66	0.43
Germany	1.25	1.57
France	1.04	1.20
India	1.00	0.29
Italy	0.98	1.15
United Kingdom	0.90	1.01
Brazil	0.79	0.45
Mexico	0.60	0.25
Canada	0.52	0.58

Source: New York Times, May 20, 1993, p. A6.

NOTE: countries of the erstwhile Soviet Union are left out of this accounting.

The purchasing power parity measures tend to stress domestic price levels rather than the ability of the local currency to buy foreign goods. China and India cannot afford to buy large quantitites of foreign goods, but their own domestic purchasing power (in terms of local currency) is high. Probably each of these measures errs in overemphasizing a single factor in the power equation. Countries with high GNP measured by international currency values could afford to buy large amounts of technology and arms abroad.

5. See Samuel Huntington, "The Clash of Civilizations?" *Foreign Affairs* 72, no. 3 (Summer, 1993): 22–49.

6. The following figures show the slender strength of these groups, even taken together. China and the Middle East as a Proportion of 1987 World GNP and in Millions of U.S. $:

	% of 1987 World GNP	Millions of US $
China	1.66	304,962
Middle East	2.00	366,116

Source: Ruth Sivard, *World Military and Social Expenditures 1991.*

In terms of purchasing power parity, however, these groups amount to about 14 percent of world GNP. (See the account in the *New York Times,* May 20, 1993, p. A6.)

7. See particularly Robert Gilpin, *The Political Economy of International Relations* (Princeton: Princeton University Press, 1987).

8. See particularly Peter J. Katzenstein, *Small States and World Markets* (Ithaca, N.Y.: Cornell University Press, 1985).

9. Here the key work is Albert Hirschman, *Exit, Voice, and Loyalty* (Cambridge, Mass.: Harvard University Press, 1978).

10. Payoffs in the Prisoner's Dilemma game are those in which two parties can benefit somewhat from cooperating with one another, but each can benefit somewhat more from "defecting" (not cooperating) if the other cooperates. Hence, both have a rational incentive *not* to cooperate. Economic growth does not present such incentives. The economic growth of one party is consistent with the (cooperative) economic growth of the other.

11. It is particularly necessary to underscore the malign effects of setting Japan adrift, both from the Anglo-Japanese Alliance and from liberal immigration into the United States, in the "Gentlemen's Agreement" of 1908.

12. See Dean Wilkening, *The Strategic Implications of START II* (Santa Monica, Calif.: Rand Corporation, in press).

13. See Richard Rosecrance, "A World Concert of Powers," *Foreign Affairs* 71, no. 2 (1992): 64–82.

14. See Richard Rosecrance, *The Rise of the Trading State: Commerce and Conquest in the Modern World* (New York: Basic Books, 1986).

15. Susan Strange, "States, Firms, and Diplomacy," *International Affairs* 68, no. 1 (1992): 1–14.

16. Michael Doyle, "Kant, Liberal Legacies, and Foreign Affairs," *Philosophy and Public Affairs* 12 (1983): 205–235.

17. Carl Kaysen, "Is War Obsolete? A Review Essay," *International Security* 14, no. 4 (1990): 42–64.

18. Richard Rosecrance, "The Prospect of World Economic Conflict: Implications for the Global System and for Europe," in Beverly Crawford, ed., *The*

Future of Economic Security (Berkeley: Regents of the University of California, 1992).

19. It was for this reason that Helmut Schmidt wanted American midrange nuclear forces stationed in Germany to offset the SS-20.

20. Cited by Richard Nixon in "Asia and the Pacific After the Cold War," address to the Los Angeles U.S.-Japan conference on the "Fragile Friendship," Biltmore Hotel, April 21, 1993.

21. See Paul Kennedy, *The Rise and Fall of the Great Powers* (New York: Random House, 1987).

3

Power: What Is It?
How Can We Best
Use It?

JOSEPH S. NYE, JR.

Power is one of the central concepts of international politics, but it is often poorly understood. Broadly speaking, *power* is the ability to achieve one's purposes or goals. Dictionaries tell us that it is the ability to do things and to control others. Robert Dahl has defined power as the ability to get others to do what they otherwise would not do.[1] But to measure power in terms of the changed behavior of others, we have to know their preferences. This behavioral definition of power is useful to analysts and historians who devote considerable time to reconstructing the past, but to practical politicians and leaders it often seems too ephemeral.

Because the ability to control others is often associated with the possession of certain resources, political leaders commonly define power in those terms. These resources include, but are not limited to, population, territory, natural resources, economic size, military forces, and political stability. The virtue of this definition is that it makes power appear more concrete, measurable, and predictable than does the behavioral definition. Throughout history, political leaders have used resource-based definitions of power, but they have often made mistakes about which power resources are most relevant in particular situations and about the ability of actors to convert their resources into usable influence or control.

Power conversion is a basic problem that arises when power is defined in terms of resources. Some countries are better than others at converting their resources into effective influence, just as some skilled card players win despite being dealt weak hands. Many apparently strong states (in terms of resources) have suffered surprising defeats at the hands of seemingly weaker states. Power conversion is the capacity to convert potential power, as measured by resources, to realized power, as measured by the changed behavior of others. Thus, one has to know about a country's skill at power conversion as well as its possession of power resources to predict outcomes correctly.

Changing Sources of Power

According to A.J.P. Taylor, the traditional test of a great power is the test of strength for war.[2] For example, in the agrarian economies of eighteenth-century Europe, population was a critical power resource because it provided a base for taxes and recruitment of infantry. The application of industrial technology to warfare had a powerful impact in the nineteenth century. Advanced science and technology have been particularly critical power resources since the beginning of the nuclear age in 1945. But the power derived from nuclear weapons has proven to be so awesome and destructive that its actual application is too strong to be useful for limited tests.

Some observers have argued that the sources of power are, in general, moving away from the emphasis on military force and conquest that marked earlier eras. In assessing international power today, factors such as technology, education, and economic growth are becoming more important, whereas geography, population, and raw materials are becoming less so.

In recent years, there has been considerable discussion of the changing role of military force as a source of power. Most large countries today find military force more costly to apply than in previous centuries. There are at least four factors that brought about this change. The most dramatic was the invention and development of nuclear arsenals after 1945. The dangers of nuclear escalation seemed to violate Clausewitz's doctrine that war was part of a political process. The enormous destructiveness of a large-scale nuclear war was disproportionate to any political goals that might be achieved. Thus, the ultimate form of military force became disconnected from actual use. Despite the history of the Cold War, there was no nuclear (or conventional) World War III. Nuclear weapons are now widely regarded as a muscle-bound form of power.

Another reason for the diminished role of military force was the difficulty of ruling nationalistically awakened populations in otherwise weak states. As local populations were socially mobilized, external rule became more costly. In the nineteenth century, European countries ruled their colonies with tiny forces. In the late twentieth century, outsiders have generally found the costs of controlling mobilized populations in weak countries to be unacceptably high. It is interesting to note that during the Cold War, the United States and the Soviet Union were both defeated by weak states with mobilized societies (Vietnam and Afghanistan, respectively).

A third cause of the changing role of force is the danger of rupturing profitable relations on other issues. For example, Commodore Matthew C. Perry could threaten Japan with bombardment in 1853 if it refused to trade, but in the complex interdependence of today's U.S.-Japan economic relations, threats of force are implausible.

Finally, there is the growth of a norm in Western democracies against prolonged and expensive military conflicts. John Mueller has traced this norm back to the late nineteenth century and argues that it has been growing steadily despite the setbacks of the two world wars. Mueller argued that in modern Western societies, war has become delegitimized just as dueling and slavery were at an earlier time.[3] Even so, the increased cost of military force does not mean that its use will be ruled out. There is a difference between a major war and a limited intervention. In some cases, the stakes may justify a costly use of force. When the United States planned Desert Storm, much higher casualties were expected than occurred, yet Congress supported the president's decision to go ahead. Moreover, as the actions against Grenada and Libya during the 1980s have shown, not all uses of force by great powers involve high costs.

Political scientists have written about pluralistic security communities in which force is not used to settle disputes. The relations between France and Germany today are in sharp contrast to what they were a half century ago. Some observers go further and argue that war is obsolete among much of the advanced industrial world.[4] However, even if the direct use of force is banned among a group of countries, military force can still play an important indirect political role. Force can be used to extend protection as well as to threaten. For example, the U.S. military role in deterring threats to allies in Europe or Asia or of assuring access to a crucial resource such as oil in the Persian Gulf means that the provision of protective force can be used in bargaining situations. Thus, force remains a source of power even among advanced industrial countries.

It has become a new cliché to say that economic power has replaced military power. Although that view contains a kernel of truth, it is much too simple. Not only is there still a need for military power, but also economic power, like other forms of power, cannot be measured simply in terms of tangible resources. Intangibles matter, too. For example, outcomes generally depend on bargaining, and bargaining depends on relative costs in particular situations and skill in converting potential power into effects. Relative costs are determined not only by the total amount of measurable economic resources a country has but also by the degree of its interdependence in a relationship. Countries may be equally sensitive to each other in a situation of economic interdependence, but if one is more vulnerable in the sense of high costs of escaping the relationship, that asymmetry provides a source of power to the less vulnerable partner.[5] For example, if the United States and Japan depend on each other but one is less dependent than the other, that asymmetry is a source of power. The United States may be less vulnerable than Japan if the relationship breaks down, and it may use that threat as a source of power.

Soft Power: Co-optative Versus Command Power

Getting other states to change might be called the *direct,* or *command,* method of exercising power. Command power can rest on inducements ("carrots") or threats ("sticks"). But there is also an indirect way to exercise power. A country may achieve the outcomes it prefers in world politics because other countries want to follow it or have agreed to a system that produces such effects. In this sense, it is just as important to set the agenda and structure the situations in world politics as it is to get others to change in particular situations. This aspect of power—that is, getting others to want what you want—might be called *indirect,* or *co-optative,* power behavior. It is in contrast to the active command power behavior of getting others to do what you want. Co-optative power can rest on the attraction of one's ideas or on the ability to set the political agenda in a way that shapes the preferences that others express. The ability to establish preferences tends to be associated with intangible power resources such as culture, ideology, and institutions. This dimension can be thought of as soft power, in contrast to the hard command power usually associated with tangible resources like military and economic strength.[6]

The distinction between hard and soft power resources is one of degree, both in the nature of the behavior and in the tangibility of the resources. Both types are aspects of the ability to achieve one's purposes by controlling the behavior of others. Command power—the ability to change what others *do*—can rest on coercion or inducement. Co-optative power—the ability to shape what others *want*—can rest on the attractiveness of one's culture and ideology or the ability to manipulate the agenda of political choices in a manner that makes actors fail to express some preferences because they seem too unrealistic. The forms of behavior between command and co-optative power range along the continuum shown in Figure 3.1.

Soft power resources tend to be associated with co-optative power behavior, whereas hard power resources are usually associated with command behavior. But the relationship is imperfect. For example, countries may be attracted to others with command power by the myth of invincibility, and command power may sometimes be used to establish institutions that are later regarded as legitimate. But the general association is strong enough to allow the useful shorthand reference to hard and soft power resources.

Command Power	coercion	inducement	agenda-setting	attraction	Co-optative Power

FIGURE 3.1 Types of Power Behavior

Balance of Power

To an extent, balance of power is a useful predictor of how states will behave; that is, states will align in a manner that will prevent any one state from developing a preponderance of power. This is based on two assumptions: that states exist in an anarchic system with no higher government and that political leaders will act first to reduce risks to the independence of their states. The policy of balancing power helps to explain why in modern times a large state cannot grow forever into a world empire. States seek to increase their power through internal growth and external alliances. Balance of power predicts that if one state appears to grow too strong, others will ally against it so as to avoid threats to their own independence.

In an age of information-based economies and transnational interdependence, power is becoming less transferable, less tangible, and less coercive. However, the transformation of power is incomplete. The twenty-first century will certainly see a greater role for informational and institutional power, but military force will continue to be a crucial factor. Economic scale, both in markets and in natural resources, will also remain important. As the service sector grows within modern economies, the distinction between services and manufacturing will continue to blur. Information will become more plentiful, and the critical resource will be the organizational capacity for rapid and flexible response. Political cohesion will remain important, as will a universalistic popular culture. As regards some of these dimensions of power, the United States is well endowed; as regards others, its relative status is questionable. But even larger questions arise for the other major contenders—Europe, Japan, Russia, and China.

No matter how power is measured, an equal distribution of power among major states is relatively rare. More often, the processes of uneven growth, which realists consider a basic law of international politics, mean that some states will be rising and others declining. Many Americans see the United States as a declining power and believe that Japan will replace the Soviet Union as the United States' primary challenger in the post–Cold War era. Some analysts even predict military conflict.[7] But those views are based on a misunderstanding of the nature of power in today's world.

Japan lacks hard military power and, in terms of soft power, its culture is highly insular. Japan has yet to develop a major voice in international institutions. The United States, on the other hand, has a universalistic culture and a major role in international institutions. Because power is relative, it is important to note that similar questions arise about the power resources of all major contenders. Although the United States has a less preponderant position in economic power resources than it did in the period immediately after World War II, no other country has as diversified a portfolio of power resources as the United States in the post–Cold War world.

The Post–Cold War Distribution of Power

For nearly half a century after 1945, the balance of power in world politics was bipolar. With the demise of the Soviet Union, the bipolar world order collapsed. What will the new distribution of power be? Different observers have claimed to discern five alternatives.

Return to Bipolarity

Before the final collapse of the Soviet Union, some argued that a newly repressive Soviet or Russian regime would create a harsh international climate and return the Cold War. But even if the August 1991 coup had succeeded, it would not have restored bipolarity. The decline of the Soviet Union stemmed from overcentralization. Stalin's system was unable to cope with the Third Industrial Revolution, in which flexible use of information has become the key to successful economic growth. The return of centralization might create a nasty international climate, but it would also continue the long-term decline of the Russian economy. The old bipolar balance would persist only in nuclear weapons, which, as argued previously, are an important but limited source of power.

Multipolarity

Multipolarity implies a historical analogy with the nineteenth century that is highly misleading. At that time, the balance involved five roughly equal great powers, and today's great powers are far from equally balanced. Russia will continue to suffer from economic weakness, and its reform is a question of decades, not years. China is a developing country and, despite favorable growth, will remain so well into the next century. Europe is the equal of the United States in population, economy, and human resources, but it lacks the political unity necessary to act as a single global power. As argued earlier, Japan is well endowed with economic and technological strength, but its portfolio of power resources is limited in the hard military area, and Japan would have to make major changes in its attitudes toward military power as well as its ethnocentricity before it would be a challenger on the scale of the United States.

Three Economic Blocs

Those who devalue military power argue that Europe and Japan will be superpowers in a world of restrictive economic blocs. An Asian bloc will form around the yen, a Western Hemisphere bloc will form around the dollar, and a European bloc (including the remnants of the former Soviet Union) will cluster around the European currency unit (ECU) or the deutsche mark.

Three problems exist with this picture of the post–Cold War balance of power. First, it runs counter to the thrust of global technological trends. Although regional trade will certainly grow, many industries will not want to be limited to one-third of the global market and will resist restrictive regionalism. Second, restrictive regional blocs run against nationalistic concerns in the lesser states that need a global system to protect them against domination by their larger neighbors. The last thing that Japan's Asian neighbors want is to be locked up alone with Japan in a yen bloc. There will continue to be a constituency for a broader international trade system.

Most important, however, this vision is too dismissive of security concerns. It ignores what was identified previously as the protective role of force. With large nuclear neighbors in turmoil, both Europe and Japan have an interest in keeping a U.S. insurance policy against uncertainty. The second Russian revolution is still in its early years, and China faces a generational transition. Yet it is difficult to imagine the United States continuing to extend security guarantees in the context of trade wars. The end of the Cold War was not marked by European and Japanese calls for withdrawal of U.S. troops. European and Japanese security concerns are likely to set limits on how restrictive the economic blocs become.

Unipolar Hegemony

According to Charles Krauthammer, the Gulf War marked the beginning of a *Pax Americana* in which the world will acquiesce in a benign U.S. hegemony.[8] The premise is correct in that the collapse of the Soviet Union left the world with only one superpower, but the hegemonic conclusion does not follow. For one thing, the world economy is tripolar and has been since the 1970s. Europe, Japan, and the United States account for two-thirds of the world's product. In economics, at least, the United States cannot exercise hegemony. The financing of the Gulf War was an interesting example of a new disjunction between U.S. military and economic power that was not in existence in the 1950s.

Hegemony is also unlikely because of the diffusion of power through transnational interdependence. To take a few examples: Private actors in global capital markets constrain the way interest rates can be used to manage the U.S. economy; the transnational spread of technology increases the destructive capacities of otherwise poor and weak states; and a number of issues on the international agenda—drug trade, AIDS, migration, and global warming—have deep societal roots in more than one country and flow across borders largely outside of governmental control. Since military means are not very effective in coping with such problems, no great power, the United States included, will be able to solve them alone.

Multilevel Interdependence

If bipolarity and unipolarity each fail to capture important dimensions of the distribution of power, we are forced to conclude that no single hierarchy adequately describes a world politics that has multiple structures. The distribution of power in world politics has become like a three-dimensional chess game. The top board is military and largely unipolar, for there is no other military power comparable to the United States. The economic middle board is tripolar and has been for two decades. The bottom board of transnational interdependence shows a diffusion of power.

None of this complexity would matter if military power were as fungible as money and could determine the outcomes in all areas, but as argued previously, military prowess is a poor predictor of the outcomes in the economic and transnational layers of current world politics. The United States is possessed of a more diversified portfolio of power resources than any other country, but the new world order will not be an era of U.S. hegemony.

The distribution of power after the Cold War is sui generis, and traditional realist analysts overly constrain their understanding by trying to force it into the procrustean bed of traditional metaphors with mechanical polarities. Power is becoming more multidimensional, structures are becoming more complex, and states themselves are growing more permeable. This added complexity means that world order must rest on more than the traditional military balance of power alone. Here the problems encountered by the Bush administration at the end of the Gulf War are illustrative. The traditional approach of balancing Iran and Iraq was clearly not enough, and U.N. Resolutions 687 and 688 (which dealt with Iraq's weapons and refugees) went deep into areas of national sovereignty.

Lessons of the Gulf War

The Persian Gulf Crisis exposed the one-dimensional nature of the supposed new superpowers, Germany and Japan. It also showed that the decline of the Soviet Union as a superpower had not removed the value of the military card in the U.S. hand. At the same time, force was only half the answer, and that is the second count on which the declinists were proven wrong by events in the Persian Gulf. The success in mobilizing an international coalition against Iraq rested on more than military force and showed that the United States retained a broader range of power resources than any other country. The position of the United States in a post–Cold War world rests on both hard and soft power.

During the Gulf War, it was important to get the hard power of the 82nd Airborne to Saudi Arabia quickly, but it was equally important to have the soft power to shape the U.N. resolutions that defined Iraq's entry into Kuwait as a violation of international law and called for enforceable sanctions. Without such resolutions, it might have been impossible for the Saudis to accept U.S. troops, for the Arab League vote that encouraged some Arab states to send forces, or for Islamic Turkey to close Iraq's oil pipeline.

After the Iraqi invasion of Kuwait, some declinists warned that past empires in decline were able to use their military for massive force projection. Some examples they gave were Spain in 1634 and Great Britain in 1900 (the Thirty Years War and the Boer War, respectively). Critics implied that U.S. action in the Persian Gulf masked a similar decline in power. They were correct in pointing out that the United States had less economic power than in the 1950s and was suffering from a low savings rate, a government deficit that ate up what savings it had, and a system of education that was inadequate for the needs of an information-age economy. But the Gulf War showed that the declinists, and their followers in the press, greatly exaggerated the rise of Germany and Japan and underestimated U.S. strength in both hard military and soft coalition-building power resources.

On the other hand, if U.S. political leaders neglect domestic reform, their power to construct a new world order will become increasingly hollow. U.S. decline could occur through a gradual long-term accumulation of political decisions favoring consumption over investment. Ultimately, America's hard and soft power resources both depend upon addressing such difficult domestic issues as the budget deficit, the savings rate, the education system, and the condition of the cities. Military strength depends on a strong economic base. Culture and ideological appeal depend on maintaining a healthy domestic society. A successful strategy for applying U.S. power will require a better balancing of internal and external concerns than was the case during the Cold War.

How Can the United States Best Use Its Power?

Given its domestic problems, why should the United States spend anything on international order? The simple answer is that in a world of transnational interdependence, international disorder can have effects that hurt, influence, or disturb the majority of people living within the United States. A nuclear weapon sold or stolen from a former Soviet republic could wind up in the United States in the hold of a freighter or the cargo bay of an airliner. Chaos in Lebanon could sustain terrorists who threaten U.S. travellers abroad. A Caribbean country's inability to control drugs or disease could mean larger flows of refugees across its borders. Release of ozone-depleting chemicals overseas could contribute to a rise in skin cancer in the United States. With more than 10 percent of its GNP exported, U.S. jobs depend upon international economic conditions. And many Americans are discomfited by the violations of human rights or mass starvations that are brought into their homes by transnational communications. The intervention in Somalia is a case in point. If the rest of the world is mired in chaos and governments are too weak to deal with their end of a transnational problem, the U.S. government will be unable to influence them to reduce the damage done to Americans.

In addition, even after the Cold War, the United States has geopolitical interests in international stability. It has a continuing interest in ensuring that no hostile power controls the continent of Europe and that no turmoil occurs that could draw it in under adverse circumstances, as happened twice before in this century. Although such events now have a much lower probability and thus can be met with a much reduced investment, a wise foreign policy still takes out insurance against low-probability events. Given the uncertainties in the aftermath of the Soviet collapse, a U.S. security presence, even at greatly reduced troop levels, has a reassuring effect as European integration proceeds. The United States has an interest in a stable and prosperous Western Europe that gradually draws the eastern part of the continent toward pluralism and democracy. The primary role will rest with the Europeans, but if the United States were to divorce itself from the process, it might find the future geopolitical situation far less stable.

The United States also has a geopolitical interest and a major role in the Pacific. It is the only country with both economic and military power resources there, and its continued presence is desired by other Asian powers that do not want Japan to remilitarize. The current political consensus in Japan is opposed to such a military role, and Japanese leaders realize it would be destabilizing in their region. The United States can help to provide reassurance in the Pacific while encouraging Japan to invest its economic power not in military but in international institutions and to help share more of the lead in dealing with transnational issues. Moreover, if the United States wishes to stem the spread of nuclear proliferation in the region, its security guarantees to countries like South Korea will be crucial.

The United States will remain the world's largest power well into the next century. Economists have long noted that if the largest consumer of a collective good (like order) does not take the lead in organizing its production, there is little likelihood that the good will be produced by others. That was the situation in the 1920s when the United States refused to join the collective security system of the League of Nations or to cooperate in preserving the stability of the international economy. Isolationist free riding in the 1920s came back to haunt and hurt Americans a decade later. There is even less room for neo-isolationism today.

Why not simply leave the task of world order to the United Nations? The answer is simple: because the United Nations is the sum of its member nations and the United States is by far the largest member. The United States can support the development of greater U.N. capabilities for small contingencies, but large-scale U.N. efforts like the repulse of Iraq will continue to require the participation of the world's largest power.

The United States correctly wants to avoid the role of world police officer. The way to steer a middle path between bearing too much and too little of the international burden is to renew the U.S. commitment to multilateral institutions that fell into abeyance in the 1980s. The use of multilateral institutions, while sometimes constraining, also helps others to share the burden that the United States does not want to bear alone. Multilateralism also limits the resentments and balancing behavior of other nations that can lead them to resist U.S. wishes and make it harder for Americans to achieve their national interests.

Ironically, while the Bush administration failed in its policies toward Iraq before and at the end of the Gulf War, its actions in organizing the multilateral coalition nicely fit the national interest in a new world order. The administration combined both the hard power of military might and the soft power of institutions to co-opt others to share the burden. Without the United Nations, however, it is unlikely that the United States could have persuaded others to foot nearly the entire bill for the war. Had there been no response to Saddam Hussein's aggression and violation of his obligations under the Non-Proliferation Treaty, the post–Cold War order would have been far more dangerous.

As has happened many times in the past, the mix of resources that produce international power is changing. What may be unprecedented is that the cycle of hegemonic conflict, with its attendant world wars, may not repeat itself. The United States today retains more traditional hard power resources than any other country. It also has the soft ideological and institutional resources to retain its leading place in the new domains of transnational interdependence. The problems for world order after the Cold War will be presented less by the new challengers for hegemony than by the new challenges of transnational interdependence and whether the largest power will play a leading role in developing international institutions and coalitions or revert to an inward orientation.

Notes

1. Robert Dahl, *Who Governs?* (New York: Yale University Press, 1961). See also James March, "The Power of Power," in David Easton, ed., *Varieties of Political Theory* (New York: Prentice Hall, 1966), and James Rothgale, Jr., *Defining Power* (New York: St. Martin's Press, 1993).

2. A.J.P. Taylor, *The Struggle for Mastery in Europe, 1848–1918* (Oxford: Oxford University Press, 1954), xxix.

3. John Mueller, *Retreat from Doomsday: The Obsolescence of Major War* (New York: Basic Books, 1989).

4. Robert Jervis, "The Future of World Politics: Will it Resemble the Past?" *International Security* 16, no. 3: 39–73.

5. Robert Keohane and Joseph S. Nye, Jr., *Power and Interdependence* (Boston: Little Brown, 1977).

6. See Joseph S. Nye, Jr., *Bound to Lead: The Changing Nature of American Power* (New York: Basic Books, 1990).

7. George Friedman and Meredith Lebard, *The Coming War with Japan* (New York: St. Martin's Press, 1991).

8. Charles Krauthammer, "The Unipolar Moment," in Graham Allison and Gregory Treverton, eds., *Rethinking America's Security* (New York: Norton, 1992).

PART TWO

The Gulf War and Its Lessons

4

The Mystique of U.S. Airpower

ELIOT A. COHEN

Airpower is an unusually seductive form of military strength, in part because, like modern courtship, it appears to offer gratification without commitment. Francis Bacon wrote of command of the sea that he who has it "is at great liberty, and may take as much and as little of the Warre as he will," and a similar belief accounts for airpower's attractiveness to those who favor modest uses of force overseas. Statesmen may think that they can use air attacks to engage in hostilities by increments, something ground combat does not permit. Furthermore, it appears that the imminent arrival of so-called nonlethal or disabling technologies may offer an even more appealing prospect: war without casualties.

This rise in airpower's stock comes from its success in the Gulf War. In the view of some, that conflict represented the opening shot of a fundamental transformation in the nature of warfare, a "military-technical revolution," as the Russians have termed it for more than a decade. Thus, the Russian military sadly read the outcome of a war that vindicated their predictions even as it sealed their profound sense of inferiority vis-à-vis the United States. Secretary of Defense Richard Cheney agreed: "This war demonstrated dramatically the new possibilities of what has been called the 'military-technological revolution in warfare.' "[1] Others, outside the Bush administration, expressed this view no less enthusiastically. William Perry, now secretary of defense, wrote in *Foreign Affairs* that "a new class of military systems . . . gave U.S. forces a revolutionary advance in military capability."[2]

The lopsided struggle with Iraq has already affected the way Americans understand modern war, inducing the ornithological miracle of doves becoming hawks. More than one distinguished commentator who had reservations about aerial bombardment in the Persian Gulf expressed a newfound belief in its utility as a tool of U.S. foreign policy in the Balkans. Thus, Anthony Lewis of the *New York Times* wrote during the Gulf War in disgust at the ruin wrought by aerial bombardment, "We should never again tolerate anyone who talks about 'surgical strikes.' " Since then he has developed a keener appreciation of airpower, asserting that "a few air strikes in Dubrovnik" would have stopped the Yugoslav horrors in 1991. According to Lewis, a "straightforward way to apply force" in Bosnia existed that involved "minimum risk" and provided a course that was not merely right but "clear and doable"—precision air attacks.[3]

Many of these individuals came away from the Gulf War with a far healthier respect for airpower believing it had made all the difference. Indeed it had.[4] Some 52,000 air-to-surface sorties delivered approximately 210,000 unguided bombs, 9,300 guided bombs, 5,400 guided air-to-surface missiles, and 2,000 antiradar missiles; U.S. forces also hurled more than 300 cruise missiles at the enemy. To what effect? Of its 700 aircraft, the Iraqi air force lost 33 in the air; approximately 140 perished in hardened aircraft shelters, and more than 120 were flown to Iran. The Iraqi air defense system succumbed within days—really, hours—to an extremely sophisticated attack, and it managed to shoot down only a tiny fraction of the attacking aircraft. The Iraqi electrical grid, oil refineries, and most of the telephone and communications system stopped functioning. The Iraqi ground forces in the Kuwait theater attracted the most attention from coalition air forces. Before the ground war began on February 24, 1991, the Republican Guard, located in the northern part of the theater, had lost nearly a quarter of its armor to air attacks, and frontline units had suffered even heavier losses. Moreover, airpower had completely disrupted Iraqi logistics and immobilized the Iraqi army. Aircraft operating around the clock crushed the one attempt by the Iraqis to launch a large-scale operation—the two-division thrust southward that barely got over the Saudi border at the town of Khafji. Although ground action necessarily consummated the ultimate victory for coalition forces, airpower had made the final assault as effortless as a wartime operation can be.

The Gulf War has an importance that goes beyond its immediate (and considerable) effects on politics there. If the claims of airpower advocates are correct, the United States has acquired a military edge over conventional opponents comparable to that exercised in 1898 by the soldiers of Lord Kitchener against the sword-wielding dervishes of the Sudan. The way would lie open to a reorientation of the defense budget in favor of an air-dominated force.[5] Indeed, if airpower continues to perform as spectacularly as it did in the Persian Gulf, the way to a U.S.-policed world order might look remarkably smooth. Was, then, the Gulf War a major departure in the history of warfare, and does it point the way to unshakable U.S. military preeminence?

Tools of War

The Gulf War saw the first extensive use of some new technologies. The F-117 stealth fighter penetrated the Iraqi radar system safely and secretly. The Joint Surveillance Target Attack Radar System, still undergoing testing, detected Iraqi trucks and tanks along highways in Kuwait, and an array of satellites provided unparalleled support to military commanders for intelligence gathering, map making, communication, navigation, meteorology, and missile-launch detection. Still, the bulk of the work came from much older systems and mundane technologies such as air refueling (which was required for three-fifths of all combat missions). Most of the weapons used in the Gulf War dated back two decades or more. The airframes of U.S. Air Force B-52 and U.S. Navy A-6 bombers had seen at least twenty years of active service, although they employed newer electronics. Guided bombs first appeared in the Vietnam War, when U.S. aircraft dropped 4,000 or so on the Vietnamese communists. Even modern, first-line aircraft such as the F-16 have been in use for almost a decade. The "military-technical revolution" sparkled in the new systems, but it drew as much on considerably more mature technologies.

The most profound change in military technology, however, was the vast increase in usable and communicable information. The Gulf War saw, for example, the first combat use of the Global Positioning System (GPS), which allows units to locate their position in three dimensions by a mere press of a button. (The Gulf War was also the last war in which only one side will have this knowledge. The technology for tapping into the GPS is widespread, easy to use, and relatively inexpensive. And even if U.S. operators were to attempt limiting access by degrading the GPS satellite signals, a clever enemy could largely circumvent such spoofing.) Space-based information-gathering systems also churn out vast quantities of data, and even a third-world country, for example, can tap into international weather satellites or buy militarily useful commercial imagery from the French satellite imaging system, commonly known as SPOT (*Satellite Probatoire d'Observation de la Terre*).

Conventional warfare depends increasingly on the skillful manipulation of electronically transmitted information. The advantage goes overwhelmingly to combatants who can bring together information from many sources, updating old databases (for example, removing from the target list a radar station already destroyed) and acting on perishable information. Countries such as the United States or, to a lesser extent, Israel have enormous and growing advantages in these areas. In the future, the struggle for information may take the place that the contest for geographic position took in the past. But the information explosion does not mean, as a casual observer might think, that war will become more transparent to those who conduct it. Clausewitz's "fog of war" may now descend on the battlefield not so much from a paucity of good information as from a plethora of half-knowledge. A fog it remains, however, and it lay heavily over the Gulf War.

Any editor knows that the advent of the personal computer and the fax machine has prompted authors to fiddle with articles constantly and to submit them at the very last moment. Similarly, the flood of combat information prompts commanders to change targets or tactics at the last possible moment. During the Gulf War, commanders changed one-fifth of all missions during the few hours between the time that staffs printed the centralized air-tasking order (ATO) and the time that aircraft took off. They made many more changes before the ATO was officially issued and still more after aircraft had left their bases. Sometimes these decisions made sense; other times they did not. In all cases, they created great uncertainty among the pilots flying the missions.

Despite the wisdom of proverbs, pictures sometimes lie or at least deceive. Coalition air planners in Riyadh tried to do their own bomb-damage assessment by looking at videotape footage of laser-guided bomb strikes. Lacking time (and in some cases, experience in photo interpretation), they sometimes misinterpreted what they saw—mistaking an exploding fuel truck or decoy for a mobile missile launcher, for example, or thinking that a bomb bursting on a concrete roof meant that the contents of the building had been destroyed. The short decision times created by modern weapons can also force quick decisions on the basis of electronically gathered information, the ambiguity of which may not be readily apparent. The shooting down of an Iranian airliner in 1988 by a U.S. naval cruiser is a case in point. Time pressure created by an abundance of data breeds longer-term problems as well. The constant pressure of the data stream, together with the growth of nighttime operations, means that leaders try to keep on top of events at the cost of sleep and acuity.

Combat information increasingly takes the form of abstract representations of reality compiled from multiple sources. It becomes harder to discriminate between different types of information when a distant, anonymous expert or even a machine has done the sifting. Since the Vietnam War, U.S. generals have decried civilian micromanagement of military operations, an indictment only partly warranted but accepted uncritically by politicians as well as soldiers. Today, however, the danger of military micromanagement looms much larger. A general in Washington, an admiral in a command ship, or a theater commander in rear headquarters may have access to almost the same information as a forward commander and in some cases more. Those distant commanders will often succumb to the temptation to manipulate individual units in combat accordingly.

Dependence on vast quantities of electronic information, of course, poses certain risks. During the Gulf War, pilots complained of having to fly missions without the kind of target graphics they had used in training. In the future, soldiers may become overly dependent on detailed, well-presented, and accurate information that simply may not exist in wartime. And as the verisimilitude of computer simulators and war games increases, future warriors may paradoxically find themselves all the more at a loss when the real world differs sharply from a familiar cyberworld.

Furthermore, the more sophisticated and expensive the information-gathering system, the greater the premium that opponents will put on disabling it with anything from electronic attack to homing missiles. The payoff for shooting down a state-of-the-art radar surveillance aircraft, for example, will surely attract intense efforts to do so. The Gulf War also demonstrated a trend toward what one might call the speciation—that is, the evolution of distinct families—of munitions. These new munitions can, in theory and often in practice, achieve effects unimaginable in comparison to conventional, high-explosive bombs. Antiradiation missiles, for example, not only destroyed Iraqi radars but also intimidated air defense crews from turning them on in the first place. Specially tipped laser-guided bombs punctured hardened aircraft shelters immune to regular high explosives.

But as air-delivered munitions have become increasingly specialized in their effects, they have also become susceptible to unintentional misuse. Air campaign planners expected extremely high kill rates against Iraqi armor, for example, based on the use of a scatterable mine, CBU-89. But the projected lethality of CBU-89 relied on calculations made for a war in Europe that would presumably have been fought against Soviet tank armies on the move. Against static, dug-in Iraqi tanks, CBU-89 had much less to offer. The speciation of munitions brings unusual capabilities, but it also poses the risk of creating forces so specialized that they lack flexibility and weapons so expensive that commanders will have only slender inventories to use when a war starts. Moreover, "dumb" (or at least relatively unintelligent) weapons will keep a place. Massive raids by B-52s raining down conventional bombs helped crush the morale of Iraqi soldiers and smash the large military-industrial facilities that figured so prominently in Saddam Hussein's aspirations for power.

War and Organization

The successes of the air campaign in the Gulf War rested almost as much on organizational innovations as on technology. To speak of a revolution in warfare as a purely technological affair is to miss half the significance of the war. In the Gulf War, for example, Lieutenant General Charles Horner, the commander of CENTAF (the U.S. Air Force component of U.S. Central Command, or CENTCOM), also controlled in some measure the airplanes of all the armed forces as well as helicopters flying above 500 feet and U.S. Navy Tomahawk cruise missiles. In this respect, he embodied a doctrine dear to military pilots for half a century: "Control of available airpower must be centralized and command must be exercised through the Air Force commander if this inherent flexibility and ability to deliver a decisive blow are to be fully exploited." "Centralized planning, decentralized execution" remains a catchphrase of U.S. Air Force doctrine, much as "Don't divide the fleet" preoccupied U.S. naval strategists in earlier times.

In practice, though, Horner's authority had its limits. The U.S. Navy controlled maritime air operations and the U.S. Marines determined the assignments of their short takeoff and landing aircraft plus at least half of their fighter-bombers, while the allies exercised discretion regarding which targets they would attack. Special operations forces—which, in effect, constitute a fifth service—continued to struggle for control of their own air operations.

Horner, directing 1,800 combat aircraft, had a staggering fleet at his command. Nonetheless, even his gently wielded centralized control elicited suspicion and hostility from officers in other services who feared that the U.S. Air Force would attempt to dominate all aerial warfare. Grudgingly conceding the necessity of a single command center, they argued that in theory it could dilute the synergy of, for example, U.S. Marine air and ground forces and that in practice it proved cumbersome and slow.

The centralized control of airpower made for a much more coherent campaign than would otherwise have occurred. But as officers from the other three services bitterly observed, the centralized control rested overwhelmingly in the hands of U.S. Air Force officers. Although the core planning staff, the so-called Black Hole, included representatives from the U.S. Navy, Army, and Marine Corps as well as the U.K. and Saudi Air Forces, its membership came predominantly from the U.S. Air Force. In theory, a joint targeting board should have selected targets; in practice, it did very little. Furthermore, much of the inspiration for the Black Hole's targeting decisions came from a U.S. Air Force staff in the Pentagon, an organization known as "Checkmate" led by Colonel John Warden, a fervent believer in airpower.

Thus, a U.S. Air Force staff (nominally under Joint Staff auspices) dominated the flow of targeting information and proposals to the theater. This certainly violated the intent, if not the letter, of a command system that in theory excluded the service staffs from operational activity. But in fact this arrangement proved fortuitous because the Air Staff could tap a far wider range of expertise than could General Norman Schwarzkopf's understaffed and overworked U.S. Air Force staff in Riyadh, which had to cope first with the task of deploying a vast force to the Persian Gulf and then with the myriad chores of daily flight activity and defensive planning. Furthermore, U.S. Air Force dominance in both Washington and Riyadh meant that the plan was conceptually consistent. Normal procedures, which give each service an equal voice in the name of cooperative participation, would not have done nearly so well.

The procedurally orthodox abhor the notion of Washington service staffs feeding operational suggestions to a theater staff. Such a practice subverts the idea—enshrined in the Goldwater-Nichols Act of 1986—of theater commanders as semi-autonomous warlords who take only the broadest strategic direction from Washington. But U.S. defense planners should look at what happened and ask whether these improvisations do not point the way to greater effectiveness. After several decades of insisting that the word *service* means "parochial," military reformers might ponder the individual merits of the services, each of which can pool a great deal of operational expertise along with a common worldview and an esprit de corps difficult to find among a mélange of officers.

The abundance of reliable and secure voice, data, and facsimile communications to (and within) the theater transformed command and control. Communications technology subverted hierarchies and rendered abundant exchanges between the theater and the United States that were both inevitable and desirable. During the Gulf War, staffs in Colorado relayed warnings of Scud launches to Riyadh and Tel Aviv, and the now-defunct Tactical Air Command near Norfolk, Virginia, managed CENTAF logistical accounts. Watching CNN and using other sources of instantaneous news, the chair of the Joint Chiefs of Staff (and, to only a slightly smaller degree, his civilian superiors) monitored the day-to-day activities of CENTCOM forces. The new technologies threaten age-old principles such as unity of command and delegation of authority. Those pieces of military folk wisdom carry with them so much tradition that they will persist in peacetime even if they must disappear in war. A new concept of high command, one that acknowledges that technology inevitably diffuses authority, will have to take root.

Information-gathering and -processing technology can help but not solve the problem of bomb-damage assessment. In many cases, commanders sent out sorties uncertain about how much damage a target had already received. Part of the problem stemmed from excessive reliance on intelligence derived from satellites rather than locally controlled reconnaissance aircraft. The theater intelligence staff was small in number and had little experience in tasking the array of satellites at its disposal. There remained, moreover, the sheer difficulty of knowing what damage has been done. From an overhead photograph, for example, it may prove difficult to figure out whether a small black hole on top of a hardened aircraft shelter indicates a hit by a dud bomb; an explosion in the thick, rubble-filled space between the shelter's inner and outer walls; an explosion within the shelter; or an artful paint job by enemy camouflage experts. And unless reconnaissance units can keep targets under near-constant surveillance from many angles and with different kinds of sensors, intelligence analysts may not know which projectile did what kind of damage. Finally, functional damage may differ sharply from physical damage. U.S. Air Force planners desired the first, hoping, for example, that a few hits on a command post would discourage the Iraqis from using it, even if according to normal measures of damage (which depend mainly on engineering criteria), the facility had not received a mortal blow. Not surprisingly, they became increasingly frustrated with intelligence reports that paid more attention to physical than functional damage.

The problem of bomb-damage assessment means that the fog of war will persist, although intelligence services will work to develop ever more sophisticated means of interpreting imagery and cross-checking damage through different sources of information. These individual uncertainties can add up to much higher aggregate levels of confusion. Hard as it may be to figure out what a particular target consists of and how to strike it, figuring out a target system—for example, how destruction of one microwave relay affects an entire telephone network—is even more difficult. It is depressing to recall that the United States began the war with two known Iraqi nuclear facilities on its target list, that it added six more during the conflict, and that another dozen were uncovered by U.N. inspectors only after the war. Furthermore, it appeared that the Iraqis had vitiated the effects of bombing by stripping these buildings of equipment and materials used in the nuclear program. This, too, was not known until after the war.

Although some aircraft, such as the F-117, had excellent videotape recorders, most could not take pictures of where their bombs or missiles had landed. And neither did the coalition have nearly enough unmanned aircraft or manned reconnaissance aircraft to do a proper job, given the magnitude of the effort. These shortfalls revealed an institutional failure before the war to accept the notion that knowing what a bomb has done is almost as important as delivering it. In future conflicts, where commanders might have less time or much smaller forces, an inability to track damage to an enemy could prove crippling. Even in retrospect, it has proven extremely difficult to decipher the air war's effects. There was no comprehensive survey of the battlefield conducted in the wake of advancing coalition forces, in part because of deficient prewar planning and in part because of CENTCOM's antipathy to visiting study teams. The U.S. armed forces could have done a far more thorough job of recording and analyzing battles as they unfolded and certainly after they were over.

The War and U.S. Influence

Reliance on airpower has set the U.S. way of war apart from all others for well over half a century. Other countries might field doughty infantry, canny submariners, or scientific artillerists comparable in skill and numbers to those of the United States. Only the United States, however, has engaged in a single-minded and successful quest for air superiority in every conflict it has fought since World War I. Air warfare remains distinctively U.S. high-tech, cheap in terms of lives lost and (at least in theory) quick. To America's enemies past, current, and potential, it is the distinctively U.S. form of military intimidation.

Air warfare plays to the machine-mindedness of U.S. civilization. Aircraft can direct massive and accurate destructive force at key points without having to maneuver cumbersome organizations on land or sea. Airpower can indeed overawe opponents, who know quite well that they cannot hope to match or directly counter U.S. strength. On the other hand, these enemies will find indirect responses. The Saddam Husseins of the world have surely learned that they need not take U.S. children hostage to deter bombardment; they can take their own citizens' young with no less effect. When F-117s struck the so-called Al-Firdos bunker—a perfectly appropriate military target—on February 13, 1991, they apparently killed the wives and children of Iraqi leaders using the facility as a shelter. For the next four days all air operations against Baghdad ceased, and when they resumed, politically motivated controls reduced the number of targets to the barest handful. Mobility, when abetted by camouflage and tight communications security, can also shield a potential opponent from harm. Publicly available evidence does not suggest that air attacks destroyed any Scud missile launchers, for example.

The soldier or marine will surely say to the airpower enthusiast that nothing can substitute for ground forces with bayonets. True, but some politically desired effects (elimination of electrical power in Baghdad, for example) required no use of ground forces. And in some cases, the United States has proved unwilling to use ground forces to achieve its objective (for example, the overthrow of Saddam). Airpower may not decide all conflicts or achieve all of a country's political objectives, but neither can land power.

All forms of military power seem likely to benefit from the imminent arrival of nonlethal or disabling technologies, which offer the prospect of war without casualties. But here, perhaps, lies the most dangerous legacy of the Gulf War: the fantasy of near-bloodless uses of force. Set aside, for the moment, the question of so-called nonlethal weapons. No military technology (indeed, no technology at all) works all the time. Inevitably, even the best-aimed laser-guided bomb will lose its fix on a target because of a passing cloud or a steering mechanism failure and hurtle into an orphanage or hospital. As one wise engineer put it, "The truly fail-proof design is chimerical."[6]

In many cases, so-called nonlethal weapons will prove to be just the reverse. The occupants of a helicopter crashing to earth after its flight controls have fallen prey to a high-power microwave weapon would take little solace from the knowledge that a nonlethal weapon had sealed their doom. Some of these weapons (blinding lasers, for example) may not kill but do have exceedingly nasty consequences for their victims. And in the end, a disabling weapon works only if it leaves an opponent vulnerable to full-scale, deadly force.

War Is Cruelty

The simple and brutal fact remains that force works by destroying and killing. In the Gulf War, the commanding generals ostentatiously, indeed obsessively, abjured Vietnam-style body counts, but that did not diminish the importance of terrifying enemy soldiers through the fear of violent death from tons of ordnance raining down on them. And fear of violent death only comes from the imminent possibility of the real thing. It is true that in the Gulf War relatively small numbers of Iraqis (perhaps 2,300 civilians and up to 10,000 soldiers) died before the ground war, although others suffered indirectly from the combined effects of air attack and the coalition embargo. That so few died reflects, among other things, the potential of the new technologies and the scrupulous regard for civilian life shown by coalition planners. But the essential ingredient of fear remained constant.

Sometimes fear does not suffice. The objectives of conflicts such as the war with Iraq will frequently mandate killing. The destruction of some 50 percent of the Republican Guard's armor (in roughly equal proportions by air and ground action) made little difference outside the Kuwait theater. The Republican Guard remained at war's end an organized force and, after drawing on ample stocks of weapons in Iraq proper, put down the Kurdish and Shi'ite uprisings. To stop that and to undermine Saddam's regime (which the Bush administration certainly wished to do) would have required killing or wounding the men who constituted the bulwark of the regime. This uncomfortable fact, long known to the Israelis, who have had few scruples about killing German rocket scientists in the past or rogue supergun designers in more recent years, sits poorly with Americans. When General Michael Dugan, Chief of Staff of the U.S. Air Force, hinted to journalists in September 1990 that the most effective use of airpower might consist of attacks on Saddam Hussein, his intimate associates, and key members of the Iraqi general staff and Ba'ath Party, he only pointed to the truth, impolitic as his outraged superiors found it.

It appears likely that civilian populations or large portions thereof will continue to be the objects of terror. General William Tecumseh Sherman described the grim purpose of his 1864 march through Georgia and South Carolina thus: "My aim then was, to whip the rebels, to humble their pride, to follow them to their inmost recesses, and make them fear and dread us. 'Fear of the Lord is the beginning of wisdom.' "[7] Sherman's troops did not massacre the inhabitants of the South; they merely ruined their private and public possessions, attacking (as a contemporary strategic analyst might antiseptically observe) the region's "economic infrastructure." In many cases today, war means bringing power, particularly airpower, to bear against civil society. Those who hope for too much from airpower desire to return to a mode of warfare reminiscent of the mid-eighteenth century in western Europe—war waged by mercenary armies isolated from society, war with (by modern standards, at any rate) remarkable efforts to insulate civilians from its effects. Sherman, reflecting the character of armed struggle in his century as well as ours, believed that in modern conditions, civil society must inevitably become a target.

As leaders attempt to use their civilians as hostages against U.S. airpower this will become ever more true, whether we like it or not. Moreover, throughout the nineteenth and twentieth centuries, military power has become increasingly intertwined with civil society. The electric generators that keep a defense ministry's computers running and its radars sweeping the skies also provide energy for hospitals and water purification plants. The bridges indispensable to the movement of military forces support the traffic in food, medicine, and all other elements of modern life for large civilian populations. Sherman faced a similar situation when he besieged Atlanta. "You cannot qualify war in harsher terms than I will," he told the hapless leading citizens of that city. "War is cruelty, and you cannot refine it."[8]

The Use of Airpower

U.S. airpower dominated the Gulf War as in no other conflict since World War II. Special circumstances helped account for this achievement, but in the end, military pilots were probably correct in their belief that this war marked a departure. No other nation on earth has comparable power, and neither will any country accumulate anything like it, or even the means to neutralize it, for at least a decade and probably much longer. U.S. airpower has a mystique that it is in the U.S. interest to retain. When presidents use it, they should either hurl it with devastating lethality against a few targets (say, a full-scale meeting of an enemy war cabinet or senior-level military staff) or extensively enough to cause sharp and lasting pain to a military and a society. But both uses of force pose problems. The first type represents, in effect, the use of airpower for assassination, a procedure not without precedent (U.S. pilots stalked and slew Japan's Admiral Isoroku Yamomoto in 1943). But it sets troubling precedents and invites primitive but nonetheless effective forms of revenge. The second involves the use of airpower in ways bound to offend many, no matter what pains commanders take to avoid the direct loss of human life. To strike hard, if indirectly, at societies by smashing communication or power networks will invite the kind of wrenching television attention that modern journalists excel at providing. Still, to use airpower in penny packets is to disregard the importance of a menacing and even mysterious military reputation. "The reputation of power is power," Thomas Hobbes wrote, and that applies to military power as well as to other kinds.[9] The sprinkling of air strikes over an enemy country will harden it without hurting it and deprive the United States of an intangible strategic asset. U.S. leaders at the end of this century have indeed been vouchsafed with a military instrument of a potency rarely known in the history of war. But glib talk of revolutionary change obscures the organizational impediments to truly radical change in the conduct of war and, worse, its inherent messiness and brutality. In the end, students of airpower will serve the country well by putting the Gulf War in a larger context, one in which the gloomy wisdom of Sherman tempers the brisk enthusiasm of those who see airpower as a shining sword, effortlessly wielded, that can create and preserve a just and peaceful world order.

Notes

1. Such a possibility seems implicit in Christopher Bowie et al., *The New Calculus: Analyzing Air Power's Changing Role in Joint Theater Campaigns* (Santa Monica, Calif.: The Rand Corporation, 1993).

2. Department of Defense, *The Conduct of the Persian Gulf War* (Washington, D.C.: Government Printing Office, 1992), 164; William Perry, "Desert Storm and Deterrence," *Foreign Affairs* 70, no. 4 (1991): 66. See also Perry's columns in the *New York Times,* February 8, 1991; June 14, August 3, and December 7, 1992; and April 12, 1993.

3. See his columns in the *New York Times,* "The Surgical Myth," February 8, 1991, p. 31; "Weakness and Shame," June 14, 1992, p. 19; "Yesterday's Man," August 3, 1992, p. 19; "What Should We Do in Bosnia," December 7, 1992, p. 19; and "The Clinton Challenge," April 12, 1993, p. 17.

4. See Thomas A. Keaney and Eliot A. Cohen, *Gulf War Air Power Summary Report* (Washington, D.C.: Government Printing Office, 1993).

5. War Department, *Field Manual 100-20, Command and Employment of Air Power* (Washington, D.C.: Government Printing Office, 1943), 3–4.

6. Henry Petroski, *To Engineer Is Human: The Role of Failure in Successful Design* (New York: Vintage, 1992), 217.

7. William T. Sherman, *Memoirs,* vol. 2 (1875; reprint, New York: Library of America, 1990), 729.

8. Ibid., 601.

9. Thomas Hobbes, *Leviathan* (1651; reprint, Harmondsworth, England: Penguin Books, 1968), 150.

5

The Ground War

JOHN KEEGAN

The victory of the coalition forces over the Iraqi army in Kuwait marked the culmination of one of the most remarkable military campaigns of modern times. At the onset of the crisis in August 1990, no forces in the region were capable of mounting a counteroffensive against the invasion. In fact, there were grave fears that Iraq might go on to violate the sovereignty of Saudi Arabia, which lacked the means to repel a large-scale thrust into its territory. Within two months, however, a dramatic logistic effort had positioned enough U.S. air and ground units in northern Saudi Arabia to ensure that further Iraqi aggression was deterred. By November, the arrival of more U.S. units and others from the anti-Iraqi coalition had shifted the advantage of force in the coalition's favor.

During the air war of January and February 1991, the combat effectiveness of the Iraqi divisions deployed in the desert was severely degraded. Finally, four days of fighting on the ground in the last week of February inflicted a devastating blow to the army of Saddam Hussein, leaving it emasculated (and him humiliated) and resulting in the outright liberation of Kuwait and the restoration of its legitimate government.

The Opposing Armies

The Iraqi army of 1990 was widely described as one of the largest and most experienced in the world, but these descriptions require qualification. During the eight years of the Iran-Iraq war (1980–1988), the army had grown to a strength of roughly one million men, organized into nearly fifty divisions. It had also successfully defended the northwest borders against a series of Iranian invasive offensives that were aimed particularly at isolating Basra, Iraq's second city, and cutting the Shatt al-Arab, the country's principal waterway. The Iraqi army's attack on Iran, with which it had opened the war, was a failure, however, and it showed little offensive capability thereafter. Moreover, its size was not matched by quality. Iraq has a male population of only 9 million, of which half is either under or over military age. The 1 million conscripted to military service, therefore, included many who were unfit for duty, and the fifty divisions were widely varied in capability. The most highly motivated and combat-ready men were incorporated into the Republican Guard, which had been formed to protect the regime and Saddam Hussein's person, and they possessed the best of Iraq's modern equipment; many of the ordinary divisions of the army were composed of young or elderly conscripts who had little experience of warfare and little enthusiasm for it. Their equipment was obsolescent; the infantry divisions had scanty artillery and no armored vehicles.

The U.S. divisions deployed to the Persian Gulf, by contrast, were the best of their kind in the world. Their soldiers were all volunteers who had been trained and equipped to a uniformly high standard, and they hailed from three separate sectors of the U.S. armed forces. One of these was the Marine Corps, which sent its 1st and 2nd Divisions, together with the 3rd Air Wing, from the United States. The second was the Army's XVIII Corps, drawn from the home strategic reserve and consisting largely of airborne and airmobile elements. The third was VII Corps, brought from Germany, where it had trained for years to resist a Warsaw Pact offensive against the North Atlantic Treaty Organization (NATO). Many other units came to reinforce this core, which was organized as the U.S. 3rd Army. What gave it such striking power, however, was the combination of high airmobile and amphibious maneuver capability and heavy armored offensive capacity contributed by the marine and army divisions.

The 3rd Army received important reinforcement in the form of ground troops contributed by eighteen members of the coalition. These contributions ranged in size from 300 Mujahideen sent by Afghanistan to 95,000 soldiers from the Saudi army. Of particular value were the contingents from Syria and Egypt, the latter deploying both an armored and a mechanized division, and the divisions assembled in theater by the United Kingdom and France. The French 6th Light Armored Division, which had been assigned to XVIII Corps, was to join in the dramatic desert deployment on the coalition forces' left flank, while the U.K. 1st Armoured Division was to take part in the breaching of the main Iraqi defended positions.

The Iraqi defenses of Kuwait did much to compensate for the qualitative inferiority of the Iraqi army and to capitalize on the high number of troops deployed therein. During the later stages of the war with Iran, the Iraqi army had come to depend increasingly upon fixed defenses to hold the Iranian offensives at bay; its engineers were skilled in constructing obstacles, and its infantry was practiced in defending them. The pattern of fortifications used by the Iraqis owed much to Soviet theory, as had the fortifications dug along the Sinai border of Israel by the Egyptian army in 1967, and although impressive, it suffered from the same defects. For example, the Iraqi fortifications tended to isolate defenders inside strongly wired positions that were also protected by minefields. As a result, defenders were unable to go to each other's assistance if a penetration occurred. Mobile defense, reinforcement, or counterattack was to be provided by reserve armor supported by artillery bombardment. No allowance had been made, however, for the effect of airpower on the movement of armor or the manning of artillery during a high-intensity battle.

The Iraqis began their fortification of the Kuwaiti border with Saudi Arabia as soon as it became clear that the invasion was not to be accepted as a fait accompli. There were no suitable topographical positions to strengthen, so the terrain was physically altered. Berms—extensive sand or earth banks—were bulldozed to form continuous barriers, fronted by wire entanglements and minefields. Some berms were also protected by trenches filled with oil, which was intended for ignition during an attack. A forward Iraqi line was constructed from roughly 3 to 9 miles inside the Kuwaiti border and was garrisoned by platoons and companies in its strong points. A second line, some distance behind the first, had similar strong points in brigade strength. Minefields varied in depth from 328 to 656 feet, the whole complex containing many millions of antipersonnel and antivehicle mines.

The defenses were thickest at these fronts: on the coast road; at the bend in the Kuwaiti border with Saudi Arabia; and on the western side of the Wadi Al-Batin, a dry desert valley crossed by the most direct route to King Khalid Military City, the Saudi base nearest to Kuwait. Strong defenses, including underwater electric cables, were laid in the water itself. The layout of the defensive systems reflected the Iraqi high command's belief that the main danger to the occupying forces in Kuwait lay along existing lines of communication. Little provision was made for the defense of the western desert flank, apparently out of disbelief that major military operations would be mounted across such remote and difficult terrain. This miscalculation was to be a principal cause of the undoing of Iraq's illegal occupation of Kuwaiti territory.

The Coalition War Plan

Breaching the Iraqi obstacle zone nevertheless became the first priority in the coalition forces' operational plan. Planning began in earnest on August 25, 1990, when the commander in chief of Central Command, General Norman Schwarzkopf, sketched out a four-phase campaign that was to end with a grand offensive into Kuwait to drive out the Iraqi forces. In an original and enlightened development, detailed planning was entrusted to a cell of officers who were all graduates of the School of Advanced Military Studies (SAMS) at Fort Leavenworth, Kansas. SAMS, in deliberate imitation of the nineteenth-century Prussian *Kriegsakademie*, selects the foremost officers of each year to study the history and theory of warfare within the context of current U.S. Army doctrine. The SAMS graduates who formed the Special Planning Group (SPG) therefore brought high intellectual ability, combined with an awareness of the latest military thinking, to the task of devising a battle-winning strategy for the Kuwaiti crisis. The SPG's initial scheme, presented to General Schwarzkopf on October 6, called for a direct assault on the Iraqi position. Because of the difficulty foreseen in breaching the obstacle zone, the plan was revised, and a new concept, which involved the deployment of two corps to envelop the enemy position from the west, was presented to the Chairman of the Joint Chiefs of Staff (CJCS) on October 11. Approved on October 22, this plan resulted in a decision to bring the VII Corps from Germany. The move was made public in President Bush's announcement of November 8 that the coalition forces in the Persian Gulf were effectively to be doubled in strength.

While reinforcements were deploying, formations already in theater began intensive training for the coming offensive, in which new arrivals joined as soon as they were reunited with their equipment. Most of the U.S. Army's units had been through the realistic program at the National Training Center at Fort Irwin, California, while the U.S. Marines had undergone similar training at their Air-Ground Combat Center at Twenty-Nine Palms, also in California. Training schedules organized inside Saudi Arabia concentrated on obstacle breaching, attack of strong points, desert navigation, night operations, and chemical defense, since the threat of Iraqi chemical attack was taken seriously right up to the moment the coalition attack was launched. A model of an Iraqi triangular strong point was built by the 82nd Airborne Division as a training aid, while the 101st Airborne (Air Assault) Division used an abandoned village for street-fighting practice. Particular emphasis was laid by all formations on the rehearsal of ground-air operations with the other units that were to support them in battle, while tank and artillery crews conducted extensive live-firing trials to ensure their ability to achieve first-hit accuracy.

While training was in progress, the logistic organization, 22nd Support Command, was stockpiling supplies brought from the ports of the upper Persian Gulf to dumps in and around King Khalid Military City, which was to be the main maintenance center. Achieved over an inadequate network of unimproved roads, this effort was not only the key to the coming offensive's successful outcome but also one of the most impressive logistic enterprises ever undertaken.

As soon as adequate stocks were in place, a similarly difficult deployment of combat elements occurred. Between January 17 and February 24, the duration of the air war, some 270,000 troops belonging to VII Corps and XVIII Airborne Corps as well as the U.K. 1st Armoured Division and French 6th Light Armored Division were shifted westward to their attack positions. The few routes available crossed each other and had to be shared with supporting logistical units, so the movement schedules required meticulous planning and execution. Vehicles were moving at 15-second intervals over distances of 150 miles for VII Corps and up to 260 miles for XVIII Corps. Ground movement was supplemented from the air; during the first thirteen days of the move, C-130s were leaving King Fahd International Airport for the staging areas every seven minutes.

The Iraqis remained in ignorance of this mighty repositioning of force throughout its course, thanks to a total denial of overflight and elaborate deception measures on the part of the coalition. The latter included amphibious demonstrations by the U.S. Marines along the Kuwaiti coast and feints by army units along the Kuwaiti border with Saudi Arabia; as well, the 1st Cavalry Division conducted a series of raids against Iraqi defenses around Wadi Al-Batin for much of the month before G-Day, the first day of the offensive. As G-Day approached, these feints evolved into aggressive penetrations of the Iraqis' former positions, particularly in the U.S. Marines' sector near the Kuwaiti coast. Obstacles were destroyed, paths were cleared through the minefields, and Iraqi observation posts were eliminated.

During the preparatory period, however, the Iraqis themselves mounted aggressive raids of their own, the most important of which was staged at Al-Khafji, near the coast and inside the Saudi border. On the night of January 30, 1991, two Iraqi mechanized brigades, with 4,000 men and 80 tanks, took possession of the small town. By high-level decision, it was left to the Saudis to organize a counterattack, which they did the following day. Supported by the 1st Marine Division, a force of one Qatari and three Saudi battalions retook the place with considerable Iraqi losses. The episode attracted great attention in the world media, which was undoubtedly Saddam Hussein's purpose, but it was of no military significance. If anything, it reinforced the coalition's intelligence assessments of the low quality of Iraqi formations.

Coalition intelligence performance in support of the ground offensive was mixed in quality. The main difficulty was encountered in establishing real-time communications. Both satellite and aerial reconnaissance were slow in transmitting their findings to local tactical commanders, and they often did so in forms the recipients found unfamiliar. The deception plan disallowed them, moreover, to seek local intelligence themselves, while sensory equipment deployed within the tactical area became overloaded by computing demands. Dissatisfaction with the patchiness of the intelligence picture provided—and with the delay in supplying it—was one of the few blemishes on an operation otherwise marked by the highest technical efficiency.

Taking the long view, however, the deficiencies of intelligence may be seen to have had a compensatory effect. Because the coalition was thereby misled into overestimating the quality—and more important, the quantity—of Iraqi forces deployed in the tactical zone, the coalition in turn overinsured against the possibility of failure by heightening its own offensive capability. The official estimate of Iraqi numbers deployed was 540,000, with half in Kuwait itself; the true figure appears to have been 250,000, of which 150,000 were in Kuwait. Instead of fighting at a disadvantage of numbers, therefore, the coalition virtually fought at a positive advantage, a factor of enormous importance in guaranteeing the success of the tactical plan.

One way in which the intelligence overestimate contributed to ensuring success was the influence it had on the scale of the preparatory bombardment of Iraqi positions. The Iraqis had 3,100 122-mm and 152-mm Soviet guns and howitzers in their fire zones, excellent artillery pieces amply provided with ordnance. For three days before the attack, however, the corps and divisional artilleries of the coalition subjected the enemy gun lines to a prolonged, sustained, and effective preparatory fire, against which the Iraqi guns made little response. By the eve of the coalition's attack, sixteen of the enemy's divisional artilleries had suffered between 75 to 100 percent degradation. The effect of the coalition bombardment was also devastating psychologically, reducing individual Iraqi soldiers to a state of trembling incapacity.

By the early hours of Sunday, February 24, the coalition forces had two corps, a large U.S. Marine force and two Joint Forces Commands concentrated in the line of departure. They consisted together of two U.S. airborne/airmobile divisions, two U.S. armored divisions and one mechanized division and two U.S. Marine divisions, one U.K. armored division, one French light armored division, one Egyptian armored and one mechanized division, one Syrian armored division, three U.S. aviation brigades and two armored cavalry regiments, and seven Saudi and other Arab brigades. They were opposed by some forty Iraqi divisions, of which five were armored and six were mechanized; but most were below strength, and the majority had suffered heavy equipment loss as a result of the air war and artillery preparation. The equipment of the infantry divisions was deficient, and the motivation of their soldiers was low.

The Ground War: Day One

The first of the coalition formations to attack was XVIII Airborne Corps, concentrated on the desert flank west of the Iraqi fortified area. Its elements formed three groups: The French 6th Light Armored Division and the 82nd Airborne struck on the left, driving towards the Euphrates River 160 miles distant; in the center, the 101st Air Assault Division had the mission of reaching the Euphrates by rapid air movement and blocking the route between Baghdad and Basra; on the right, the 24th Mechanized Division and 3rd Armored Cavalry Regiment was also to drive to the Euphrates and then turn eastwards to destroy Iraqi forces in the Kuwaiti theater of operations.

All these missions were achieved with success and dispatch. The French reached their objectives in seven hours, fighting a brisk battle with the Iraqi 45th Division en route. They engaged tanks with missile-firing Gazelle helicopters and took 2,500 prisoners. The 82nd Airborne followed up to secure a highway that was to become the main operating route of the XVIII Corps. The 101st, delayed at first by fog, then leapfrogged to deliver one of its brigades to a base nearly a hundred miles inside Iraq. Over three hundred helicopter sorties were flown in what was the largest military helicopter mission in history. The base, codenamed Cobra, then became a logistic and refueling center for further advances. By February 26, 380,000 gallons of fuel were stockpiled there, much of it having been flown forward in helicopter belly tanks.

Meanwhile, the 24th Mechanized Division, with the 3rd Armored Cavalry Regiment and a reinforced squadron of the 2nd Armored Cavalry Regiment, mounted a full-scale armored assault to the coast. Supported by eighteen Apache helicopters, the division attacked with one brigade leading, with its two armored battalions leading in line abreast. It also transported in its train over 2.5 million gallons of fuel and 17,000 metric tons of ammunition. Although impeded by heavy sand- and rainstorms, the division had reached all its objectives and taken 2,500 prisoners as well.

To the west of XVIII Corps, VII Corps had both the heaviest task but also the strongest force—the U.S. 1st and 3rd Armored Divisions, the 1st Cavalry and 1st Infantry, and the U.K. 1st Armoured, supported by an aviation brigade and the 2nd Armored Cavalry Regiment. This solid mass of tanks and infantry fighting vehicles was to engage and destroy the enemy's main counterattack force—the Republican Guard and the Iraqi Army tank divisions. Because the enemy armor was deployed both to protect the fortified front and to guard the western flank, VII Corps' mission was a complex one: two divisions—the U.S. 1st Infantry and U.K. 1st Armoured—were respectively to breach and exploit through the fortifications, while the U.S. 1st and 3rd Armored Divisions were to roll up the right flank, preventing the Republican Guard from advancing to contest the break-in. This was a classic tank maneuver, but it demanded meticulous coordination, both of covering fire power with the movement of formations and of the sequence of attack by the formations themselves.

The success of XVIII Airborne Corps moved General Schwarzkopf to launch VII Corps fifteen hours earlier than planned. It began its mission on the afternoon of February 24 with the most testing of all the component operations of Desert Sabre, a deliberate assault and obstacle clearance of the Iraqi fortified zone. The task fell to the combat engineers of the U.S. 1st Infantry Division. As luck had it, the chosen point of assault fell at the boundary of two Iraqi divisional positions, those of the 26th and 48th. Artillery preparation for this undertaking had been heavier than that used during the whole of the U.K. 8th Army's attack before the battle of Alamein in November 1942, and the 26th Division had already been paralyzed by its effect. There was no resistance, therefore, to the reconnaissance teams that were helicoptered across the sand berms as an advance force or to the armored bulldozers that followed them to drive breaches; sixteen lanes altogether were opened in a 2-mile front. Behind the bulldozers and their supporting tanks appeared mine-clearing parties, which fired "snakes" of explosive hose to detonate mines along a 200-foot track; the snakes also opened passages in the barbed wire entanglements. When mine-free lanes had been driven across the whole depth of the obstacle zone, other combat engineers advanced to make good the passageways, fill ditches, and mark routes for the advance of VII Corps' main striking force.

The obstacle-clearing operation was the greatest single triumph of the whole operation. It had rightly been anticipated as the most difficult but also the most crucial element of the plan, since its success would determine whether the goal of the entire endeavor would be met—quick and crushing defeat for the enemy. It had succeeded beyond expectation, at almost no loss to the brave and exposed combat engineers of 1st Infantry Division.

In their wake, the tanks of the division advanced to fall on the Iraqi 4th Division, which, devastated by air and artillery bombardment and largely abandoned by its officers, rapidly disintegrated. In the tracks of the Americans, the U.K. 1st Armoured Division followed to exploit the advantage already won. Standing in its path was the Iraqi 12th Armored Division, positioned and tasked to mount a counterattack against precisely such a break-in as the Americans and British had now achieved. It did not, however, make any move to do so, but remained frozen in its complex of bunkers and trenches. The British had assigned three objectives to themselves, which were codenamed Copper, Zinc, and Platinum. At Copper, a large Iraqi communications center, concerted resistance was met for the first time during VII Corps' attack. It was overcome by the combined efforts of a tank-infantry team formed from the Royal Scots Dragoon Guards and the Staffordshire Regiment. Objective Zinc was taken by another tank-infantry team, and these successes took the whole 7th Brigade of the U.K. 1st Armoured Division to its final objective, Platinum, ahead of schedule. Meanwhile, the 4th Brigade overran an Iraqi brigade position to achieve its planned phase-line also. This comparatively heavy fighting had opened the way for VII Corps' other strong armored element, the U.S. 1st and 3rd Armored Divisions, to maneuver rapidly across the desert flank from west to east, thus securing ground initially penetrated by the 2nd Armored Cavalry Regiment, which advanced 45 miles that day.

The first day of the offensive also saw the 1st U.S. Marine Expeditionary Force and the two Arab Joint Forces Commands committed to action on the coastal sector and in the heavily defended Iraqi front south of Kuwait City. On the coast, Joint Forces Command East, largely Saudi in composition, opened six lanes through the obstacle belt and captured large numbers of prisoners. On the left, Joint Forces Command North, of which the Egyptian 3rd Mechanized and 4th Armored Divisions formed the spearhead (the Syrian division was held in reserve for political reasons), brought forward its attack to exploit the advantage won by XVIII Corps and the marines. After an initial success, it was temporarily halted when it lost direction in the obstacle zone and was subjected to Iraqi artillery fire, but it regrouped and carried on with decisive effect. Joint Forces Command North quickly secured the surrender of the whole defensive Iraqi division and succeeded in clearing free passage through what was later estimated to have been the densest sector of the obstacle zone.

The U.S. Marines, attacking between the two Joint Forces Commands' sectors, were actually the first of the coalition forces to move off. They did so under cover of a ruse that brought the 2nd Marine Division from the coast to the left flank of the 1st Marine Division. Together, the two were tasked not to attack the front directly before them, as the Iraqis had been led to expect, but rather to bring their forces to bear on the bends in the Kuwaiti border with Saudi Arabia further to the west, known respectively as the "elbow" and "armpit," because the divisions were weaker in organic armor than their army equivalents. The 2nd Brigade of the 2nd Armored Division was attached to provide greater weight.

The U.S. Marines' offensive began under cover of darkness, when the 16-inch guns of the battleships *Wisconsin* and *Missouri* brought the Iraqi fortified zone under fire, together with the divisional artilleries, at 1:00 A.M. The Iraqis replied, but ineffectively, since preparatory fire had caused heavy casualties among their gun crews, and the survivors were reluctant to man their weapons. The U.S. Marine engineers succeeded in opening lanes through the obstacle belt, releasing the armored columns supported by marine aviation, to move forward between 4:00 and 5:30 A.M. They met some resistance but within a few hours of departure had overrun the positions and destroyed the Iraqi 7th, 14th, and 29th Divisions. Many of the enemy survivors had clearly been waiting for the opportunity to surrender and ran forward to meet the attackers waving white flags. Very shortly, prisoners had been taken in such numbers that their management became the U.S. Marines' chief operational difficulty.

The Advance Continues

Sunday, February 24, could be counted a complete success. All objectives had been taken. In some sectors, progress had exceeded expectations, and the final second line was further forward than the plan required. The Iraqis had almost nowhere put up a fight, and where they did, their resistance had been easily overcome. Prisoners had been collected in large numbers. The weather, a mixture of sand- and rainstorms accompanied by unseasonably low temperatures, had been the principal impediment to progress. On the following morning, progress accelerated dramatically, particularly in XVIII Airborne Corps' sector. Starting from the Cobra logistic base established the day before, 300 helicopters lifted a complete brigade of the 101st Air Assault Division 130 miles in a single bound, positioning it across Highway 8 and thus severing direct contact between Baghdad and Kuwait City. The move appears to have taken the Iraqi high command completely by surprise, thanks to the severe damage to their communications system inflicted during the air war. The 24th Mechanized Division profited from this breakdown to race ahead of schedule some 200 miles into Iraqi territory. By the evening of February 25, it had exceeded its phase-line by 36 hours and was established in territory far behind Iraqi lines.

VII Corps had also sustained the advance begun the previous day. The U.K. 1st Armoured and U.S. 1st Infantry Divisions met pockets of stiff resistance at isolated points, including one where an Iraqi battalion engaged the U.K. 7th Brigade for some time. By pressing along the western edge of the Wadi Al-Batin, instead of up the wadi itself as the Iraqis had expected, they bypassed the heaviest concentrations of enemy troops; by maintaining a series of short, rapid blows on the many positions encountered, they distracted the enemy from any attempt to launch a counterattack across the long tail of logistic vehicles that followed them. Indeed, they were now themselves bringing the Iraqi reserves under attack, ensuring the unobstructed advance of the U.S. 1st and 3rd Armored Divisions to their west. These divisions, led by the 2nd Armored Cavalry Regiment, reached northward throughout the day to seize by nightfall the road center at Al Busayyah, thereby positioning themselves for an eastward advance against the Republican Guard divisions that constituted the Iraqis' final and stronger reserve. On the coastal flank, meanwhile, the U.S. Marine divisions had also sustained progress, meeting and defeating the Iraqi 5th Mechanized Division, while the Egyptians, pressing forward into a thickening pall of smoke from the oil wells vindictively ignited by the Iraqis that were rapidly turning the overcast day to gloomy night, approached the outskirts of Kuwait City.

On the morning of Tuesday, February 26, the U.S. Marines resumed the advance that would carry them by evening through Kuwait International Airport to positions north of Kuwait City itself. The decision had been taken to allot the liberation of the city to the Kuwaiti forces of Joint Forces Command East as soon as they could extricate themselves from the traffic jams on the coastal route that were impeding progress. On the western flank, XVIII Airborne Corps, spearheaded by the 24th Mechanized Division, found visibility reduced at times by a raging sandstorm to 80 feet but finally reached the Euphrates valley and became embroiled in a battle for a large logistic base defended by four Iraqi battalions. Here the enemy attacked the division's vehicles with small arms and antitank weapons at close range. Calling in artillery fire, which proved devastating, the crews forced a way through to join the airborne troops already positioned across Highway 8, thus denying the main force of the Iraqi army in Kuwait any hope of an orderly withdrawal into the Mesopotamian plain. In any case, the armor of VII Corps was about to engage the best of the Iraqi army, the Republican Guard, in decisive battle.

The core of the Republican Guard was formed by the Medinah and Tawakulan ("Trust in God") Divisions, respectively mechanized and armored, supported by several army divisions. All were dug into strong positions, the armor positioned behind berms that concealed all but the top of the tank turrets. As the U.S. 1st and 3rd Armored Divisions and the U.K. 1st Armoured Division, which had joined forces with the 2nd Armored Cavalry Regiment, approached the fortifications, the worst of the sandstorms to afflict the coalition throughout the land battle descended, blotting out the landscape to the naked eye. The attackers' satellite positioning system continued to function, however, as did their thermal-imaging and image-intensifying lights. As a result, tank crews were able to identify the Iraqi entrenchments from their maps and to locate targets with their fire-control equipment. Engaging at slightly under two miles, gunners quickly began to destroy Iraqi vehicles, whose occupants were unaware that they lay under threat. In a few hours of one-sided destruction, the Tawakulan and an Iraqi tank division were destroyed, and the Medinah Division was reduced to half its strength. Some 308 Iraqi tanks and 318 armored vehicles were destroyed, and perhaps 10,000 Iraqi soldiers were killed or wounded. U.S. losses amounted to only a few dozen wounded, less than ten killed, and a handful of armored vehicles disabled in a battle fought at odds of ten to one.

The battle to liberate Kuwait was now effectively at an end, though the city itself was not occupied until the following day, Wednesday, February 27. The crux of the action was centered on the Mutala Ridge, on which runs the highway from Kuwait City northwards, the Iraqi army's only remaining route of escape. There the fleeing Iraqis were caught between the fire of the 1st Armored Division and the 2nd Marine Division and under the hail of relentless attack by the coalition air forces. At the height of the battle, a 25-mile traffic jam of trapped and often burning vehicles occupied the road northward from Kuwait City, and the devastation was only heightened by the unavailing efforts of surviving units of the Iraqi Hammurabi and Medinah Divisions to hold their enemy at bay.

President Bush, as head of the coalition, now decided that further offensive effort against the broken and fleeing Iraqis would serve neither politics nor humanity, and he accordingly declared the land battle at an end at its hundredth hour, 5:00 A.M., Thursday, February 28. Estimates of Iraqi combat losses remain in dispute: The U.S. Defense Intelligence Agency suggested a figure of 100,000, with an error factor of 50 percent; other estimates lie between 60,000 and 100,000. The Iraqi government has issued no figures of its own, however, and the coalition undertook no systematic registration of graves. If the real total of Iraqi forces in the theater before the ground war was above 360,000, and it is known that 86,000 were taken prisoner, then the quoted casualty lists seem high. The figures look even less realistic if the normal proportion of wounded— between two and three for each fatality—is taken into account; to do so is to arrive at a casualty list of at least 150,000, which approaches 50 percent mortality. Such a figure would be unprecedented in so short a war. Even allowing for the intensity of coalition firepower, it requires revision downward.

A corrective factor is supplied by equipment losses, which amounted to 3,847 tanks, 1,450 armored vehicles, and 2,917 artillery pieces, for a total of 8,214 items in all. On the one hand, experience indicates that when a tank is hit, one crew member is killed and one is wounded; on the other hand, a direct hit on an armored personnel carrier with a missile or tank round tends to kill all the occupants. If it is presumed that all Iraqi fighting vehicles lost were hit—and that is not a sustainable presumption—then losses in the armored units would amount to some 4,000 tank crew killed and 14,000 killed in other armored vehicles, for a total of 18,000. It seems probable, however, that the majority of Iraqi vehicles taken by the coalition forces were abandoned, so that figure would fall to below 10,000 killed in the armored formations. The latter comprised a quarter of all Iraqi formations in the theater; applying the same ratio of fatalities to the total, therefore, a maximum of 40,000 Iraqi soldiers killed appears the highest figure that could be sustained statistically. The actual figure is probably lower and, including the wounded, might amount to no more than 60,000.

This is still appalling high, particularly when contrasted with coalition losses: 148 in combat among Americans, less than 20 among the British (the majority to "friendly fire"), only 2 French, and 14 Egyptians.

Assessing the Battle

The Persian Gulf ground war had therefore resulted in one of the most unequal conclusions ever recorded. The outcome should, nevertheless, have surprised no one but Saddam Hussein and his circle of military and political confidants. Their army, though large in numbers and plentifully supplied with modern Soviet equipment, was insufficient to oppose those that the coalition had assembled. Its experience in combat against the Iranians during the eight years of the Iran-Iraq war had been no preparation for the ordeal to which Hussein's ill-judged invasion of Kuwait had exposed it. The enemy in the Iran-Iraq war not only lacked airpower but also ground firepower and the ability to apply armored shock on narrow fronts of attack. The Iranians, indeed, had fought in essentially First World War style, depending on the use of vast masses of infantry, advancing in rigid wave formations, to overwhelm the Iraqis' entrenched positions. Such offensives had been consistently checked by investment in fortification, including inundation, which, though entailing a steady drain of losses in defense, had resulted in a casualty exchange rate very much in the Iraqis' favor.

It appears to have been their experience in the Iran-Iraq war that persuaded the Iraqi high command to believe their army would be capable of resisting the shock of a coalition offensive into Kuwait, though their adherence to the Soviet doctrine of defense, which also laid heavy emphasis on the importance of entrenchments, mine-laying, and obstacle-building, was also a contributory factor. What the Iraqis had omitted from their calculations was the likely reaction of the U.S. and other NATO contingents of the coalition to the military problem of assaulting a Soviet-style fortification system. The U.S. and U.K. divisions deployed to Saudi Arabia in particular had, of course, trained for years on the presumption that they might eventually have to fight a Soviet army. They knew the characteristics of Soviet weapons and the precepts of Soviet defensive and offensive tactical doctrine in detail.

The Iraqi miscalculation was, therefore, a double one. They had presumed that their defenses, which had worked on their eastern border with Iran, would work equally as well on Kuwait's southern border with Saudi Arabia, despite the marked topographical differences between the two regions. They had further presumed that tactics that had served to repel the attacks of an ill-trained and ill-equipped third-world enemy would serve also against the high-tech armies of developed powers. And they had made a third and perhaps more fundamental miscalculation. Though they had attempted to penetrate the psychological makeup of their enemies, they had misunderstood it. In the Iranians they had met warriors who appeared to compensate for their technological inferiority by fortitude of will or fanaticism of belief. In the U.S. and other Western contingents, they believed they were confronted by soldiers whose technological superiority was a mask for absence of belief and feebleness of will. Saddam Hussein is known to have convinced himself, by his misunderstanding of the repercussions of the Vietnam War in the United States, that Western democracies lacked the strength of purpose to persist in military operations that entailed high casualties. He had convinced himself that "a mother of battles," even if fought by the Iraqis at a material disadvantage, would nevertheless yield victory, because the shock of the first casualty lists would deter their enemies from persisting with an offensive bound to lengthen the roll of the dead.

It can be argued that Saddam Hussein might have been proven correct if he had succeeded in prolonging his "mother of battles"; it can equally be argued that the coalition would have shown a greater resilience than he expected. What is inarguable is that Schwarzkopf's confidence in his own ability to mount and orchestrate an offensive that would rob the Iraqis of the chance to prolong the conflict into a battle of attrition was well founded. Risks there were, but the coalition's plans were designed to minimize them to the greatest extent possible, while its capabilities made the prospect of such minimization realistic.

Yet it would be unsafe to conclude from the course and outcome of the Gulf War that high-technology operations guarantee unlimited success in all circumstances. The results of the Gulf War were limited in two important respects. The first was geographical: The February victory did not lead to the occupation of Iraq, which would undoubtedly have brought about the downfall of Saddam Hussein's regime. That was because the coalition high command rightly concluded, for strictly logistic reasons, that the terrain of Mesopotamia in the wet season precluded any continuation of the high-intensity operations it had conducted so successfully in the dry, open desert of Kuwait and western Iraq. On the banks of the Euphrates and Tigris and in the plain between them, the spring snowmelt causes inundations that might bog down even the most mobile—and airmobile—of modern armies. Huge areas disappear under water, wide detours are necessary to find passable terrain for tracked vehicles, villages and even towns become islands, and whole road networks are swamped. Successful offensive operations in springtime Mesopotamia would require an amphibious capability for which no army in the world is equipped or is likely to be made so.

The second respect in which the Gulf War's results were limited was psychological. The failure to occupy Iraq allowed Saddam Hussein to proclaim, and perhaps even to believe, that he had not been truly defeated. Had climate and topography, among other factors, not persuaded the coalition to desist from a deep penetration of his territory, the fact of his defeat would have been undisguisable. There may, however, have been other reasons that caused the coalition to hold back from concluding its offensive with an outright occupation. One was the humanitarian restraint that President Bush declared. Another that was almost certainly present in the coalition's calculations was its unwillingness to take up the burden of administering a hostile and highly nationalistic Arab state. This burden would not merely have been short term. In the long run, such an occupation would have entailed a return to some form of the imperialism that has failed everywhere in the twentieth century, most recently and spectacularly in the Soviet Union. Imperialism requires the imposition of one culture upon another. Although Western culture is supremely adept at the organization and execution of decisive military operations, it is no more adept than any other at transforming military victory into an instrument of fundamental cultural domination, and nothing less than a transformation of a culture as fundamentally Islamic as Iraq's would ensure its subordination to Western ideals of good-neighborliness and respect for international order in the Persian Gulf region. War has many uses, but the restructuring of cultures is rarely one of them. That may be seen as the most abiding lesson of the coalition's victory in the Gulf War.

6

Implications of the Gulf War for Future Military Strategy

John H. Cushman

The Gulf War was but one of many events and developments—such as recent military experiences; the breakup of the Soviet Union and its bloc; the end of the Cold War; the emergence of the United States as the sole military superpower; and political, military, economic, environmental, and social changes worldwide—with implications for the future military strategy of the United States.

From Washington, D.C., to distant places of U.S. concern, the military component is but one of many elements of U.S. influence and power. It is guided in harmony with all the other elements by means of national military strategy, which governs both the generation of military capabilities and their employment, should it be called for. Executive decisionmakers and members of Congress collectively determine the kinds and amounts of forces and other capabilities to be generated, given the resources available and the perceived needs.[1] In contrast, decisions regarding the employment of capabilities—defining precisely when, where, how, and what forces and other capabilities are to be employed and for what purposes—are formulated in concert at Washington and in the area of operations.

A new administration was voted into power in 1992 and with it came a searching review of U.S. national security objectives. How will the sole military superpower fit into the world scheme? Is the United States to take a proactive role in the emerging era? Is it to be the world's policeman? An enforcer of good behavior by rogue nations? The guarantor of regional stability worldwide? The United Nation's conscience and motivating agent? The backbone of each military coalition that gets called into play around the world? Or a provider of forces to operate under U.N. direction?

In the Gulf War, the United States led the way, and the coalition, masterfully built and directed, followed. Operation Provide Comfort, aimed at assisting the Kurds in northern Iraq, was a similar performance by a U.S.-led multinational force. Is the implication here that the United States is so politically, indeed logistically, dependent upon its friends and allies that the option of "going it alone" no longer exists? And if only multinational action is acceptable, is the United States denied independent freedom of action? What about Operation Just Cause, Panama 1989–1990? Or Urgent Fury, Grenada 1983? Or Eldorado Canyon, Libya 1986? The United States clearly must preserve the prerogative to act independently in the future.

Since U.S. disengagement does not appear likely, it seems a good idea for the Clinton administration to continue to generate forces that would be ready for, if not all, most of the eventualities cited—and for others like them around the world. And it seems right for the United States to build forces and other capabilities that can carry out unilateral action, always seeking to employ military force in multinational action but employing it unilaterally if need be.

In generating forces for the future, the first rule is to balance innovation and vision with caution. The army went for a radically new "pentomic" divisional organization in 1956 only to reverse its decision three years later; the navy downplayed minesweepers in the buildup by Secretary of the Navy John Lehman to its later regret; in the 1950s, the air force neglected conventional weaponry when national policy ordered reliance on massive nuclear retaliation. At the least, such bad judgment can produce an embarrassing inability to act; at worst, it can be catastrophic, as was the case for France in 1940. Cost cutting in the late 1940s left the United States grossly unprepared for Korea in 1950 and barely able to stave off disaster.

In contrast, to have judged rightly, or almost so, can save a situation and even change the direction of history for the better. Right judgment can come from good luck; for reasons far removed from a possible Iraqi invasion of Kuwait, the United States in August 1990 had on hand the right mix of forces for success in just such an event. But this was happenstance; those forces' development over decades had been aimed primarily at the Soviet Union, which at the time of the Gulf War was in the process of folding, and time was available for their assembly and final preparation. Good fortune like that is not guaranteed.

The implications of all the preceding are as follows: The United States should generate the right forces and other capabilities. It should aim to optimize them across a well-calculated range of potential requirements. And it should cover reasonably well each important need and build in a safety factor.

Gulf War Lessons

The Gulf War has been the subject of comprehensive analysis within the U.S. government and from outside.[2] The generally accepted judgment is that it was a success, although not an unqualified one. Its ultimate implication might be this: If the United States wants to influence a situation decisively, it must, as in the Gulf War, have both the means to act and the will to act; and then it has to use those means very well.

The following specific and enduring lessons of the Gulf War should be kept in mind when generating and employing military forces. First, General Colin Powell is right: Overwhelming force gets the job done quickly and saves lives. The United States should have such force available for rapid assembly and use.

Second, if freedom of air and naval action is not already present, the first order of business must be to achieve it. Unless land forces are engaged from the outset (as might happen when they are already deployed) or the situation is desperate, they should not be committed into combat until air supremacy is gained, the enemy's command and control is beaten down and its intelligence assets are neutralized, and the battlefield is prepared through precision air and artillery attack. In the Persian Gulf, command of the air was absolute from the first hours of combat, as was the uncontested application of coalition airpower (meaning the attack aviation and cruise missiles of both air and naval forces) and its precision weaponry. This created the necessary conditions for a lightning air/land campaign that, with remarkably few casualties, sealed the enemy's destruction and gained control of the land.

Third, the complex of ports and airfields provided by Saudi Arabia was invaluable but probably unique. The United States should seek actual or potential base locations around the globe and should press on with their development, but it cannot count on their being as near the action, or as complete, as were those of Saudi Arabia.

Fourth, U.S. command of the sea lanes was undisputed; in like situations for decades to come, there will be no enemy to contest it seriously. Establishing inshore maritime supremacy is, however, another matter; the United States should reorient its maritime forces and influence those of its potential coalition partners to operate close to shore.

Fifth, the timely assembly of forces and their remarkable proficiency in battle was made possible by the generous time that was available for movement, training, and preparation. This cannot be guaranteed in future situations. Ample airlift and rapid sealift must be provided. Through joint training, the readiness of forces to hit the ground running must be ensured.

Sixth, the interim Department of Defense report observed that the intelligence staff "was not structured for a deployment or conflict on the scale of Desert Storm. . . . It was not [adequately] staffed or equipped."[3] Similarly, the report by the House's Committee on Armed Service states,

"Operation Desert Storm revealed significant problems in intelligence support."[4] It is vital to correct these deficiencies before the next conflict.

Seventh, although all U.S. services and the special operations contingent displayed superlative operational and tactical proficiency, their performance could be improved. For example, the navy and the marines lacked the night-fighting capabilities demonstrated by the army and air force. As well, the Scud hunt took too long to organize and execute. These and other shortcomings call for correction.

Eighth, the U.S. emphasis on high-technology weaponry proved itself in the Stealth fighter and its precision munitions, the Patriot and Tomahawk missiles, the JSTARS (joint surveillance and targeting system) aircraft, and others. With plenty of time to put it in place, U.S. command and control technology came through; emergency production of the satellite-based Global Positioning System, for example, which gave individual tanks and aircraft their precise locations, saved the day in the featureless desert. But many areas need more work: communications interoperability, battlefield air mobility, positive battlefield identification of friendly forces, equipping carrier aviation with smart weapons, and so on.

Ninth, the Gulf War was a logistical triumph. It made clear once again that without logistics, operations cannot succeed.

Tenth, joint expeditionary forces are here to stay; the various services' forces mutually reinforce each another, and shrinking budgets and forces make multinational operations increasingly more necessary.

Eleventh, a striking feature of the war was its remarkably few casualties, especially in light of predictions before the event.[5] Public anguish over even these few losses was amplified when a rear area barracks was struck catastrophically by a Scud missile in the war's final days and upon learning later of the undue numbers of frontline troops struck by friendly fire. The American people accept far fewer casualties from war than they once did. In the desert, technology and overwhelming force coupled with superb troop proficiency saved lives. The Gulf War set new standards both for skill and for cost in lives.

The U.S. military establishment, by and large, did very well in the Gulf War. Next time, whenever and wherever that may be, those responsible must strive to have the U.S. military equally ample, skilled, and ready. And next time there will almost certainly be less time to prepare.

Command and Control Arrangements

In this new era, U.S. forces had better be ready to fit into imaginative arrangements for multinational command or action. In World War II, the United States and the United Kingdom developed a binational field command responsive to the Combined Chiefs of Staff. An elaborate superstructure that was multinational all the way to corps level with three military commands evolved in NATO. In the Korean War, the U.N. Security Council (its sessions boycotted by the Soviet Union over China's representation) named the U.S. president as its executive agent for a U.N. field command, and South Korean President Rhee quickly placed his forces under General MacArthur. After the war, the United States and South Korea established a permanent Combined Forces Command under a U.S. general. Each of these precedents gave the coalition unity of command in the theater.

But in the Persian Gulf, although the U.K. and French governments agreed that General H. Norman Schwarzkopf, commander in chief of the U.S. Central Command, could lead their contingents in operations, Saudi Arabia and the other Moslem nations did not. To cope with the high-tech, swift, and violent fighting expected in the war with Iraq, General Schwarzkopf was forced to use what he called a "C³IC"—a Coalition, Coordination, Communications, Integration Center.

The C³IC was the brainchild of Lieutenant General John J. Yeosock, commander of Schwarzkopf's army forces. When Iraq attacked on August 2, 1990, the only U.S. military presence in Saudi Arabia was the U.S. Military Training Mission, under an air force major general, and the project manager for the Saudi Arabian National Guard (PMSANG). Yeosock, who had once been PMSANG, immediately saw the need for Saudi-U.S. coordination of both the buildup and the plans for defending Saudi territory. Using officers from the PMSANG and the training mission, Yeosock formed the C³IC.

Lieutenant General Yeosock headed the U.S. side of the C³IC. His Saudi counterpart was Lieutenant General Khalid, son of that nation's minister of defense and a member of the royal family. Each had a full-time deputy. General Khalid's deputy would always be a trusted Saudi general officer able to negotiate on his own. General Yeosock brought in Major General Paul Schwartz, "another old Saudi hand distinguished by his infinite patience and ability to work problems as the Saudis do," to be his deputy. Schwartz was designated as Vice Commander ARCENT because that had a meaningful ring for the Arab side.[6]

General Schwarzkopf had been an advisor to South Vietnam's airborne division, had been exposed in his youth to Arab ways through his father's assignments in the area, and had just spent eighteen months as commander in chief, U.S. Central Command, visiting Arab countries and leaders. He knew how to handle himself with the Saudis.[7] He also knew a good thing when he saw it and quickly made the C³IC his own.

The implication of all this is as follows: It helps very much to have people available who are used to dealing with allies, who seek to understand their ways, and who are willing to accommodate. This kind of talent does not arise automatically; it must be developed. Developing and nurturing it is a function of military strategy.

But in the type of warfare faced by General Schwarzkopf, would using a C³IC to direct operations get the job done when negotiation, cooperation, and coordination were the watchwords for much of his force, including the Saudis? Schwarzkopf's challenge was to organize for coherent, high-tech, fast-moving, and all-dimensional warfare a mushrooming array of multiservice/multinational forces in which the forces of the United States, which he did command, were dominant and would be decisive.

General Schwarzkopf's U.S. forces came to him in components—ARCENT (3rd U.S. Army), MARCENT (1st Marine Expeditionary Force), NAVCENT (7th Fleet), and CENTAF (9th Air Force), each with a three-star commander.[8] (The commander of ARCENT had three three-star subordinates: the commanders of VII Corps, XVIII Airborne Corps, and the 22nd Support Command.) General Schwarzkopf wielded important new team-building authority over these components per the 1986 Goldwater-Nichols legislation. Among the powers he was able to employ were the following: "authoritative direction over all aspects of military operations . . . prescribing the chain of command . . . organizing [subordinate] commands and forces as he considers necessary . . . employing forces as he considers necessary . . . [and] assigning command functions to subordinate commanders."[9] But Schwarzkopf had no such authority over the other coalition members' forces. With them, he could use only leadership, persuasion, and appeals to their self-interest.

For his air forces, General Schwarzkopf benefited from Pentagon reforms triggered by the Goldwater-Nichols Act, which had led to joint doctrine whereby any U.S. joint force commander could designate a single air authority, known as the JFACC (joint force air component commander), for the "planning, coordination, allocation and tasking" of all the air units in the joint force, regardless of its service component.[10] Using that authority, he designated Lieutenant General Charles A. Horner as the JFACC. This provided a single command and control center for the air war into which air contingents of other nations had no choice but to join if they wanted to benefit from coalition intelligence or to have their air missions "deconflicted"—in other words, to have them fly without running into other aircraft or being shot down by coalition air defenses.[11]

Similarly, while placing sea-launched cruise missiles and carrier aviation under the tasking authority of the JFACC, Schwarzkopf called on his naval component commander to direct the sea campaign. He charged Vice Admiral Henry A. Mauz, Jr.—later succeeded by Vice Admiral Stanley R. Arthur—to conduct sea and coastal operations with the U.S. Navy forces that Mauz commanded as well as with other U.S. forces (Coast Guard, marine units, and army helicopter elements on occasion) over which Mauz had operational control and to pull together other nations' maritime contingents in the coalition's sea effort.[12] In operations like the reflagging and escort of Kuwaiti tankers three years earlier, the U.S. Navy in the Persian Gulf had become adept at coordinating such multinational sea operations.

Land forces differ in nature from those of the air and sea. They do not range widely. Below the level of brigade or battalion, formations of different nations and services do not mix well. Their required teamwork is intricate, their detailed ways of fighting differ from nation to nation and army to marine, and force proficiency comes only by working together at length.

The marine contingent could fit well in a plan that placed it near the Persian Gulf coast and marine logistic bases, where it would also be in a position to link up with deeper amphibious operations should that be called for and where, with Arab forces, it could breach the Iraqi barriers and retake Kuwait City.[13] The army's VII and XVIII Corps, with their stronger logistic structure (and control of the U.K. and French divisions), could be moved westward over land and sustained in a deep envelopment of the Iraqi defenses. With this lineup, General Schwarzkopf could allow the two main Arab commands—Joint Forces Command North (between VII Corps and the 1st Marine Expeditionary Force) and Joint Forces Command East (along the Persian Gulf)—to come directly under General Khalid, staying within their boundaries in a common scheme.

But coordinating the operations of land forces and making possible their effective use of intelligence, air support, and logistics in fast-moving situations requires more than simply lining them up in formation. Here General Yeosock made another crucial contribution; he organized liaison parties from his army-provided resources to go with the two Arab formations—the North and East commands—and with other formations of Schwarzkopf's command.

General Yeosock saw these liaison parties for the Arab allies as similar to the C³IC in concept. They would be

> not just . . . a means of communication, but an instrumentality to influence how the allies did business, even to assist them in complex staff work if necessary. . . . [They provided] interface with the Special Operations Forces assigned from CENTCOM to provide advice and training . . . [produced] a communication and command information net in the Arab forces more reliable than that possessed by the Northern and Eastern commands . . . [and] assisted in planning and obtaining deep targeting support from [tactical air], provided tactical commanders with intelligence not otherwise available, [and] provided immediate "ground truth" for [higher commanders].[14]

Invaluable both in planning and operations, these teams "became a means of working out a variety of coalition problems."[15] They were a tribute to the insight and ingenuity of General Yeosock, who put them into place.

Although much smaller, Operation Provide Comfort, which took place during April and May of 1991 in Turkey and northern Iraq, was an equally cogent example of cooperation among the United States and its allies.[16] The operation's initial purpose was to provide humanitarian relief to Kurds who had been driven into the mountains by Iraqi tanks and armed helicopters after Saddam Hussein's surrender in early March. The commander in chief of U.S. European Command, General John R. Galvin, U.S. Army, who was responsible for the U.S. part of the effort, appointed Lieutenant General John M. Shalikashvili, U.S. Army, to be the task force commander. Shalikashvili had a U.S. Air Force deputy, a Marine Corps chief of staff, and a hastily assembled all-service staff. By the end of May, he was directing a 20,000-strong coalition force, of which 11,000 were Americans.

Lieutenant General Shalikashvili's mission quickly expanded beyond airdropping food and other necessities. He was told to organize camps, supervise distribution of food and water, and help with sanitation and medical care. He was also to use U.S. and other nations' military forces to guarantee camp security, establish a protected security zone in Iraq, operate a combat air patrol over Iraq, and engage in combat with Iraqi forces if necessary.

Shalikashvili's organizing principle was simple: Give key subordinates the disparate U.S. and international elements for a given function and then hold them responsible for pulling that function together. He made his air force commander responsible for coordinating all air delivery, with jurisdiction over U.S. Army cargo helicopters and those of other nations. He gave the U.S. Army commander a mix of U.S. Army, U.S. Air Force, and Marine Corps logistic units and told him to manage support operations for the multinational task force. He told the commander of Task Force Bravo, Major General Jay M. Garner, to build camps for the refugees; in turn, Garner made the commander of the army's 18th Engineer Brigade responsible for this effort and placed under him the mixed bag of U.S. and coalition engineers, including a Seabee battalion.

To provide area security in his zone inside Iraq and to move civilians into camps, Garner gave one area each to the senior French commander, the Italian brigadier, the Spanish force commander, the Royal Marine brigadier, and the commander of the U.S. Marine component, assigning each a composite force. For U.S. Marines, this consisted of a U.S. Army Airborne Battalion, some Italian special forces teams, and an Air Force explosive ordnance disposal unit.

Each national contingent came with its own commander—a major general for the larger ones. Each national commander established liaison with General Shalikashvili at his command post in Incirlik and, in turn, with Shalikashvili's subordinates. There were no memoranda of understanding; Shalikashvili simply told each national commander that he expected to exercise *tacon* (tactical control), a well-known NATO term. Each commander immediately accepted that, asking only what he could do to help— and the troops went about their business.

Service and national command chains were relied upon for administration and support and as the channels through which operational instructions were passed. The operational orders would go something like this: "Take your unit, and report to so-and-so [the Brit, or the marine, or the special forces commander]. He'll tell you what to do; I'll stay in touch."

The organizational and leadership talents demonstrated by Generals Schwarzkopf, Yeosock, Shalikashvili, and Garner did not develop overnight. Like Lieutenant General Horner, who pulled together the Gulf War coalition air effort, and Vice Admirals Mauz and Arthur, who did the same for the naval effort, these officers had studied their trade in successive assignments with allies and other services.

These successes imply that the United States should develop forces for command and control that are ready for unexpected missions and unusual arrangements. It should also place a high value on commanders who are knowledgeable, flexible, and prepared to bring together disparate service and coalition forces in coherent operations.

Forward Engagement Zone

In the future, the kinds of talents just mentioned can be developed (and will be needed) in the forward engagement zones of a twenty-first-century *Pax Americana;* that is, in those places where the United States will want to promote stability in what will surely continue to be a trouble-riddled and crisis-prone world. To do so will involve, among other things, the use of U.S. military capabilities and expertise in cooperation with the military establishments of struggling nations to help the latter build and protect healthy and stable societies. The aims of this cooperative endeavor will be to foster healthy national development, to identify and take care of incipient trouble spots before they develop into crises, and—if necessary—to deal with those crises quickly and effectively before they require force commitment.

In many developing nations, the military is a major, if not *the* major, component of the governing structure. Military institutions, in our own nation and in others, have long been recognized as potentially helpful in coping with problems of national and regional economies, education, health and sanitation, and evolution toward democratic processes. Although helpful of themselves, however, the military aspects of this endeavor will by no means be paramount; they will complement other thrusts of U.S. foreign, economic, and national security policy—all within a mutually accepted understanding of the situation and with conceptual unity governing the effort. The military means available to the United States to achieve these aims include frequent reciprocal visits, officer exchanges, combined exercises, military advice and assistance, the development and maintenance of area expertise and language proficiency, and similar activities—all pulled together in a subtle, consistent, and adequately resourced enterprise without an overbearing U.S. role but with cooperation based on self-interest being the rule.

For example, the U.S. Pacific Command has long had programs of liaison and cooperation with the military establishments of the Asia-Pacific region to promote what has been variously called "civic action" or "national assistance." The United States could establish an Institute for National Military Cooperation in Hawaii, the aim of which would be to provide a means for the military establishments of its friends in Asia and the Pacific to work together among themselves and with the U.S. military toward the improvement of conditions in their nations and in the area generally. The institute's director could be one of the many U.S. officers who has served as an advisor and area specialist and is fluent in some of the area's principal languages. The institute could have a small multiservice and civilian research staff and teaching faculty as well as linkages with academia. The United Kingdom, Japan, and Australia could provide liaison officers. A U.S. foreign service officer could serve as the director's political advisor.

The institute might conduct research, sponsor seminars, take part in instructional programs, and the like—all in a multinational, cooperative framework. It could carry out a program of analysis, reciprocal visits, information and expert exchange, and production of publications. Inasmuch as unsettled conditions in a nation may breed terrorism and similar aggressive actions, often instigated from outside its borders, the theory and practice of effectively dealing with low-intensity conflict would be one of the institute's primary concerns.

For example, consider Country X, with a poor economy, a military dictatorship that is out of touch with its people, and insurgents forming in the countryside. One of the institute's objectives in this case would be to help the military leaders to realize that their country cannot have military security without good government, genuine land reform, and social justice. Perhaps the central government, with help from local military units in the field and with U.S. advice and assistance, could begin to carry out a comprehensive program of rural development and land redistribution combined with military security in villages.

The insurgents could well react with violence, cutting roads and utility lines, killing local officials, and mixing propaganda with attempts at intimidation. But if the military stayed on a steady course, locating the insurgent hideouts, ambushing their night movements, infiltrating their organization, monitoring their communications, and denying them secure bases in the countryside—then after many months, even years, of patient work, the tide could eventually turn.

Perhaps a U.S. officer, with a background of experience and study in low-intensity conflict and national development, could become the faculty advisor to a group of officers from Country X who were participating in a two-week seminar. Fluent in their language, he could build rapport, spend time on temporary duty in the country, and in a low-profile mode assist its military establishment in understanding its situation, developing a comprehensive program to cope with the situation, and carrying out that program.

Capabilities for military action and influence in the low end of conflict will be more important in years to come. Although no two situations will be alike, one feature common to all will be an ambiguous and complex interaction among social, political, economic, and military forces and interests.[17] Thus, future U.S. military strategy would do well to focus on the development of capabilities and institutions for achieving stability in crisis-prone regions so that situations do not deteriorate to the point where the United States must intervene with military force.

Objectives

Should military force become necessary, as General Powell has observed, "[one] must begin with a clear understanding of what political objective is being achieved" and then determine the proper military means for doing so.[18]

The objectives of military intervention were on the mind of Secretary of Defense Weinberger when, in November 1984, he set out six conditions to be met before the United States commits its forces abroad. These criteria, made public when speculation was rife that the United States might send troops to El Salvador, were clearly the result of post-Vietnam soul-searching within the Pentagon:

1. The United States should not commit forces to combat overseas unless the particular engagement or occasion is deemed vital to our national interest.
2. If such a commitment is made, we should do so wholeheartedly and with the clear intention of winning.
3. We should have clearly defined political and military objectives. We should know precisely how our forces can accomplish those clearly defined objectives.
4. The relationship between our objectives and the forces we have committed, their size, composition and disposition, must be continually reassessed and adjusted if necessary.
5. There must be some reasonable assurance we will have the support of the American people and their elected representatives in Congress.
6. The commitment of U.S. forces to combat should be seen as a last resort.[19]

As applied to the Gulf War, the first of these criteria was easily met. Secretary of Defense Cheney and General Powell found the second one to be of paramount importance, and so President Bush decided in early November 1990 to double U.S. might in the Persian Gulf. The fifth and sixth criteria were less easy to satisfy initially, but they were adequately met in due time. But the third and fourth criteria, dealing as they do with military strategy, merit the closest consideration here, especially as the Gulf War served as an excellent case study for their application.

The process of defining and achieving military objectives can be called "the direction of war." It is a process of transcendent importance and profound complexity. It has four dimensions: political, strategic, operational, and tactical.[20]

In principle, political/strategic direction should be the product of a nation's or coalition's highest political and military authorities working in concert, with leadership in political guidance being the domain of the former and strategic direction being the area of expertise of the latter. A theater commander would join the high military authorities in formulating strategic direction; once that was established, he would turn his attention to in-theater strategic direction. In action, however, the institutions and processes for political and strategic direction are so closely linked that the two forms of direction should be looked at together.

Strategic direction defines operational conditions to be achieved and establishes campaign purposes and sequencing to achieve those conditions. In principle, the formulation of political/strategic direction takes place at the seat of government. But defining (more specifically) operational conditions to be achieved and establishing (in more detail) campaign purposes and sequencing to achieve those conditions is also the duty of the field commander, consistent with the guidance given to him. So the field commander and, in the U.S. system, Washington share responsibility for strategic direction, with the field commander reinforcing and expanding on what he has been told to do by higher authorities. And there is usually only one chance to do it right.

The presence of a coalition considerably complicates the direction of war, both for the high political-military authorities of the nations involved and for the coalition's field command, however it is constituted. Most fundamentally, nations may disagree on the objectives for which the coalition should fight. But even when agreeing on ultimate objectives, nations may differ on how to achieve them. During the 1950s, for example, the NATO coalition agreed to defend Western Europe, but its member nations disagreed on whether that defense should be placed well forward, giving up the minimum of territory in West Germany, or should be allowed more depth.

No counterpart to the Combined Chiefs of Staff of World War II existed for the Gulf War coalition. The Military Staff Committee of the U.N. Security Council was incapable of serving as a coalition staff; its procedures called for the armed forces chiefs of staff of the five permanent members to agree on every product. During the Cold War it had never been used, and for this war it simply got in the way.

The United States provided by far most of the forces, so the U.S. Joint Chiefs of Staff became the primary military staff for the Gulf War coalition. General Powell, using the Joint Staff, working with other members of the Joint Chiefs of Staff, and advising the secretary of defense and the president and responsive to them, developed military instructions for General Schwarzkopf, the field commander of U.S. forces and the coordinator responsible for the coalition effort. (Legally, General Schwarzkopf was a direct subordinate to the secretary of defense.) After obtaining the approval of Secretary Cheney—and of President Bush when appropriate—Powell then issued those instructions.

Contacts with other members of the coalition took place, for political direction, at the level of heads of government and their relevant ministries. To coordinate strategic direction from each nation's seat of government, the U.S. secretary of defense and Joint Chiefs of Staff were in touch with their counterparts in other nations. For strategic and operational direction in the area of operations, General Schwarzkopf worked with the coalition's commanders in the field. Of these, only the British and, finally, the French would be under his operational control. In effect, President Bush and his advisors, including the Joint Chiefs of Staff, were thinking for the coalition. But they were also doing a job for the United States.

At 1:00 A.M. (Kuwait time) on August 2, 1990, Iraq's armored forces invaded Kuwait; by 4:30 A.M., they had reached Kuwait City, and news of the invasion had reached the White House, where it was 8:30 P.M., August 1. Within ninety minutes, President Bush had received a request from Kuwait for assistance and had decided to take the case to the United Nations. Reached by telephone in New York, Thomas Pickering, U.S. ambassador to the United Nations, began drafting a resolution to lay before the U.N. Security Council that night.[21]

At 6:00 A.M. on August 2 (New York time), the U.N. Security Council passed its Resolution 660:

The Security Council . . .

1. Condemns the Iraqi invasion of Kuwait;
2. Demands that Iraq withdraw immediately and unconditionally all its forces to the positions in which they were located on 1 August 1990. . . .[22]

That morning President Bush and Secretary of State James A. Baker (who was meeting in Irkutsk with Soviet Foreign Minister Eduard A. Shevardnadze) began to assemble the coalition that would, under the mantle of the United Nations, fight the Gulf War.

On August 6, the Security Council voted its Resolution 661, stating its determination "to restore the sovereignty, independence, and territorial integrity of Kuwait" and to institute an embargo and begin the isolation of Iraq.[23] Sanctions went into effect, the Desert Shield buildup began, the coalition grew, but Saddam Hussein remained defiant. On November 29, in Resolution 678, the Security Council authorized "member states . . . unless Iraq on or before 15 January 1991 fully implements [all previous] resolutions, to use all necessary means to uphold and implement resolution 660 and all subsequent relevant resolutions and to restore international peace and security in the area."[24]

The United States had, in four months, used its moral authority, the commitment of its military might, and the machinery of the United Nations to build a coalition of Arab and Western powers that was now prepared to go to war—for three basic objectives:

1. The unconditional withdrawal of Iraqi forces from Kuwait (Resolution 660, reaffirmed in Resolution 678)
2. The restoration of the sovereignty, independence, and territorial integrity of Kuwait (Resolution 661, reaffirmed in Resolution 678)
3. The restoration of international peace and security in the area (Resolution 678)

The arena for presidential persuasion now moved to the U.S. Congress. After convening in early January 1991 and debating fervently in both houses, Congress provided the president the practical equivalent of a declaration of war on January 14. The Senate, by a vote of 52 to 47, and the House of Representatives, by a vote of 250 to 183, approved a resolution saying that the president was authorized (pending his notification of the House and Senate that peaceful means to obtain Iraq's compliance would not succeed) "to use United States Armed Forces pursuant to United Nations Security Council Resolution 678."[25]

Masterfully managing the crisis, building a coalition, and developing popular support, the president had brought about a situation in which the objectives of the United States and those of the United Nations coincided and were adopted by Congress.[26] Yet the United States had retained for itself a degree of freedom of action. Resolution 678 gave it authority to determine for itself—as a member state—what would be the "necessary means . . . to restore international peace and security in the area." Within limits, the United States could further define its own objectives and act toward realizing them. A delicate balance would be necessary. The United States could not stray too far from a consensus; certainly it needed to keep the five permanent members of the Security Council and the major Arab nations reasonably on board.

But were the three *political* objectives enough for the *strategic* direction of the force? Strategic direction defines the operational conditions to be achieved and establishes campaign purposes and sequencing to achieve those conditions. If by January 15 Saddam Hussein had yielded to coalition pressure with an "unconditional withdrawal of Iraqi forces," that political objective would have been achieved without the coalition's use of force. Should force be required, however, that political objective would translate into a coalition strategic *military* objective: "Expel Iraq from Kuwait." Either way, the third political objective—"Restore the government of Kuwait"—would follow.

But what about the third political objective, if force were to be necessary? What precise military end-condition would most probably restore international peace and security in the area? Might it be an end-condition such as a dismantled Iraqi military machine and the elimination of its chemical, biological, and nuclear means or the removal of Saddam Hussein from power? Unlike the situation in Panama 1989, when Noriega was a specific target, Saddam Hussein was not, at least not directly. His future depended in large part on how far the United States wanted to go in weakening Iraq. An Iraq left too weak by the war might tempt its neighbors—Iran, Turkey, and Syria—to move in or allow Iraq's Kurdish and Shi'ite sections to break away. But if Iraq were left strong enough for a central regime to control its people, then Saddam Hussein would probably be in control of that regime.[27]

Secretary Weinberger's third criterion stated that the United States should "have clearly defined political and military objectives [and to] know precisely how our forces can accomplish those clearly defined objectives."

Defining the operational conditions to be achieved is a task shared by political and military authorities in Washington and the theater commander, with—inasmuch as political and strategic direction are so closely linked—primacy in establishing basic end-conditions residing in the hands of the former.

Calibrating the application of force and precisely stating operational goals to be achieved for political purposes is problematical. War is not amenable to precise calculations. But—going along with Secretary Weinberger's advice that "the relationship between our objectives and the forces we have committed, their size, composition and disposition, must be continually reassessed and adjusted if necessary"—it may be useful to play out an imaginary vignette to illustrate what could be involved in tailoring operations to a definite end.

Imagine that at some time between mid-January and mid-February 1991, the president, meeting with his key advisors, including Secretary Cheney and General Powell, is reviewing General Schwarzkopf's plan for the war's ground phase. General Powell describes General Schwarzkopf's mission—to destroy Iraqi armed forces in and near Kuwait and then to liberate Kuwait—and says that Schwarzkopf is authorized to enter Iraq as necessary to do so.

He displays Schwarzkopf's operation plan and explains it: "The all-armor VII Corps will make the main effort. Along with the 24th Mechanized Division of XVIII Airborne Corps, it will strike deep, sweep east toward Basra, and engage and destroy the Republican Guard divisions in and near Kuwait while the marine divisions and Arab forces drive up from the south. The XVIII Airborne Corps' 101st Airborne Division (Air Assault) with its helicopters will establish a forward operating base from which it can launch assault forces and Apaches to control Highway 8 south along the Euphrates. It will then leapfrog to a new base, from which it can range as far as Basra and the highway north of Basra. The 82nd Airborne Division and the French 6th Light Armored Division will protect the left flank."

Let's say that the president asks, "What is the plan for the end game?"[28] It turns out that the plan depends on the goal sought and that the desired goal at this time is the destruction of the Republican Guard divisions in or near Kuwait and the ejection of all Iraqi forces, which will liberate Kuwait. Discussion moves to the subject of the U.N. (and U.S.) objective to restore international peace and security in the area. The question surfaces: What operational end-condition would best achieve this objective?

Now, imagine that the president says, "Suppose I told you that my view of what would most contribute to peace and security in the area is to bring about Saddam Hussein's removal from power." He continues, "Saddam is cunning; he is ruthless; he is a survivor. How can we put a stranglehold on this man out of which he can't wriggle? How can we control postwar events inside Iraq? That's what I want to be able to do—but I don't want to get embroiled among the population as we were in Lebanon." He then asks, "Can we calibrate a military end-condition that would do that?" The meeting ends without an answer. Within a day the president receives a new option, briefed by Colin Powell.

"Sir," the general says, "this option is contingent on near-total collapse of Iraqi forces; this may well occur within days of our ground attack.[29] This option aims to trap the Republican Guard south of the Euphrates, where most of it is now, by blocking, initially with airmobile forces on the ground, the highways north of Basra and any other escape routes.

"This option also tells General Schwarzkopf to plan to place a force astride the Baghdad-to-Jordan highway—to be executed on your order should the moment be right. Provided Iraqi forces have essentially collapsed, this option is feasible. We can establish a two-brigade lodgment in the desert on the Baghdad-Jordan highway, with airborne or heliborne forces or both.[30] We can support such a lodgment, and given our air supremacy, we can defend it without difficulty. The risk can be made small, and casualties few.

"This option will both trap the Iraqis south of the Euphrates and establish a force on the Baghdad-Jordan highway, leaving no doubt of our victory—or of our ability to dictate terms to Saddam Hussein, no matter how he tries to manipulate his way out. The Arabs may think this option goes too far. It can be argued, however, that because it will cut Saddam Hussein down to size, the move is in the interest of the coalition's common objective as established in Resolution 678—peace and security in the region. This option may give rise to a perception that the United States is committing itself to an unwanted and unsustainable long-term presence in the area. A counterargument is that the United States has been rotating its units on peacekeeping in the Sinai since the Camp David accords; a deployment here for a period of time is similarly sustainable. In any event, this is an end-condition option to consider."

Of course, the president received no such option. The secretary of defense's order to General Schwarzkopf, issued on December 29 as a warning and then ordered for execution on January 15, was the first plan outlined—one that called simply for destroying the Republican Guard and ejecting Iraqi forces from Kuwait. It also permitted entry into Iraq as necessary.

General Schwarzkopf launched the ground phase of Desert Storm at 4:00 A.M., Kuwait time, on February 24. Iraqi resistance at the front quickly crumbled. By February 27, VII Corps was driving eastward to the Kuwait-Basra highway; it was clogged with fleeing Iraqis under ferocious, even horrifying, air attack—reported on live television. The Republican Guard was being destroyed; coalition casualties were surprisingly few. That day at 9:00 P.M., local time, General Schwarzkopf gave the world his "mother of all briefings." Ninety minutes or so later, General Powell had him on the telephone, indicating the president's wish to stop the attack as soon as possible, mentioning 5:00 A.M., local time, as the hour visualized and asking if there was any military reason not to do so. General Schwarzkopf polled his commanders and gave General Powell his assent. From the moment he queried General Yeosock, an irreversible movement began in VII and XVIII Corps to stop the fighting. Hostilities ceased at 8:00 A.M., February 28.[31]

When General Schwarzkopf heard back from his commanders at approximately midnight on February 27, he knew that he had no ground formations near Basra; in that area was only an enemy in chaos. Planes and Apache helicopters had, without restraint, been attacking Iraqi forces there all day. He knew that VII Corps' north boundary, running east-west, was south of Basra. He had been led to believe that units of VII Corps were on the ground on the highway to Basra, just north of the Kuwaiti border (he learned the next morning that they were not). He knew that the four bridges in Basra were either open, closed but repairable, or replaceable with pontoon bridges and that the causeway to the west was in Iraqi hands. In other words, he knew that the "gate" through Basra and across the Euphrates "was not closed."

But General Schwarzkopf believed, or so he said, that he had accomplished his mission—the destruction of the Republican Guard.[32] So he agreed to a cease-fire to go into effect early in the morning of February 28. The remnants of the Republican Guard south of the Euphrates immediately began to flow north. Two days later, a chart of General Yeosock's morning briefing had this to say about the Iraqi forces: "*Major trends:* . . . Continue moving out of the Basra pocket across the Euphrates River. *Probable Intent:* . . . Continue to establish hasty defensive positions inside Iraq, while conducting hasty and deliberative river crossings to save remaining forces."[33]

But by then it was two days too late for General Schwarzkopf and his commanders to do anything about the Iraqi withdrawal; they could only watch the Iraqis reconstitute—and perhaps regret the coalition's lost opportunity. Among those who may have regretted most sorely would surely be the commanders of XVIII Airborne Corps and of its 24th Mechanized and 101st Airborne Divisions. As the corps commander, Lieutenant General Gary E. Luck, was being queried by General Yeosock at midnight on February 27, his 24th Mechanized Division, with the 2nd Armored Cavalry Regiment attached, was refueling and rearming in preparation to continue the attack eastward to destroy the Republican Guard in its zone and to seize the causeway crossing over the Euphrates. They faced a demoralized and ineffective enemy. About 3:30 A.M., the division commander learned that a cease-fire had been called; he suspended offensive operations.[34] The causeway remained in Iraqi hands.

On the morning of February 27, Luck's 101st Airborne Division (Air Assault) established Forward Operating Base (FOB) Viper. All day, four battalions of Apache attack helicopters (about 72 Apaches total) from Viper had been mercilessly striking Iraqi columns.[35] That evening, the 101st was preparing to launch a brigade task force from FOB Cobra further west. The task force was to refuel their helicopters at Viper and at mid-morning of February 28 was, with Apache and air support, to air assault to block the highways out of Basra to the north.[36] Except for an eastward movement of the 24th Mechanized Division—which occurred after the official cessation of hostilities and included seizing the causeway—none of these planned actions took place.[37]

Conclusion

The Gulf War's end brought an eruption of national pride, praise for everyone from the president to the fighting troops, and welcome-home celebrations such as had not been seen in the United States for decades. There was special praise for the president's assembly of an unprecedented and unified Mideast coalition and for General Schwarzkopf's handling of that coalition's effort in the field. Overwhelming force coupled with superb troop proficiency had made for a swift and stunning ending of the war at a very low cost in lives. The contrast between the Gulf War's quick and satisfying triumph and the Vietnam War's long agony and eventual defeat could not have been more striking.

Yet within hours of President Bush's decision to end the fighting, fears began to emerge that important objectives had not been achieved; that the war's outcome had been less than satisfactory; that somehow, in the war's final hours and afterward, Saddam Hussein had been able to preserve too much of his army. As the brief account related in the previous section indicates, those fears were justified. General Schwarzkopf could have made the coalition's victory unequivocal, and he should have.

There is no intent here to call the Gulf War a failure. The war's outcome fundamentally changed, favorably for U.S. interests and those of the people of the region, the complexion of the Middle East. If the war did not take Iraq out of military commission completely, it did diminish, and perhaps eliminate, its ability to browbeat its neighbors for a long time to come.

The Gulf War was a success, but it could have been more so. It can be convincingly argued that when Saddam Hussein got away with too much of his army, the leverage available to the United States, the coalition, and the United Nations to make him and Iraq behave in the war's aftermath suffered. Although such a view can be called Monday-morning quarterbacking or niggling at the details of what was a success, the intent here is simply to look honestly at what happened and to learn. Insights gained from thinking objectively about the Gulf War's success in achieving its goals could be of value in any future commitment of U.S. forces. Then, as in the Persian Gulf, there will be only one chance to do it right.

The question is this: What was done wrong? The answer is that neither the president and his key advisors in Washington nor General Schwarzkopf and his people in the theater thought through and established the desired end-condition or -conditions needed to meet the political objectives sought. The fault did not lie in the political objectives. In an interview on November 1, 1990, General Schwarzkopf said:

> There are alternatives to destroying Saddam Hussein or to destroying his regime. I like to think that the *ultimate objective is to make sure that we have*

peace, stability, and a correct balance of power in the Middle East. . . . There are many ways you can accomplish that. One way would be the total destruction of Iraq, but I am not sure that is in the interest of the long-term balance of power in the region. . . . I do think there are alternatives to having to drive on to Baghdad and literally dig out the entire Baathist regime and destroy them all in order to have peace and stability in the area. (emphasis added)[38]

But when it came down to deciding, the plan to achieve the coalition's political objectives on the ground (leaving aside the destruction of Iraq's nuclear, chemical, and biological capabilities) was simply to "destroy the Republican Guard" (which would, of course, "eject Iraqi forces from Iraq"). This was an inadequate end-condition. Others could have been found. The coalition could have set up a decisive lodgment on the Baghdad-Jordan highway as Iraq reeled from defeat, just before placing into effect a cease-fire. Or before any cease-fire went into effect, it could have placed armor on the causeway exit and air assault forces on the highways north of Basra. General Schwarzkopf had tools in hand to do these things. He should have used them or at least have made plans to use them; not making plans ruled them out.

War is a brutal undertaking, not readily amenable to finesse, but artful employment of available forces has its place. General Schwarzkopf may well have had a mindset against any use whatsoever of airborne assault in Desert Storm. If so, that is unfortunate; it deprived him of a unique and useful capability. But after three days of intense battle, when the president, like the public, the press, and members of Congress, was sickened by the killing and wanted to talk cease-fire, General Schwarzkopf's mindset did not admit of the possibility to trap what he had not destroyed, even though he had the forces on hand to do just that.[39]

If he had been thinking in terms of trapping as well as destroying when queried late in the evening of February 27 about a cease-fire, General Schwarzkopf could (without polling his commanders) have replied to General Powell, "Give me until noon tomorrow. By then I'll have the Basra highway blocked and the causeway secured, and we'll have the Iraqis trapped; that will be a better outcome. [And if you give the go-ahead on that airborne operation, for which we are fortuitously ready, we'll have by noon a lodgment on the Baghdad-Jordan road, and then we'll really have Saddam by the short hairs.]" And history would have been different. Saddam Hussein would have been more surely in our grip, and there would have been no nagging aftertaste of not having done Desert Storm quite right.

Notes

Part of this chapter draws upon *Issues of Mideast Coalition Command and the Future of Force Projection,* prepared by the author for the Program on Information Resources Policy, Harvard University.

1. *Capabilities* seems a better term than *forces,* which connotes fighting organizations only. Other capabilities would include space-based intelligence systems, military assistance, and advisory groups, linguists, commanders, and staff officers prepared to serve in multinational agencies and headquarters, and so on.

2. The official Department of Defense studies on this subject are the *Interim* (July 1991) and *Final* (April 1992), *Reports to Congress on Conduct of the Persian Gulf War* (Washington, D.C.: Government Printing Office). A congressional study, *Defense for a New Era: Lessons of the Persian Gulf War* (Washington, D.C.: Government Printing Office), was prepared by the staff of the Committee on Armed Services, U.S. House of Representatives, for its chairman and ranking Republican member and published March 30, 1992. In July 1991, the Center for Strategic and International Studies, Washington, D.C., published *The Gulf War: Military Lessons Learned.* A host of other private studies and books have also addressed this subject.

3. Department of Defense, *Interim Report to Congress on Conduct of the Persian Gulf War* (Washington, D.C.: Government Printing Office, 1991).

4. Committee on Armed Service, *Defense for a New Era: Lessons of the Persian Gulf War* (Washington, D.C.: Government Printing Office, 1992).

5. U.S. Senator Edward M. Kennedy went on record as saying: "Most military experts tell us that a war with Iraq would not be 'quick and decisive' as President Bush suggests; it will be brutal and costly. It will take weeks, even months, and will quickly turn from an air war to a ground war with thousands perhaps even tens of thousands of American casualties. The administration refuses to release casualty estimates, but the 45,000 body bags the Pentagon has sent to the region are all the evidence we need of the high price in lives and blood we will have to pay. . . . In other words, we are talking about the likelihood of 3,000 American casualties a week, with 700 dead, for as long as the war goes on." *Congressional Record,* 102nd Cong., 1st sess., 1991, 137, pt. 6:126–127.

6. From the draft Army history of the Gulf War being prepared by the Center for Military History at the U.S. Army Command and General Staff College, Fort Leavenworth, Kansas, 42–44.

7. This sensitivity apparently did not carry over into General Schwarzkopf's book, *It Doesn't Take a Hero* (New York: Bantam, 1992). A *New York Times* article (October 21, 1992, p. A8) reported that General Khalid "accused General H. Norman Schwarzkopf of presenting a self-serving, inaccurate account of the war that exaggerates General Schwarzkopf's role and diminishes Saudi Arabia's contribution to the victory."

8. ARCENT stands for U.S. Army Forces, Central Command; NAVCENT refers to CENTCOM's U.S. Navy forces; MARCENT refers to its U.S. Marine Corps forces; and CENTAF stands for its U.S. Air Force forces. U.S. Coast Guard forces in the theater, although part of the Department of Transportation, operated under U.S. Navy command and with U.S. Navy logistic support. The commander of ARCENT also had the title Commander, 3rd U.S. Army; similar designations, in parentheses, apply to other component commanders.

9. *Goldwater-Nichols Department of Defense Reorganization Act of 1986,* Public Law 93-433, October 1, 1986, chapter 6, section 164(c).

10. Office of the Chairman, JCS, Joint Publication 1-02, 197.

11. As theater air defense authority, General Horner also had control of the U.S. Army Patriot battalions.

12. Operational control (often called *opcon*) "normally provides full authority to organize commands and forces and to employ those forces as the commander

in operational control considers necessary to accomplish assigned missions. . . . [It] does not, in and of itself, include authoritative direction for logistics or matters of administration, discipline, internal organization, or training" (Joint Publication 1-02, 263).

13. The aim of the plan was also to make the Iraqis think that the marines were the main attacking force.

14. Author--Please supply a note to identify the source of this quote.

15. Quotes are from the draft Army history of the Gulf War, 193–196.

16. For a more complete account of Operation Provide Comfort, see John H. Cushman, "Joint, Jointer, Jointest," *U.S. Naval Institute Proceedings* 118, no. 5 (1992): 78–85.

17. The foregoing is taken in part from John H. Cushman, "Requirements for U.S. Military Capabilities: Asia-Pacific Region, 2005–2015," working paper, The Rand Corporation, 1989.

18. *New York Times,* September 28, 1991, p. 1.

19. *New York Times,* November 29, 1994, p. A1.

20. These terms are used in Allan R. Millett and Williamson Murray, eds., *Military Effectiveness,* 3 vols. (Boston: Allen & Unwin, 1988), an illuminating and mostly discouraging study of the political, strategic, operational, and tactical effectiveness of Germany, Italy, Japan, the Soviet Union, France, the United Kingdom, and the United States in the two world wars and in the period between them.

21. Unless otherwise noted, the source for this narrative recounting of the events leading to the Gulf War is *Triumph Without Victory,* published in January 1992 by the editors of *U.S. News and World Report.* Prepared by the magazine's staff from news reports, official papers, and interviews, it is generally viewed as an authoritative account.

22. Resolution 660 passed by a vote of 14 to 0 (with Yemen abstaining). Appendix A of *Triumph Without Victory* provides the full text of all U.N. resolutions relating to Iraq's invasion of Kuwait.

23. Resolution 661 was passed by a vote of 13 to 0, with Cuba and Yemen abstaining.

24. Resolution 678 was passed by a vote of 12 to 2, with China abstaining and Cuba and Yemen against.

25. *Triumph Without Victory,* 450.

26. When President Bush told the world on August 8, 1990, that he had ordered the 82nd Airborne Division and U.S. Air Force Fighters to Saudi Arabia, he said that "four simple principles guide our policy." The first three of these were that "the immediate, unconditional, and complete withdrawal of all Iraqi forces from Kuwait" be achieved, that "Kuwait's legitimate government . . . be restored," and that "[the United States be] committed to the security and stability of the Persian Gulf." The president's first two objectives paraphrased Security Council Resolutions 660 and 661; the third foreshadowed Resolution 678, yet to come. The president's fourth principle—"I am determined to protect the lives of American citizens abroad"—was a warning to Iraq not to mistreat Americans or to retain them as hostages. (By the end of December, Saddam Hussein had released all hostages of every nation.)

27. The president made clear that, although removing Saddam Hussein from power was not a specific U.S. objective, he would be pleased if it came about. For example, on February 15, 1991, he said that "another way for the bloodshed to stop" was for "the Iraqi military and Iraqi people to take matters into their own

hands and force Saddam Hussein to step aside" (The *New York Times,* February 16, 1991, p. A6). He also said, "We do not seek the destruction of Iraq. . . . We do not want a country so destabilized that Iraq itself could be a target for aggression" (The *New York Times,* January 29, 1991, p. A13).

28. "**end game** . . . The stage of a chess game following serious reduction of forces" [*Webster's New International Dictionary of the English Language,* 3rd ed. (Springfield, Mass.: Merriam-Webster, 1971), 748].

29. Five days before the ground attack, General Schwarzkopf said that the Iraqi army (presumably not including the Republican Guard) was "on the verge of collapse" (*The Washington Post,* February 20, 1991, p. 1).

30. Use of airborne forces would have required time to bring parachutes and other air items from the United States; the 82nd Airborne Division deployed to the desert without them. A practice airborne assault would also have been necessary. However, an objective area astride the Baghdad-Jordan highway was reachable by helicopters, by establishing a desert refueling point halfway from Saudi territory.

31. These two paragraphs summarize the account in the draft Army history on the Gulf War, 392–400.

32. At General Schwarzkopf's 9:00 P.M. briefing on February 27, a reporter asked, "You said the gate was closed. Have you got any ground forces blocking the roads to Basra?" Schwarzkopf answered, "No." The reporter continued, "Is there any way they can get out that way?" The answer: "No. That's why the gate is closed" (*The Washington Post,* February 28, 1991, p. A37). In his book, *It Doesn't Take a Hero,* Schwarzkopf wrote (p. 470) of his affirmative answer that night to Powell: "[W]e'd kicked this guy's butt, leaving no doubt in anyone's mind that we'd won decisively, and we'd done it with very few casualties. Why not end it? Why get somebody else killed tomorrow? That made up my mind." He also wrote that he told Powell, "Our objective was the destruction of the enemy forces, and for all intents and purposes we've accomplished that objective." Powell then went ahead with plans for the president to announce at 8:00 A.M., local time, cessation of hostilities. Schwarzkopf related that he later called Powell and told him, "If we call this cease-fire, we're going to see Republican Guard T-72s driving across pontoon bridges." He added, "Powell came back later and said that the White House now understood that some tanks would get away and decided to accept it."

33. Briefing for General Yeosock, March 2, 1991, taken from the official record of COMUSARCENT briefing held at the U.S. Army Command and General Staff College, Fort Leavenworth, Kansas.

34. XVIII Airborne Corps Situation Report, February 27, 1991, from 262100 Z Feb to 272100 Feb (midnight to midnight, local time), *A History of the 24th Mechanized Infantry Division Combat Team During Operation Desert Storm* (Fort Stewart, Ga.: Headquarters 24th Infantry Division, 1992), 32.

35. *Mercilessly* is not the right word; pilots were appalled at the carnage wrought on the Iraqis, who were by then almost unable to defend themselves.

36. XVIII Airborne Corps Situation Report, February 27, 1991; *101st Airborne Division (Air Assault) Operations Desert Shield/Desert Storm Command Report* (Fort Campbell, Ky.: Headquarters, 101st Airborne Division, 1991), 56–59.

37. The draft army history on the Gulf War (pp. 427–435) describes an action that began the night of March 1, 1991, with the 24th Division moving forward to a north-south line four miles west of the causeway "looking for abandoned equipment." This action triggered a company-sized fight (escalating to battalion,

then brigade) with the Iraqi columns that had been using the causeway to flee north. The result was the destruction of 81 Iraqi tanks, 95 personnel carriers, 8 wheeled armored vehicles, 5 artillery pieces, 11 Frog missile launchers, and 23 trucks. The division lost 1 tank (the result of an Iraqi tank exploding alongside it), and only one soldier was wounded. By the time the action ended on March 2, the division had moved six miles forward, "enough to control the causeway line of withdrawal." The behavior of the division commander, Major General Barry R. McCaffrey, calls to mind Horatio Nelson's "holding his telescope to his blind eye" at Copenhagen [A.T. Mahan, *The Life of Nelson*, vol. 2 (Boston: Little Brown, 1897), 90] and of George Patton making "rock soup" when his 3rd Army had to halt because fuel ran out in early September 1944 [George Patton, *War As I Knew It* (Boston: Houghton Mifflin, 1947), 125]. McCaffrey's admirable action closed the causeway exit.

38. *New York Times,* November 2, 1990, p. A8.

39. General Schwarzkopf made this statement on November 14, 1990, to the two- and three-star commanders who would execute Desert Storm: "And finally, all you tankers, listen to this. We need to destroy—not attack, not damage, not surround—I want you to *destroy* the Republican Guard" (Schwarzkopf, *It Doesn't Take a Hero,* 381; emphasis in the original). Schwarzkopf gave the following instructions to Lt. Gen. Luck, XVIII Corps commander, on February 26, the third day of the ground attack: "I want to make sure you understand your mission. . . . It is to inflict maximum destruction, *maximum destruction,* on the Iraqi military machine. You are to destroy all war-fighting equipment. Do not just pass it on the battlefield" (Ibid., 462; emphasis in the original). On February 27, he told General Powell, "I want to continue the ground attack tomorrow, drive to the sea, and totally destroy everything in our path" (Ibid., 469). In his interview with David Frost, broadcast March 27, 1991, General Schwarzkopf said of the decision to halt the offensive: "My recommendation had been, you know, continue the march. I mean we had them in a rout and we could have continued to, you know, reap [sic] great destruction on them. We could have completely closed the door and made it in fact *a battle of annihilation*" (The *New York Times,* March 28, 1991, p. A18; emphasis supplied). Two days later he told reporters, "If I could do [the interview] over again I would change the word 'recommend' to say 'we initially planned.' Because that's what it was. We initially planned [a battle of annihilation] (The *New York Times,* March 30, 1991, p. A4).

PART THREE

Elements of Future Military Strategic Thought

7

The Role of
Nuclear Weapons

THOMAS C. SCHELLING

Half a century has passed since the first—and the last—nuclear weapons were used in warfare. These five decades of nonuse are a stunning achievement. And they are possibly the result of some stunning good luck.

It is plausible that the very existence of these weapons inhibited military adventure, suppressing opportunities for their use. But there has never been any real doubt about their military effectiveness or their potential for terror, and some (or perhaps a very large part) of the credit for their not having been used must go to the "taboo" that Secretary of State John Foster Dulles perceived to have attached itself to these weapons as early as 1953, a taboo that he himself deprecated.

The title of this chapter could have been "The Status of Nuclear Weapons," because their status has determined their role. The weapons remain under a curse, a now much heavier curse than the one that bothered Dulles in the early 1950s. The word *conventional* is used to describe most other weapons, and that word has two quite distinct senses. One meaning is "ordinary, familiar, traditional"; in this context, it is a word that can be applied to food, clothing, or housing. The more interesting sense of *conventional* refers to something that arises as if by compact or agreement. It is simply an established convention that nuclear weapons are unique. And the main thing that makes these weapons unique is that they are perceived to be unique.

It is true that their fantastic scale of destruction dwarfs the conventional weapons. But as early as the end of the Eisenhower administration, nuclear weapons could be made smaller in yield than the largest conventional explosives; thus, an overlap existed between their ranges of capability. There were military planners to whom "little" nuclear weapons appeared untainted by the taboo that, in their minds, was more properly attached to weapons like the ones used at Hiroshima and Bikini. But by then nuclear weapons had become a breed apart; size was no shelter from the curse.

This abhorrence of nuclear weapons was certainly not limited to the general public. Senior officials, civilian and military, acknowledged and expected that if the nuclear "threshold" were ever crossed by either side in a war, the other might feel instantly released from inhibitions, and there might be no telling how far escalation would go. No one, at least in Western countries, appears to have been immune to the perception that there was something generic about nuclear weapons.

This tradition that took root and grew over these past five decades is an asset to be treasured. It is not guaranteed to survive, and some possessors or potential possessors of nuclear weapons may not share it. The questions, How to preserve this inhibition, what kinds of policies or activities may threaten it, how it may be broken or dissolved or bypassed, and what institutional arrangements may support or in some fashion weaken it are worth careful consideration. How did this inhibition arise, was it inevitable, was it the result of careful design, was luck involved, and should we assess it as robust or vulnerable for the coming decades?

A Brief History of Nonuse

The first occasion when nuclear weapons might have been used was the initial stage of the Korean War. Americans and South Koreans had retreated to a perimeter around the southern coastal city of Pusan and appeared in danger of being unable either to hold out or to evacuate. The nuclear-weapons issue arose in public discussion in the United States and in parliamentary debate in the United Kingdom. Prime Minister Clement Atlee flew to Washington to beseech President Harry S. Truman not to use nuclear weapons in Korea. The visit and its purpose were both public and publicized. The House of Commons, considering itself to have been a partner in the enterprise that produced nuclear weapons, considered it legitimate that the United Kingdom have a voice in the U.S. decision.

The successful landing at Inchon obviated the question whether nuclear weapons might have been used if the situation in the Pusan perimeter had become desperate enough. But at least the question of nuclear use had come up, and the upshot was in the negative.

More than enough reasons may exist to explain the nonuse of nuclear weapons at that time in Korea. There was strongly voiced opinion on the unwisdom of bombing Asians once again with atomic bombs; there was concern not to deplete the strategic inventory; and there may have been a poor match between weapons and available targets on the battlefield. The possibility of nuclear escalation would not have been an issue, as no such weapons were available to the other side. I neither find nor recall evidence that an important consideration, for the U.S. government or the U.S. public, was apprehension over the consequences of demonstrating that nuclear weapons were "usable," of preempting the cultivation of a tradition of nonuse.

Nuclear weapons again went unused in the debacle in North Korea upon the entry of Chinese armies, and they were still unused during the bloody war of attrition that accompanied the Panmunjom negotiations. Whether they would have been used, where and how they might have been used, and what subsequent history would have been had they been used in North Korea or in China if the war had ground on for many months are, of course, purely matters for speculation. Whether the threat of nuclear bombardment influenced the truce negotiations remains unclear.

But the ambiguity expressed in the title of this chapter—that of the word *role*, which connotes an active presence, as applied to nuclear weapons—became vivid at that time. Nuclear weapons have not been dormant for fifty years; they have been, as it were, wide awake and alert. Their potential role in compelling, as well as deterring, became visible.

A recent book by McGeorge Bundy has documented the fascinating story of President Dwight D. Eisenhower and Dulles and nuclear weapons.[1] At the National Security Council (NSC) on February 11, 1953, "Secretary Dulles discussed the moral problem in the inhibitions on the use of the A-bomb. . . . It was his opinion that we should break down this false distinction."[2] The concept of "false distinction" is an interesting one; if enough people make the distinction, it becomes real! I do not know of any analysis of that time within the U.S. government of actions that might tend to break down this distinction or of what actions or inactions would preserve and strengthen it. But evidently Secretary Dulles believed, and may have taken for granted, that all members of the NSC were of the opinion that the restraints were real even if the distinction was false and that they were restraints not to be welcomed.

On October 7, 1953, Dulles reiterated his position, using the word that has since become familiar: "Somehow or other we must manage to remove the *taboo* from the use of these weapons" (emphasis supplied).[3] Just a few weeks later, the president approved, in a Basic National Security document, the following statement: "In the event of hostilities, the United States will consider nuclear weapons to be as available for use as other munitions."[4] This statement surely has to be read as more rhetorical than factual, even if the NSC considered itself to constitute "the United States." Taboos are not easily dispelled by pronouncing them extinct, even in the mind of the one who does the pronouncing. Six months later at a restricted NATO meeting, the U.S. position was that nuclear weapons "must now be treated as in fact having become conventional."[5] Again, saying so cannot make it so; tacit conventions are sometimes harder to destroy than explicit ones, existing as they do in potentially recalcitrant minds rather than on destructible paper.

According to Bundy, the last public statement in this progress of nuclear weapons toward conventional status occurred during the Quemoy crisis. On March 12, 1955, Eisenhower said, in answer to a question, "In any combat where these things can be used on strictly military targets and for strictly military purposes, I see no reason why they shouldn't be used just exactly as you would use a bullet or anything else."[6] Bundy's judgment, which I share, was that this again was more an exhortation than a policy decision.

Was Ike really ready to use nuclear weapons to defend Quemoy or Taiwan itself? It turned out he didn't have to. The conspicuous shipment of nuclear artillery to Taiwan was surely intended as a threat. Bluffing would have been risky from Dulles's point of view; leaving nuclear weapons unused while the Chinese conquered Taiwan would have engraved the taboo in granite.

At the same time, Quemoy may have appeared to Dulles as a superb opportunity to dispel the taboo. Using short-range nuclear weapons in a purely defensive mode, especially at sea or on beachheads devoid of civilians, might have been something that Eisenhower would have been willing to authorize and that European allies would have approved; in this case, nuclear weapons might have proved their worth as ordnance to be used "just exactly as you would use a bullet or anything else." The Chinese did not offer the opportunity.

On the status of nuclear weapons, the Kennedy and Johnson administrations were a sharp contrast to the Eisenhower administration. There was also a change in roles within the cabinet. Hardly anybody born after World War II remembers the name of Eisenhower's secretary of defense, but most people who have studied any U.S. history know the name of John Foster Dulles, his secretary of state. A bit of research into Bundy's book shows the contrast. In its index are thirty-one references to Dulles, two to Charles Wilson, and nine to Admiral Arthur W. Radford, the chairman of the Joint Chiefs under Eisenhower. Looking at it another way, eighty pages contain references to Dulles; two pages, to Wilson; and ten pages, to Radford. Under Presidents John F. Kennedy and Lyndon B. Johnson, the score is reversed; the index lists forty-two references to Secretary of Defense Robert McNamara, which cover sixty-one pages, and twelve references to Secretary of State Dean Rusk, which cover twenty-one pages.

The antinuclear movement in the Kennedy administration was led from the Pentagon (with encouragement from the White House), and in 1962 McNamara began his campaign—with President Kennedy—to reduce reliance on nuclear defense in Europe by building expensive conventional forces in NATO. During the next couple of years, McNamara became associated—again, presumably, with encouragement from the White House—with the idea that nuclear weapons were not usable at all in the sense that Eisenhower and Dulles had intended and even with the idea—stunning to some in Congress who heard his testimony—that the United States should prefer that the Soviets construct expensive, invulnerable strategic forces to stabilize the nuclear balance; undoubtedly, the traumatic events of October 1962 contributed to the revulsion against nuclear weapons held by some of Kennedy's key advisors and Kennedy himself.

The contrast between the Eisenhower and Kennedy-Johnson attitudes toward nuclear weapons is beautifully summarized in a statement of Johnson's from September 1964: "Make no mistake. There is no such thing as a conventional nuclear weapon. For 19 peril-filled years no nation has loosed the atom against another. To do so now is a political decision of the highest order."[7] This disposed of the notion that nuclear weapons were to be judged by their military effectiveness. It disposed of any "fakeness" in the distinction that Dulles abhorred: "a political decision of the highest order" compared with "as available for use as other munitions."

I am particularly impressed by the phrase "19 peril-filled years." Johnson implied that since 1945, the United States had resisted the temptation to do what Dulles had wanted the United States to be free to do where nuclear weapons were concerned. The implication was not that, no occasion having arisen in nineteen years, it would be a shame to spoil that unblemished record by using some nuclear weapons. The United States, or collectively the United States and other nations with nuclear capabilities, had an investment, accumulated over nineteen years, in the nonuse of nuclear weapons, and those nineteen years of quarantine for nuclear weapons were part of what would make any decision to use them a political decision of the highest order. Had Truman said in December 1950 that for five peril-filled years nobody had used nuclear weapons and that he, for that very reason, did not intend to use them now, it would have been hard to understand what he had in mind; Johnson had no doubt that his audience would know what he had in mind when he adverted to a precious investment in nineteen years of nuclear abstention.

A Basis for the Distinction?

It is worth a pause here to consider just what might be the literal meaning of the assertion that there is "no such thing as a conventional nuclear weapon." Specifically, why couldn't a nuclear bomb no larger than the largest blockbuster of World War II—or a nuclear depth charge of modest explosive power for use against submarines far at sea, or nuclear land mines to halt advancing tanks or cause landslides in mountain passes—be considered conventional? What could be so awful about using three "small" atomic bombs to save the besieged French at Dien Bien Phu as was discussed at the time? What is so wrong about using nuclear coastal artillery against a Communist Chinese invasion flotilla in the Gulf of Taiwan?

I think there are two distinct types of answers that this question has received, one mainly instinctive and the other more analytical but both resting on a belief or a feeling—a feeling somewhat beyond reach by mere logic—that nuclear weapons were simply and generically different. The more instinctive, intuitive response can probably best be formulated, "If you have to ask that question, you wouldn't understand the answer." The generic character of everything nuclear was simply—as logicians might call it—a primitive, an axiom; analysis was therefore seen as being as unnecessary as it was futile. The other, more analytical, response took its argument from legal reasoning, diplomacy, bargaining theory, and theory of training and discipline, including self-discipline. This argument emphasized bright lines, slippery slopes, salami tactics, well-defined boundaries, and the stuff of which traditions and implicit conventions are made. (The analogy to "one little drink" for a recovering alcoholic was sometimes heard.) But both lines of argument arrived at the same conclusion: Nuclear weapons, once introduced into combat, could not—or probably would not—be contained, restrained, confined, or limited.

Sometimes the argument was explicit in maintaining that no matter how small the weapons initially used, the size of weapons would ineluctably inflate, there being no natural stopping place. At other times, the argument was that the military needed to be held in check and once they were allowed to use nuclear weapons, it would be impossible to stop that use from escalating.

The case of the neutron bomb is illustrative. Because of their very small size and the materials of which they are constructed, these bombs emit "prompt neutrons" that can be lethal at a distance at which blast and thermal radiation are comparatively moderate. As advertised, they kill people—military personnel—without great damage to structures. The issue of producing and deploying this kind of weapon arose during the Carter administration, evoking an antinuclear reaction that caused it to be left on the drawing board. But the same bomb—at least, the same idea—had been the subject of even more intense debate fifteen years earlier, and it was then that the argument against them that was used in the 1970s was first honed, an argument that was simple and surely valid, whether or not it deserved to be decisive. Those opposed to the development of the neutron bomb held that it was important not to blur the distinction—the firebreak, as it was called—between nuclear and conventional weapons; they feared that either because of its low yield or because of its "benign" kind of lethality, there would be a strong temptation to use this weapon where nuclears were otherwise not allowed and that its use would pave the way for nuclear escalation.

This argument is not altogether different from that against so-called peaceful nuclear explosions (PNEs). The decisive argument against PNEs was that they would accustom the world to nuclear explosions, undermining the belief that nuclear explosions were inherently evil and thereby reducing the inhibitions on using nuclear weapons. The prospect of blasting new river beds in the northern Soviet Union or a bypass canal for the waters of the Nile generated concern about "legitimizing" nuclear explosions.

A revealing demonstration of this antipathy was in the virtually universal rejection by U.S. arms controllers and energy-policy analysts of the prospect of an ecologically clean source of electrical energy, proposed in the 1970s, that would have involved the detonation of tiny thermonuclear bombs in underground caverns to generate steam. I have seen this idea unanimously dismissed without argument, as if the objections were too obvious to require articulation. As far as I could tell, the principal objection was always that even "good" thermonuclear explosions were bad and should be kept that way. (I can imagine President Eisenhower opining, "In any energy crisis where these things can be used on strictly civilian sites for strictly civilian purposes, I see no reason why they shouldn't be used just exactly as you would use a ton of coal or anything else." And Dulles would add, "Somehow or other we must manage to remove the taboo from the use of these clean thermonuclear energy sources.")

But it is important not to think that nuclear weapons alone have this character of being generically different, independently of quantity or size, from other tools of war. Gas was not used in World War II. The Eisenhower-Dulles argument could have been applied to gas: "In any combat where these gases can be used on strictly military targets and for strictly military purposes, I see no reason why they shouldn't be used just exactly as you would use a bullet or anything else." But as Supreme Commander of the Allied Expeditionary Forces, General Eisenhower, as far as we know, never proposed any such policy. I conjecture that if you had asked him at the time why he didn't favor the use of gas when it might be militarily effective, he would not have had a ready answer. After some thought, however, he would have responded that if U.S. forces used gas, the enemy would and if U.S. forces did not, the enemy might not. And if you had pursued the issue and asked him why he hadn't calculated which side would come out the better if both were to use gas, he might have adverted to the patients in veterans' hospitals all over the United States still suffering from lung damage received in World War I. Maybe if he had been put through the exercise at the time, General Eisenhower would have convinced himself not that gas should never be used but that gas was at least different from bullets and that its use raised strategic issues. And ten years later, President Eisenhower might have recalled that line of thinking when he (reluctantly, I suspect) let his secretary of state urge doing for nuclear weapons what he himself apparently never thought of doing for gas in the European theater.

Some other things in warfare have this all-or-nothing quality. Nationality is one; for a long time it was thought, and I believe even was policy, that if uniformed U.S. and Soviet troops, however few in number, deliberately fired at each other, it meant "war."[8] The Chinese did not visibly intervene in the Korean War until it was time to intervene in force. U.S. military aid personnel have always been cautioned to avoid appearing to engage in anything that could be construed as combat, the notion being that such contamination could not be contained. There was some consideration of U.S. intervention in Indochina at the time of Dien Bien Phu, but not on the ground, and it was thought that aerial reconnaissance would count less as "intervention" than would bombing. Typically, the notion is that to provide military assistance in the form of equipment is much less participatory than to provide it in the form of people; we arm the Israelis and provide ammunition even in wartime, but so much as a

company of U.S. infantry would be perceived as a greater act of participation in the war than US$5 billion worth of fuel, ammunition, and spare
parts.

I mention all this to suggest that there are persistent perceptual and
symbolic phenomena that, if examined, help to make the nuclear state of
affairs less puzzling. And I find it remarkable how these perceptual constraints and inhibitions cross cultural boundaries. During the Chinese
phase of the Korean War, the United States never bombed air bases in
China; the "rules" were that Chinese bombing sorties originated from
North Korea, and to abide by the rules Chinese aircraft originating in
Manchuria touched down briefly at North Korean airstrips on the way to
bombing their U.S. targets. That reminds us that national territory is like
nationality; crossing the Yalu, on the ground or in the air, is a qualitative
discontinuity. Had General Douglas MacArthur succeeded in conquering
all of North Korea, even he could not have proposed that penetrating just
a little bit into China proper wouldn't have mattered much because it
was only a little bit.

Still, these qualitative all-or-nothing thresholds are often susceptible to
undermining. People who wish, as did Dulles, that a taboo did not exist
might not attempt to get around it only during crucial situations. They
might also apply their ingenuity to dissolving the taboo during relatively
unimportant occasions in anticipation of later times when the taboo would
be—to their minds—a genuine embarrassment. Bundy suggested that in
discussing the possibility of using atomic bombs in defense of Dien Bien
Phu, Dulles and Radford had in mind not only an immediate, local strategic goal but also that of "making the use of atomic bombs internationally
acceptable."[9]

The aversion to nuclear weapons—one might even say the abhorrence
of them—can grow in strength and become locked into military doctrine
without being fully appreciated or even acknowledged. The Kennedy administration launched an aggressive campaign for conventional defenses
in Europe on the grounds that nuclear weapons certainly should not be
used, and probably would not be used, in the event of a war in Europe.
(The no-first-use idea emerged later as a reflection of this same principle.)
Throughout the 1960s, the official Soviet line was to deny the possibility
of a nonnuclear engagement in Europe. Yet the Soviets spent great
amounts of money developing nonnuclear capabilities in Europe, especially aircraft capable of delivering conventional bombs. This expensive
capability would have been utterly useless in the event of any war that
was bound to become nuclear. It reflects a tacit Soviet acknowledgment
that both sides might be capable of nonnuclear war and that both sides
had an interest—an interest worth a lot of money—in keeping war nonnuclear by having the capability of fighting a nonnuclear war.

Arms control is often identified solely with limitations on the possession or deployment of weapons; it is often overlooked that this recipro-
cated investment in nonnuclear capability is a remarkable instance of un-
acknowledged but mutual arms control. This fact reminds us that the

inhibitions on first use may be powerful without declarations, even if one party refuses to recognize its own participation for what it is. (I have thought for many years that the inhibition on any president's authorizing the use of nuclear weapons was already far stronger than any no-first-use declaration [or even treaty] could make it; an official public announcement of a no-first-use policy would have the same effect as adding a hemp rope to an anchor chain.)

With the possible exception of the ABM (Antiballistic Missile) Treaty, this conventional buildup in Europe was the most important East-West arms agreement until the demise of the Soviet Union. It was genuine arms control, even if inexplicit, even if denied—as real as if the two sides had signed a treaty obliging them, in the interest of fending off nuclear war, to put large amounts of treasure and personnel into conventional forces. The investment in restraints on the use of nuclear weapons was real as well as symbolic.

That the Soviets had absorbed this nuclear inhibition was dramatically demonstrated during their protracted campaign in Afghanistan. I never read or heard public discussion about the possibility that the Soviet Union might shatter the tradition of nonuse to avoid a costly and humiliating defeat in that relatively undeveloped country. The inhibitions on use of nuclear weapons are such common knowledge, the attitude is so confidently shared, that not only would the use of nuclear weapons in Afghanistan have been almost universally deplored but it also wouldn't even have been thought of.

But that may be because what had been a nineteen-year nuclear silence for President Johnson had stretched into a fourth and then a fifth decade, and everyone in responsibility was aware that this unbroken tradition was a treasure held in common. We have to ask, Could that tradition, once broken, have mended itself? Had Truman used nuclear weapons during the Chinese onslaught in Korea, would President Richard M. Nixon have been as impressed in 1970 by the nineteen-year hiatus as Johnson was in 1964? Had Nixon used nuclear weapons, even ever so sparingly, in Vietnam, would the Soviets have eschewed their use in Afghanistan? Would Margaret Thatcher have chosen to use them in the Falklands? Would the Israelis have resisted the temptation to drop them on the Egyptian beachheads north of the Suez Canal in 1973?

The answer, surely, is that we do not know. One possibility is that the horror of Hiroshima and Nagasaki would have repeated itself and the curse would have descended again with even more weight. The other possibility is that nuclear weapons would have emerged as militarily effective instruments and, especially when used unilaterally against an adversary who had none, as a blessing that reduced casualties on both sides of the war, as some think the bombs on Hiroshima and Nagasaki did. Much might have depended on the care with which weapons were confined to military targets or used in demonstrably defensive modes.

The United States was spared from temptation in the Persian Gulf in 1991. Iraq was known to possess, and to have been willing to use, "unconventional" chemical weapons. Had these been used with devastating effect on U.S. forces, the issue of appropriate response would have posed the nuclear question. I am confident that had the president, in that circumstance, deemed it essential to escalate the level of conflict, battlefield nuclear weapons would have been the military choice. Nuclear weapons are what the army, navy, and air force are trained and equipped to use; their effects in different kinds of weather and terrain are well understood. The U.S. military profession traditionally despises poison. A strong urge would have arisen to respond with the kind of unconventional weapon we know best how to use. To have done so would have ended a period of forty-five peril-filled years. We can hope that no U.S. president has to face such a "political decision of the highest order." I've no doubt that any president would recognize the kind of decision that would be.

Into the Future

I have devoted this chapter to where the world stands and how it got there as regards the status of nuclear weapons in the belief that the development of that status has been as important as the development of nuclear arsenals. The nonproliferation effort, concerned with the development, production, and deployment of nuclear weapons, has been more successful than most authorities can claim to have anticipated; I consider the accumulating weight of tradition against nuclear use to be no less impressive and no less valuable. The United States depends on nonproliferation efforts to restrain the production and deployment of weapons by more and more countries; it may depend even more on universally shared inhibitions on nuclear use. Preserving those inhibitions and extending them, if possible, to cultures and national interests that may not currently share them will be a crucial part of U.S. nuclear policy.

I would like to punctuate my chapter at this point by quoting an editorial that Alvin M. Weinberg, the distinguished nuclear physicist, wrote on the fortieth anniversary of the bombing of Hiroshima and Nagasaki in *Bulletin of the Atomic Scientists* (December 1985). After saying that he had always been convinced that both U.S. and Japanese lives were saved by the use of the bomb in Japan, he gives another reason for his belief that the bombing of Hiroshima (but not Nagasaki) was fortunate: "Are we witnessing a gradual sanctification of Hiroshima—that is, the elevation of the Hiroshima event to the status of a profoundly mystical event, an event ultimately of the same religious force as biblical events? I cannot prove it, but I am convinced that the 40th Anniversary of Hiroshima, with its vast outpouring of concern, its huge demonstrations, its wide media coverage, bears resemblance to the observance of major religious holidays. . . . This sanctification of Hiroshima is one of the most hopeful developments of the nuclear era."

A crucial question is whether the antinuclear instinct so exquisitely expressed by Weinberg is confined to Christian, or even Western, culture.

I believe that this set of attitudes and expectations about nuclear weapons is more recognizably widespread among the people and the elites of the more developed countries, and as the United States looks to North Korea, Pakistan, Iran, or Iraq as potential wielders of nuclear weapons, it cannot be sure that they inherit this tradition with any great force. But it is comforting that there was no assurance that the leadership of the Soviet Union would inherit the same tradition or participate in cultivating it. Not many Americans in the 1950s would have thought that, were the Soviet Union to engage in and lose a war in Afghanistan, it would behave there as if nuclear weapons did not exist.

The United States can be grateful to them for behaving that way in Afghanistan, adding one more entry to the list of bloody wars in which nuclear weapons were not used. Forty years ago, some might have thought that the Soviet leadership would be immune to the spirit of Hiroshima as expressed by Weinberg, immune to the popular revulsion that John Foster Dulles did not share, immune to the overhang of all those peril-filled years that awed President Johnson. In any attempt to extrapolate Western nuclear attitudes toward the areas of the world where nuclear proliferation looms on the horizon, the remarkable conformity of Soviet and Western ideology is a reassuring point of departure.

Notes

1. McGeorge Bundy, *Danger and Survival: Choices About the Bomb in the First Fifty Years* (New York: Random House, 1988).

2. Ibid., 241.

3. Ibid., 249.

4. Ibid., 246.

5. Ibid., 268.

6. Ibid., 278.

7. *New York Times*, September 8, 1964, p. 18.

8. Maxwell D. Taylor, *The Uncertain Trumpet* (New York: Harper and Brothers, 1960), 7–10, 38–39.

9. Bundy, *Danger and Survival*, 268.

8

What Do We Want to Deter and How Do We Deter It?

ROBERT JERVIS

An effective military policy requires appropriate political foundations. In their classic analysis and critique of deterrence during the Cold War, Alexander George and Richard Smoke argued persuasively that in all too many cases, U.S. heads of state used deterrence as a substitute for, rather than a tool of, general foreign policy.[1] Analysts and political leaders could easily fall into the same trap again. Indeed, the experience of the Gulf War might lead to either of two misguided reactions. Because the United States did not seek to deter Iraq from invading Kuwait, some might suppose that worldwide deterrence was called for. Others, seeing that military victory was possible at a relatively low price (and, indeed, perhaps at a financial and political profit), might argue that military superiority allows the United States to ignore deterrence and rely on its capability for dealing with challenges after they arise.

This chapter will focus on deterrence and threats, but this is not to imply that these are the only, or even the most effective, tools for securing U.S. interests. The whole range of political, economic, social, and diplomatic instruments can and should be brought to bear. The most obvious contrasts—and often, complements—to deterrence and threats are promises and reassurances. Put more broadly, exercising political leadership involves a large measure of trying to reduce others' grievances and give them less reason to use force. Indeed, in some circumstances, a policy of deterrence can increase, rather than decrease, conflict by setting off or exacerbating an unnecessary spiral.[2] But here I will concentrate on the possible uses of deterrence.

Political Roots of Deterrence

Deterrence is too costly, dangerous, and distorting to apply without discrimination; it is, however, generally cheaper than using military force, and it has a vital role to play. We need to ask, Who and/or what does the United States want to deter?[3] This is the most crucial question concerning the political setting for U.S. military policy. Furthermore, it is one that the United States did not have to ask during the Cold War. Of course, there were fierce debates over specific aspects of deterrence policy during that period—for example, what areas of the world were really vital to the United States? Did it need to fight in Vietnam? Would its allies or adversaries discount U.S. promises and threats if the Soviet-backed faction won in Angola? Should the nuclear strategy that supported extreme deterrent threats be based on counterforce or countervalue targeting? But it was generally agreed that the only menace to U.S. vital interests was Soviet power and that containment, backed by deterrent threats, was to be a core of U.S. security policy.

As the Gulf War made clear, it is no longer easy to determine what the United States needs to deter. Before August 1990, Iraqi power did not seem much of a menace. Indeed, to a large extent Iraq was a welcome counterbalance to Iran. As late as July 1990, U.S. officials explained that the United States was not committed to protecting Kuwait.[4] But the invasion, combined with an implicit threat to Saudi Arabia, quickly changed U.S. perceptions of what was necessary to defend its vital interests, if not the conception of those interests themselves. Such reevaluations have occurred before—when North Korea attacked South Korea, U.S. political leaders decided that, contrary to what they had said and believed before, the United States had to fight—and they may well happen again. Events and decisionmakers' instinctive reactions often shape definitions of vital interests, rather than preexisting definitions shaping behavior. Psychologists have found that people adopt beliefs that explain and rationalize their previous behavior, thereby setting them on a course that they had not previously sought and that cannot be explained by their deepest values and most careful analyses of the world. Moved by the press of events, people often act first and then ask themselves, "What sorts of values and beliefs did I have to have in order to make rational what I just did?"[5] The Bush administration appeared to have proceeded in this way. That is, the Pentagon's draft *Defense Guidance* (as leaked to the media) inferred U.S. interests from the cases in which the United States had used force in the recent past. The paper listed the following interests for which the United States may have to fight: access to vital raw materials, primarily Persian Gulf oil; curtailing the proliferation of ballistic missiles and weapons of mass destruction; threats to U.S. citizens from terrorism or local conflict;

and threats to U.S. society from narcotics trafficking.[6] This definition of interests seems derived from the Gulf War as well as the U.S. interventions in Grenada and Panama. In the absence of the latter intervention, which overthrew Noriega, it seems unlikely that the threat from drugs would have been included in this list.

It is easy to see that this presentation of the threats that the United States needs to deter is inadequate; however, it is harder to do better. Even after the fact, it is often difficult to determine what interests are vital and how various events will affect the state. One can even dispute whether Nazi Germany posed a direct menace to the United States.[7] Now that it lacks a challenger of roughly equal power to itself, the United States has an unusually wide range of choices in its security policy. In part, this stems from the unusual nature of the current international system. It clearly is not bipolar—an arrangement that provides an easy identification of adversaries. But neither is it multipolar, at least not in the classic sense. In such a system, states may be forced to defend the interests of their allies in order to keep their coalition together.[8]

In the current system, by contrast, the United States lacks both dominant adversaries and vital allies. It is not surprising, then, that so many questions of what the United States needs to deter remain unanswered. For example, some have argued, consistent with traditional theories of international politics, that it needs to strive to maintain primacy.[9] Particularly relevant here is the ancillary claim that in order to discourage other countries (most obviously Germany and Japan) from seeking to increase their power, the United States needs not so much to seek to deter them directly—conflicts of interest are not that severe—as to deter potential adversaries of these countries, thereby removing their need to increase their military power.[10]

Scenario-Driven Planning and Its Alternatives

Perhaps the most obvious way to consider what the United States wants to deter is to think of possible scenarios: specific events, kinds of events, or even chains of events that, if they occurred, would be very damaging to it. This requires imagining situations that are dangerous and likely (or at least not totally unlikely). Such an approach would concomitantly lead one to exclude certain eventualities as sufficiently remote to be unworthy of worry; for all the discussion of "worst-case analysis," heads of state in multipolar worlds have always done so. The almost unlimited number of adversaries—that could also combine with each other—means that military planning would be impossible unless it were bounded by judgments of political plausibility. Thus, in 1924, Winston Churchill opposed the Admiralty's argument that more ships had to be built to meet the menace from Japan with these words: "A war with Japan! But why should there be a war with Japan? I do not believe there is the slightest chance of it in our lifetime."[11]

During the Cold War, the automatic identification of the adversary meant that even those who argued that nothing could be taken for granted did not seek nuclear forces that would be secure against a combined strike from the Soviet Union, China, the United Kingdom, and France: the United States was spared both the risk of Churchill's error and some of the pressures for building up forces unnecessarily. But, of course, there were other such pressures. As Bernard Brodie put it with his normal asperity: "All sorts of notions and presuppositions are churned out, and often presented for consideration with the prefatory words: 'It is conceivable that . . .' Such words establish their own truth, for the fact that someone has conceived of whatever proposition follows is enough to establish that it is conceivable. Whether it is worth a second thought, however, is another matter."[12] During the Cold War, many of these "notions" concerned complex nuclear strategies. Now they are more likely to involve the identification of possible adversaries and unpleasant situations.

It appears that, at least in the Bush administration, the construction of possible threatening scenarios indeed formed the basis of U.S. military planning.[13] This is not to say that these intellectual exercises strongly affect the size of the U.S. armed forces, however. The "base force" of 1.6 million troops was established before the Soviet Union disintegrated. (This is not surprising; during the Cold War as well, rationales for the size and composition of the U.S. military establishment changed much more rapidly than the size and configuration of the military itself.[14]) But it is at least possible that the development of scenarios could influence U.S. deterrence policy. It could make sense to decide on what guarantees and threats to issue by trying to determine what possible events fit three criteria: likelihood, harm to the United States if they should occur, and the ability of the United States to reduce their likelihood by issuing deterrent threats. It is not clear, however, whether the scenarios apparently being discussed within the government in recent years are being thought of in these terms. For example, one such contingency discussed in 1992 was a joint attack by Russia and Byelorus on Lithuania and Poland.[15] As far as one can tell from the public record, little thought had been given to whether the United States should seek to deter such an attack by making a commitment to defend Poland. Furthermore (and perhaps this is one reason why there has been little discussion of such a commitment), one can question how much the United States would be menaced by such an attack. It lived quite comfortably with the Soviet occupation of Poland during the Cold War; although a return to this situation would be deeply regrettable, would such an attack be a sufficient infringement on core U.S. values to merit the use or threat of force?

It may well be that the difficulty in answering questions like this will drive a wedge between military planning and deterrence planning. That is, because cases like a Russian attack on Poland are not clearly a menace to the United States, it is not likely to commit itself to fight on Poland's behalf (and such a commitment, even if undertaken, might not be believed). But to say that neither the United States nor others could be sure that it would fight for Poland is not to say that it is clear that the United States would *not* fight. This not only purchases some deterrence but also means that military planners have to be prepared for this eventuality: they cannot place too much faith in the fact that civilian decisionmakers deem areas as not vital (such as South Korea in 1950) or as not menaced (such as Kuwait forty years later). Thus, the military is not being entirely unreasonable or self-serving in seeking forces that can handle contingencies that the government is not willing to seek to deter.

At the present time, it is hard to think of scenarios that meet the criteria just set forth of being somewhat likely, menacing U.S. values if the events should occur, and potentially deterrable. But this does not mean that the world is serene or that all the most troublesome issues are beyond U.S. influence. It may reflect the failure of imagination. Or, perhaps to say the same thing another way, even unlikely events occur. Before August 1990, few people thought that Iraq would invade Kuwait. Any policy based on scenarios is vulnerable to attack on the grounds that the threats are exaggerated. This may undermine domestic support for such a policy but does not make it unreasonable.

The alternative to scenario-driven military policy is "planning for uncertainty." Rather than thinking in terms of specific contingencies, the United States would try to be prepared to meet a range of situations that could not be foreseen far in advance. This approach makes some sense in terms of military procurement, but the implications for deterrence are troublesome. Unless the United States were willing to say that it would act to prevent or punish all instances of aggression—and perhaps all instances of large-scale civil unrest as well—this stance implies that it would have "timely warning" (to borrow a useful concept from arms control) of problems as they develop and be able to stake out its deterrent position before potential aggressors had become committed to a disruptive policy. As I will show, it is far from clear whether this is a realistic assumption. This chain of reasoning, then, leads back to the need for the extremely difficult task of clarifying U.S. interests so that some areas and issues are marked out as calling for the use of force if that should prove necessary.

But a sharp line is even less possible now than it was during the Cold War. The existence of gray areas may not be entirely unfortunate, however; others do not have to be completely certain that the United States will intervene in a particular dispute in order to be deterred. A probability—in some cases even a low probability—may suffice. Furthermore, the damage to U.S. credibility is less when the United States does not intervene in instances like this than when it fails to live up to a clear commitment. Here as elsewhere, ambiguity has great value.[16] But this does not mean that the United States can happily ignore the need to clarify its interests.

Deciding who, what, and when to deter is further complicated by the fact that with few exceptions, what menaces the United States is not the direct consequences of aggression but rather the delayed or second-order effects that could grow out of the spread of the conflict to new areas and participants. For example, the civil war among the various fragments of

Yugoslavia, unfortunate as it is for those directly concerned, poses no threat to traditional U.S. interests as long as it stays limited to that territory. But Western European states might be drawn in—in the most dangerous case, on opposite sides—if the fighting led to the exodus of large flows of refugees. Equally troublesome, although at this point harder to imagine, would be Russian support for Serbia. The spread of the fighting to Albania could also set in motion dynamics that would be extremely worrisome for Western Europe and, at least indirectly, for the United States. Indeed, given the conflict between the republic that wants to call itself Macedonia and Greece, Western European interests are perhaps no more than one step removed from the internal fighting. Similarly, although the United States does not have much direct interest in Nagorno-Karabakh, it must be concerned about the danger that Armenian success in linking its territory to this enclave could lead to active Turkish support for the Azerbaijanis, which in turn could lead to Iranian or Russian involvement.

In cases like these—and the 1990s are likely to see many more of them—the United States must try to predict the course of the conflict to determine whether the stakes are sufficiently high and whether the prospects for success if it acts are sufficiently great to call for deterrence. But deterrence of who and of what? Should the United States seek to prevent the outbreak of the conflict or deter others from joining once it has started? I doubt if any general answer can be given, and the judgments in any particular case are likely to be very difficult. But the question is important because conflicting answers often point to very different policies. The Yugoslav situation again presents a disturbing example. Initially, the United States sought to keep the country together (as it did the former Soviet Union), telling the non-Serbian republics that their futures would be bleak if they broke away. Of course, the United States did not threaten to use force, but its clear preference for a unified Yugoslavia and its prediction that the outlying republics would not benefit by its dismantling implied, at the least, that it would not assist the republics. Perhaps one reason why the Serbians felt betrayed by the later U.S. policy of pressures and sanctions was that they had been encouraged by the previous U.S. policy. The attempt to discourage secessionist movements may then conflict with the attempt to deter violence if the region does fragment. It will therefore be hard to make either set of threats credible, and the expectation of one position will undercut the other.

Dual Deterrence and Other Dilemmas

More generally, the United States is likely to face situations that require what might be called *dual deterrence*—the deterrence of two countries or factions that are in conflict with one another. This is more difficult than what we have come to see as the standard case, in which the defender seeks to deter a particular adversary from taking particular actions. This situation occurs in clear-cut contexts in which one state can readily identify another as the potential troublemaker, as was true in much of the Cold War. But even then, the situation was not always appropriate for this kind of deterrence, and when it was not, U.S. policy often failed. Thus, it is now clear that in the year preceding the outbreak of the Korean War, the United States sought to deter both North and South Korea because each had the desire and the capability to undermine or attack the other. This meant that the United States had to try to give each side the impression that the United States would oppose it if and only if it moved against the other.[17] Such a message is difficult to get across, however. It is easier to convince another state that you are its adversary and will block it at every turn or, conversely, that your interests and those of the other are congruent and that you will protect it. Complex, conditional threats and promises are much more difficult to make credible, and it is not surprising that the United States was unable to do so in this case. The failure of U.S. policy toward Iraq in the years before the Gulf War has a similar explanation. If all the United States had had to do was to deter that country, it might have succeeded. But it wanted to see that neither Iran nor Iraq dominated the area, and this required trying to show each of them that the United States would support it if it were moderate and restrained but oppose it if it sought regional hegemony. Such a policy, even if carefully crafted (which the U.S. policy was not), faces severe hurdles. It is not entirely surprising that on the one hand, Saddam Hussein seems to have interpreted some actions of the United States and other countries associated with it as indicating great and unconditional hostility and that on the other hand, he apparently saw U.S. restraint and friendly overtures as indicating weakness. Although Saddam Hussein's regime may have been unusually evil and his grasp of reality unusually tenuous, the general problem is likely to recur in other cases of dual deterrence.

The United States could try to deter both sides in a dispute by arguing that it will support the state that is reasonable and will seek to block anyone who resorts to force. But even if U.S. interests are deeply involved in maintaining the peace, three problems arise. First, the facts of the situation are almost always difficult to obtain and ambiguous. If fighting breaks out, it may be difficult to determine who started it or, even more, whether the side that struck first had been intolerably provoked. Second, the relevant judgments, especially of who was and was not reasonable, are notoriously subjective. Not only will the burden on U.S. intelligence—in the general sense of the term—be very great, but it will also be difficult for the states in the dispute to be sure what behavior of theirs and of their adversary will be acceptable. Indeed, given common biases in perception, each side is likely to think that its behavior meets U.S. standards and that its adversary's does not. Each is then likely to expect U.S. support, and at least one of them will be disappointed.

The third problem arises even when the United States seeks only to deter one side: Security guarantees tend to freeze the status quo. Indeed, this is usually their purpose. But they can also discourage peaceful change.

This was not a problem for the U.S. guarantees to Western Europe during the Cold War, but it did complicate U.S. policy in the third world, where adjustments between neighbors were often called for and repressive internal politics were often part of the problem. Thus, Douglas Macdonald's study of U.S. policy toward corrupt and threatened Asian states shows that the United States often fell into what he calls the "commitment trap." The United States felt it could not permit countries like Vietnam to fall to communism, but becoming committed to providing large-scale assistance enabled these countries to resist U.S. pressures for reform because they knew that even if they did not comply, the United States would not abandon them.[18] In the current situation, to provide security guarantees to a country could have the unintended effect of making it less willing to negotiate with its neighbors or grant human rights to its ethnic minorities within its borders. If the United States were to guarantee Ukraine's security, for example, it might increase the chance of a war with Russia by giving Ukraine the confidence to stand firm in its position on issues like economic arrangements with Russia and the status of Crimea.

Not all the problems that the United States faces concerning deterrence are new. One familiar and important one is the basic deterrence trade-off: U.S. commitments and threats are likely to decrease the chance that the target state will take the undesired action, but assuming that the United States was making a threat and not a warning (that is, it would prefer not to take forcible action had it not committed itself to doing so), commitments also increase the price it will have to pay if the other does move.[19] In contrast, abstaining from threats and guarantees, while enabling the United States to stay out of any conflict that develops, increases the chance that it will occur.

Domestic Support

An effective deterrence policy must be rooted in domestic as well as international politics. It will do no good for policymakers to discern U.S. interests, creatively wield threats and promises, and chart the best course if the U.S. people remain unconvinced. Of course, domestic support can be cultivated, if not created: it does not have to exist before the policy is developed. During the early years of the Cold War, large segments of U.S. public and elite opinion resisted an active containment policy. The Truman administration therefore had to spend much time and effort to convince people that the Soviet threat was real and could be adequately met by interventionist international policy. Indeed, the administration may have "oversold" both the extent of the danger and the likely efficacy of the proposed solutions.[20] As a result, in the 1950s the U.S. government found that policies previously regarded as too belligerent were now seen as excessively soft. Negotiations with the Soviet Union were inhibited, relations with allies were strained, and international tensions may have been unnecessarily increased.

The Bush administration's response to the need to align foreign policy and domestic politics was to veer from one extreme to the other. As the Soviet threat diminished and then all but disappeared with the revolution in Eastern Europe, the administration gave little guidance about what U.S. interests would be in the new era. Then, after it decided to expel Iraq from Kuwait, the Bush administration made far-reaching claims about the need for and possibility of a "new world order."[21] The effect of this campaign was not entirely clear. Judging by the press commentary, some found it alarming, others wanted to push it further in the direction of serving values such as human rights and democratization, and still others found it quite unconvincing. The third group may well have been the largest.[22] Perhaps as a cause or an effect of this reaction, soon after the Gulf War was concluded, the Bush administration abandoned this rhetoric. Indeed, after early 1991 the administration said remarkably little about foreign policy. Within the government, of course, consideration of the broad outlines of U.S. interest and deterrence policy continued, as is shown by the versions of the *Defense Guidance* that were leaked to the press. Whatever one may think of the contents of these documents, it is clear that the idea of trying to keep U.S. policy secret makes no sense. Deterrence cannot rest on commitments that remain private; a policy that is not vigorously and continuously defended in public will lack the support necessarily for its implementation.[23]

The Clinton administration has so far followed the pattern of the later Bush years, which served it so well during the presidential campaign. Since Clinton could only lose by talking about foreign policy and making it more salient, during the campaign he spoke about it as little as possible. In office, he has responded as necessary to pressing issues, especially in the Balkans, but has avoided discussion of general foreign policy principles and priorities. The issues are of course highly complex, and in a rapidly changing world a significant degree of improvisation is necessary. But it is to be doubted that either specific policies or the level of sophistication of the U.S. public will benefit from prolonged silence on the part of national leaders.

For the U.S. public, the question of whether policy is to be pursued multilaterally or unilaterally may be only slightly less important than the question of what interests are worthy of defense. Much has been written about the isolationist tradition in U.S. foreign policy, but for many purposes and in a number of eras, the unilateralist strand in U.S. thinking was equally prominent. Although it is common to refer to the "isolationist" wing of the Republican Party in the early years of the Cold War, "unilateralist" catches this group's approach better; although they did not favor binding ties to European allies, they strongly supported intervention in Asia. What they wanted above all was that U.S. foreign policy not be beholden to others and that the United States be free to pursue its interests as it saw them without the need to adjust to allies. Of course, they lost the struggle for leadership of the Republican Party in 1952, and although they continued to be a thorn in President Eisenhower's side, the need for

allies became widely accepted. But throughout the Cold War, the United
States was the dominant member of its coalition. Although the allies
usually received a respectful hearing and often influenced aspects of U.S.
policy, almost all crucial decisions were made in Washington. This is not
to deny that the approval of allies was important for both international
and domestic politics. Indeed, even if the Gulf War had been militarily
and logistically possible without a large coalition, it is questionable
whether Bush could have led the country into war—or perhaps even into
an economic embargo—without worldwide support. But the Gulf War
was not a true instance of multilateralism in the sense of a policy developed
by several countries. The United States led; others followed in part because
they approved of what the United States was doing, in part because they
needed U.S. support, and in part because their attempts to fashion a
competing policy failed, due in large measure to Saddam's errors. It is
not clear that the U.S. public would have tolerated a more equal division
of decisionmaking responsibilities. It is similarly not clear whether U.S.
opinion would tolerate a policy of deterrence that was strongly shaped
by the interests and perspectives of allies.

If the United States is to sharply cut its defense budget, however, it
may not be able to avoid multilateralism. Indeed, one might turn this
point around and argue for deep reductions to ensure that any large-scale
military operation would have to be a multilateral. It is hard for me to
conceive of an interest that would be vital enough for the United States
to merit the use of force on a scale larger than that of the operation in
Panama that also did not involve the interests of major allies. If others
will not threaten or use force, one can question whether the United States
should.

Classical theorists of the balance of power noted that even the most
benign state cannot be trusted with excessive power. As Edmund Burke
put it in the early stages of the struggle with revolutionary France:

> Among precautions against ambition, it may not be amiss to take one pre-
> caution against our *own*. I must fairly say, I dread our *own* power and *our*
> ambition; I dread our being too much dreaded. It is ridiculous to say we
> are not men, and that, as men, we shall wish to aggrandize ourselves in
> some way or other. . . . If we should come . . . to be absolutely able, without
> the least control, to hold the commerce of all other nations totally dependent
> upon our good pleasure, we may say that we shall not abuse this astonishing
> and hitherto unheard-of power. But every other nation will think we shall
> abuse it. It is impossible but that, sooner or later, this state of things must
> produce a combination against us which may end in our ruin.[24]

François Fénelon, a French thinker of the late seventeenth century,
made a similar argument noting that no matter what a state's intentions
and domestic politics and society, it will not behave with moderation and
decency if it is not checked by others.[25] Waltz draws the important conclusion about the effect of the crumbling of Soviet power: "Despite good
intentions, the United States will often act in accordance with Fénelon's

theorem."[26] If the United States were to bind itself to act multilaterally by denying itself the capability to use large-scale force on its own, it would by so doing provide a safeguard against the excessive use of its power. This might benefit the United States as well as the rest of the world: it would not be able to act on its own worst impulses; others would share the costs of interventions; and others would be less fearful of it, which would reduce the danger of their forming a coalition against it and make productive cooperation easier.

Requirements of Deterrence

Successful deterrence requires a combination of capabilities and credibility. These two sets of factors are not entirely separate; the ability to block the adversary at low cost increases credibility. Indeed, it is largely this reason that leads to the general spirit of optimism concerning the prospects for the United States to be able to deter a wide range of undesirable behavior on the part of many other countries.

Capabilities

The adequacy of U.S. capabilities for deterrence cannot be judged apart from the question of who and what the United States is trying to deter. But overall, it would seem that deterrence should be easier now that the Cold War is over. When the United States faced the Soviet Union, many of its threats would have been extremely costly to carry out because doing so might have led to nuclear war. This will rarely be the case in the foreseeable future. It is even difficult to imagine that the United States would have to fight a long, large-scale conventional war. Indeed, in some cases the costs might be low enough that the United States would need only to issue warnings, not threats. We should not exaggerate the strength of the U.S. position, however. First, even if using force would be less costly than was the case in the Cold War, it may still be quite costly indeed. Desert Storm might have turned out quite differently; some future adversaries of the United States are likely to have nuclear weapons; and interventions in civil wars are not likely to be quickly terminated. Second, as the terrible vision of nuclear war recedes from sight, costs that seemed relatively slight by comparison (in other words, those of fighting even a small war) may loom psychologically larger.

In many cases, it may be useful to distinguish between the capabilities required for deterrence by denial and those that permit deterrence by punishment.[27] More than was true during the Cold War, the United States may now be able to deter undesired adventures by possessing the capability to prevent them from succeeding. Deterrence by denial—which generally equates with the ability to physically defend territory in dispute—was the main form of deterrence in the prenuclear era and perhaps will be again in the future. Whether this is the case cannot be determined in the abstract;

it is highly sensitive to the particular adversary, the particular scenario, and the particular U.S. policy being followed. But even a much smaller U.S. military than we now have could beat back many instances of aggression, especially it was able to act in cooperation with allies.

Perhaps the main inhibitor of the U.S. threat to punish others—especially with nuclear weapons—is not retaliation by the adversary but rather the expected adverse response on the part of world and U.S. public opinion. Although these forces did not operate strongly in the Gulf War, in part because the efforts combined denial and punishment, I suspect that unless the provocation were viewed as extreme, many would be outraged at massive death and destruction visited upon an offending third-world country. Again, much would depend upon the circumstances and the way in which the punishment was exacted (blockades may produce as much suffering as bombing, but they are much less dramatic), but the fact that the United States is relatively immune to direct counterpunishment does not mean that this form of violence can easily be used.

The increased U.S. capabilities, coupled with the difficulty in identifying U.S. interests ahead of time, may mean a smaller role for deterrence in the narrow and technical sense and a larger role for offense and compellence. The Gulf War may be symptomatic of this. Until the invasion, the United States was unable to understand that it had important interests that were being menaced. During the Cold War, such an error might have been fatal. Once the Soviet Union had moved into an area, it could usually deter any U.S. attempt to dislodge it. But Iraq lacked strength to do this; the United States was able to forcibly expel Iraqi troops from Kuwait and, if it had chosen, probably could have unseated Saddam Hussein. In the future, the United States may find similar instances of the threat or use of offensive force. For reasons that remain somewhat unclear, its threats to force Iraq out of Kuwait were not effective. But possibly in future cases, the United States could convince another state that unless it reversed its course, stopped objectionable behaviors, or withdrew from territory it had seized, the United States would use military force against it. Some of the impediments to the credibility of deterrent threats discussed in the next section would not apply because the actual transgression would have clarified U.S. interests and commitments in a way that the possibility of it did not.

Credibility

Capability, of course, contributes to the credibility of threats, but it is neither necessary nor sufficient for it. Capability is not always necessary because others may overestimate the state's ability to act. More important here, capability is not sufficient because there is much the United States could do that others—sometimes with good reason, sometimes not—do not expect it to do. During the Cold War, the main impediment to the credibility of U.S. threats was the prospect of Soviet retaliation. But the removal of this menace does not make all U.S. threats highly credible. Indeed, four impediments are greater than they were in the past. First, I have suggested that it will be difficult for the United States to decide what interests are sufficiently important, menaced, and susceptible to effective deterrence. Explicit commitments, most clearly and dramatically in the form of treaties of guarantee and even the stationing of troops, might be effective, but the arguments and domestic pressures against doing so are strong. It follows that in many instances, the United States will not be able to make its interests and commitments clear to others. There is a bright side to this problem, however, in that inadvertent deterrence is possible. That is, others might believe that the United States would act in instances in which it actually would not. Given the fact that it might take a transgression to clarify U.S. interest in the minds of its leaders and general public, others would have to realize that, as in the case of the Iraqi takeover of Kuwait, the absence of a commitment does not mean that the United States would not act. But in part because countries that feel great pressure to move are likely to overestimate their ability to do so successfully and underestimate the likelihood that others will block them, more frequently others will make the opposite error; especially in the absence of a U.S. commitment, they are likely to believe that the United States will stay on the sidelines.

Of course, the United States can declare its commitments as threats develop. That is, it could use what Patrick Morgan called "immediate deterrence."[28] But this brings up the second problem, which is one of timing. To be most effective, threats must be issued before the other side has committed itself—psychologically and politically—to move. Decisions, even tentative ones, are not easily reversed. Once a state's leader has decided that it is important to take certain acts, he or she will not be easily dissuaded. This is especially true if the leader's political fortunes have been staked on the course of action. Under these conditions, furthermore, he or she is not likely to accurately perceive any threats that others may issue.[29] Thus, I doubt whether anything Ambassador April Glaspie could have said to Saddam Hussein on the eve of the invasion of Kuwait would have done much good. Similarly, President Kennedy warned Nikita Khrushchev not to deploy missiles in Cuba only after the weapons were on their way.

Threats are likely to be much more effective if they are issued earlier, when the other side is perceptually ready to hear them and politically able to act on them. But this requires that the United States be able to identify its interests and the potential menaces to them before the dangers have started to emerge. This is probably asking too much of intelligence, in the general sense of the term. For example, it is only in retrospect that we can clearly see that the United States should have shifted its policy toward Iraq much earlier and made clear its determination to rebuff Iraqi aggression. The evidence was far from clear at the time, and the reasons for seeking to conciliate Iraq were not foolish. In part, the United States was misled by its preoccupation with the threat from Iran. This is likely to be all too typical of future disturbances. In a multipolar world, the sources of menace to U.S. interests are diffused, and U.S. attention cannot be carefully focused on one potential aggressor.[30]

Furthermore, detecting threats in a timely manner is especially difficult if acting on this perception requires a sharp change in policy. This was one of the major problems in the summer of 1990, and it is not likely to be unique. If a state that the United States has supported starts to menace U.S. interests, political and perceptual inhibitions again are likely to prevent a quick recognition of the situation. It is hard for decisionmakers to see that their policy is failing and indeed may have been misguided for quite some time. In anticipation of this, intelligence officials will not be quick to provide analysis that flies in the face of established policy.

Earlier I noted that the costs for the United States of carrying out threats are likely to be less than they were in the past. But although this increases their credibility, the opposite side of this coin constitutes the third impediment to credibility: The benefits that the United States will gain by deterring others are also less than they were during the Cold War. This is merely another way of saying that few imaginable disputes will engage vital U.S. interests. To a first approximation, the credibility of a threat is determined by the ratio of the costs the state will suffer if it does not act to the benefits it will receive if it does. Because both the numerator and the denominator have been simultaneously lowered, the net effect is not easy to determine.

The problem is compounded by the fact in most future disputes, the interests of the United States and its adversaries are likely to be asymmetric; they will be more important to the latter than to the former. For example, the United States has some interest in preventing or limiting Serbian attacks on the other republics of what was Yugoslavia and, perhaps, in convincing Serbia to make some concessions as well. But for the local actors, the interests are vital—literally worth dying for. In general, they will then be more highly motivated than the United States, and the "balance of interest" so important for determining the outcome of bargaining will favor them.[31] States that care deeply about the issue at stake will be willing to spend a disproportionate share of their resources to prevail. Furthermore, in situations that resemble the game of Chicken (in other words, in which the failure to reach an agreement is the worst outcome for both sides), such a state will have reason to expect the other side to back down. Psychological factors enter in as well; actors who are strongly motivated to prevail are likely to perceive information about the situation and others' likely responses in a way that systematically pushes them toward taking a "hard line" in bargaining.[32] These forces will all undercut the credibility of U.S. threats.

A fourth factor that could reduce the credibility of U.S. commitments is related to the change in the structure of the international system. In the bipolar world, the United States sought to deter Soviet adventures along the peripheries of the system by staking its reputation on preventing those peripheral countries from falling under Soviet domination. Although in the first analysis the threat to respond to such challenges by force would be incredible because the fate of the menaced small state did not deeply affect the United States, deterrence was possible through the interconnections provided by reputation. That is, for a state to break a commitment or act weakly in one area of the world is to undercut its commitments throughout the globe.[33] To the extent that the other side believes this, it will be deterred because it will expect the defender to act strongly, not because of the intrinsic value of the issue or territory at stake but because the state needs to safeguard its reputation.

In a multipolar world, however, it is far from clear whether the reputational effects of behavior fit this model. Under bipolarity, the main audiences that the United States needed to impress were the Soviet Union and a manageably small number of allies; in the current era, challenges could come from almost anyone, and so the number of actors the United States needs to impress is much larger. Under bipolarity, the crucial audiences paid a great deal of attention to the disputes in the peripheries; with many more actors involved and many more concerns, attention will be diffused. The result will be to decrease the credibility of U.S. threats because acting strongly in one case or living up to one commitment will not have as beneficial and widespread reputational effects as could be expected in the bipolar world. Thus, the U.S. victory in the Gulf War seems to have little influence on the parties to the Yugoslav civil conflict and probably would not have even if the U.S. had sought to exercise explicit deterrence. If U.S. leaders realize this, they will be less likely to make commitments or to live up to them if they are challenged—which may help explain why the U.S. did not direct many threats to the aggressors in what had been Yugoslavia.

Finally, the United States may now need to be prepared to deter unconventional actors. Disruptions from states certainly cannot be excluded, but it must also be prepared to deal with types of actors that, although familiar to it, are different from those that have dominated traditional international politics. The differences are likely to be significant for deterrence; factions, ethnic groups, protostates, secessionist movements, and religious or ideological groups may all be very highly motivated to change the status quo or act in ways that menace U.S. values. Yet because they lack territory, a standing army, a large formal bureaucracy, or other attributes of statehood, they are difficult targets for military power. Deterrence by denial is a very demanding task against elusive adversaries whose aim is to disrupt and impose costs rather than to take territory; deterrence by punishment is difficult without suitable targets for retaliation.

Nuclear Weapons

The credibility of threats is not inversely proportional to the magnitude of the other side's possible retaliation against the state. Because punishing others that are weak may be costly in terms of domestic and world opinion, it is probably true, although ironic, that U.S. strategic nuclear weapons are more relevant to deterring nuclear than nonnuclear states. The threat to destroy cities of a third-world challenger—or at least to do so with atomic bombs—may simply be too horrible to be credible. Moral inhibitions are also likely to be present, as will be the pragmatic fears that such use might lead nonnuclear states to see that these weapons do indeed have high utility.

The threat to employ tactical nuclear forces against the adversary's armed forces would be at least a bit more believable because their use would not be so disproportionate to the provocation. But there would be a great pressure to use these weapons only if the United States faced an adversary whose army it could not defeat with conventional forces or that could inflict high casualties on U.S. forces if it did not resort to nuclear use. The former problem is unlikely, but the latter is not. Even when there would be real military advantages to using tactical nuclear weapons, however, the political and psychological inhibitions would be great. The net effect, I suspect, is that although explicit U.S. threats to employ tactical nuclear weapons would not be highly credible, neither could an adversary completely discount this possibility. This may mean that a cautious adversary, which probably would have been deterred in any event, will find additional reasons not to move but that a very strongly motivated adversary might not be much affected.

With the exception of Russia, no adversary would have the capability to destroy the United States. But some could be armed with nuclear weapons. Since even having one of its cities destroyed would be the greatest disaster in U.S. history (excepting only the Civil War), one can argue that the United States would be deterred from using its own nuclear weapons. During the Cold War, it was often said that mutual second-strike capability meant that the "sole purpose [of strategic nuclear weapons] is to deter the other side's first use of its strategic forces" and that, therefore, extended nuclear deterrence was not possible.[34] Similarly, it can be argued that although the United States will be able to continue to deter other nuclear powers from menacing its territory, it will not be able to credibly threaten to use nuclear weapons in response to attacks on allies. On closer examination, however, neither empirical evidence nor logic supports this argument; extended deterrence is indeed theoretically possible and operated quite robustly during the Cold War.[35] The basic reason for this was that no one could be sure that a confrontation or, even more, a conventional war between two nuclear-armed powers would not escalate into all-out violence. This would also be true for conflicts in the future. Indeed, since the pressures to escalate and preempt are more likely to operate when both sides have nuclear weapons, extended deterrence may be more effective against a nuclear-armed opponent than against one that lacks these weapons. Even if this is not the case, one can at least reach the negative, but not unimportant, conclusion that U.S. nuclear weapons can help deter even nuclear-armed adversaries from moving against U.S. interests.

This is not to deny that U.S. threats would be more credible if the United States were not vulnerable to nuclear attacks. Partly for this reason, some analysts and public figures call for a version of the Strategic Defense Initiative (SDI). The obvious problem, however, is that even if it were possible to defend against a small number of ballistic missiles, this is not the most likely means by which new adversaries would try to strike the United States.

Tools of Deterrence—What Is to Be Threatened?

Because this is a book about military policy, I have concentrated on the potential use and limits of military threats. But in closing, I should mention other instruments that might be employed and other sanctions that might be threatened. This discussion will not only be brief but, as I noted at the beginning of this chapter, will also mention only negative inducements, ignoring diplomacy, conciliation, rewards, and the attempt to reduce disturbances by meeting others' legitimate grievances.

The obvious alternative—or prelude—to force is economic sanctions. Often scorned by analysts who neither grasped the multiple objectives of using this tool nor compared its effectiveness with that of the alternatives, sanctions have been useful in the past and are likely to be even more so in the future.[36] A wide range of actions are possible, from total boycotts to banning the sale or purchase of some materials, increasing tariffs, and severing air connections. The fact that none of them are likely to roll back a conquest made by a powerful and strongly determined state does not mean that they cannot be of major value in less-demanding circumstances. The prospects for success, furthermore, are greater now that the Cold War has ended because of the increased feasibility of putting together a large or even universal coalition, thereby reducing the possibilities for alternative sources of supplies and markets. Neither target states nor parties that seek to resist the pressure to join the coalition can avail themselves of the threat to "go communist" if the pressure is too severe. Although the vulnerability of countries to economic sanctions can only be determined on a case-by-case basis, it seems probable that changes in the world economy may increase the efficacy of sanctions. More countries are coming to see the need for deep involvement in the international economy; a side effect is that they are likely to be more vulnerable because they will suffer more from being cut off.

Economic sanctions are usually coupled with denunciations from international and regional organizations. It has often been a commonplace to scorn the efficacy of the adverse reaction of world opinion, but one should not be too quick to dismiss this tool in the current context. If the great powers can work together and build a consensus that includes many of the leading third-world states as well, outcast states will pay a high price for being excluded. Of course, this will have little impact on regimes that are strongly driven to take unacceptable actions, shun the standards of the wider community, and preside over populations they either control or that share their outlook, but a number of potential disturbers of the international system may be open to influence.

These tools require heavy use of diplomacy and international institutions in order to create and maintain a coalition. As noted earlier, the U.S. diplomatic tradition is more unilateral than multilateral. During the Cold War, the perception of a terribly dangerous adversary helped convince U.S. political leaders and public opinion that there was no alternative to working with others, even at some cost to U.S. preferences and values. During the Gulf War, allies were both necessary and, with the exception of some ineffective French and Soviet initiatives, left most of the decisionmaking to the United States. But the future may require a somewhat different U.S. outlook and approach. Developing a large coalition requires that the interests to be defended and the values to be fostered be ones that are widely shared and that diverse perspectives and views be not only considered but also accommodated. The challenge to U.S. intellectual resources, leadership at home and abroad, and domestic institutions will be great.

Notes

1. Alexander George and Richard Smoke, *Deterrence in American Foreign Policy* (New York: Columbia University Press, 1974).

2. See Robert Jervis, *Perception and Misperception in International Politics* (Princeton: Princeton University Press, 1976), chapter 3. More recent findings from several fields of study are summarized in Paul Stern et al., eds., *Perspectives on Deterrence* (New York: Oxford University Press, 1989).

3. Unless otherwise indicated, I will use the term *deterrence* broadly in the sense of the use of threats to achieve desired objectives. This can include compellence—that is, the use of threats to stop the other side from continuing a course of action—as well as deterrence proper—the use of threats to inhibit the other side from doing something. Many cases, such as U.S. attempts to restrain Serbia in the Yugoslav civil war, partake of both categories.

4. For a discussion of the ambiguous and contradictory messages the United States sent in the pre-invasion period, see Janice Stein, "Could War Have Been Avoided? Crisis Prevention and Management in the Gulf, 1990–1991," in Stanley Renshon, ed., *The Political Psychology of the Gulf War: Leaders, Publics, and the Process of Conflict* (Pittsburgh: University of Pittsburgh Press, 1993).

5. Daryl Bem, "Self-Perception Theory," in Leonard Berkowitz, ed., *Advances in Experimental Social Psychology,* vol. 6 (New York: Academic Press, 1972), 1–61. For an excellent application of this argument to foreign policy, see Deborah Larson, *The Origins of Containment: A Psychological Explanation* (Princeton: Princeton University Press, 1985).

6. "Excerpts From Pentagon's Plan: 'Prevent the Re-Emergence of a New Rival,' " *New York Times,* March 8, 1992, p. 12. It is not clear whether this section of the document was left unrevised; see Patrick Tyler, "Pentagon Drops Goal of Blocking New Superpowers," *New York Times,* May 24, 1992, p. 1. A later public document is vaguer but consistent with this stance: Department of Defense, *De-*

fense Strategy for the 1990s: The Regional Defense Strategy (Washington, D.C.: Department of Defense, 1993).

7. Bruce Russett has done so in *No Clear and Present Danger* (New York: Harper & Row, 1972).

8. Kenneth Waltz, *Theory of International Politics,* (Reading, Mass.: Addison-Wesley, 1979), 161–176; Glenn Snyder and Paul Diesing, *Conflict Among Nations* (Princeton: Princeton University Press, 1977), 429–470.

9. For further discussion, see Robert Jervis, "International Primacy: Is the Game Worth the Candle?" *International Security* 17 (Spring 1993): 52–67, and "The Future of World Politics: Will It Resemble the Past?" *International Security* 16 (Winter 1991/1992): 61–73.

10. This argument, made by the draft *Defense Guidance* (*New York Times,* March 8, 1992) was apparently softened in the final version (*New York Times,* May 24, 1992), but it is not clear what U.S. policy will actually be.

11. Quoted in Martin Gilbert, *Winston S. Churchill,* vol. 5, *1922–1932* (London: Heinemann, 1978), 76.

12. Bernard Brodie, "The Development of Nuclear Strategy," *International Security* 2 (Spring 1978): 83.

13. Patrick Tyler, "War in the 1990's: New Doubts," *New York Times,* February 18, 1992, p. 7.

14. The classic study is Warner Schilling, "The Politics of National Defense: Fiscal 1950," in Warner Schilling, Paul Hammond, and Glenn Snyder, *Strategy, Politics, and Defense Budgets* (New York: Columbia University Press, 1962), 5–266.

15. Patrick Tyler, "Seven Hypothetical Conflicts Foreseen by Pentagon," *New York Times,* February 17, 1992, p. 5.

16. For further discussion, see Robert Jervis, *The Logic of Images in International Relations,* 2nd ed. (New York: Columbia University Press, 1989), chapter 5.

17. Bruce Cumings, *The Origins of the Korean War,* vol. 2 (Princeton: Princeton University Press, 1990), especially part III. Much of the rest of Cumings's interpretation is badly flawed, but this point sheds a great deal of light on U.S. policy and unfolding events.

18. Douglas Macdonald, *Adventures in Chaos* (Cambridge: Harvard University Press, 1992).

19. Thomas Schelling, *The Strategy of Conflict* (Cambridge: Harvard University Press, 1960), 123–125.

20. Theodore Lowi, *The End of Liberalism* (New York: W.W. Norton, 1969), chapter 6.

21. See, for example, Secretary of State Baker's testimony to Congress reported in the *New York Times,* September 5, 1990, p. 8. A comprehensive analysis of the alternative meanings of "new world order" is provided in Stanley Sloan, "The U.S. Role in a New World Order: Prospects For George Bush's Global Vision," *Congressional Research Service Report,* March 28, 1991.

22. See the data reported in *Time,* October 7, 1991, p. 15, and in R.W. Apple, "Majority in Poll Fault Focus by Bush on Global Policy but Back New Order," *New York Times,* October 11, 1991, p. A8.

23. For a similar argument, see Zbigniew Brzezinski, *Power and Principle* (New York: Farrar, Straus, and Giroux, 1983), 445–446.

24. Edmund Burke, "Remarks on the Policy of the Allies with Respect to France," *Works,* vol. 4 (Boston: Little Brown, 1899), 457.

25. Herbert Butterfield, "The Balance of Power," in Herbert Butterfield and Martin Wight, eds., *Diplomatic Investigations* (Cambridge: Harvard University Press, 1960), 140.

26. Kenneth Waltz, "America as a Model for the World? A Foreign Policy Perspective," *PS: Political Science and Politics* 24, no. 4 (December 1991): 699.

27. Glenn Snyder, *Deterrence and Defense* (Princeton: Princeton University Press, 1961), 12–16.

28. Patrick Morgan, *Deterrence* (Beverly Hills, Calif.: Sage, 1977), chapter 2.

29. Richard Ned Lebow, *Between Peace and War* (Baltimore: Johns Hopkins University Press, 1981); Robert Jervis, Richard Ned Lebow, and Janice Gross Stein, *Psychology and Deterrence* (Baltimore: Johns Hopkins University Press, 1985).

30. For the interesting (but, I think, unconvincing) argument that this makes multipolar world more stable than a bipolar one, see Karl Deutsch and J. David Singer, "Multipolar Power Systems and International Stability," *World Politics* 16 (April 1964): 390–406.

31. Glenn Snyder, " 'Prisoner's Dilemma' and 'Chicken' Models in International Politics," *International Studies Quarterly* 15 (March 1971): 66–103; Robert Jervis, "Bargaining and Bargaining Tactics," in J. Roland Pennock and John Chapman, eds., *NOMOS*, vol. 15, *Coercion* (Chicago: Aldine Atherton, 1972), 272–288.

32. Lebow, *Between Peace and War;* Jervis, Lebow, and Stein, *Psychology and Deterrence.*

33. There is remarkably little empirical research about reputation. See the essays by Robert Jervis, Deborah Larson, Douglas Macdonald, Ted Hopf, and Douglas Blum in Robert Jervis and Jack Snyder, eds., *Dominoes and Bandwagons: Strategic Beliefs and Great Power Competition in the Eurasian Rimland* (New York: Oxford University Press, 1991) and Jonathan Mercer, *Broken Promises and Unfilled Threats: Resolve, Reputation, and the Deterrents* (Cornell University Press, forthcoming).

34. Robert McNamara, "The Military Role of Nuclear Weapons," *Foreign Affairs* 62 (Fall 1983): 68.

35. Robert Jervis, *The Illogic of American Nuclear Strategy* (Ithaca, N.Y.: Cornell University Press, 1984), chapter 5, and *The Meaning of the Nuclear Revolution* (Ithaca, N.Y.: Cornell University Press, 1989), chapter 3.

36. The best analysis of economic sanctions is David Baldwin, *Economic Statecraft* (Princeton: Princeton University Press, 1985).

9

Force Projection/
Crisis Response

JEFFREY RECORD

For over half a century, from the mid-1930s to the late 1980s, U.S. security interests were threatened on a global scale by one or more large, hostile, totalitarian empires. The United States accordingly created an unmatched capacity to project and sustain its military power overseas. Among the outstanding elements of that capacity were a long-range bomber force, navy, and body of amphibious infantry second to none; a large fleet of intercontinental-range military transport aircraft; the pre-positioning ashore and afloat of vast quantities of military supplies in regions of anticipated trouble; and a robust network of U.S. bases along the western, southern, and eastern rims of Eurasia.

Recent and ongoing events at home and abroad, however, are profoundly altering calculations of future U.S. requirements to project military power beyond the Western Hemisphere. The Soviet Union's disappearance removes the only remaining state capable of challenging U.S. interests on a global scale; it also removes any significant prospect of a major war in Europe, preparation for which has long dominated U.S. strategic planning. Additionally, the collapse of Soviet power and influence in the third world, highlighted by the disintegration of many of its African, Asian, and Arab client regimes, strips much of the third world of its strategic significance to the United States. Except for those few states intrinsically valuable to the United States (such as Saudi Arabia), what happens in this one or that one matters much less than it seemed to during the Cold War, because there is no longer a chance of their becoming bases of Soviet power.

The Cold War's demise by no means eliminates the U.S. demand for overseas force projection capacity. The Persian Gulf crisis of 1990 to 1991 demonstrated the potential suddenness and scale of that demand in the post–Cold War world. In that crisis, U.S. force projection and sustainment capacities created largely to meet the demands of an East-West conflict in Europe were unexpectedly employed in a North-South conflict outside Europe. Moreover, the Gulf War was in several respects a reminder of the increasing scarcity of politically assured U.S. military access ashore overseas. The scale and modernity of Saudi air bases and ports, most of which were built in the 1970s and 1980s with U.S. assistance and to U.S. military specifications, have no equal elsewhere in the third world. Neither Desert Shield nor Desert Storm would have been feasible without them, and Saudi permission to come ashore, even when granted, was conditioned on a U.S. pledge to withdraw its forces from the kingdom upon Desert Storm's conclusion. The Saudi government even refused to permit U.S. retention of a single heavy division's worth of equipment and supplies. Riyadh's behavior testifies, along with Manila's termination of U.S. basing rights in the Philippines in 1992, to mounting political sensitivity on the part of third-world governments to hosting even a token Western military presence, especially a U.S. presence.

The Gulf War experience also revealed much about the state of U.S. force projection capacity in 1990 and 1991. The air wings, ground divisions, and carrier battle groups necessary to guarantee Desert Storm's success were in fact available in the force structure, and they were moved to the Persian Gulf in time for Desert Storm's initiation. But the deployment process consumed six months, even though it was granted a completely free ride by an adversary that apparently could think of nothing better to do than to remain passive as the United States amassed overwhelming military power on its very doorstep. Desert Shield also revealed serious deficiencies in militarily useful shipping, as did Desert Storm in countermine warfare. The shortcomings in the latter, attributable to decades of conscious U.S. Navy neglect, compromised prospects for an amphibious assault, a major force projection option in Desert Storm.

The combination of a logistically flush host country and a strategically incompetent enemy is not likely to be encountered again, if for no other reason than the lessons that future adversaries are certain to draw from the Gulf War itself. The Gulf experience certainly contrasts sharply with the U.S. experience in World War II and the Korean and Vietnam Wars. In those conflicts, U.S. military power often had to be projected ashore forcibly, and logistical infrastructures had to be created from scratch on the spot, a process requiring years of effort. In Europe and East Asia, the United States also faced truly powerful, alert, and innovative enemies who either effectively competed with U.S. military power on its own terms or devised alternative styles of warfare aimed at neutralizing U.S. military strengths and exploiting U.S. political weaknesses.

The strategic, operational, logistical, and other conditions that so favored U.S. arms in the Persian Gulf were nearly ideal, but the phenomenon that gave rise to the Gulf War is not. Although the horizon seems clear of any power capable of supplanting the breadth of the military challenge once posed by the Soviet Union, the latter's very extinction seems to have promoted the ambitions of aspiring regional hegemons in the third world, including some former Soviet client regimes now free of their old patron's restraining influence. Moreover, the third world's half-dozen or so large and militarily ambitious states have increasing access, via their own efforts and transfers from abroad, to hyperlethal munitions and to effective means of delivering them over ever-increasing distances. The Gulf War inflated the attractiveness of highly destructive ordnance and ballistic missile technologies to third-world countries with imperial ambitions at odds with important U.S. security interests. The Gulf War demonstrated the futility of non-Western attempts to challenge modern conventional military power (a Western invention) on its own terms; Iraq's attempt to buy into conventional military modernity by acquiring its outward trappings provided impressive-looking ground and air forces with little actual fighting power—except against other third-world opponents also beset by crippling cultural and political obstacles to achieving conventional military effectiveness (Iran) or simply too small to resist (Kuwait).

But Saddam Hussein did have one weapon that proved not only strategically significant but also impossible for the United States to suppress completely. Unlike his air force, which effectively vanished after its first few encounters with U.S. airpower, and unlike his large army in Kuwait, which was battered into a coma from the air and then quickly trampled to death on the ground, Saddam's mobile Scud ballistic missile force escaped destruction and throughout the conflict posed the only significant threat to the coalition's political cohesion. Needless to say, had Iraqi Scuds carried chemical warheads, their political and even military effects would have been greatly magnified. In ballistic missiles and hyperlethal munitions, Saddam clearly saw what other aspiring third-world hegemons have also seen: a path to regional military preeminence and a relatively cheap and easy means of at least partially offsetting conventional Western military strengths.[1]

Pre–Gulf War U.S. force projection operations in the third world did not have to contend with either ballistic missile threats or the prospect of chemical and biological munitions attacks. The proliferation of these technologies among the likes of Libya, Syria, Iraq, Iran, and North Korea does not fundamentally endanger U.S. capacity to project its military power overseas. Antiballistic missile technologies are unfolding, and the United States retains powerful conventional and other means of retaliation against states tempted to employ hyperlethal munitions against U.S. forces; there is in fact significant evidence that U.S. nuclear and other threats may have contributed to Iraqi passivity with respect to using its vast chemical weapons arsenal.[2] However, the very presence of these new capabilities in a third-world adversary's arsenal will pose new challenges to the projection of U.S. military power. The Iraqi Scud threat imposed a significant diversion of the Desert Storm air campaign's attention away from preferred targets, and Iraqi chemical attacks, had they been mounted against Saudi ports and air bases, could have severely disrupted both Desert Shield and Desert Storm.

Whatever the likely future demand for power projection capability, a significant decline in its supply is certain. Almost as certain is that the force projection environment overseas will in some respects be more difficult than in the past. U.S. defense expenditure has declined significantly since the mid-1980s and will continue to do so until at least the mid-1990s. Moreover, the pace of decline may accelerate in the near term. The Pentagon's proposed Base Force, devised before the Soviet Union's final disintegration, may not command an adequate constituency among a public and Congress thoroughly preoccupied with domestic issues, although military industrial base and job maintenance considerations could serve to block a wholesale assault on planned defense spending. The result has been, and will continue to be, a contraction in U.S. conventional force levels by a minimum of 25 percent and as much as 50 percent of their late-1980s strengths. Of course, not all components of the force structure will be slashed equally, but few major categories of forces, including such projection components as long-range bomber, naval, and amphibious assault forces, will escape major cuts. There will, in short, be substantially less force to project. How much will be enough to meet future contingencies is impossible to determine with any assurance, given the uncertainties of the post–Cold War, and now post-Soviet, world. Some believe the requirements of Desert Shield and Desert Storm offer an adequate benchmark, since they are not likely to be exceeded in any reasonably foreseeable contingency not involving a militarily resurgent former Soviet entity. The Base Force will be capable of replicating Desert Storm, although its capacity to cover more than one major regional contingency simultaneously is not self-evident.

Less force may well be sufficient, but the general conditions in which it will operate will differ from those of the past. The United States is dismantling much of its once robust network of overseas garrisons that for so long contributed to the containment of Soviet military power. In Northeast Asia and especially Europe, hundreds of U.S. bases are being closed, and hundreds of thousands of U.S. troops are being sent home. This drawdown, though permitted by the Soviet Union's disappearance, dramatically reduces a standing U.S. presence in the Eastern Hemisphere, elements of which were often called upon, because of their proximity, to participate in the kind of force projection operation entailed in Desert Shield—witness the transfer of the U.S. Army's Germany-based VII Corps to the Persian Gulf. This evacuation of Cold War garrisons on or along the rim of the former Soviet empire, together with the continued decline in U.S. military access ashore in the third world, contains significant implications not only for the Pentagon's investment in strategic mobility but also for the relative emphases traditionally accorded to various categories of forces specifically tailored or otherwise suitable for the force projection mission. The contraction of overseas garrisons and basing rights may alter the relative values traditionally accorded to such simultaneously complementary and competitive clusters of capabilities as airlift and sealift; onshore and maritime prepositioning; long-range and tactical airpower; land-based and sea-based aviation; heavy, medium, and light ground forces; and amphibious and nonamphibious ground forces.

The Separation of Threats

Judging these matters requires some sense of the future threat spectrum, particularly as regards those threats that could be expected to elicit a violent U.S. military response. Customary Cold War threat analysis routinely postulated three conflict environments, based on their anticipated intensity. The first was high-intensity conflict, which was virtually synonymous with a global nuclear or conventional war with the Soviet Union. The second was mid-intensity conflict, generally associated with regional powers and waged on a conventional basis. Low-intensity conflict was—and remains—a catch-all for everything else: special operations for combatting terrorism and narcotics traffic; punitive actions against militarily helpless dictators like Manuel Noriega; intervention in primarily civil conflicts of the guerrilla variety; and operations, like Eastern Exit of 1991 in Mogadishu, aimed at rescuing endangered U.S. and foreign nationals.[3]

Today, the prospect of U.S. involvement in a high-intensity conflict seems to have vanished altogether. With what major industrialized state could the United States realistically find itself drawn into a deliberate nuclear exchange or large-scale conventional war? There are simply no plausible candidates left now and for the foreseeable future. The major European powers, including Russia, are all allies or friends, and for Russia to return to a hostile military resurgency of Cold War scope would require decades. Japan is likely to remain self-deterred from any form of bellicose behavior for quite some time, and it is difficult to postulate a realistic *causus bellum* with China or India.

Unlike prospects for a high-intensity war, the bottom end of the spectrum contains many plausible conflict scenarios. The issues here, however, are whether they would seriously tax U.S. military resources (as opposed to ingenuity), and more important, the likelihood of U.S. involvement. Even a force structure significantly smaller than the Bush administration's planned Base Force would be more than capable of repeating such operations as those mounted in Grenada in 1983, Panama in 1989, and against Libya in 1986. The change in the third-world political landscape caused by the end of the Cold War, however, has drained many present and prospective low-intensity conflicts of their strategic significance to the United States. Since there is no chance of a Grenada, Dominican Republic, Panama, Ethiopia, or Angola becoming an outpost of Soviet power, the likelihood that events in such countries (other than anarchy threatening U.S. citizens) would elicit U.S. military intervention diminishes, except for humanitarian purposes. Moreover, memories of Vietnam continue to caution against direct involvement in other countries' internal wars.

Even in Europe, prospects for significant U.S. military operations of other than the humanitarian variety appear remote. Communism's collapse from the Elbe to the Neva has liberated long-suppressed ancient ethnic and national antagonisms in Eastern Europe (especially in the Balkans) and the former Soviet Union itself. Civil war has already erupted in what was Yugoslavia, and other potential flashpoints abound, including the Polish-Slovak dispute over claims to Silesia, Serbian-Albanian tensions over Kosovo province, the Romanian-Hungarian dispute over the rights of ethnic Hungarians in Transylvania, and Greek bitterness over the name and territorial scope of the new Republic of Macedonia. None of these potential conflicts, however, directly engages core U.S. security interests in Europe and are therefore most unlikely to prompt U.S. military intervention; the United States also certainly will steer clear of conflicts among former Soviet republics.[4]

This leaves mid-intensity conflict outside Europe as the category deserving the greatest force-planning attention. In terms of resources, such conflicts are much more demanding than low-intensity ones, and the Cold War's demise has hardly discouraged the quest for regional hegemony on the part of such hostile states as Libya, Syria, Iraq, Iran, and North Korea (and conceivably, a politically radicalized Algeria, Egypt, and even Saudi Arabia). Since 1945 the United States has fought three such wars—in Korea, Southeast Asia, and the Persian Gulf, and the continued presence in the Persian Gulf region of vital U.S. interests and aspiring regional hegemons hostile to those interests portends further major conflict.

Some have argued that the very example of Desert Storm will deter future assaults on U.S. interests and client states in the region. There is no question that Desert Storm demonstrated the unassailable superiority of the United States in modern conventional military power in circumstances where it has the time and space to deploy sufficient force. There is every reason to believe, however, that the Gulf War will caution adversaries to avoid making the same kinds of mistakes that Saddam Hussein did. Those included gobbling up Kuwait in one fell swoop (a limited advance into the disputed border areas would have given him most of what he wanted without provoking an effective U.S. military response); failing to push on into Saudi Arabia's Eastern Province (which would have given him control of most of the ports and air bases critical to Desert Shield); refusal to evacuate Kuwait before Desert Storm (which would have left his military power and nascent nuclear capability intact); and failure to find means of inflicting casualties on U.S. forces sufficient to undermine U.S. public and congressional support for the war.[5]

Desert Storm's political impotence also must be recognized. A defiant Saddam Hussein and much of his military power survived the war; and the war has, if anything, heightened tensions between the rich southern Persian Gulf states and their largely oilless Arab neighbors. The war also seems to have excited an expansion of hostile Islamic fundamentalist sentiment in Morocco, Algeria, Tunisia, Sudan, Libya, and Jordan. Finally, the war has paved the way for yet another Iranian bid for hegemony in the Persian Gulf.

Nowhere in the third world outside the Persian Gulf is there such an intersection of vital U.S. interests, explosive regional stability, and lack of militarily significant surrogates for U.S. power. Alone or collectively, the southern Gulf states, below whose deserts lies so much of the oil that fuels the Western economy, lack populations and social systems necessary to balance the military power and potential of Iraq and Iran—both of which, for different reasons, seek to expunge U.S. power and influence from the region.

Requirements for Military Operations

From a domestic political standpoint, however, Desert Storm did fulfill three imperatives of successful post-Vietnam military interventions: brevity, casualty minimization, and clarity and persuasiveness of objectives. These imperatives dominated the planning and execution of Desert Storm and are likely to do so for the foreseeable future, with Desert Storm inevitably serving as the yardstick for success.[6] But these same imperatives also will serve to inform adversaries of U.S. weaknesses deserving exploitation. Indeed, hypersensitivity to casualties—both U.S. military and enemy civilian—may now be the single greatest comparative military disadvantage of the United States on the battlefield, especially against third-world adversaries prepared to inflict them at almost any cost. The political imperative of casualty minimization largely determined Desert Storm's force requirements, the timing of its initiation and termination, the sequencing of air and ground operations, and such choices as the decision to eschew an amphibious assault in favor of alternative ground operations inland.

In Korea, Vietnam, and Lebanon, our enemies fatally eroded the U.S. will to prevail by prolonging combat and inflicting much loss of U.S. life. Saddam Hussein may have had no illusions about the ultimate fate in store for his forces in Kuwait, but he clearly expected, or at least hoped, that they would fight longer and harder than they did and thereby weaken U.S. resolve. That he failed to do so was testimony to his utter ignorance of modern warfare, not of U.S. political sensitivities. Saddam also faced a U.S. force with clear, convincing, and achievable formal objectives— Kuwait's liberation and Iraq's partial disarmament. Such objectives were notable for their absence in Vietnam in the 1960s and Lebanon in the early 1980s, and they may elude the United States in future interventions.

Indeed, the requirement for brevity and casualty minimization may preclude U.S. intervention even when important and well-understood security interests are at stake. It is doubtful that the Bush or any other administration would have launched Desert Storm had it been convinced that hostilities would be prolonged and U.S. losses high. Therefore, any future adversary that can credibly threaten to impose extended and sanguinary combat on U.S. forces may deter U.S. intervention altogether or at least restrict it to air and naval action. Even Saddam Hussein understood that ground combat is the primary source of casualties in war, and it is no coincidence that the United States relied mainly on airpower, followed by an abbreviated land offensive, to destroy Iraqi forces in the Kuwaiti theater of operations (KTO). The Pentagon may have discarded the body count as a measure of success, but for astute third-world adversaries, counts of U.S. bodies are likely to become a paramount strategic objective in wartime.

Some airpower proponents believe that the several heavy U.S. Army divisions deployed to the Persian Gulf were superfluous to Desert Storm's outcome and that airpower's performance in the Gulf War portends a revolution in warfare that by implication will permit the United States to prevail quickly and cheaply over any third-world conventional military challenge.[7] This judgment, if valid, would not only free the United States of any significant Vietnam-style risks in future interventions but would also permit the substitution of airpower for heavy ground forces, which already compare unfavorably with airpower in terms of strategic mobility.

There is no question that airpower, broadly defined, was the dominating and determining instrument of victory in the Persian Gulf. Moreover, a case can be made, certainly in retrospect, that the amount of U.S. and allied ground force amassed in Saudi Arabia for Desert Storm far surpassed that needed to fulfill the mission of Kuwait's liberation; the preliminary air campaign did, in fact, serve as a significant, if not total, surrogate for the massive heavy ground forces originally thought to be necessary to ensure a rapid and decisive victory in the KTO. Modern airpower's future importance relative to surface forces may well increase.

But such judgments must be tempered by an understanding of what airpower *failed* to accomplish in Desert Storm and of the disparities among third-world states and their armies in vulnerability to a quick and effective takedown by U.S. airpower. In the Persian Gulf, U.S. air operations clearly isolated and crippled Iraqi forces in the KTO, but those forces remained in place and did not attempt to withdraw or surrender en masse until they were attacked on the ground. Moreover, as a Department of the Air Force study concluded, the strategic bombardment component of the air campaign, though it destroyed much of Iraq's economic infrastructure while consuming only about 10 percent of total coalition air sorties, failed to find and destroy much of Iraq's vast and well-concealed or -protected military-industrial complex—the result in part of faulty intelligence. And neither did strategic bombing, despite contrary hopes, provoke desired changes in Iraq's political leadership.[8] In fact, airpower alone has never toppled a totalitarian regime.

Thus, there were serious qualifications to airpower's success in the Persian Gulf, even though it was employed in ideal conditions, including an abundance of aviation assets, an enemy state physically isolated and lacking an air force worth the name, and an enemy military establishment utterly exposed to air attack by weather, terrain, a conventional force structure, and static defense mentality. Iraq almost seemed determined to serve up its vulnerabilities on the ground to U.S. strength in the air.

If only every future U.S. adversary in the third world offered U.S. airpower a challenge amounting to little more than a live-fire training exercise with real targets. Unfortunately, few third world countries and military establishments are, or are likely to remain, as vulnerable to rapid defeat by U.S. airpower as was Iraq in the Gulf War (Libya being a prominent exception)—although many third-world national economic infrastructures remain open to disruption or destruction from the air. Airpower's application in Korea and Vietnam was frustrated by rugged or heavily foliated terrain, foul weather, primitive enemy economies, and logistically austere enemy field forces that operated in a manner designed to thwart detection and attack from the air. North Korea, still regarded as the main threat to peace and stability in Northeast Asia, would likely prove relatively impervious to swift and decisive air attack, given its rugged topography and the degree to which it has, more than any other country, buried its military-industrial complex and even operating forces beyond the reach of all but nuclear munitions. The country's exceedingly closed society also suggests that air campaign planners would confront an intelligence failure far larger than they faced in Desert Storm.

Even in Southwest Asia, potential adversaries are, for one reason or another, less vulnerable to paralysis from the air. Take Iran, for example. That country is three times the size of Iraq and lacks that country's pre–Desert Storm economic modernity, thereby making it less vulnerable to swift economic paralysis from the air. Key military and other targets are distant and far apart, and Iran's topography provides far more cover for field forces than that of the KTO. On the other hand, Iran's oil industry, critical to its economic and military potential, will remain highly exposed to a determined air assault.

There is, too, the very practical question of how the United States could again assemble the kind of vast air armada required to conduct an air campaign of Desert Storm's scope and intensity. That campaign rested on an overseas deployment of aviation assets unprecedented since World War II. Yet the deployment to the Persian Gulf of 2,800 U.S. and 650 allied aircraft itself hinged on an unprecedented political decision by the House of Sa'ud, which itself was confronted with a direct threat to its survival unprecedented in its history. The entire affair was so unusual as to suggest the virtual impossibility of ever again repeating a similar campaign, although the economically devastating strategic bombardment component of coalition air operations consumed relatively few resources in terms of aircraft and sorties. What other third-world client state of the United States could logistically—and would politically—accept so vast an amount of U.S. force on its territory for the purpose of attacking a neighboring state?

To say that another air campaign like Desert Storm is most improbable does not mean that another such air campaign will be required or that airpower will revert to becoming a mere accessory of surface forces. Airpower will remain the weapon of choice as a means of punishment in circumstances where commitment of ground forces is infeasible or undesirable and where the primary objective is economic disablement. Much will depend not only on the strategic and operational environments but also on the scope and nature of regional challenges and of U.S. objectives in regional crises.

Future interventions, like past ones, can be grouped into three basic categories, none of them mutually exclusive. Punitive interventions are designed to punish a hostile state or group for an act or acts already committed. They are usually one-time affairs, like the 1986 air strikes on Libyan targets, and are directed against targets associated with the offense committed. Punitive strikes can be conducted with land- or sea-based aviation and commonly do not involve the employment of ground forces.

A second form of intervention involves attempts to overturn or block actual or anticipated forcible changes in the territorial status quo. This was the ostensible basis of the Bush administration's decision to intervene in the Persian Gulf following Iraq's invasion of Kuwait, and it formed the rationale for U.S. intervention in Korea and Vietnam. Intervention in this case almost invariably requires the commitment of ground forces, either to deter an expected enemy advance or to roll back one that already has taken place.

A third type of intervention aims at the overthrow of the enemy regime itself via the destruction of its field forces, the conquest of its territory, or direct attacks on its leadership and supporting political institutions. The success of these interventions, which also customarily require ground force action, seems to vary inversely with the political and military resilience of the target regime. Panama and Grenada succumbed quickly to irresistible U.S. power, but stronger, totalitarian regimes—those of Kim Il Sung, Ho Chi Minh, and Saddam Hussein—managed to survive assaults that decimated their field forces and destroyed their economies. Such regimes may be more or less impervious to displacement via conventional military action, unless the United States is prepared, as it was not in the Persian Gulf and Indochina, to carry the war on the ground directly to the regime's territorial center of political authority and then to impose a new political order. Such an objective risks long casualty lists as well as exposure to charges of imperial aggrandizement.

A desire to avoid such risks led the Bush administration to eschew an advance on Baghdad and to proclaim unilaterally a cease-fire only 100 hours after the beginning of the coalition ground offensive against Iraqi forces in Kuwait. These decisions, together with the air campaign's failure to eliminate the institutional foundations of Saddam Hussein's power— the Republican Guard, secret police, and Ba'ath Party apparatus—made it possible for Saddam to prevail over post-cease-fire Shi'ite and Kurdish challenges to Sunni rule in Iraq.

To these traditional categories of U.S. intervention must now be added a fourth: preventive war. Though long opposed in policy and practice by the United States, Desert Storm was in fact more of a preventive war than it was a traditional intervention to reverse an aggression. By January 1991, Kuwait's liberation had become but a convenient pretext for Desert Storm, whose overriding objective was the elimination of Iraq as a future military threat to regional stability, especially in regards to its nascent nuclear weapons capability. It was this objective that accounted for the massive strategic bombardment campaign against military-industrial and economic infrastructure targets deep inside Iraq—targets whose elimination was more or less superfluous to the ability of Iraqi forces in the KTO to offer effective resistance to coalition air and ground forces dedicated to theater operations. Saddam's invasion of Kuwait, at the time an anti-U.S. country to which the United States had not the slightest shred of a defense obligation, provided the United States an opportunity to demolish an even greater future threat to its security interests in the Persian Gulf.[9]

Whether the preventive character of Desert Storm is a portent of interventions to come remains to be seen. On the one hand, Desert Storm represents a major and in many respects disturbing departure from centuries of U.S. condemnation of preventive war (as opposed to preemptive military actions like the invasion of Grenada); on the other hand, understandable concern expressed in recent years over the proliferation among rogue third-world states of hyperlethal munitions and their increasingly long-range means of delivery and the very ease with which Desert Storm eliminated Iraq as an at least near-term future threat, along with the departure of the last remaining state capable of providing a restraining military counterweight in regional disputes—all may encourage preventive military action as a perceived solution to the problem posed by renegade regimes seeking "forbidden" weapons. If so, then the frequency of U.S. military intervention in the third world, otherwise likely to decline for another set of reasons, could increase; a policy of militarily preventing aspiring regional powers from acquiring such capabilities will require repeated use of force or at least threats to use force. Such a policy would moreover inflate airpower's relative importance to land and naval power, since airpower is likely to remain the preferred means of quickly and effectively destroying an enemy state's military-industrial complex and economic infrastructure.

The principal obstacles to adopting such an avowed policy of preventive military action as an instrument of nonproliferation are political; preventive war, unless artfully disguised as something else, is not likely to command much enthusiasm among a U.S. public and Congress that have long associated this institution with outright aggression on the part of their enemies. And neither is much of international opinion likely to view such a policy as anything more than an assertion of naked imperialism in a new guise. The policy's demand for frequent threatened or actual use of force would certainly provoke strong domestic political resistance. Finally, the policy, once adopted, would provoke potential target states to bury, disperse, conceal, and otherwise shield their suspect activities from possible air attack, thereby rendering effective preventive action ever more difficult.

The New World Disorder

The burden of this discussion so far has been to suggest that future U.S. power projection force planning and operations against regional third-world threats will be governed by the following internal and external general conditions: (1) comparative resource scarcity, (2) threat unfamiliarity and unpredictability, (3) diminished onshore U.S. military access overseas, and (4) hypersensitivity to incurring casualties. We now turn to a discussion of these conditions and their implications for U.S. force projection.

Comparative Resource Scarcity

Comparative resource scarcity refers to the on-going budget-driven contraction in U.S. force structure inherited from the Cold War. From 1990 to 1995 alone, planned force cuts include a 20 percent drop in total active-duty military personnel (29 percent for the army, 19 percent for the air force, and 13 percent each for the navy and marines). In terms of major force units, the army will move from 29 (18 active) to 18 (12 active) divisions; navy aircraft carriers, from 16 to 13; carrier air wings, from 15 to 13; total battle force ships, from 545 to 451; air force tactical fighter wings, from 36 (24 active) to 26 (15 active); and strategic bombers, from about 300 to less than 200.[10]

Moreover, it is far from clear that the Defense Department's post-1995 Base Force, which was calculated before the Soviet Union's dissolution, will command adequate and sustained congressional support; both the House and Senate Armed Services Committees have called for additional cuts in defense spending over the next five years on the order of US$40 billion to US$50 billion, and sentiment for even greater reductions is strong. Clearly, some key force projection and supporting capabilities will suffer significant contraction, though others will actually register modest increases.

Of particular concern is the decline in the long-range bomber force, whose size has been shrinking for decades despite the air force's new emphasis on "Global Reach, Global Power." The fate of the B-2 program, which originally called for a force of 132 aircraft but was capped in 1992 at a maximum of 20, portends a mid-1990s bomber force of no more than 200 aircraft. Moreover, the force will hardly be optimized for the kind of projection operations undertaken in the Gulf War, since it will be composed of only about 70 aging B-52G/H bombers configured for conventional strike operations, with the balance consisting of newer B-1Bs and B-2s designed primarily for nuclear attacks on a Soviet Union that no longer exists.

Amphibious presence and assault capabilities, perhaps the epitome of U.S. force projection capacity, also will be slashed. Each of the Marine Corps' three active division will lose at least one and probably more of its nine maneuver battalions, and major reductions in key U.S. Navy supporting capabilities, notably levels of attack aviation, amphibious shipping, and gunfire support, are now in progress or planned.

The productivity of U.S. carrier-based aviation, already unsatisfactory as manifested in Desert Storm, is also certain to suffer further diminution. Aside from ongoing reduction in the number of carriers and carrier air wings, the structure of the latter still reflects a lingering Cold War–derived obsession with fleet air defense and antisubmarine warfare operations at the expense of attacking targets ashore—notwithstanding the experience of three wars (in Korea, Indochina, and the Persian Gulf) against enemies, characteristic of those we are likely to continue to face in the third world, incapable of seriously threatening U.S. carriers at sea. (Not since the Battle of Okinawa in 1945 has a U.S. carrier been subjected to hostile air or submarine attack.)

Worse still is the crisis in naval attack aviation itself, highlighted by the cancellation in 1992 of the A-12, the designated replacement for the thirty-year-old A-6 Intruder. This leaves the navy with no near-term or even mid-term dedicated strike aircraft—only its old A-6s and the newer, hybrid F/A-18s, whose range and payload compare poorly with both the A-6 and competing U.S. Air Force aircraft. The crisis is compounded by another serious deficiency made manifest in Desert Storm: a comparative scarcity within naval aviation of modern precision-guided air-to-surface ordnance, especially heavy munitions required to destroy hardened targets of the kind the U.S. Air Force so often successfully attacked in Iraq. It is also to be noted that naval aviation's declining productivity has serious implications for the Marine Corps' ability to carry out its most distinctive mission, especially in contingencies where land-based airpower is unavailable; carrier aircraft provide indispensable fire support for amphibious assault forces' movement to shore and initial beachhead consolidation.

Still another navy deficiency impeding amphibious assault and the navy's own ability to operate effectively, particularly in such strategically critical confined waters as the Persian Gulf, the Red Sea, and the Sea of Japan, has been chronic underinvestment in countermine warfare. Sea and shallow-water mines are cheap and effective weapons of choice for third-world countries, and the penalties of the navy's relative inattention to countermine warfare were evident in both Operation Earnest Will (the reflagging/escort operations in the Persian Gulf of 1987 and 1988) and Desert Storm. During the latter, Iraqi mines severely damaged two large U.S. warships; the presence of mines also was a major consideration behind General H. Norman Schwarzkopf's decision not to authorize an amphibious assault along Kuwait's Iraqi-held coastline. To be sure, two new classes of mine-sweeping and mine-hunting vessels are under construction, but they are few in number and remain low on a severely budget-constrained navy's list of procurement priorities. Given the disintegration of the only country capable of challenging U.S. naval power on the high seas, as well as the likelihood that the navy will again be called upon to conduct operations in mine-infested waters in such confined areas as the Persian Gulf (as it has twice already in the past seven years), a major overhaul and expansion of U.S. countermine capabilities would seem imperative if the United States is not to forfeit the full potential effectiveness of a major component of its future force projection capability.

The same may be said of inshore warfare. The navy's Cold War focus on large-scale engagements on the high seas with the now defunct Soviet fleet bred decades of inattention to dealing with the kind of threat now posed increasingly by third-world states equipping themselves with relatively small but very fast antiship missile-armed patrol boats—craft that also, if packed with explosives, could provide a terrorist organization's dream weapon. That such vessels in Iraqi hands proved ineffective was attributable less to any inherent impotence than it was to Iraq's severely constrained access to the Persian Gulf and the overwhelming coalition armada arrayed against it. Operating along an extensive and jagged coastline like Iran's, such craft, especially if crewed by fanatics willing to die to achieve a collision with a U.S. warship, could prove a nasty threat. This suggests the need for greater investment in small and swift coastal patrol craft.

Against these unfavorable trends must nevertheless be counted some highly positive developments. Strategic mobility—airlift, sealift, and prepositioning—is the basic currency of force projection, and the outlook here is far more encouraging than in many other force projection budget accounts. Desert Shield and Desert Storm profited immensely from the vast increases in U.S. strategic airlift and maritime prepositioning (for three Marine Corps expeditionary brigades) undertaken in the late 1970s and throughout the 1980s. The Gulf War also reaffirmed the need for additional and more modern airlift capacity in the form of the C-17 program as well as the need to extend the concept of maritime prepositioning to components of selected heavy U.S. Army units—traditionally the most strategically immobile elements of U.S. conventional force structure. Plans have been drawn up and funds requested for both, including 9 prepositioning ships for army combat and support equipment.

Desert Shield also drew attention to a longstanding major strategic mobility deficiency: inadequate sealift, especially fast sealift of the roll-on/roll-off variety. But for heavy reliance on large numbers of chartered foreign vessels, Desert Shield could not possibly have delivered programmed forces for Desert Storm by the time the coalition ground offensive was actually launched. Fortunately, the very experience of Desert Shield has prompted Defense Department requests for additional fast sealift, including 11 new vessels designed to move heavy army divisions rapidly overseas.

In sum, U.S. strategic mobility capabilities overall proved adequate by virtue of great foresight shown in the 1970s and 1980s, though Desert Shield promoted new initiatives aimed at correcting residual deficiencies. Given continued cuts in force structure, this will produce a Base Force— or something smaller—far richer in strategic mobility per unit of force than was available for the larger Cold War U.S. military establishment.

Unfamiliar and Unpredictable Threats

During the Cold War, U.S. force planners became accustomed to dealing with one primary, familiar, and relatively predictable adversary. Even the Korean and Vietnam Wars were regarded as products of Soviet expansionism via third-world surrogates, and the failure of U.S. arms to prevail in both was attributable in large measure to North Korea's and North Vietnam's access to Soviet and other external communist military assistance. Conversely, most Soviet third-world client states were subject to varying degrees of restraint from Moscow (including Iraq during the Iran-Iraq War), and none had significant arsenals of hyperlethal munitions or ballistic missiles. The Cold War also engendered a preoccupation on the part of the U.S. intelligence community with developments in the Soviet Union and its communist allies. This preoccupation came at the expense of intelligence gathering on noncommunist countries like Iraq, Iran, Lebanon, and Grenada, where events routinely caught the United States by surprise and where related U.S. military actions were commonly plagued by intelligence deficiencies ranging from lack of militarily useful maps to gross misunderstanding of local political developments precipitating confrontations and hostilities.

The post–Cold War security environment is one of comparative threat unfamiliarity and unpredictability—witness the Persian Gulf crisis. Before August 2, 1990, the United States knew relatively little about Iraq; it grossly overestimated the Iraqi army's fighting power while at the same time grievously underestimating both the true scope of Iraq's "forbidden" weaponry programs and the political resilience of the Ba'athist regime in Baghdad. Saddam Hussein's regional ambitions and willingness to act upon them were discounted; until August 2, he was regarded as a "force for moderation" who, whatever his quarrel with Kuwait, could be "managed" into a nonviolent resolution of it. His invasion of Kuwait came as much of a surprise as had the Ayatollah's overthrow of the Shah of Iran, another country where a continuation of the status quo was taken for granted because of a basic unfamiliarity with the political pressures for radical change and their potency.

In the future, moreover, the United States will be contending with third-world adversaries unfamiliar in two other respects. The Soviet Union's demise means that adversaries like Iraq will not have the benefit of external superpower assistance, though they may enjoy some aid from regional allies. This will serve to simplify both the military and political burdens of intervention. It will make adversaries more militarily isolable and therefore theoretically more easily beatable, although probably not to the degree that Iraq was trounced during Desert Storm. Isolation from superpower succor also will remove a major source of civil-military tension that flourished in both the Korean and Vietnam conflicts, where the issue of permitting U.S. forces to attack either the source of that external support (for example, trans-Yalu targets in Manchuria) or their points of entry (such as Haiphong harbor and the rail links along the Sino-Vietnamese border) became a major source of public discontent over both wars' management. Iraq's complete military isolation rendered moot the issue of sanctuaries.

Be all that as it may, the United States can expect to face adversaries having military capabilities that Pyongyang and Hanoi lacked. Iraq's prewar nuclear weapons development programs, its use of chemical weapons against Iran, and subsequent Scud attacks on Saudi Arabia and Israel underscore the continuing proliferation among "problem" third-world states of hyperlethal munitions and ballistic missiles. In such weaponry is seen a means both of achieving regional military preeminence and of partially offsetting U.S. and Western conventional military strengths, especially modern airpower, with which no third-world country can hope to compete with the West on its own terms.

Desert Storm marked the first time since 1944 that U.S. field forces and their operating bases overseas were subjected to ballistic missile attack, though Iraq did not employ chemical or biological munitions against coalition forces. Baghdad was not, however, deterred from launching its Scud missiles, which proved to be its only strategically significant weapons as well as the only ones that the coalition never fully suppressed. If anything, the relative success of the Iraqi Scuds, along with the manifest vulnerability of Saudi ports, air bases, and cities to ballistic missile–delivered hyperlethal munitions, will accelerate the demand for such capabilities by third-world countries having ambitions at odds with U.S. security interests. Certainly such technologies are far cheaper to acquire and operate, in terms of both money and skilled labor, than the kind of robust air forces fielded by the United States; the difficulties the coalition encountered in suppressing Scud launches and then intercepting them in flight, together with persistent inadequacies in U.S. defenses against chemical and biological agents, argue strongly for the conclusion that improved ballistic missile defenses, ranging from counterstrike to terminal defense capabilities, must of necessity become major components of future U.S. force projection operations.

Deterrence is always preferable to denial, of course, though it is not self-evident that the principles and instruments of nuclear deterrence that managed to thwart direct armed conflict of any kind between the United States and the Soviet Union during the Cold War will be as efficacious and politically acceptable in deterrence of wartime use of hyperlethal munitions by rogue third-world states. Threatening nuclear retaliation to deter chemical or biological attacks may lack credibility, given the almost certain disproportionality of effects involved, strong U.S. aversion to inflicting excessive collateral damage, and the enormous political and moral inhibitions that have arisen since 1945 around the use of nuclear weapons for any purpose other than retaliation against a nuclear attack on the United States itself. A U.S. nuclear riposte against any third-world state would have inescapably racist and imperialist overtones and would probably be unacceptable in all circumstances short of a nuclear attack on U.S. contingency forces. And neither is the United States prepared to respond effectively in kind to chemical and biological weapons attack; it is rapidly dismantling its arsenal of the former and has renounced possession and use of the latter.

However, Desert Storm demonstrated that *under the right conditions,* modern conventional airpower, in which the United States has an unassailable lead, can quickly disable a modernizing, nonagrarian country's essential economic functions, including its commercial intercourse with the outside world (the maintenance of which is vital to such countries as Libya, Iraq, and Iran)—and do so at a relatively low cost in terms of friendly military and enemy civilian casualties. Iraq in 1990 was no primitive, preindustrial society but rather a model in many respects of the very kind of third-world country upon which U.S. proliferation concerns have focused: economically advancing countries that contain well-developed and highly exposed communications, transportation, and energy production and distribution centers and that are critically dependent on exports and outside assistance to finance and support their military ambitions.[11] Thus, if Desert Storm is any guide, the United States now has at hand a potentially very effective nonnuclear tool of intrawar deterrence of third-world use of nuclear and other weapons of mass destruction if not of conventionally armed ballistic missiles. The prospect of having decades of costly and painful economic modernization quickly erased cannot but provide a disincentive to any future "Iraq" contemplating employment of unconventional weapons against U.S. contingency forces.

The very ability to gain and maintain air supremacy swiftly over a third-world state's economic and political heartland affords other benefits as well. Iraq remains under effective "air occupation" by the United States; it was only the explicit threat of resumed U.S. air action against it that permitted U.S. forces to provide a sanctuary in northern Iraq for Kurdish refugees and allowed unarmed U.N. inspection teams to carry out their missions free from assault by Iraqi forces. As a potential tool of intrawar and postwar deterrence of dangerous third-world behavior, the concept of air occupation, which ironically dates back to Royal Air Force operations in Iraq in the 1920s, deserves further study. Even in the absence of war, the ability to seize another country's airspace could provide an effective tool of compulsion, especially in situations where alternative forms of military action are unfeasible or undesirable.

Airpower as a means of compulsion, however, has limitations as well as strengths. Saddam Hussein's continued defiance of the United Nations, notwithstanding U.S. disablement of Iraq's economic infrastructure and that country's inability to control its own airspace, reveals a characteristic common to many—though not all—third-world tyrants: subordination of their country's national interest to the preservation of their own political authority at any cost. Against a regime willing to sacrifice economic progress and even regional military preeminence in order to ensure its own survival, the air option may prove ineffective. This, in turn, suggests that, in some cases at least, elimination of a regime's political authority—or at least credible threats to do so—may be a more effective means of altering that regime's behavior than focusing on economic or even military targets.

Targeting a regime's intentions (in other words, its leadership) rather than its feared military capabilities, however, poses problems of its own. U.S. law prohibits assassination of foreign leaders; there is never a guarantee that the new leadership will be more pliable than the old; and paranoid personalities of the likes of Mu'ammar Gadhafi and Saddam Hussein take great care to conceal their movements and to protect their persons via bodyguards and deep underground bunkers.

But the power of even the most absolute of dictators rests on institutions whose disruption or destruction could topple the dictator himor herself. Those institutions commonly include, as they do in Saddam Hussein's Iraq, a secret police (*Mukabarat*), party apparatus (Ba'athist officialdom), and elite military units valued primarily for their loyalty to the regime (the Republican Guard). The fact that none of these institutions were forcefully or systematically attacked during Desert Storm (other than Republican Guard units in the KTO) ensured the postwar survival of Saddam Hussein and his loyal band of Tikritis throughout the police, party, and army. In future confrontations with such regimes, consideration should be given to political targeting—that is, targeting the institutional foundations of the regimes' political authority. This, of course, will require comprehensive knowledge of the enemy's political system and of the loci (both physical and institutional) of that authority's key elements.

In sum, the combination of improved ballistic missile defenses (which may require space-based sensors), together with modern conventional airpower capable of quickly reversing a state's military and economic progress and of threatening the institutional foundations of the target regime's political authority, may suffice to deter and even deny wartime use of hyperlethal munitions against U.S. contingency forces and host country population centers. In any event, a focus on intrawar deterrence would seem a more practical and far less politically messy strategy than one of preventive military action aimed at thwarting third-world acquisition of such weapons in the first place.

Declining Onshore U.S. Military Access Overseas

The recession of U.S. Cold War garrisons and continuing termination of U.S. basing rights in the third world (as in the Philippines in 1992 and Panama by 2000) has rightly prompted increasing emphasis on forward presence as opposed to forward deployment. *Presence* implies the scarcity of, or undesirability of maintaining, large U.S. ground and land-based air force deployments overseas and reliance instead on a combination of offshore sea-based projection forces and rapidly deployable air and ground forces withheld in the United States. It was a mix of these forces that conducted Desert Storm, though their capacity to do so rested almost entirely on politically unprecedented access to Saudi ports and air bases.

Had that access been denied either by the Saudis or by Iraqi military action, a forcible entry into the kingdom (via amphibious assault and air assault operations) would have been required.

Indeed, politically uncertain U.S. access onshore in third-world trouble spots places a premium on three specific categories of force projection capabilities: sea-based airpower, long-range land-based airpower, and forcible entry forces (mainly amphibious assault)—all of them relatively free of dependence on in-theater bases and local political goodwill. Unfortunately, the outlook for such forces, in part because they are very expensive to buy and operate, is not encouraging. Mention already has been made of the crisis in naval strike aviation, which is unlikely to be resolved until the late 1990s at the earliest, when a replacement for the A-6 (and cancelled A-12) can be fielded. A smaller carrier force lacking modern attack aircraft may not be able to provide a sufficiently potent on-station presence to cover, deter, or defeat potential violent challenges to U.S. security interests in the third world, especially in situations where it can expect no help from land-based tactical aviation. Even enhanced investment in sea-launched/land attack cruise missiles, while desirable, offers only a partial solution (except in punitive, one-time strikes like the 1986 U.S. reprisal attacks on Libya), given their nonrecoverability and high ratio of system cost per pound of ordnance delivered.

Note also has been made of the continuing inadequacy of or ongoing decline in other Navy capabilities—amphibious shipping, gunfire support, and countermine warfare—essential to support a robust and effective Marine Corps amphibious assault capability. However, other aspects of the Marine Corps and its most distinctive mission deserve review in any attempt to maximize the overall effectiveness of future U.S. force projection capabilities. There is, first of all, the fact that preparation for that mission has imposed significant penalties on Marine Corps ground force structure in terms of organic firepower and tactical mobility relative to army units. In Desert Storm, it was deemed advisable to bolster the firepower and mobility of marine units operating ashore via assignment of a heavy U.S. Army brigade to the marines area of operations as well as substitution of army M-1 Abrams tanks for the marines' much less capable M-60s. Marine Corps force structure is not optimized for combat against tank- and artillery-heavy foes. (Against such opponents, the army's Light Infantry Divisions are complete nonstarters; none participated in Desert Storm, and their utility is questionable in other than very low-intensity conflicts, in which U.S. involvement is likely to diminish in the future.) Of course, the Marine Corps' comparative firepower and tactical mobility deficiencies have been and will continue to be of little consequence against all but "heavy" third-world adversaries, of which there are few in number, and in circumstances, like Desert Storm, where army forces are present in abundance; but nonetheless, they are deficiencies that demand redress.

More significant are questions that have arisen around the utility of the amphibious assault mission itself. To be sure, the very threat of a major assault on Kuwait's Iraqi-held coastline played a critical role in contributing to Baghdad's miscalculation of the loci and character of the coalition's ground offensive, tying down as it did at least eight powerful Iraqi divisions to a defense against a seaborne assault that never came. On the other hand, Desert Storm marked the beginning of the fifth decade since the Marine Corps was last called upon to conduct a major ship-to-shore landing on a defended coastline (during the Inchon assault of 1950). This suggests that planned U.S. investment in amphibious assault capabilities, even though declining, may still be excessive in light of likely future requirements. Some measure of investment—perhaps a brigade's worth or two—would seem essential for purposes of deterrence, deception, and limited descents on hostile shores. But amphibious assault traditionally has been an option of last resort because it is among the most difficult of all military operations and because it invites relatively high casualties. In Desert Storm, an amphibious assault was rejected because other, more attractive alternatives were available and because it promised high casualties among both assault forces and the Kuwaiti civilian population in the landing areas.

Modern Marine Corps amphibious doctrine calls for avoidance of heavily defended enemy coastlines (not an option in Desert Storm) in favor of descents "where the enemy ain't," or at least "ain't" in significant strength. But this welcome emphasis on seeking unopposed or lightly opposed landings serves to move the traditional concept of amphibious assault far in the direction of administrative landings requiring little in the way of costly Iwo Jima–style preparatory air and naval gunfire bombardment, mine clearance, and specialized assault shipping. In so doing, it opens the door to the substitution of much of present U.S. amphibious assault capacity by cheaper alternative investment in administrative ship-to-shore delivery assets such as marine and army forces prepositioned aboard specialized cargo vessels capable of using conventional port facilities and, if necessary, lighterage for direct over-the-beach movement—the very way every marine moved ashore in the Gulf War.

With respect to long-range airpower, there is an affordable complement to the present bomber force, which is poorly configured to meet the requirements of future U.S. force projection operations. For the past thirty years, the air force has sought to replace the manned strategic bombardment capacity once represented in its peak B-52, 744 of which were built between 1954 and 1962. No actual or planned successor aircraft, however, proved adequate in either numbers or performance. The B-58, of which only 116 were procured, lacked the range and payload of the B-52; the B-70 (2 prototypes) and B-1A (4 prototypes) programs were cancelled for reasons of cost and lack of mission persuasiveness; the B-1B program was capped at 100 planes, all of which remain troubled by performance problems; and the once-planned fleet of 132 B-2 bombers has been terminated at a maximum of 20 aircraft.[12]

Several factors have combined to doom prospects for maintaining a significant U.S. intercontinental-range penetrating bomber force. The emergence of intercontinental-range ballistic missiles (ICBMs) and submarine-launched ballistic missiles (SLBMs) in the 1960s relegated bombers to a secondary role as contributors to the mission of nuclear deterrence against the Soviet Union. Congressional and public support for a penetration force has steadily eroded since the B-52 program, as successive new programs registered exponential cost increases largely attributable to penetration requirements. At the same time, the very need for a penetrating bomber force has been called into question by the emergence of highly accurate, long-range cruise missiles, which can be fired from stand-off bombers or ships. More recently, and most important, the Soviet Union's collapse has greatly deflated the relative significance of nuclear deterrence and its associated forces as well as voided the rationale for a large penetration force.

Another factor has been the Gulf War experience. On the one hand, the so-called great Scud hunt underscored the ability of very primitive mobile targets to elude the most determined aerial search and bombardment efforts—a mission that formed the last, desperate rationale for maintaining a robust force of penetrating bombers. At the same time, the war also offered a dramatic demonstration of the potency of nonnuclear, precision-guided stand-off munitions against "strategic" targets once believed vulnerable only to traditional penetrating bombers armed with nuclear weapons.

All of this suggests that a major and growing portion of future U.S. strategic bombardment requirements can be satisfied by a combination of stand-off conventional munitions and aircraft capable of simply carrying and launching them in desired quantities from preferred distances. This, in turn, opens the door to reliance on relatively inexpensive transport aircraft, military and perhaps even commercial, such as the C-5B and C-17. A force of such aircraft, convertible to stand-off bombardment, would not only offer an eventual replacement for the present B-52G/H force but would also permit retention of the B-1B/B-2 force for whatever long-range penetration/nuclear strike requirements may persist. Almost by definition, aircraft of this type would also be suitable for such other combat missions as aerial mining and antiship operations.

Hypersensitivity to Casualties

All future U.S. force projection operations will be sternly conditioned by the political imperative of minimizing both U.S. military and enemy civilian casualties—with Desert Storm providing the yardstick by which such operations invariably will be compared. The effects of the casualty minimization imperative in situations not involving supreme U.S. security interests are likely to be pervasive. They range from outright abjuration of intervention in circumstances where the price of intervention appears to be a politically unacceptable loss of life; to avoidance, once hostilities commence, of certain kinds of inherently casualty-prone military enterprises such as amphibious assault, urban warfare, and counterinsurgency operations; and to stringent tactical rules of engagement designed to spare noncombatants even at the expense of operational efficiency.

Generally speaking, the casualty minimization imperative will favor reliance on air and naval power over ground operations and, with respect to airpower itself, preference for stand-off air-to-surface attacks over placing manned bombing platforms directly over targets. To be sure, there will be situations in which airpower alone will not satisfy the specific force projection requirements at hand; Desert Storm never came close to vindicating the prophesies of Douhet, Mitchell, and Trenchard that airpower would soon render surface forces obsolete. Desert Storm did, however, demonstrate that under the right conditions, including a highly vulnerable enemy, airpower can go a long way toward providing the decisive military clout customarily thought to repose primarily in large, heavy (and casualty-prone) ground forces. Is it still necessary, in each and every instance, to pit a U.S. armored division against an enemy heavy ground force, or could a U.S. Air Force tactical fighter/bomber wing do the same job? Modern airpower still cannot take and hold territory (though it can occupy the air space above it), but can it not significantly reduce ground force requirements for doing so?

Desert Storm also revealed the obvious advantages that accrue from being able to put in place overwhelming force before hostilities begin. It was this very overwhelming force that guaranteed a relatively short duration of combat as well as a scarcity of casualties among coalition ranks. Moreover, the very example of Desert Storm, the first war in which the United States was able to chose the time and place to fight, is likely to encourage, for reasons of casualty avoidance, the amassing of overwhelming force, if not before hostilities commence (the enemy is likely to make that decision), then certainly before the United States initiates major offensive operations.

This, of course, is not always going to be possible. As in the Korean War, both time and the enemy may not permit it, confronting the United States with the unpleasant choice of not intervening at all or feeding forces into combat piecemeal—a recipe for prolonged combat and long casualty lists. Unfortunately, although Desert Storm's spectacular brevity and cleanliness (that is, dearth of friendly military and enemy civilian casualties) will inescapably provide the benchmark by which future major U.S. force projection operations will be compared, it is a benchmark probably impossible to replicate ever again. If pre–Desert Storm U.S. military force planning was haunted by the disastrous legacy of Vietnam, post–Desert Storm planning will be plagued by the specter of falling short of the splendid and relatively painless performance of U.S. forces in the Persian Gulf in 1991. Indeed, Desert Storm's very painlessness may exert some quite perverse effects on U.S. propensity to intervene in regional contingencies. For much of the uninformed U.S. public and their elected representation, Desert Storm seems to have created the illusion that war against third-world opponents from now on can be had on the quick and cheap—the old Vietnam syndrome in reverse; yet senior military professionals, who know better, may find themselves counseling against prospective combat action for fear of those operations' being unable to match the now impossibly high standards of success established by Desert Storm.

At the very least, future third-world adversaries can be expected to seek to avoid Saddam Hussein's egregious strategic and operational mistakes—and especially to raise the price in blood as high as possible, and by any means, in any encounter with U.S. forces. Moreover, options for pursuing the latter will not likely be confined to the actual battlefield. Countries like Libya, Syria, Iraq, and Iran have long demonstrated a willingness to engage in terrorism against U.S. innocents abroad (including taking resident Americans as hostages), and a capacity to threaten civilian population centers in countries hosting U.S. forces could also adversely affect U.S. military choices in a crisis.

Closing Thoughts

The Soviet Union's disintegration ends a half-century-long chapter in U.S. force planning. Not since the 1920s has the U.S. military establishment lacked a hostile great power upon which to focus its attentions.[13] Moreover, now, as in the post–World War I era, public and congressional support for high levels of defense expenditure has collapsed, as Americans turn increasingly toward remedying pressing economic and social problems at home.

The United States cannot and will not turn its back militarily on a world that is a far more complicated and dangerous place than the world of the 1920s, in which a handful of states controlled the entire planet's destiny. Since the late 1940s, the international state system has expanded beyond all recognition. The number of independent military actors has mushroomed, and some of them are well-armed, implacably hostile to Western values, and recognize no distinction between the ends and means of state policy. Thus, the United States will still need to project its military power overseas, although the incidence of intervention in the post–Cold War era is likely to decline and to take place increasingly in a North-South rather than East-West context. Additionally, the combination of the Cold War's demise, the experience of both the Gulf and Vietnam Wars, and critical domestic agendas will place a premium on a force projection capacity that can prevail in combat quickly and cleanly.

Notes

1. See Michael W. Ellis and Jeffrey Record, "Theater Ballistic Missile Defense and U.S. Contingency Operations," *Parameters* 22, no. 1 (1992): 11–26.

2. See McGeorge Bundy, "Nuclear Weapons and the Gulf," *Foreign Affairs* 70, no. 4 (1991): 83–94.

3. See Jeffrey Record, *Revising U.S. Military Strategy, Tailoring Means to Ends* (Washington, D.C.: Brassey's, 1984).

4. See Jeffrey Record, "The Future of the U.S. Military Presence in Europe," in Ted Galen Carpenter, ed., *NATO at 40: Confronting a Changing World* (Lexington, Mass.: Lexington Books, 1990).

5. See Jeffrey Record, "Defeating Desert Storm (and Why Saddam Didn't)," *Comparative Strategy* 12, no. 2 (1993): 125–140.

6. H. Norman Schwarzkopf with Peter Petre, *It Doesn't Take a Hero* (New York: Bantam Books, 1992), 291–408.

7. See Joe West, "Air Power Backers Feel Vindicated by Gulf Win," *Air Force Times,* April 1, 1991, p. 4.

8. *Gulf War Air Power Survey: Summary* (Washington, D.C.: Department of the Air Force, April 15, 1993).

9. See Jeffrey Record, *Hollow Victory: A Contrary View of the Gulf War* (Washington, D.C.: Brassey's, 1993), 43–56.

10. These and other data are contained throughout in the *Annual Report to the President and the Congress* (Washington, D.C.: Department of Defense, February 1992).

11. See Helen Chapin Metz, ed., *Iraq: A Country Study* (Washington, D.C.: Federal Research Division, Library of Congress, 1990).

12. See Jeffrey Record, *Strategic Bombers: How Many Are Enough?* (Washington, D.C.: Institute for Foreign Policy Analysis, 1986).

13. For an excellent review of the interwar period's relevance to post–Cold War U.S. force planning, see Caroline F. Ziemke, "Military Planning Beyond the Cold War: Lessons for the 1990s from the 1920s and 1930s," *Washington Quarterly* 14, no. 1 (Winter 1991): 61–76.

10

The Future of Command and Control: Toward a Paradigm of Information Warfare

C. KENNETH ALLARD

The Gulf War will stand as a watershed event in military history for many of the reasons discussed elsewhere in this book: as a triumph of advanced weaponry, as a vindication of the American military institution, as a long overdue setting-to-rest of the Vietnam syndrome, and as the harbinger of a new and uncertain era in the aftermath of the Cold War. This triumph of arms certainly represented all of those things, but Desert Storm may be better remembered as the first war to demonstrate the means, the methods, and the awesome lethality of combat in the information age. Despite the uncertainties of defense reductions, budget austerities, and an organizational structure that seems singularly ill suited to the new demands of large-scale technological integration, I argue that one of the major legacies of Desert Storm will be a continuing effort by the U.S. defense establishment to exploit the potential of advanced technology and precision weaponry in an emerging paradigm of information warfare.

The ultimate significance of this paradigm is reflected in a recent statement by Paul Nitze, one of the architects of American postwar strategy, who argued that the United States may be able to shift its reliance upon nuclear weapons to a "more credible deterrence" emphasizing the new

The views expressed in this chapter are those of the author and do not necessarily represent the official positions of the National Defense University or the Department of Defense.

generation of highly precise conventional weaponry. As he explained his rationale: "The Gulf War offered a spectacular demonstration of the potential effectiveness of smart weapons used in a strategic role. Against Iraq, such weapons rapidly rendered useless the military forces of a powerful dictator, in particular by neutralizing his command, control and communications facilities."[1]

If such a dramatic shift in the role of nuclear weapons were not by itself a startling development, consider this bold statement by two RAND analysts: "Warfare is no longer . . . a function of who puts the most capital, labor, and technology on the battlefield, but of who has the best information about the battlefield. What distinguishes the victors is their grasp of information."[2]

Although an appreciation for accurate weaponry and an understanding of the importance of knowledge as power are hardly new concepts, the term *information warfare* suggests a qualitative difference in the way that an opponent can be attacked—psychologically as well as physically. The basic concept is well illustrated in an anecdote told by Senator Bill Bradley. Recounting his experiences as a member of the 1964 U.S. Olympic basketball team, the senator recalled how he had committed a single Russian phrase to memory in anticipation of the ultimate game in this long-standing rivalry. Early in the game, a collision with an opposing player caused the future senator to blurt out the only Russian phrase he knew. "Hey, big fella, watch out!" But at that point, wrote Bradley, "[a] funny thing happened. Up until that moment, the Soviets had called all their plays verbally; but after that moment, since they thought I understood Russian, they stopped talking to each other. And so we went on to win the gold medal."[3]

Desert Storm was not the conflict with the Soviet adversary that had been the sine qua non of defense planning throughout the Cold War, but it did involve a former Soviet client state that had adopted the rigid, centralized command structure characteristic of Warsaw Pact armies. U.S. forces had long studied how to attack such structures, devising methods somewhat similar to the one improvised by Senator Bradley. When Desert Storm began, the televised images of this new style of warfare were seared into public consciousness with an immediacy that was itself one of the primary distinctions between the Gulf War and all those that had gone before it. No other war in history had begun with live coverage of its first shots instantly transmitted to worldwide audiences. Television subsequently brought home equally dramatic images of Tomahawk cruise missiles striking their targets with pinpoint accuracy after flights lasting many hundreds of miles. Some of the most sobering depictions of technologically assisted carnage came at the very end of the war, after JSTARS electronic reconnaissance aircraft detected Iraqi columns retreating from Kuwait and vectored coalition aircraft to attack what later became known as the Highway of Death.

For America's armed forces, this victory in the desert was the culmination of more than two decades of post-Vietnam renewal, but it was also the payoff for an investment strategy that had consciously sought to offset enemy strengths with technological expertise. The hi-tech weapons meant to counter the now-defunct armies of the Warsaw Pact proved their deadly effectiveness against a lesser but still formidable foe. Computer-assisted weapons intended to kill at great ranges with a single shot were now the stock-in-trade of the frontline soldier. He was supported by commanders and staffs who used "battle management" systems to monitor the status of enemy forces, friendly forces, and the all-important movement of logistics. Strategic direction in the form of information, intelligence, orders, and advice arrived in a river of digital data that flowed incessantly from the continental United States to the theater of operations—much of it in real time. These fielded technologies effectively provided U.S. forces with what has since become known as *information dominance*—the use of information systems to provide tactical, operational, and strategic advantages that come together in a whole that is more than the sum of its parts.

If these linkages conveyed superior agility and initiative to the side that had information dominance, an especially cruel fate awaited the have-nots. Coalition airpower was systematically used to blind the Iraqi command and control system in the opening hours of the war, an initial advantage that inexorably led to a succession of others:

- Overall air superiority that was maintained throughout the war
- The flanking movement of coalition ground forces to the west and its concealment from Iraqi observation
- The systematic destruction of the linkages between Baghdad and Iraqi ground forces in Kuwait, effectively depriving those forces of both the orders and information needed for coherent defense.

Ultimately, this progression culminated in the invasion of Iraq itself by a combined-arms force that, during a furious 100-hour assault, destroyed the vaunted Republican Guard, liberated Kuwait, and effectively ended the war. The real significance of information dominance was well summed up in a personal observation to the author by the commander of a U.S. cavalry squadron that had penetrated deep into the Euphrates Valley: "The first inkling the Iraqis had that we were there came when their tanks started exploding."

Guided by this recent combat experience, it is not particularly surprising that information warfare has emerged from the shadows to become the hottest of Pentagon hot topics. Centers for information warfare have sprung up in each of the service bureaucracies as well as in the Office of the Secretary of Defense, all of them marked by more than the usual amount of frenetic activity. The National Defense University is now offering an experimental, year-long course in information warfare and strategy designed to train promising midcareer officers to be the "information warriors" of the future. Most telling of all, it has become necessary for the Pentagon to put forward a prospective definition of information warfare: "Actions taken to preserve the integrity of one's own information systems from exploitation, corruption, or destruction, while at the same time exploiting, corrupting, or destroying an adversary's information systems and in the process achieving an information advantage in the application of force."[4] This spare terminology belies the potential that many see for information warfare, a potential that some liken to such revolutionary military developments as the battle tank, the airplane, and the aircraft carrier. Others suggest that this focus on the implements of war is too conservative a view and that the real significance of the information revolution is that it will inevitably transform the nature of warfare itself.

First-Order Expectations

It is consequently important to place such expectations in context by emphasizing that information has always been one of the classical components of warfare; indeed, it could be argued that there was nothing new under the sun, no matter how much the technological implements might have changed. "All warfare is based on deception," wrote Sun Tzu in the third century B.C. "Therefore, when capable, feign incapacity; when active, inactivity. . . . Offer the enemy a bait to lure him; feign disorder and strike him. . . . Therefore I say: Know the enemy and know yourself; in a hundred battles you will never be in peril."[5]

Information is also central to the thought of Clausewitz, who argued that the absence of accurate and timely information on the battlefield was an intrinsic part of the "friction" that contributed to the "fog of war." In book one of *On War,* he wrote that because "many intelligence reports in war are contradictory, even more are false, and most are uncertain," the seasoned judgment of the commander was all-important in correctly assessing battlefield situations. "This difficulty of accurate recognition constitutes one of the most serious sources of friction in war, by making things appear entirely different from what one had expected."[6] There is a direct line of continuity between these classical pronouncements and more contemporary reflections. In 1985, for example, Martin van Creveld suggested that "from Plato to NATO, the history of command in war consists essentially of an endless quest for certainty"—a search that he largely regarded as futile: "Present-day military forces, for all the imposing array of electronic gadgetry at their disposal, give no evidence whatsoever of being one whit more capable of dealing with the information needed for the command process than were their predecessors a century or even a millennium ago."[7]

Such reflections suggest nothing so much as the proverbial and prodigal sixteen-year-old who returned home at twenty-one only to be amazed at how much his parents had learned in five years; either van Creveld's assessment was unduly pessimistic or the U.S. military had improved greatly between 1985 and its deployment to the Persian Gulf in 1990. In reality, however, this "array of gadgetry" merely represented the latest evolutionary steps in the long and convoluted history that has seen the electron used in ever more ingenious ways to extend the span of battlefield control. Beginning with the telegraph in the nineteenth century and continuing with radio and radar in the twentieth, these "nerves of war" gradually accompanied the development of air, naval, and land forces of unprecedented destructive power—forces that were eventually deployed on a global scale. During the Cold War, the military structures of both blocs were linked to their respective command authorities by electronic networks that allowed a high degree of peacetime micromanagement and—at least in theory—positive control over each escalatory step all the way to the initiation of nuclear war.[8]

Paced by the need to exert positive control over the forces of a potential Armageddon, the marriage of computers, satellites, and communications pathways was gradually changing the nature of battlefield command. More and more data, flowing faster and faster, was becoming available at lower and lower levels. In his excellent book *The First Information War,* Alan D. Campen argued, "Information technology unveiled in the Persian Gulf war gave combat forces a tantalizing glimpse of what commanders have hungered for since the dawn of human conflict: a 'bird's eye' view of the battlefield."[9] This "tantalizing glimpse" of something better is what made Desert Storm unique, both as a military victory in its own right and as a harbinger of things to come.

Those developments were summarized in a *Foreign Affairs* article in late 1991 that took on additional importance when its author, Dr. William Perry, subsequently became secretary of defense in the Clinton administration. Perry argued that U.S. forces in the Gulf War had exacted a thousand-to-one combat advantage over their Iraqi adversaries due to their employment of a class of weapons originally developed around an "offset strategy" intended to blunt the numerical advantage of Warsaw Pact armies.[10] This strategy had given U.S. forces a decisive technological edge in the following three critical areas.

- **Command, Control, Communications, and Intelligence (C³I).** A diverse suite of intelligence, communications, and navigation systems gave U.S. field commanders better "situational awareness," meaning that they had a more precise idea of their own dispositions as well as those of the enemy. Much of this advantage resulted from the exploitation of space satellites that provided the information used to "generate data for maps, locate military units, identify military systems, and pinpoint . . . [Iraqi] air defense and command and control installations."[11] Global positioning satellites also provided pinpoint navigation information at the tactical level, while reconnaissance aircraft such as JSTARS and AWACS (Airborne Warning and Control System) played critical roles in locating such diverse targets as tanks, Scuds, and fleeing Iraqi aircraft.
- **Air Defense Suppression.** Stealth bombers, Tomahawk cruise missiles, and antiradiation missiles were used to blind the Iraqi air de-

fense system through a combination of innovative tactics that destroyed its main sensors systems (principally radars) as well as the command and control centers that were supposed to tie them together. Iraqi gunners were thus forced to fire blindly at aircraft that generally remained well out of effective range, with the result that "coalition air forces were able to fly 2,000 to 3,000 sorties per day with losses averaging less than one aircraft per day."[12]

- **Precision-Guided Munitions (PGMs).** The combination of Stealth bombers and PGMs meant that effective bombing could take place not only with far fewer collateral civilian casualties than ever before but also with a quantum jump in overall effectiveness. Of the 2,100 bombs delivered by the Stealth aircraft, some 1,700 were believed to have fallen within 10 feet of their targets—an effectiveness rate of over 80 percent.[13] Perry emphasized as well the interdependence of each component: "The effectiveness of the coalition's defense suppression tactics depended upon the precision-guided weapons; the effectiveness of the precision-guided weapons in turn depended on the intelligence data that identified and located targets; and the very survivability of the intelligence systems depended on the effectiveness of the coalition's defense suppression systems."[14]

The critical linkages between all these elements were of course provided by communications systems, and although interdependence was one way to think of this new reality, the larger truth was that the integration of joint combat power into a synergistic whole depended upon the free flow of information, much as the human brain depends upon the free flow of blood for its functioning. The communications systems and pathways in Desert Storm were—by several orders of magnitude—more effective at providing top-down, bottom-up, and side-to-side communications than any in military history. According to Lieutenant General James S. Cassity, the Joint Staff's top communications officer during the war, "The services put more electronics communications connectivity into the Gulf in 90 days than we put in Europe in 40 years."[15] Another official likened the hastily built theater communications system to "a mini-AT&T."[16] Because military communications specialists were forced to link diverse generations of equipment, this hybrid system became a model of high-pressure improvisation as well as high-tech components, but it ultimately proved capable of handling more than 700,000 telephone calls and 152,000 messages per day, in addition to managing over 35,000 tactical radio frequencies.[17]

This communications infrastructure was essential to the functioning of the advanced weaponry that had been placed in the hands of the American military during the 1980s. The army's M-1 Abrams tank, for example, is capable of cross-country speeds of over 30 miles per hour. Thanks to its thermal sights and laser range-finders, it is also capable of shooting on the move, often achieving first-round hits at ranges between 1 and 2 miles.

These speed and range capabilities, however, complicated the task of command and control, especially when considering that a single U.S. corps in the ground attack deployed over 1,400 M-1s in an arc covering thousands of square miles across a largely trackless desert. Tactical computers, part of the Maneuver Control System, helped to track these fast-moving forces, while a new generation of tactical radios (known as SINCGARS) helped to speed both voice and data communications around the battlefield. Commanders in the field were also equipped with the new MSE (mobile subscriber equipment) system—the military version of the cellular phone—as well as tactical satellite terminals that brought unprecedented range and clarity to radio communications that had previously been notorious for failures on both counts.[18]

More effective communications—especially involving satellites—were not only crucial in controlling fast-moving, far-flung forces but also in operating the improved sensor systems needed for all classes of precision munitions. Coalition air operations were controlled by AWACS aircraft that featured not only long-range, "look-down, shoot-down" radars but also secure radio systems that transmitted both data and voice communications. Naval forces—including a new class of all-seeing Aegis-class cruisers and upgraded sensor suites on all embarked aircraft carriers—were linked by a command and control system that had featured digital data flows since the 1950s. Although it was only a prototype, the debut of the Joint Stars aircraft brought a quantum (and long overdue) improvement in the surveillance of ground targets. Possessed of special radars that could see over 150 miles into enemy territory, JSTARS was linked with AWACS and other aircraft to provide a battlefield portrait of unparalleled clarity. The downlinking of these images to tactical ground stations allowed for real-time decisions that directly affected battlefield outcomes. In addition to its most visible role in detecting the Iraqi retreat that became the Highway of Death, JSTARS was credited with detecting and neutralizing a Republican Guard counterattack during the liberation of Kuwait, locating mobile Scud launchers, and preventing fratricide between adjacent U.S. Marine and U.K. armored units.[19]

However, there is probably no better example of the importance of the relationship between sensors and communications than the NAVSTAR Global Positioning System, or GPS. NAVSTAR is a system of satellites that transmits navigation data to any point on the earth; by simply turning on a receiver that compares the signal from several of these satellites, the user's position can be pinpointed to within less than 300 feet. This capability underlay much of the tactical and technical mastery displayed by the United States in the Gulf War. The Pentagon's final report on the war singled out these receivers as "lifesavers" for troops operating in a featureless desert, but it also noted that the equipment was similarly useful, among other things, for improving aircraft navigation on many different platforms, pinpointing the location of Iraqi radio transmitters, reducing the emplacement times of Patriot missile batteries, and providing the precision data needed by the navy's Tomahawk cruise missile.[20]

There are numerous examples of technical wizardry that played important roles in Desert Storm, many of which have a direct tie-in to information warfare: the proliferation of night vision devices, software modifications that turned the Firefinder radar and the Patriot missile into Scud hunters, multispectral imagery in aerial reconnaissance, digital terrain mapping, and much else. However, none of these implements nor the ones mentioned previously would have had the same effect had it not been for the people who made them work, an admittedly commonsense observation that takes on additional significance when placed in the context of policy, organization, and doctrine.

A succession of public policy choices, for example, meant that the men and women of Desert Storm were members of a military service that, in the aftermath of Vietnam, had evolved from a draft-induced force to a volunteer force before ultimately becoming a professional force. Because the new professionals were smarter, better educated, and more highly motivated, they could be trained to operate more complex equipment, often through the use of advanced simulators and teaching methodologies that outstripped those available in the private sector. The renascence in military training that marked the 1980s could clearly be seen during Desert Storm, when thousands of off-the-shelf personal computers appeared in all sectors of the battlefield. Regardless of whether or not they were formally authorized, these computers were brought along by soldiers, sailors, airmen, and marines determined to use in war the tools with which they had trained in peace.[21] The widespread innovations in the tactical applications of spreadsheeting, word processing, and data transfer that contributed so much to the war effort would have been unthinkable in a military system that lacked the improvisational and even entrepreneurial talents of this youthful cadre of uniformed professionals.

Another act of public policy had adjusted the always troublesome organizational balances of centralization and decentralization that were the underpinnings of the command and control system. The Goldwater-Nichols Act of 1986 realigned the chain of command, reaffirming the direct line of authority from the president and secretary of defense to the theater commander (the CINC) and giving him virtually complete authority to adjust his organization (including its command and control system) to mission requirements. The same act also clarified the role of the Chairman of the Joint Chiefs of Staff, making him the principal military advisor to the president and granting him additional authority to direct the work of the Joint Staff. The CINC's combatant authority as well as the means of strategic direction were thus clarified as they had not been since the Defense Department was created by the National Security Act of 1947. Because the Gulf War brought the first wartime test of the new arrangements, General Norman Schwarzkopf's assessment is relevant: "Goldwater-Nichols established very, very clear lines of command authority and responsibilities over subordinate commanders, and that meant a much more effective fighting force in the Gulf. The lines of authority were clear, the lines of responsibility were clear, and we just did not have any problem in that area—none whatsoever."[22]

The advantages of effective policy and organization were further complemented by the development of a body of thought in both the army and the air force that was especially well suited to the prosecution of information warfare. Although doctrine has always been one of the cornerstones of army professionalism, it was never more important than in the aftermath of the Vietnam War and the Middle East War of 1973, the latter conflict featuring unprecedented levels of destruction made possible by the first widespread use of PGMs. Both events sparked a wrenching internal debate between the army's traditional orientation toward massive, attrition-style warfare and a rival school of thought that argued for greater emphasis on maneuver. The "maneuver warriors" stressed the new possibilities for mobility suggested by the armor and helicopter systems then coming into service and were much influenced by the thought of a former fighter pilot named John Boyd. Boyd's greatest contribution to the debate was the notion that combat essentially consisted of four basic functions: observation, orientation, decision, and action. Completing this decision cycle (which, in the acronym-rich environment of Pentagon jargon, tragically became known as the "OODA loop") more rapidly than the opponent allowed one to gain the upper hand by maintaining the initiative, establishing control, and eventually paralyzing the enemy's command structure.[23] By 1986, the army had refined its new Airland Battle Doctrine to reflect the best of both the maneuver and attrition schools of thought, a doctrine well suited to exploit the capabilities of the new generation of tanks, armored fighting vehicles, and attack helicopters that had finally arrived. Although the OODA loop was never mentioned by name, the new doctrine stressed the need for initiative, agility, depth, and synchronization.[24] Implicit in all of these things was the importance of thinking faster and more effectively than the enemy, of "turning inside his decision loop," and of indirectly attacking his ability to command.

A more direct attack on the enemy command structure was independently developed by Air Force Colonel John Warden using a wholly different set of assumptions. Warden is a latter-day exponent of the classical airpower theories originally developed by Giulio Douhet and Billy Mitchell. In a major restatement of the offensive primacy of airpower, his book *The Air Campaign* provides a theoretical and historical template for applying airpower as a decisive force against key enemy strong points or centers of gravity. Although it is not the only such strong point, "command, with its necessarily associated communications and intelligence gathering functions is an obvious center of gravity, and has been from the earliest times: As the death of the king on the field of battle meant defeat for his forces, so the effective isolation of the command structure in modern war has led to the rapid defeat of dependent forces."[25]

Warden also broke command down into three basic functions—information, decision, and communications—and argued that each could be attacked either directly or indirectly as part of an overall air superiority campaign.[26] But what makes this formulation of more than academic interest was the application of these theories to the planning and execution of the air war against Iraq, both through Warden's own role as the leader of an elite planning cell on the Air Staff in Washington and through the contributions of his disciples who helped carry out those plans in the Joint Forces Air Component Command in Riyadh.

Inevitable tensions arose during Desert Storm over the use of airpower to carry out the strategic air campaign envisioned by Warden versus the ground attack missions supported by classic Airland Battle theory. There is a good deal of evidence that these were nontheoretical and highly emotional arguments for those involved in making these choices when lives hung in the balance.[27] However, the larger point is that both the army and air force approaches recognized the importance of disrupting and destroying the enemy's command structure—and that this became one of the coalition's major strategic objectives. It is also worth noting that much of what was done in prosecuting the war is consistent with Warden's conception of attacking basic Iraqi command functions—everything from the blinding of its information and intelligence systems to the systematic attacks on command centers all the way from Baghdad to frontline Iraqi observation posts. Although Iraq's information and decision functions were clearly singled out for attack, the third element in Warden's trilogy of command functions was equally well represented by the concerted air campaign against a laundry list of Iraqi communications facilities: microwave relays, telephone switching centers, and even bridges carrying coaxial communications cables.[28] The importance of what had been achieved, as well its implications for the future, was summarized by General Schwarzkopf: "Desert Storm confirmed that state-of-the-art equipment is required to counter threats in many regions of the world. Our superiority in stealth, mobility, and command, control, communications, and computers proved to be a decisive force multiplier."[29]

Second-Order Implications:
The Military-Technical Revolution

It is in the nature of the U.S. way of life that the euphoria of victory quickly gave way to more critical assessments of what had been achieved in the Persian Gulf. Many of these assessments had a "good news, bad news" quality about them. Improvisation, for example, had worked wonders in the quick adaptation of high-technology weapons to the harsh demands of desert warfare. The bad news was that the Iraqis had let us do it, erroneously believing that time was on their side and allowing U.S. forces to attack only after the extended period required for a leisurely fine-tuning of our advanced but fragile equipment. As a result, said one critique, "The Gulf war provided little conclusive evidence regarding the effectiveness of high-technology weapons in combat."[30] Such overstatements reflected a fundamental misunderstanding of the nature of combat, well summarized in an adage from the sports world: You take what your opponent gives you. The Iraqis had given the coalition the priceless gift of time, and credit rather than criticism was merited when this advantage was used with such devastating effect.

But if that much was clear, what vulnerabilities required correction before the inevitable "next time," especially because no future opponent was likely to repeat Iraqi strategic blunders? In the years since the end of the war, attention has centered on three closely related areas summarized here: interoperability, communications infrastructure, and intelligence.

Interoperability

Interoperability is the technical term for the continuing tendency of U.S. military communications systems to be different. This is an old problem, having much to do with not only the histories, strategies, and structures of the four military services (when the marines are counted) but also their legal mandate to procure the weapons and equipment for the forces deployed to combatant commands worldwide. Because this responsibility includes the acquisition of command and control systems, the usual practice is to put service needs first and joint requirements second. As Figure 10.1 illustrates, these priorities do not reflect bureaucratic knavery as much as they do a recognition that the operating environments, organizational structures, and basic command responsibilities differ greatly between the

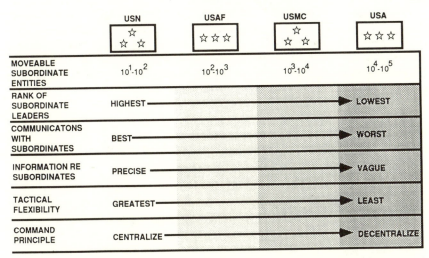

FIGURE 10.1. Service organizational differences and their relevance to command and control. This chart illustrates some of the effects which differences in service organizational and leadership principles have on command and control.
Source: Author, from Command, Control and The Common Defense (after Gen. Paul Gorman).

respective service components. As the diagram suggests, even the most fundamental element of the military structure—the numbers of forces that must be commanded and controlled—vary widely between the services. Consequently, other things differ as well: rank structures, the ability to exchange information with subordinates, and even basic organizational principles. Navies, for example, tend to be suspicious of centralized control at any level above the ship's quarterdeck. Since the time of the Caesars, however, armies have been built around hierarchical systems in which control is centralized at the top and decentralized downward.[31]

The problem is always most acute whenever these differing systems must be linked during joint operations, that is, those requiring the services to work together. During Desert Storm, for example, the Air Tasking Order—a thousand-page document containing the daily attack requirements for all coalition aircraft—could be transmitted only through air force communications channels. Because the electronic linkages with the navy were more limited, it became necessary to print the Air Tasking Order every day and fly it to each aircraft carrier in the Red Sea and the Persian Gulf. Different service requirements for secure voice (a radio system that prevents enemy eavesdropping) in air-to-air communications made it more difficult for the air force AWACS to control navy fighters.[32] These and similar examples show why improvisation—and the time to patch such work-arounds together—was so important in making the Desert Storm communications system operate at all. In the aftermath of Goldwater-Nichols, improvements in communications standards and protocols had helped to ease interoperability problems, but a new dimension arose when the scope of Desert Shield became apparent. The only way to manage its vast communications demands was with the help of commercial companies, both for basic satellite capacity and for mobile ground stations. In most cases, these interoperability problems were exacerbated by the fact that commercial technologies had outpaced those of the military.[33]

Communications Infrastructure

The U.S. communications gear that provided the infrastructure for Desert Storm command and control was heavy, bulky, and hard to transport. Much of it had never been intended for such a large-scale contingency operation; just the air force portion of the communications package eventually required over 200 sorties of C-141 aircraft.[34] But if time was once again on the side of coalition in overcoming the lift problem, an equally important element in the functioning of the Desert Storm communications infrastructure was the utter absence of determined Iraqi countermoves. Although the Iraqis maintained a Soviet-style command and control system, they followed none of its characteristic "radio-electronic combat" procedures that emphasized aggressively jamming, intercepting, or destroying enemy transmitters. There has been considerable speculation as to why Iraq did not apply any of these options to interfere with a U.S. communications system that was already overstressed by exponential growth.[35] A postwar congressional report, for example, pointedly noted that the reliance on commercial telecommunications "made theater communications vulnerable to jamming, saturation, and sabotage."[36] But regardless of the means of attack, the sprawling and electronically conspicuous centers of the Desert Storm communications lash-up would be obvious and highly lucrative targets for any future enemy.

Finally, some of the most vexing problems of the communications infrastructure involved the technical limitations of many tactical radio systems. In addition to the interoperability problems noted previously, the modernization of communications equipment has always proceeded by fits and starts, leading not only to differences between the services but within them as well. Some army units, for example, had the new SINCGARS radios, while many others did not. Older, FM-voice radios—in addition to being vulnerable to jamming and interception—were so limited in range that they were ill suited to the fast-moving armored warfare that characterized the ground assault.

Intelligence

Much of the publicity surrounding the use of intelligence in the Gulf War has focused on the controversy between analysts in Riyadh and Washington over the issue of bomb-damage assessment and what it suggested about the efficacy of the air campaign on Iraqi ground forces. Other issues, however, may have more lasting significance. Although U.S. intelligence systems collected reams of information that provided commanders with a remarkably accurate view of enemy forces and dispositions, the Gulf War experience also underlined the continuing importance of an old lesson: Problems in communications inevitably lead to problems in disseminating intelligence. The reason is time, because intelligence delayed by communications hang-ups quickly becomes history—useful for writers and analysts but not terribly helpful to hard-pressed commanders. Calling access to tactical intelligence a "serious flaw," the congressional analysis of the war noted that "the failure of the intelligence system to keep warfighters properly supplied with information underscores the vast increase in tailored, current intelligence required by weapons with one-target, one-bomb accuracy."[37]

Although the unprecedented numbers of computers brought to the battlefield stressed a communications system not set up to handle such data streams, the major problem was the insatiable demand for imagery used for targeting information, bomb-damage assessment, reconnaissance, and a host of other purposes. It is an article of faith among signal officers that "a little bit of photo eats up a whole lot of data." However, the root of the problem was the lack of effective alignment between the sensors deployed by each of the services and the communications pathways needed to deliver this information to those who needed it. Alan Campen suggested that the emphasis in sensor technology has been on developing more powerful capabilities for "detection and discrimination" rather than on considering how the resulting data could be made comprehensible and sped to the user in time to make a difference.[38] As a result, it was difficult to link these individual reconnaissance "systems" into interlocking pieces, much less to weave them seamlessly into a larger whole.

Underlying both the capabilities and limitations of the new style of warfare was the computer—or more properly, the microchip—which had now found its place at every level of combat, from individual weapons to the theaterwide databases that kept track of everything from electronic order of battle to the time-phased deployment of the troops, their equipment, and the supplies that sustained them. In the aftermath of Desert Storm, however, there has been a growing realization that the seemingly awesome technology deployed in the war actually represented a look through the rearview mirror. Given the vagaries of government procurement, many of the systems deployed in the 1980s were conceived using 1970s technologies. One example is the Patriot missile. Although its Scud-busting properties have come in for postwar revisionist critiques, it is worth remembering that the Patriot was actually conceived and developed as an anti-aircraft weapon during the Carter administration. Modifications in its software allowed the Patriot to be used to intercept missiles, although a bug in this same software also allowed the last Scud fired in the war to slip through undetected and kill 28 U.S. soldiers in a cantonment area outside Dhahran.[39]

Newer technologies of the information age offer seemingly limitless possibilities to correct such problems and to usher in a whole range of unprecedented military capabilities. The pace of development for producing, disseminating, and storing electronic data is such that entirely new generations are being produced by the commercial marketplace every twelve to eighteen months. The cheaper, more powerful, and more ubiquitous computers of the 1990s promise not only active collaboration with individual users but also a shift in the machine's basic purpose from calculation to communication. This "ultra-large scale integration" envisions the emergence of computers as "software agents" roaming a global information network to communicate freely with smart, interactive databases.[40] Dr. Alan B. Salisbury has suggested that improvements in artificial intelligence, image systems, machine translation, flat-panel displays, and holographic storage are helping to create this global network by fueling the integration and fusion of multiple technologies into new products and services.[41] The improvements in computers parallel those in communications. Although 64,000 bits of information per second are commonly transmitted via the telephone system, the advent of fiber-optics networks will raise this number to 150 megabits per second. And by the year 2000 even this standard may be eclipsed by one measured in gigabits. As Michael L. Dertouzos of MIT summarized these developments: "Independent of each other, computing and communicating tools have been improving at the annual rate of 25 percent for at least the last two decades. This relentless compounding of capabilities has transformed a faint promise of synergy into an immense and real potential."[42]

This potential has attracted a great deal of attention from the international security community in discussions of what has been termed the "military-technical revolution," or MTR. Surprisingly, some of the most attentive observers have been members of the armed forces of the former Soviet Union, suggesting that the Russian approach to the disciplined study of military science that preceded the October Revolution may have survived it as well. Hudson Institute analyst Mary C. Fitzgerald has argued that the Russian military views the U.S. performance during the Gulf War as a qualitatively new stage in the history of warfare—equivalent to that which ushered in mechanized combat earlier this century. In the Russian formulation, this first "space-age war" was decided by two factors: satellite reconnaissance and other forms of surveillance and target acquisition, which led to a 300 to 400 percent increase in combat effectiveness; and "intelligent" command and control systems linked to the delivery of precision-guided and Stealth munitions. Accordingly, success in future warfare will be determined by the side exercising superiority in these systems to gain—in the following order—superiority through the airwaves (electronic warfare), in the air itself, and only then by the operations of ground forces.[43]

The comparison between the MTR and the dawn of armored warfare is one of a number of metaphors that have also been drawn by several U.S. studies. These studies have emphasized that the real potential of the tank and the helicopter was realized only after these emerging technologies were effectively integrated with other elements of the military force structure to produce a quantum leap in combat capability—the blitzkrieg and airmobile warfare, respectively. The true potential of the MTR will be similarly hard to judge until the information-based technologies profiled in Desert Storm are effectively united with new force structures.[44] In a similar vein, the merging of the tactical, operational, and strategic levels of warfare is said to have been one of the characteristic features of Desert Storm, signifying a form of warfare that "integrates and synchronizes multiservice warfighting systems in simultaneous attacks on the enemy throughout his entire depth and in the space above him as well."[45]

If the importance of effective integration across different systems and levels of warfare is one of the central tenets of the MTR, then another is the concept of "information dominance"—a term first used in a 1993 study on the MTR by the Center for Strategic and International Studies (CSIS). Placed in the context of future regional contingency operations by U.S. forces, the CSIS study argued that an integrated system of powerful and pervasive sensors linked to an integrated network of tough, lightweight computers is essential both to providing American forces with information as a combat multiplier and to denying this advantage to the enemy. The aspect of denial, with the object lesson of the blinding of Iraqi intelligence, is important as a lesson for the future:

> Information denial can be done passively, through the use of stealth, concealment, and hard-to-detect electronic signals, or it can be done more thor-

oughly through active means: the use of electronic warfare to jam enemy radars or radios, concentrated early attacks on enemy command and control nodes . . . and, more radically, using such advanced techniques as electromagnetic pulse weapons to wreck the enemy's electronic systems and computer viruses to incapacitate its software.[46]

The calm tone used in delivering this invocation of the merits of electronic mass destruction should not mask its significance, both as a deadly harbinger of the future and as a departure point for all subsequent discussions.

The CSIS study, like so many others that have examined the relationship between warfare and information, draws upon some of the classical formulations of Dr. Thomas P. Rona. A career engineer at Boeing, Rona's writings in this field—though mostly unpublished—are nevertheless to would-be information warriors what John Boyd's were to maneuver warriors. He links information warfare to all forms of military plans and operations as well as the larger issues of national strategy, a fact of life that must be understood in the context of increasing information flows and technological sophistication. He has also warned constantly of the dangers of hubris, since technological proliferation means that competitors may gain some of the same capabilities the United States now considers to be uniquely its own: "The enemy also has the capacity to learn lessons." His concept of "the extended weapon system" (see Figure 10.2) represents the interdependent linkages between the PGM and its environment as well as the supporting structure of weapons platforms (aircraft, for example), sensors, and communications pathways needed to guide the PGM to its target. It is precisely in the spiderweb of linkages required by the extended weapon system that information warfare takes place. As shown in Figure 10.3, information warfare exists as an elaborate interplay of moves and countermoves in which each side tries to interfere with, manipulate, or exploit the extended weapon system of the adversary while attempting to prevent such actions against its own systems. The side that most effectively balances the offensive actions needed to exploit the linkages of the enemy's extended weapon system with the defensive actions needed to protect its own can be said to enjoy the competitive advantage that will be the prerequisite to victory in future warfare. The quest for this "information differential" is fundamental, as is the corollary principle that Rona has constantly cited: The basic purpose of command and information systems is to destroy *other* command and information systems.[47]

A more visionary approach to the MTR has been offered by Martin Libicki, who argued that advances in computer manufacturing will lead to "free silicon" (in other words, pervasive and ubiquitous computing) in the twenty-first century, leading in turn to wider applications of robotics, including the evolution of PGMs into large numbers of "smart ants." The principal implications are that "seekers" will become more dominant than "hiders" as information grids make masking more difficult; that the larger the weapon, the easier it is to detect and kill, so smaller is better; and that large numbers of smart ants will be the equivalent of

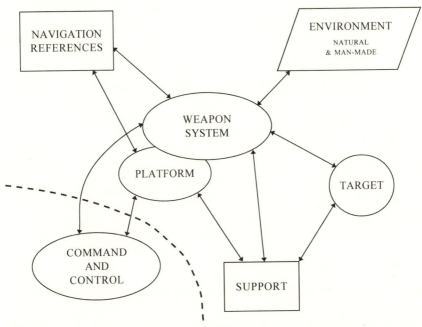

FIGURE 10.2. The extended weapon system. Note the capabilities for both extended command and control—through the complex linkages between systems—and enemy interference with these same links.
Source: Dr. Thomas Rona

intelligent and deadly minefields—meaning that defense will dominate the offense.[48] So profound are these changes that the traditional balance between information and force is being altered, with firepower becoming a mere appendage to information. There is consequently a need, in Libicki's opinion, for the American defense establishment to enter a new era of joint warfare and contemplate the need for profound organizational changes, including the formation of a new "Information Corps."[49]

Institutional Responses

It may be assumed that the enthusiasm of the Department of Defense (DoD) for the creation of such a new military service—especially from the ranks of the computer-driven *corps d'elite*—will remain under firm control, if for no other reason than the considerable difficulties of designing new uniforms or composing the appropriate fight songs. There have been, however, a number of institutional responses by the DoD that suggest some important directions for the future.

One of the most important of these occurred as a feature of the Defense Management Review put in motion by Secretary of Defense Dick Cheney.

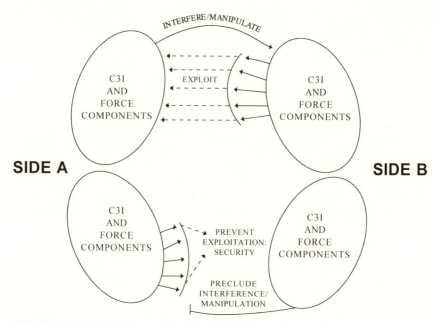

FIGURE 10.3. The information war concept. The essence of the information war concept is the balance between offensive actions designed to exploit enemy linkages and the defensive measures needed to preclude such actions against one's own forces.
Source: Dr. Thomas Rona

One of those initiatives, known as Defense Management Review Decision (DMRD) 918, was a frank acknowledgment that despite average annual expenditures of more than $20 billion, DoD business information systems were simply not up to the challenges of radical increases in information flows, primarily because they had not been designed to work together. Like the discontinuities in operational command and control systems, information exchanges between these disparate business systems—for finance, administration, logistics, and training—were difficult and required unnecessary expenditures of time, labor, and money. The DMRD initiative eventually gave rise to the DoD program on Corporate Information Management, or CIM, a concept most closely identified with Paul Strassmann, appointed by Cheney as the first director of defense information. Strassmann's frequent briefings on CIM reflected not only the emphasis on saving money as the DoD was downsized but also the need to tailor the department's information systems to provide end-to-end support from the Pentagon to joint task forces in the field. This was a radical departure, because it appeared to wipe away the traditional dividing line between the centrally managed business information systems largely run by DoD and the command and control systems procured by the services.[50]

Two DoD directives issued at the end of the Bush administration codified the new directions. The most sweeping change came in DoD Directive 8000.1, which stressed that "data and information shall be corporate assets structured to enable full integration and interoperability across DOD activities."[51] The Assistant Secretary of Defense for C³I was named as the official responsible for the department's information management program while the Defense Information Systems Agency (or DISA, formerly the Defense Communications Agency) was given broad authority to enforce "integrated information technology standardization."[52] DoD Directive 4630.5 further strengthened the existing emphasis on interoperability by declaring that all C³I systems developed for use by U.S. forces were to be considered for joint use.[53] The ability to enforce these interoperability standards made DISA into a powerful player for all future procurements of both information as well as command and control systems. The Clinton administration added to that authority still further by giving the agency the lead role in rationalizing the existing DoD information infrastructure—including more than four hundred financial systems, 300 matériel management systems, and (at least) 10,000 command and control systems.[54] Implicit in this authority was not only the approval of new systems but also the identification and forcible retirement of redundant old ones—all of which are critical development functions historically performed by the military services. Although these far-reaching policy changes are certain to face difficulties in implementation, they have already transformed DISA into the de facto architect for the entire defense information community.

The Joint Staff, its stature already enhanced by Goldwater-Nichols, also benefited from the lessons of Desert Storm and the increased emphasis on interoperability. It has revised its policy on "command and control warfare" to reflect the need to decapitate the enemy command structure while protecting one's own ability to communicate, plan, and act more quickly than the adversary. Intelligence contributes to these objectives by compiling databases that identify the critical "C2 nodes, links, and sensors of potentially hostile nations."[55] Equally important is the emphasis that this new operational doctrine places on the conscious exploitation of the improvements in command and control technology, which offer "the potential for an exponential increase in the efficient application of military power . . . in a focused joint strategy."[56] Joint commanders in future operations will therefore be expected to focus the technologies and practices of operations security, deception, electronic warfare, and even psychological operations through tightly integrated campaign plans.[57] Although all these activities have previously had their place in U.S. military operations, those places have generally been secondary; their combination into a whole larger than the sum of its parts suggests their importance for the future.

If the emphasis on command and control warfare can be seen as an effort to exploit existing capabilities in new ways, one of the most visible approaches to the future of information warfare has come with an initiative known as "C4I For The Warrior." In briefings, brochures, and several official publications, this concept has been advanced as a vision of technology focused around a joint, completely interoperable, global information grid—"the infosphere." Warriors of the future, it is said, will be able to take advantage of flexible C4I modules and common operating environments and receive "over-the-air updating" of mission orders and target information, perhaps through the use of multicasting or similar receiver-oriented communications. These are interesting capabilities, and the overall objective is worthy: to give the Joint Warrior of the future the information he needs when he needs it. The reality is somewhat more mundane; in spite of Goldwater-Nichols, DoD directives, and all the rest, it is still the military services that procure C4I systems and not the Joint Staff. Until that reality changes, glitzy visions of the future and simple salesmanship—however worthy the purpose—amount to much the same thing. What remains to be seen, of course, is the extent to which the enhanced authority of the JCS Chairman to advise the civilian leadership on program and budget decisions can translate this vision into incremental realities.

Of the three services, the air force approaches the future of information warfare with the best track record. Its demonstration of technological prowess in the Gulf War and vision of itself as the custodian of "theater battle management" have validated such programs as AWACS and JSTARS while providing powerful incentives to pursue similar innovations in the future. In such places as the Electronic Systems Command at Bedford, Massachusetts, and the Air Intelligence Agency at Kelly Air Force Base in Texas, highly automated approaches to command and control warfare are being brought to bear against an array of that services's key challenges: theater missile defense, advanced mission planning, and battlespace management among a number of others. The common objective of these diverse efforts is better situational awareness leading to the application of decisive force at the decisive point—a concept that is a passable working definition of information dominance.[58] According to the commander of the Air Intelligence Agency, "For those who ignore the importance of information dominance, the consequences will be the same as for those who . . . ignored the need to achieve air superiority."[59] Despite the occasional tendency of airpower advocates to equate both these terms to the exclusion of all other arms, the focus of these efforts appears to be resolutely joint. One point in evidence: the prospective combining of the Air Intelligence Agency and the Joint Electronic Warfare Center into the new, multiservice Joint Command and Control Warfare Center.

The navy's thirty years of experience with high-technology digital systems has recently resulted in a vision of the future that is of more than passing interest. Under the leadership of recently retired Vice Admiral Jerry O. Tuttle, the navy has articulated a concept of "Space and Electronic Warfare" (SEW) that is remarkable in its clarity and elegance. The navy declared SEW a "major warfare mission area" in 1989, centered around the by-now familiar objective of targeting the enemy leadership, separating them from their forces and even their people. The navy SEW concept also stresses that information is the key to this form of warfare, with targets that can be subjected to "hard kill" (destruction), "soft kill" (disruption), or "very soft kill" (deception) by sensors and weapons systems that may operate on land, sea, air, and space as well as the electromagnetic spectrum. Not only will this warfare be joint, but also its success depends on focusing different sensors from national to tactical levels to support a form of warfare that is best seen as a continuum.[60]

As illustrated in Figures 10.4 and 10.5, the navy approach encompasses many of the concepts embodied in emerging command and control warfare doctrine, the basic functions of deception, operations security (presented here as countersurveillance), and electronic warfare generating the specific means to defeat the opposing command structure. The command and control structure necessary to carry out this style of warfare is not, however, the one in place today, the present system being somewhat notorious for its reliance on top-down, paper-driven message traffic. "Tactically, the commander at sea, in effect, is forced to read the equivalent of all editions of the *New York Times*—every day, every page, every column—in order to glean the information he needs."[61]

The theoretical sophistication of this policy is matched by the practicality of the "Copernicus Architecture," a name deliberately chosen to imply that the center of the universe is changing as the new navy command and control system is put in place. Planned as a decade-long "investment strategy," the objectives of Copernicus include central direction of standardized technological components, the jettisoning of outdated programs, and the installation of systems and networks that will connect fleet operations to command centers at the joint, allied, and national levels. The guts of the system will be tactical nerve centers in operational units linked to CINC command complexes via flexible "virtual networks" at the tactical and global levels.[62] In order to implement the strategic objectives of SEW and to guide increasingly scarce procurement dollars, the fundamental organizing principle of Copernicus is to allow naval commanders at all levels to choose the kind of information they will need in carrying out their missions. Although the advent of a new form of receiver-oriented communications (for the first time since the wireless was sent to sea early in this century) would undoubtedly be a welcome development throughout the fleet, it is important to appreciate the bureaucratic and technical obstacles that will have to be overcome. Like every other service, the navy is faced with hard programmatic choices of "nerves versus muscle" as command and control systems are forced to compete with weapons systems for funding priority. And even when those choices have been made, the pace of modernization can present its own problems. A recent navy publication candidly noted that just after the carrier USS *George Washington* was commissioned, the ship's communications processor was removed because it had become obsolete upon installation. "Similarly, the Trident submarine USS *Kentucky* recently slipped from her ways with

Definition	Function	Means
Operational Deception • Is intended to influence enemy plans, execute a stratagem, induce reactions over a short period, and apply pressure to act	• To influence enemy plans, dispositions and expectations; • To induce reaction over a short period of time; • To apply pressure to act	• **Stratagem** (campaign level deception plan) • **Cover and security** (discourage interest) • **Feint** (maneuver before main operations) • **Technical deception** (stratagem continuity and reinforcement through communications; radar, navigation, recognition, acoustical, and electro-optical systems)
Counter-Surveillance • Targets enemy surveillance	• To deceive, degrade, evade, attack sensors and sensor platforms	• **Evasion and concealment** (denial of detection) • **Diversion and simulation** (divert detection) • **Deception** (technical means) • **Jamming and saturation** (overcome detector) • **Destruction**
Counter-C4I • Targets enemy C4I	• To deceive, delay, degrade, or destroy elements of hostile C4I from sensor platforms to weapons carriers • To deceive, delay, degrade, or destroy enemy command and control links and nodes	• **Deception** (manipulative deception of own communications) • **Deception** (imitative deception of hostile communications) • **Saturation** (overwhelm C2 systems) • **Jamming** • **Destruction**
Electronic Combat • Targets enemy weapons and weapons systems	• The coordination of all offensive and defensive measures across the force to provide counter-weapon protection to the force	• **Counter-targeting** (radar deception, IR deception, signals management) • **Counter-platform** (hard-kill request to ASUWC, AAWC, ASWC) • **Counter-weapon/terminal phase** (platform deception, decoys, jamming, hard-kill request to other commander) • **Jamming** • **Destruction**

FIGURE 10.4. This chart illustrates the continuum of warfare and supporting operations in the space and electronic warfare arena.
Source: Office of the Chief of Naval Operations (OP-094), *Space and Electronic Warfare: A Navy Policy Paper on a New Warfare Area* (Washington, D.C.: Government Printing Office, 1992).

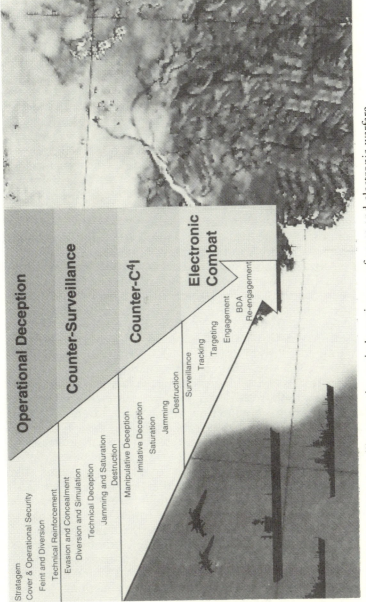

FIGURE 10.5. This chart illustrates the tactical continuum of space and electronic warfare. *Source:* Office of the Chief of Naval Operations, *Space and Electronic Warfare.*

KW-7 cryptographic machines installed, more than a year after active ships in the Fleet removed them from their radio rooms."[63]

The army has traditionally occupied third place in the annual three-way race for defense dollars, a fact of life that has made modernization dollars hard to come by, especially those earmarked for command and control. The service has gamely made do with existing resources, but its tactical operations have often been conducted either as if the airplane and the reconnaissance satellite had never been invented or as if these products were of no conceivable use to the soldier. Fortunately, this has begun to change. General Gordon R. Sullivan has used his position as Army Chief of Staff to stress the importance of information-based warfare and to prompt a number of key initiatives: establishment of a broad effort aimed at "digitizing the battlefield," preparation of a new field manual on information operations, and the orchestration of a series of training maneuvers aimed at testing out the operational implications of new information technologies.[64]

Although these larger initiatives are meant to suggest a broad institutional commitment, some of the most important practical developments have recently taken place within the army's intelligence establishment. This branch—always yielding pride of place to the elite combat arms—has for more than a decade grappled with one of the toughest problems in command and control: how to engineer the common sensor languages and software architectures needed to keep track of the 30,000 enemy "movers, shooters, and emitters"? The Desert Storm experience suggested that this measurement—originally derived from the canonical Soviet-style combined arms force typically facing a U.S. Army corps commander—was still valid for many regional conflict scenarios.

The answer to this continuing problem has come with the maturing of a number of closely related technologies: the increasing processing power of 486/Pentium computer microprocessors, advances in software algorithms to accommodate greater complexity, and the extension by satellite and computer of digital data pathways from the strategic to the tactical level. The first two technological advances have moved the army's long-awaited All-Source Analysis System from dream to reality, whereas the third represents the Information Age equivalent of rural electrification. Consequently, ground commanders will soon have the ability to collate nearly instantaneously information derived from their own sensors (including digitized frontline reports as well as the downlinks from long-duration, remotely piloted aircraft) with those of theater systems (such as JSTARS) and to compare those results with databases and other intelligence holdings at the highest national levels.[65] The foreseeable effects include turning tactical intelligence from a craft to something approaching a science; however, the potential also exists for this new form of "electronic cavalry" to supplant the more traditional one.

The institutional responses summarized here suggest that the capabilities exhibited during Desert Storm have created a revolution of rising expectations within the defense establishment. Far from preparing for the last war, would-be information warriors in every department and defense agency are preparing for the inevitable "next time," whether it results from a second North Korean invasion or an as-yet-unnamed "major regional contingency" elsewhere in the world. It should be recognized that these efforts result not only from recent wartime experience but also from a strong sense that information technology represents a way—possibly the only way—to enhance future American combat effectiveness in the midst of severe defense cutbacks. The new fiscal austerity raises a troubling paradox: At the very moment when technological possibilities gleam brightest, the likelihood of getting them has seldom been dimmer. These cutbacks also have the potential to turn troublesome budget rivalries into turf fights of Darwinian proportions, with force structure reductions raising even more basic questions about service roles and missions. Under such conditions, how will it be possible to maintain the high levels of cooperation necessary to avoid stand-alone, single-service approaches ("stovepiping") in new command and control systems while building the consensus needed to kill others that are obsolete or redundant?

There are several reasons to avoid falling back into the pitfalls of interservice rivalry, beginning with the fact that there simply is not enough money to go around. The following is a brief summary of some of the others.

Operational Factors

As shown by the Gulf War, the services are operating inside a tighter operational "box," with traditional dividing lines between land, sea, and air forces increasingly blurred. Not only do weapons strike from longer ranges, but the extended lines of support suggested by Thomas Rona also involve progressively higher levels of coordination and rapid exchange of information. Under those circumstances, interoperability becomes the sine qua non of all future combat.

Cultural and Generational Factors

The significance of Goldwater-Nichols becomes ever more apparent, representing a change in direction that becomes more noticeable in retrospect. It has prompted the development of a truly joint culture, particularly among younger officers for whom joint teamwork represents a well-understood constant of contemporary military life. Equally important has been the creation of joint military institutions that have become organizational counterweights to the traditional autonomy of military services. The Joint Staff and such high-level bodies as the Joint Requirements Oversight Council have become increasingly influential players in determining defense policy, and they are likely to become even more so in the future.

Commercial and Industrial Factors

The defense procurement system is an unwieldy structure whose manifold inefficiencies have been the subjects of seven major studies, the latest of which documented the astounding fact that more than six hundred laws and untold numbers of regulations govern defense procurement.[66] In 1993, this study became the underpinning for the sweeping reforms of federal procurement proposed by the Clinton administration under the rubric of "reinventing government." The resulting legislation, the Federal Acquisition Streamlining Act of 1994, amends some 225 statutes that inhibit the purchase of commercial products by the Defense Department— steps that are essential if the DoD is to be able to save money and to take advantage of the latest commercial technologies.[67] Although much remains to be done to rationalize or simply get rid of unnecessary defense procurement regulations and military specifications, it is clear that commercial products, practices, and standards will largely determine the means by which the department develops its potential for information warfare. This means in turn that the services must be prepared to enter the commercial marketplace of future command and control systems with the firm understanding that they are no longer in business for themselves.

Reflections

In addition to these institutional responses, the technology displayed in the Gulf War highlights some new perspectives on the ancient principle of command. What was perhaps most notable was the demonstration that the command and information functions—once virtually identical—have begun to separate as more and more information has been required at lower and lower levels. John Keegan has written that the two classic functions of command are to see and to know.[68] To this must be added two other functions: to decide and to enforce those decisions. This point is significant because deciding and enforcing are hierarchical functions; seeing and knowing are not. Both were clearly essential in Desert Storm; however, much of the information on which the command structure depended came in distinctly nonhierarchical ways. The free-flowing information pathways in the Gulf War suggest ad-hocracies as units scrambled to communicate by faxes and PC modems in ways that simply bypassed the traditional top-down architecture of the military communications system.

Perhaps there is something about the electron and its pathways that is inherently subversive of hierarchies, much as the printing press inevitably altered the established order during the first information revolution. Arquilla and Ronfeldt made much this same point in their essay on "cyberwar," noting that the information revolution "diffuses and redistributes power . . . crosses borders . . . [and] redraws the boundaries of offices and responsibilities," expanding "the spatial and temporal horizons" that decisionmakers at all levels must consider.[69] They also made the sensible observation, however, that both hierarchical and nonhierarchical information flows will continue to coexist for some time to come—something that is especially important in understanding the tensions imposed upon information-age command structures. There are excellent political and military reasons underlying the hierarchical ordering of command relationships, but there are equally good ones validating the more chaotic, "one-interface-stands" of free-form electronic networking. Although the rapidly evolving differences in the command and information functions pull in opposite directions, both are essential to the modern military organization. A rule of the road for the short term appears to be that command structures should be kept as flat as possible (something that goes against the grain of any hierarchy), while the organized chaos of information-gathering should be encouraged to seek its own levels (which it will do anyway).

Closely linked to the principle of command is the question of central control. Some observers see information warfare as a great mechanism of central control because they believe that the lethality of indirect fire (through remotely directed standoff weapons) will allow them to replace or significantly supplement direct fire. If this is true, there would be ample grounds in military history on which to base strong concerns. J.F.C. Fuller, for example, wrote scathingly of World War I commanders who attempted to control the battlefield from the rear with the latest implement of contemporary information warfare, the field telephone, by "talking, talking, talking in place of leading, leading, leading!"[70] The fact is that both direct and indirect fire (with their respective differences in command and operating principles) will be reverse sides of the same coin for some time to come because each of these classes of weapons brings unique capabilities to the extended battlefields of the future. Information warfare is best thought of as the binding agent for an integrated campaign (rather than a mere succession of target lists) in which both direct and indirect fires are selectively employed. The same information differential that allows a missile to be guided by a global positioning satellite to its target also permits the Abrams tank commander to site and destroy his enemy at extended ranges. This principle was articulated by the army in the aftermath of the 1973 Middle East War, the first conflict to feature the large-scale use of PGMs: What can be seen can be hit, what can be hit can be killed. [71]

One of the many great unknowns in information warfare is the question of future organization: How will military force structures accommodate the changes brought about by increasing spans of control? Difficult as it is, the answer becomes considerably harder if the discussion is couched in terms of "systems," "systems of systems," "architectures," and possibly even "architectures of architectures." The late Congressman Bill Nichols had a better perspective in 1986 as he opened the hearings that ultimately produced the landmark law named in his honor: "We can never forget that organization, no less than a bayonet or an aircraft carrier, is a weapon of war. We owe it to our soldiers, our sailors, our airmen, and our marines to ensure that this weapon is lean enough, flexible enough, and tough enough to help them win if, God forbid, that ever becomes necessary."[72]

The command structure is the one part of a military organization that, more than any other, must function as a weapon of war. It must either be a lethal, predatory weapon, capable of preying upon and killing other command structures—or else it it runs the risk of becoming a bizarre, expensive techno-gaggle more likely to generate friction than to reduce it. The American military will be another decade or more in coming to grips with the techniques of organizing, equipping, and training such command structures, but a rough consensus seems to be emerging on two points: (1) Information systems are helpful only to the extent that they reduce the fog of war, and (2) The command structure must be capable of winning even after the computer dies.

The issue of computer vulnerability is only one of the many caveats surrounding the possible outcomes of the focus on information warfare. It is far from clear what the utility of information warfare may be in low-intensity conflict. In Somalia, for example, published reports have suggested that Mohammed Aideed and his followers communicated using a combination of couriers, low-power cellular phones, and drums. At the opposite end of the spectrum, the rise of democracy in the former Soviet Union has lessened the urgency (though not the necessity) of doomsday planning. Nevertheless, the problem of nuclear proliferation has increased concern that electronically dependent U.S. forces might be vulnerable to the circuit-frying electromagnetic pulse (EMP) of even a low-yield nuclear weapon. Information may indeed underlie all forms of warfare, but it seems that the United States enjoys a clear information differential only in the realm of mid-intensity conflict.

Another caveat comes in the area of information denial put forward by the CSIS study on the military-technical revolution: How easily can denial be accomplished in an information-intensive world? If the United States considers EMP a potential threat, how much sense does it make to blithely suggest that we might initiate such warfare ourselves—a question that also applies to computer viruses? Even if these obviously extreme possibilities are discounted, the role of the media is still left unaccounted for. As was shown by Desert Storm, control over the flow of information by the media was critical in protecting the coalition's planned "left hook" because CNN was virtually the only source of information Saddam had left. Control over the media was assured through physical control over the territory from which the attack was being staged. However, what happens when the focus shifts from land to space, as will surely happen when the news media acquire their own satellite reconnaissance capability? Would future information warfare doctrine suggest that the satellite be interfered with—or destroyed? How far would a democratic country have to go to exert active information denial measures—and at what ethical and moral costs?

Despite these questions, information warfare appears to represent a uniquely U.S. approach to combat—a mixture of technical expertise, improvisation, offensive spirit, and a preference for direct results. It is, moreover, a course on which the defense establishment has already embarked.

The uncertain and awkward language used by many of its practitioners to describe the new direction—"infosphere," "cyberspace," and "coherent battlefield"—suggests not only the novelty of the subject but also the absence of paradigm. Thus, there are any number of good reasons "to make haste slowly," recognizing that this is a field whose true significance and dimensions are as much a challenge to contemporary observers as the elephant was to the six blind men of Hindustan. If it is wise to avoid the pitfalls of technological hubris, it is equally important to ensure that leadership in exploring the field of information warfare is not surrendered to technocrats, who tend to view these matters as engineering problems in which the actions of any future enemy are somehow irrelevant. This is an area of endeavor that cries out for continuing experimentation and dialogue between the military technologist and the warrior, with effective operational employment as the ultimate standard.

Finally, if information technology is truly to become a weapon of war, it must be a joint weapon: but most of our weapons and all of our paradigms reflect specific service roots. In one of my earlier works, the reader's attention was invited to the fact that the U.S. defense establishment has a long history of strategic concepts that fall short of capturing the essence of what it means to be a superpower with land, sea, and aerospace forces as well as global interests.[73] The information war paradigm—inchoate, uncertain, and indistinct though it may be—represents a possible alternative, precisely because it embraces each of these operational environments as well as the electromagnetic spectrum. It remains to be seen if the new paradigm will find a Clausewitz to articulate its true meaning and potential, but it is likely that he or she will regard the development of information warfare in Desert Storm as a true turning point.

Notes

1. Paul H. Nitze, "Is It Time To Junk Our Nukes?" *Washington Post*, January 16, 1994, p. C1.

2. John Arquilla and David Ronfelt, "Cyberwar Is Coming!" *Comparative Strategy* 12, no. 2 (1993): 141.

3. Senator Bill Bradley, "For the Record," *Washington Post*, April 21, 1992, p. A24.

4. Dr. Frank B. Horton III, principal deputy assistant secretary of defense (C^3I), "Intelligence from the Sensor to the Shooter," panel discussion, Annual Convention of the Armed Forces Communications and Electronics Association, Washington, D.C., June 8, 1994.

5. Sun Tzu, *The Art of War,* trans. Samuel B. Griffith (New York: Oxford University Press, 1982), 66, 84.

6. Carl von Clausewitz, *On War,* trans. and ed. Michael Howard and Peter Paret (Princeton: Princeton University Press, 1976), 117 (original emphasis). Later, he summed up the problem this way: "The general unreliability of all information presents a special problem in war: all action takes place, so to speak, in a kind of twilight, which like fog or moonlight, often tends to make things seem grotesque and larger than they really are. Whatever is hidden from full view

in this feeble light has to be guessed at by talent or simply left to chance. So once again for lack of objective knowledge one has to trust to talent or luck" (140).

7. Martin van Creveld, *Command in War* (Cambridge: Harvard University Press, 1985), 264.

8. See Paul Bracken, *The Command and Control of Nuclear Forces* (New Haven: Yale University Press, 1983), and Bruce G. Blair, *Strategic Command and Control* (Washington, D.C.: The Brookings Institution, 1985).

9. Alan D. Campen, "Communications Support to Intelligence," in Alan D. Campen, ed., *The First Information War* (Fairfax, Va.: AFCEA International Press, 1992), 58.

10. William J. Perry, "Desert Storm and Deterrence," *Foreign Affairs* 70, no. 4 (1991): 66–82.

11. Ibid., 69.

12. Ibid., 75.

13. Ibid., 76. Subsequent scholarship has inevitably caused these figures to be reevaluated as more details of "friction" become available. See Rick Atkinson, *Crusade: The Untold Story of the Persian Gulf War* (Boston: Houghton Mifflin, 1993), especially 216–236. See also Thomas A. Keaney and Eliot A. Cohen, *Gulf War Airpower Survey: Summary Report* (Washington, D.C.: Government Printing Office, 1993)..

14. Perry, "Desert Storm and Deterrence," 76.

15. Quoted in Department of Defense, *Conduct of the Persian Gulf Conflict: Final Report to the Congress* (Washington, D.C.: Government Printing Office, 1992), 559.

16. Dick G. Howe, quoted by Peter Grier in "The Data Weapon," *Government Executive* 24, no. 6 (1992): 21.

17. Department of Defense, *Conduct of the Persian Gulf Conflict*, 559–560.

18. Ibid., 563–568. Satellite communications were so important in Desert Storm that they ultimately provided 75 percent of all SHF connectivity to the forces in the theater (Ibid., K-32).

19. Thomas S. Swalm, "Joint STARS in Desert Storm," in Campen, *The First Information War*, 167–170. See also two related articles in *Signal* 45, no.12 (1991): "Gulf's Electronic Marvels Set for Multiple Upgrades," 53–55, and "Soldiers Contribute Battle Data for Tactical Control," 46–48.

20. Department of Defense, *Conduct of the Persian Gulf Conflict*, 569–570.

21. See Joseph S. Toma, "Desert Storm Communications," in Campen, *The First Information War*, 105.

22. Department of Defense, *Conduct of the Persian Gulf Conflict*, 546.

23. See my treatment of this subject in *Command, Control and the Common Defense* (New Haven: Yale University Press, 1990), 173–180.

24. U.S. Army, *Field Manual 100-5, Operations* (Washington, D.C.: Headquarters, Department of the Army, 1986), 12–18. For a fuller discussion of the evolution of the doctrine, see John L. Romjue, *From Active Defense to Airland Battle: The Development of Army Doctrine 1973–1982* (Fort Monroe, Va.: U.S. Army Training and Doctrine Command, 1984).

25. John A. Warden, *The Air Campaign* (Washington, D.C.: NDU Press, 1988), 51.

26. Ibid., 53–54.

27. Army–air force tensions during the air campaign are reported extensively in Atkinson, *Crusade*, 216–240 et passim.

28. Department of Defense, *Conduct of the Persian Gulf Conflict*, 98.

29. General H. Norman Schwarzkopf, "Why Desert Storm Was a Success," prepared statement to the Senate Appropriations Committee, June 13, 1991.

30. Gene I. Rochlin and Chris C. Demchak, "The Gulf War: Technological and Organizational Implications," *Survival* 23, no. 2 (1991): 262.

31. This argument is discussed in Allard, *Command, Control and the Common Defense,* 241–264.

32. U.S. Congress, House Armed Services Committee, *Defense for a New Era: Lessons of the Persian Gulf War* (Washington, D.C.: Government Printing Office, 1992), 22–23.

33. See the interview with Lieutenant General James S. Cassity of the Joint Staff, "Command, Control Advances Permeate Combat Success," *Signal* 45, no. 9, (1991): 121–126.

34. Campen, *The First Information War,* 25.

35. Ibid., 171–177.

36. House Armed Services Committee, *Defense for a New Era,* 23.

37. Ibid., 37.

38. Campen, *The First Information War,* 56.

39. See Atkinson, *Crusade,* 416–421.

40. Lawrence G. Tesler, "Networked Computing in the 1990s," *Scientific American* 265, no. 3 (1991): 54–61.

41. Dr. Alan B. Salisbury, presentation to the annual convention of the Armed Forces Communications Electronics Association, Washington, D.C., June 25, 1992.

42. Michael L. Dertouzos, "Communications, Computers and Networks," *Scientific American* 265, no. 3 (1991): 31.

43. See Mary C. Fitzgerald, "The Impact of the MTR On Russian Military Affairs," vols. 1 and 2 (Washington, D.C.: Hudson Institute, 1993); "Russia's New Military Doctrine," *RUSI Journal* (October 1992): 40–48; and "The Soviet Military and the New Air War in the Persian Gulf," *Airpower Journal* 5, no. 4 (1991): 64–77.

44. See Frank Kendall, "Exploiting the MTR," *Strategic Review* 20, no. 2 (1992): 23–30, and Major Michael R. Macedonia, "Information Technology in Desert Storm," *Military Review* 72, no. 10 (1992): 34–41.

45. Lieutenant Colonel Douglas A. Macgregor, "Future Battle: The Merging Levels of War," *Parameters* 22, no.4 (1992): 42.

46. Michael J. Mazarr et. al., *The Military Technical Revolution: A Structural Framework* (Washington, D.C.: Center for Strategic and International Studies, 1993), 20.

47. Dr. Thomas P. Rona, presentation to the Information Resources Management College, National Defense University, Washington, D.C., December 3, 1992.

48. Martin C. Libicki, "Silicon and Security in the Twenty-First Century," *Strategic Review* 20, no.3 (1992): 62–65.

49. Martin C. Libicki and James A. Hazlett, "Do We Need an Information Corps?" *Joint Forces Quarterly* 1, no.2 (1993): 88–97.

50. See the following articles on CIM and Strassmann's tenure in the DoD: Robert McCashin, "Pentagon Peruses Mastery of Corporate Data Systems," *Signal* 45, no. 11 (1991): 81–84; Lisa Corbin, "DOD Inc.," *Government Executive* 24, no. 6 (1992): 36–39; and Diane Hamblen, "Paul Strassmann: Turning Our Upside Down World Right Side Up," *Chips* 10, no. 4 (1992): 4–8.

51. U.S. DoD Directive 8000.1, October 27, 1992.

52. Ibid., paragraph E.5(a).

53. U.S. DoD Directive 4630.5, November 12, 1992.

54. Assistant Secretary of Defense (C³I) Emmett Paige, Jr., "Re-engineering DOD's Operations: Information Management Impact," address to the Federal Sources, Inc., executive breakfast, Vienna, Va., September 14, 1993.

55. Chairman, Joint Chiefs of Staff, Memorandum of Policy No. 30, "Command and Control Warfare," Washington (March 8, 1993).

56. U.S., Joint Chiefs of Staff. *Joint Publication 3-13 (Draft), Joint Command and Control Warfare Operations,* Washington, D.C., January 15, 1994, 2-1.

57. Ibid., 2-2–2-19.

58. See Clarence A. Robinson, Jr., "Information Dominance Edges Toward New Conflict Frontier," *Signal* 48, no. 12 (1994): 37–40.

59. Ibid., quoting Major General Kenneth A. Minihan, USAF, 37.

60. Office of the Chief of Naval Operations (OP-094), *Space and Electronic Warfare: A Navy Policy Paper on a New Warfare Area* (Washington, D.C.: Government Printing Office, 1992).

61. Chairman, Joint Chiefs of Staff, *Joint Command and Control Warfare Operations,* 2-9.

62. Director of Space and Electronic Warfare, Office of the Chief of Naval Operations (OP-094), *The Copernicus Architecture, Phase I: Requirements Definition* (August 1991), chapter 3.

63. Office of the Chief of Naval Operations (OP-094), *Sonata,* Washington, D.C., n.d., 70.

64. See, for example, General Gordon R. Sullivan and Colonel James M. Dubik, "War in the Information Age," *Military Review* 74, no. 4 (1994): 46–62; see also U.S. Army, *Field Manual 100-6, Information Operations* (Draft), Headquarters, Department of the Army, Washington, D.C., July 22, 1994.

65. These advances in the army's intelligence community are well covered in a pair of articles by Clarence A. Robinson, Jr., "Commanders Pull Intelligence in Information War Strategy" and "Digital Intelligence Extends Army Force Projection Power," *Signal* 48, no. 12 (1994): 29–35.

66. See U.S. Department of Defense, *"Streamlining Defense Acquisition Laws" Executive Summary: Report of the DOD Acquisition Law Advisory Panel* (Washington, D.C.: Government Printing Office, 1993).

67. U.S. Congress, House, Conf Report, *Federal Acquisition Streamlining Act of 1994,* 103rd Cong., 2nd sess., Report No. 103–712, Aug. 21, 1994. See also Pat Towell, "Pentagon Banking on Plans to Reinvent Procurement," *Congressional Quarterly* 52, no. 15, (1994): 899–904.

68. John Keegan, *The Mask of Command* (New York: Viking, 1987).

69. Arquilla and Ronfelt, "Cyberwar Is Coming!" 143–144.

70. Major General J.F.C. Fuller, *Generalship: Its Diseases and Their Cure,* (Harrisburg, Pa.: Military Service Publishing Company, 1936), 61.

71. Paraphrased from Department of the Army, *Field Manual 100-5, Operations* (Washington, D.C.: Government Printing Office, 1976), 2–6.

72. U.S. Congress, *Reorganization of the Department of Defense, Hearings before the Investigative Subcommittee of the Committee on Armed Services,* 99th Cong., 2nd sess. (Washington, D.C.: Government Printing Office, 1987), 8.

73. Allard, *Command, Control and the Common Defense,* chapter 8.

11

U.S. Military Strategy in Europe

LARRY D. BUDGE

Since the establishment of the United States as a nation, its interests have been closely intertwined with those of the major powers in Europe. However, in the years preceding 1941, the United States was politically involved with Europe only intermittently. Nevertheless, in 1945 the United States committed itself not only to the leadership of a peacetime alliance to protect the security of Western Europe but also to the rebuilding of both friend and foe from the destruction of World War II. The strategy of containment, which underlay the commitment to Western Europe, came to a conclusion in 1989 with the collapse of the communist governments in Eastern Europe, the subsequent rapid collapse of the Warsaw Pact, and the dissolution of the Soviet Union. The Atlantic Alliance, led by the United States, had won the Cold War.

Although the West has triumphed in Europe and there remains no nation capable of directly threatening the security of Western Europe, the United States retains significant vital interests that require its continued involvement in Europe. The most important of these are (1) the maintenance of democracy within those nations already democratic and the spread of democracy to those that are emerging from totalitarian rule, (2) the maintenance of a flourishing European economy and an increasingly free trade between Europe and the remainder of the world, (3) the reduction of political instability in Europe, (4) the prevention of any state from attempting to threaten future European security, and (5) the encouragement of European participation with the United States in safeguarding common vital interests outside Europe.

U.S. Security Strategy in Europe

National strategies are no longer, if they ever were, solely concerned with security issues. A nation's strategy consists of several components, and the nation that integrates all of these into a coherent whole will be more successful in achieving its interests than one that does not. U.S. economic and political strategy toward Europe will be particularly important in the future, certainly equal in importance to its security strategy. However, considerations of space necessitate that this chapter focus on U.S. security strategy in Europe.

Given the U.S. national interests considered just previously and by Dr. Rosecrance in his chapter, U.S. security strategy in Europe should aim at achieving a series of specific objectives. First, it must encourage the completion of the Russian military withdrawal from Eastern Europe and the Soviet successor states. Second, it should maintain the capability to deter a resurgent, authoritarian Russia until Russia has made the transition to democracy and formed an acceptable relationship with the remainder of Europe. If Russia does not make this transition, the West must retain the capability to deter subsequent threats. Third, the United States must provide a secure and stable environment for the Eastern and Central European states and the Soviet successor states in their transition to democratic regimes. This objective requires an effective capability to prevent conflict; to engage in peacekeeping; and where necessary, to implement sanctions and to engage in peacemaking operations.[1] Fourth, the U.S. should support the evolution of an effective European security structure that incorporates a secure Germany and maintains the Atlantic partnership. This evolution should include an increased European contribution to the security structure so that Europe ceases to be a net importer of security from the United States, except for strategic nuclear deterrence. Finally, the United States should aim to establish an effective Atlantic partnership to safeguard those vital interests that are common to both the United States and the European members of the partnership but that lie outside of Europe.

Since at least 1947, the focus of U.S. security policy in Europe has been to deter the Soviet Union and ensure the freedom of Western Europe. Through the efforts of the United States and the Western European states, that policy has succeeded. Yet the demise of the Soviet threat does not mean that the United States no longer has major security interests or objectives in Europe. The United States retains a number of such interests, and in many ways, the pursuit of these interests has become considerably more complex in the new multipolar world than it was in the previous bipolar world. Deterring the Soviet Union was expensive but relatively clear-cut; pursuing U.S. security interests in the current Europe may be less expensive but considerably more frustrating.

Deterring a Resurgent Russia

The Red Army is no more. The armed forces of the former Soviet Union are in the process of withdrawing from Eastern and Central Europe to a

Russia with few barracks in which to house them. Soldiers are leaving the former Soviet Army to join the newly formed armed forces in the successor states. The vast military-industrial complex, whose primary purpose was to support the military, is largely intact but faced with severe reductions in defense spending. Robert Gates, former director of the CIA, testified, "My brief characterization of these forces is that the threat to the United States from [the conventional and strategic forces of the former Soviet Union] has all but disappeared for the foreseeable future."[2]

In spite of this assessment, Russian forces still retain significant military potential. Even after agreed-upon reductions, Russia will remain one of only two nuclear superpowers in the world. After the destruction of the treaty-limited weapons required by the Treaty on Conventional Armed Forces in Europe (CFE), Russia will still possess the largest conventional forces in Europe. Moreover, in addition to the conventional forces allowed under CFE, Russia retains enormous stockpiles of modern equipment—including over 10,000 tanks—which were removed east of the Urals, out of the CFE area, prior to the final accounting of forces subject to CFE.[3]

The United States should continue to press the Russians to meet the agreed-upon timetable for withdrawing their forces. It should be made clear that future Western aid and assistance is directly contingent on meeting the withdrawal schedule. At the same time, however, the West should avoid giving the Russians the perception that it is trying to take advantage of the situation. The West should increase military-to-military contacts with the Russians to persuade them to accept the role that professional military forces have traditionally played in Western democracies. Assistance should also be provided to educate Russian civilians in defense matters from a Western perspective and in the Western concept of civilian control of military forces.

For the longer term, the United States must take the lead in ensuring that the West maintains the military capability necessary to convince the Russian General Staff that even a resurgent Russia would not be successful in launching a preemptive strike at any portion of Western Europe. The West may reduce its force levels, but it must retain the capability, in the event of warning, to mobilize reserves and reconstitute additional forces. Most importantly, the United States must commit itself to the retention of nuclear weapons in support of Western Europe, and both the United States and Western Europe must continue to modernize their conventional weapons systems. The Russian General Staff recognizes nuclear weapons and modern, high-technology conventional weapons as the major factors that would serve to disrupt any possible Russian offensive operations launched against the West.[4]

Creating a Stable Europe

Although the Cold War is over, instability is increasing in Eastern and Central Europe and in the Soviet successor states. This instability is a complex phenomenon; it can be thought of as either intrinsic or extrinsic to the transition process that these states are undergoing. Intrinsic instability is caused by stresses inherent to the transition from an authoritarian to a democratic form of government and from a socialist, command economy to a private, free-market economy. Symptoms of such stress are a crisis in state authority, a lack of legitimacy for new institutions, and stiff competition between groups, some of which are nondemocratic, for control of the government. Economic problems—such as obsolete plants, heavy foreign debt, and a general lack of a free-market, capitalist culture— often compound the political stress. From the West's perspective, the solution to intrinsic instability lies in providing political and economic assistance aimed at reducing internal stresses and supporting the democratic, free-market forces against other groups. Normally, this type of instability does not require the intervention of outside security forces.

Extrinsic instabilities, however, are caused by factors that are not inherent in the transition process, such as nationalism, ethnic conflicts, and border disputes. Many of these conditions existed before 1945 or even 1917, but they were suppressed by the Soviets and the communist governments in Eastern and Central Europe. These conflicts have now been reignited by the breakup of the Soviet Union and the demise of the local communist regimes and may occur between groups within a state, as in the former Yugoslavia, or between the states themselves. A serious source of potential conflict within the former Soviet Union is the 26 million Russians living in what are now independent states. Formerly among the elite within these republics, many are now treated as second-class citizens or threatened with expulsion. Russia, which cannot afford to accept 26 million refugees, is applying strong pressure on the former republics to accommodate the local Russians. It is not inconceivable that Russia could initiate military operations to protect its citizens.

A successful transition of the Eastern and Central European states and the Soviet successor states will be difficult enough to accomplish in the face of the intrinsic instabilities. Extrinsic instabilities increase the stress, and when these instabilities lead to open conflict, the transition process is almost certain to fail. Authoritarian leaders find greater opportunities to assume power when nationalism is running high. Precious economic resources needed for development are consumed in pursuing the conflict or are destroyed by the conflict. And conflicts may spread to neighboring states, delaying, if not halting, the orderly development of free and pluralistic states throughout a much wider area.

Several caveats must be kept in mind when considering the proper U.S. security strategy for dealing with these extrinsic instabilities. First, the United States cannot undertake this task alone; it must be done in concert with other European states. The United States has neither the available resources nor the political will to undertake a unilateral effort in an area that should be of primary interest to the Europeans. However, recent experience in what used to be Yugoslavia indicates that it may be necessary for the United States to take the lead at least in the near term. Second, the allies must "pick their fights." It will be impossible to right every wrong and resolve every conflict within the European arena. Instead, the allies must focus their efforts to deal first with those conflicts that have turned violent or are close to violence. Third, the United States and its European allies should establish a variety of instruments to deal with instability and conflict at the appropriate level. These must include (1) a capability for mediation and conflict resolution to halt conflicts before they become violent or to bring a halt to fighting, (2) peacekeeping forces to separate the warring parties and enforce peace agreements as a part of a conflict-resolution process, and (3) if necessary, peacemaking forces to halt the fighting and force the belligerents to negotiate.

Mediation and Conflict Resolution

Mediation and conflict resolution are designed to bring the parties in conflict to the negotiating table either before or after the conflicts have become violent. The Conference on Security and Cooperation in Europe (CSCE), consisting of all fifty European states plus the United States and Canada, has the potential to perform this role under some circumstances, but it suffers from significant weaknesses. It has relatively few resources in comparison to the scope of the potential problem. Its large membership; the wide variation in the interests, values, and traditions of its members; and the requirement for unanimity almost guarantee that the CSCE will be unable to intervene forcefully to halt conflicts. And although NATO has agreed to consider CSCE requests for peacekeeping forces, the requirement for unanimity will limit the employment of these forces to those situations in which all parties to the conflict have reached some level of agreement. The strength of the CSCE, however, lies in the very fact it does represent European and North American opinion. As such, it provides a unique forum in which to focus that opinion against either one or all of the participants in a conflict.

Even though the current CSCE has little real power to enforce stability, there are steps that the United States can take to improve the situation, both within the CSCE and outside of it. First, the United States should support the CSCE by bringing issues before that body and by pressing to expand the CSCE's role to include mediation and the supervision of peacekeeping operations. Second, if the CSCE is unable to make progress in dealing with a specific conflict, the United States should encourage and support the European Community (EC) in taking an early lead to mediate the dispute. If the EC is unable or unwilling to act, the United States should not hesitate to take the lead in bringing together an ad hoc group of states or, more likely, the NATO Council of Ministers to attempt to resolve the situation. The key in this process is to bring the states in conflict into the conflict-resolution process sooner rather than later. Although it is unlikely that the CSCE would be able to implement effective sanctions, economic or otherwise, against one or more of the parties to the conflict, the EC or NATO may have a better prospect of doing so.

Peacekeeping

Along the spectrum of conflict resolution, peacekeeping lies between me-diation and peacemaking. Peacekeeping usually comes into play only after the conflict has begun, but peacekeeping forces also can be deployed to halt a conflict that is imminent. Peacekeeping requires the agreement of both sides of the conflict in order to be successful. If the peacekeepers must mount a significant military operation to separate the warring parties, the situation has become one requiring peacemaking, not peacekeeping. In addition to being possible targets of low-level, random violence, peace-keeping forces risk being caught in the "quagmire effect." Once peace-keepers are in place, the parties to the conflict may lose their motivation to resolve the conflict, but the peacekeepers may find that they cannot withdraw for fear of reigniting it. To avoid the quagmire and increase the chances for a successful operation, the insertion of the peacekeeping forces must be followed by negotiations and unrelenting political pressure by outside parties to bring the conflicting parties to an agreement or to de-escalate the conflict so that the peacekeeping force can be withdrawn safely.

NATO members possess the forces to accomplish peacekeeping oper-ations, but it may be more acceptable in some circumstances for these forces to come from the non-NATO CSCE members. If non-NATO forces are used, their effectiveness can be improved by providing them with NATO-supplied equipment, such as night vision devices and intelligence support from U.S.- or NATO-controlled sensors. In the future, the Eu-ropean Union may also provide peacekeeping forces under the CSCE banner or its own. NATO should not necessarily become the peacekeeper of choice, and the United States should press the Europeans to take the lead wherever possible. However, the United States must be prepared to assume the leadership role when there is no other alternative and its vital interests are threatened.

Peacemaking

Peacemaking represents the most difficult option because it requires the United States and each of the participating nations to determine that stability in a particular situation is a sufficiently vital interest as to require sending soldiers into combat. In many cases, it may not be; Europe, after all, has survived earlier periods of instability. The United States and its allies must chose their fights carefully, both in terms of vital interests and in terms of possible consequences. Some conflicts may be just too risky for a peacemaking operation. A limited Russian incursion into a neigh-boring state to protect its nationals may represent too much risk for the expected gain. Consequently, the West may be forced to employ political and economic sanctions or other measures to persuade the Russians to withdraw and accept mediation. On the other hand, a Russian attempt to reincorporate a former Soviet republic against its will may have such enormous consequences that it is worth the risk of a larger conflict in order to stop it.

Three other considerations apply in making the decision to conduct peacemaking operations. First, there is the potential for the quagmire effect, particularly in peacemaking operations that involve highly nationalistic or ethnic conflicts. For example, the initial conventional conflict into which the peacemakers intervene may subsequently dissolve into a guerrilla war that drags on without settlement. Second, the state on whose behalf the peacemaking operation is launched may not require the commitment of the full range of military forces but may need only air support, intelligence, or logistics. Third, there is the likelihood that successful peacemaking operations will beget further successes; potential aggressors will then prefer to negotiate rather than fall victim to another successful peacemaking operation.

Currently, there is no single organization within Europe that has assumed the role of conducting peacemaking operations. Although the CSCE may be able to take the initiative in some peacekeeping operations, it is unlikely that the CSCE as currently organized will be able to take the lead in peacemaking operations. The interests and goals of its member states are just too divergent. Moreover, the unanimity rule allows a single state to veto any operation. If it can generate the necessary collective political will, the European Union has the potential to become an effective peacemaking organization in the future. Currently, NATO is the most likely peacemaking organization. Its members possess the necessary forces, equipment, and command and control to successfully undertake these operations. Peacemaking may be conducted under Article 4 of the Washington Treaty by those NATO members that choose to participate. When used for operations under Article 4, however, NATO members' forces function legally as a coalition of national forces and not as a NATO coalition per se. And rather than being a mere ad hoc alliance, any coalition of NATO members would share a commitment to European security based on fifty years of mutual involvement and sacrifice. On the practical level, the defense establishments of a NATO coalition are interoperable to a much higher degree than a non-NATO coalition because of the very extensive NATO operational infrastructure that has been developed over the past fifty years.

European Security Organizations

Three considerations must be kept in mind when evaluating European security organizations. First, a number of security and security-related functions must be performed in Europe and in those parts of the world that are important to both the United States and Europe. There is no reason why these functions cannot be performed by multiple organizations. A single organization may provide simplicity, but negotiating such a structure may be far from simple. Second, effective military alliances do not spring into being overnight. They require a great deal of effort and practice at working together, and this investment should not be dismissed lightly. Third, the strength of security structures depends less on the details of the organizations than on the way in which the major powers define their vital interests in Europe's future. By themselves, institutions are poor substitutes for real commitments by nation states. If commitment is lacking, almost any institutional arrangement is bound to fail if subjected to stress.

The Conference on Security and Cooperation in Europe

As discussed earlier, the CSCE has the potential, if properly resourced, to fill an important role in Europe by spotlighting potential trouble spots, providing mediation services, furnishing a forum for conventional arms control, and organizing peacekeeping operations, possibly using forces provided by NATO. Nevertheless, this potential remains seriously limited by the divergent interests and lack of consensus among the CSCE members at this time. If the Eastern and Central European states and the Soviet successor states complete the transition to democratic regimes and their interests and values converge with the Western members, then the CSCE may be able to assume more extensive responsibilities. In the meantime, the United States should support the CSCE by pushing for additional resources and capability and by bringing issues before it. The CSCE provides a unique forum by bringing together all the European states with the United States, serving as another reminder of the unique relationship between them. Although West European states belong to a plethora of European organizations, CSCE represents the only European organization to which many of the other states belong. The CSCE thereby provides an opportunity for these states to act upon a larger stage and to voice their concerns in regards to European security.

The Western European Union

The economic integration of the European Community is an accomplished fact, and despite several bumps on the road to the ratification of the Maastricht Treaty, political integration is moving forward, albeit not as swiftly as some had imagined. Although further distractions will arise, there is little doubt that the movement towards greater political integration as agreed at the Maastricht Summit will continue. The goal is to develop a common foreign policy and a common security policy within the European Union, followed by a common defense policy that will be implemented by the WEU as the defense component of the European Union. The current member governments of the WEU have agreed that it would be developed "as the defense component of the European Union and as a means to strengthen the European Pillar of the Atlantic Alliance."[5] The NATO Foreign Ministers also agreed to support the new role of the WEU, while inserting an important caveat emphasizing the continuing role of NATO: "We emphasize . . . that the primary responsibility of forces answerable to the WEU will remain NATO's collective defense under the Washington Treaty."[6]

Given the inevitability of European political integration, the United States cannot afford to oppose the planned development of the WEU. Some fear that the growth of the WEU will diminish U.S. influence in NATO and Europe, ultimately resulting in the withdrawal of the United States from both. However, to oppose the development of the WEU would almost certainly create a rupture between the United States and many of the Western European states. The time has come for the Europeans to play a greater role in European security and to carry a greater share of that burden. A strong European pillar within NATO should also increase European confidence, enabling the Europeans to serve as partners with the United States in dealing with common security interests outside Europe.

However, a risk for both the United States and Western Europe lies in whether the political integration planned in the Maastricht Treaty will, in fact, enable the European Union to play a stronger role in Europe and the world. The Maastricht Treaty is intended to establish a European Union in which member states would agree on common foreign and defense policies, largely on the basis of consensus. If all of the member states are united in a common perception that their vital interests are best supported by a strong security policy, the WEU should be able to play a strong role in Europe and in the world. But if these perceptions are not shared by most of the members of the European Union, the requirement for unanimity could produce a security policy based on a "lowest common denominator" political compromise. Unfortunately, there are indications, based on their responses to the conflict in what used to be Yugoslavia and to the U.S. call for assistance in the Persian Gulf, that some of the European members of NATO now define their vital security interests in very narrow terms, limited to the direct defense of their own homelands.[7] The proposed widening of the European Union will also admit neutral states, such as Sweden and Austria. Although these states must give up their neutrality upon joining the union, their assessment of vital security interests may differ significantly from those of the NATO members and serve to further dilute support within the union for pursuing more assertive security policies.

The United States must support the European Union and the development of the WEU as its defense component. To do otherwise would place the United States in conflict with most of the European membership of NATO, thereby possibly jeopardizing their support for NATO. At the same time, however, the United States should exert strong pressure to ensure that the Atlantic Alliance and NATO remain the defining paradigm for European security. In the event that the WEU fails to play an effective role, a functioning NATO will exist to provide the framework within which the United States and the major Western European states will still be able to pursue their vital security interests.

The North Atlantic Treaty Organization

The Atlantic Alliance is the oldest and most successful of the security organizations in Europe. It is the only organization that specifically commits the United States, along with its nuclear capability, to the defense of the European members of NATO. This commitment has permitted Germany to rearm and reunify while obviating the need for it to possess nuclear weapons. As Michael Howard points out, NATO solves the "German problem":

> There is a German problem. It may only be a problem of perception, but it exists none the less. An Alliance without the United States would be an Alliance dominated by Germany. The peoples of both Central Europe and the Soviet Union, rightly or wrongly, would see this as a threat. Even the West European allies would be uneasy. . . . So long as these feelings are strongly held, there will be an equally strong need for the United States to remain entangled in the Alliance, to balance German as well as Soviet power. We may regret these sentiments, but they do undeniably exist.[8]

In operational terms, NATO represents a major investment by its members for almost half a century in building the physical, psychological, and intellectual infrastructure that is essential for an alliance to deal successfully with unexpected crises. Generations of soldiers, sailors, and pilots from each of the member nations have become familiar with the doctrine, plans, and operational procedures that tie NATO together into a functioning whole. NATO has established one of the most extensive command, control, communications, and intelligence infrastructures in the world. All of this could be reproduced by another security organization, but only at great expense in terms of both time and money.

As discussed earlier, the United States and Western Europe have a continuing interest in ensuring against the resurgence of a hostile Russia. Given the demands of such a deterrence role, the United States must play a leading role, and NATO is the only existing organization through which that can be accomplished. Moreover, NATO's heads of government also see the Atlantic Alliance as continuing to play other key roles in the evolution of European security. NATO has developed a new strategy that reaffirms the basic purpose of the alliance to provide European security while recognizing that "risks to Allied security are less likely to result from calculated aggression against the territory of the Allies, but rather from the adverse consequences of instabilities that may arise from the serious economic, social, and political difficulties, including ethnic rivalries and territorial disputes, which are faced by many countries in central and eastern Europe."[9]

NATO forces are being reorganized from their Cold War defensive organizations facing the former inter-German border and the Czech border into reaction forces capable of moving quickly anywhere in Europe. These reaction forces are backed by larger defense forces that can be ready for combat within weeks.[10] This new organization, with its emphasis on strategic mobility and highly capable forces, is well suited to engage in either peacekeeping or peacemaking operations.

To assist the Eastern and Central European states and the Soviet successor states in making the transition to democratic regimes, NATO has established a variant of the North Atlantic Council called the North Atlantic Cooperation Council (NACC), which includes the Eastern and Central European states and the Soviet successor states as members. The intent is to establish avenues for consultation and cooperation on security and related issues such as defense planning, conceptual approaches to arms control, democratic concepts of civil-military relations, and the conversion of defense production to civilian purposes. The Eastern and Central European states and the Soviet successor states have also established permanent liaison missions at NATO Headquarters in Brussels.

NATO and its members have moved surprisingly quickly to meet the changing security requirements of a post Cold War Europe. However, much remains to be done to allow NATO to continue to play the role as the centerpiece of European security.

First, the United States must continue to maintain its leadership role in NATO for at least the near term. Likewise, support for NATO must remain near the top of the very crowded list of U.S. security priorities. Second, the United States must encourage the Europeans to play an increasing role in the management of NATO, while supporting European efforts to develop a European pillar within the Alliance. Third, NATO force structure requirements are rightly being reduced as a result of reductions in the immediate threat. However, there are indications that some NATO members are reducing below these new levels. The United States must continue to fully support its share of the reduced force structure requirements while pressuring other NATO members to do so as well. There is a danger that NATO could, over time, become a "hollow" alliance of understaffed and underequipped forces. Fourth, the United States must continue to modernize its forces and press other NATO members to do likewise so that NATO maintains its current technological lead over potential adversaries. NATO's modernization was a key factor in persuading the Soviets to seek an accommodation with the West in the 1980s, and it will remain a key factor in deterring a potentially resurgent Russia. Fifth, as the most capable and best-organized forces available, the United States must continue to support the use of NATO forces, as appropriate, in a peacekeeping role. The United States should also press the other members of NATO to agree, in principle, to the use of NATO forces in a peacemaking role, including the announcement of such a commitment prior to the outbreak of hostilities. Sixth, the United States should take the lead and encourage other NATO members to go beyond current arrangements and significantly increase the interchange among military officers in the Eastern and Central European states and the Soviet successor states. The goal should be to influence the younger generation of officers in these countries to adopt the value system of the Western officer corps.

As with many other organizations in Europe, security organizations are also undergoing profound change. The Warsaw Pact has disappeared, while the CSCE, which represents every nation in Europe plus the United States and Canada, has grown in both membership and functions. Formerly almost dormant, the WEU has been given a potentially far-reaching charter as the defense component of the new European Union and as the future European pillar of the Atlantic Alliance. NATO remains a defensive alliance, but it is adapting by developing new strategies and structures to meet the challenge of a Europe faced with changing security requirements.

Although some argue that NATO is a relic of the Cold War, it remains the single most effective security organization on the European continent. Moreover, it is the only security organization that ties U.S. forces and the U.S. nuclear deterrent to Western Europe. Although NATO may not represent the final answer, it would be a serious mistake for either the United States or Western Europe to jettison such a secure anchor. The United States and Europe must continue to rely on NATO until they are confident that the world has really changed or that more effective organizations are prepared to assume the NATO role.

Safeguarding Vital Interests
Outside Europe

The most recent version of the *National Military Strategy of the United States* posits that in the future, U.S. forces will increasingly be deployed in multilateral operations under the auspices of international security organizations or ad hoc coalitions.[11] The Gulf War provided an example of the new national strategy while at the same time demonstrating U.S. dependence on coalition support. During that war, France and the United Kingdom provided combat forces, several other NATO members provided support forces, and the NATO staff helped coordinate the movement of U.S. forces from Germany to the Persian Gulf. It would have been almost impossible for the United States to mount that operation without significant assistance from allies, both Arab and non-Arab. Considering the future defense cuts already programmed by the Bush and Clinton administrations, the capability of the United States to conduct independent operations at a distance from U.S. shores will likely be even more constrained in the future than in the past.

Given the experience of the Gulf War and assuming that NATO member states see it in their interest, is it possible for NATO to assume a continuing operational role outside of the immediate European area? In answer to this question, there are three possible options for the United States and NATO to consider.

Option 1: Revise the Washington Treaty to permit NATO to conduct out-of-area operations utilizing NATO facilities and infrastructure. The revision would include a weighted voting procedure and an escape clause to allow individual nations to opt out of any particular operation. If successful, this option would permit detailed contingency planning and a rapid response. However, the chances of success for this option are relatively low. It would require the negotiation of a new NATO treaty at a time when Europe is caught up in the throes of ratifying the Maastricht Treaty and establishing the European Union. Western Europe's plate is just too full at the moment. Moreover, many of the NATO members have begun to look inward; it is not at all clear that all of them would consider such a treaty revision in their vital interest. In summary, this option is probably not feasible at this time but may bear reexamination if the Maastricht Treaty and the European Union are successful in producing a Western Europe that is capable of acting decisively in pursuit of its interests.

Option 2: Continue to seek solutions on an ad hoc basis as was done in the Gulf War—when a crisis erupts, fashion a coalition as quickly as possible from those countries with a common perception of their vital interests and a willingness to pursue them. This is the simplest option for the present, but it may involve significant delay before operations can be mounted. Moreover, detailed planning is virtually impossible until the ad hoc coalition comes together.

Option 3: This is a compromise between Options 1 and 2. Under this option, the United States would advance an interpretation of the Washington Treaty that supports a coordinated out-of-area role by NATO members. Although this treaty established security guarantees that apply only within the territory of the member states, it does not specifically prohibit military operations by elements of NATO outside that territory. Under this interpretation, member states could not be required to participate in such an operation, but coordination and contingency planning could take place within the NATO organization, and NATO infrastructure could be used to support the forces.

Clearly, if Option 1 is untenable at this time, Option 3 is the preferred course of action and the one that the United States should pursue. Acceptance of this interpretation would allow planning and coordination to go forward with the NATO structure. However, even if the United States were successful in achieving agreement that the Washington Treaty permits out-of-area operations, a basic challenge remains. No matter what the organizational innovations established, NATO members states will join the United States in an out-of-area operation only if they are convinced that the operation supports their vital interests. The United States must still identify those vital interests and persuade at least some of the other NATO members of the validity and importance of these interests and of the necessity of their participation.

U.S. Military Policy

Force Levels

During the height of the Cold War, the United States kept over 300,000 troops stationed in Europe. This force served not only as a deterrent but also as tangible proof of U.S. commitment to Western Europe. Now that the Soviet threat has been replaced by the threat of instability in Eastern Europe or by threats to interests outside of Europe, what should be the level of U.S. forces stationed in Europe in the future?

Dr. Don Snider of the Center for Strategic and International Studies in Washington analyzed the problem in considerable detail.[12] As a basis for determining force levels, he identified three roles that U.S. forces in Europe must perform in the future.

First, U.S. forces must serve as a forward presence. As expressed in *National Military Strategy,* the primary purpose of forward presence forces in Europe is to provide a visible demonstration on a continuous basis of commitment on the part of the United States to its vital interests in Europe. By reinforcing this commitment, forward presence forces provide increased leverage for other policy instruments. To borrow a term from the game of poker, forward presence forces are the "table stakes" that the United States pays to get into the game. Forward presence forces are not just for show. To be credible, they must be well trained, well equipped, and prepared to function as a force by themselves or as the leading edge of larger crisis-response forces coming from the United States. These forces must also plan and train with other NATO forces to maintain their capability for combined operations.

Second, these forces must fulfill U.S. troop commitments to NATO. As its share in the force structure designed to support the new NATO strategy, the United States is currently committed to providing the following forces: a battalion-sized airborne force to the Immediate Reaction Force, a combat aviation brigade and other support units to the Rapid Reaction Corps, and a two-division corps to the Main Defense Forces. The corps headquarters, corps support forces, and one division of the corps are to become the nucleus of a U.S.-led multinational corps, while the other division will be attached to a German-led multinational corps. U.S. forces will thus be assigned to all major components of the restructured NATO forces. U.S. ships will also be assigned on a rotating basis to NATO's combined naval forces. In addition to these specified forces, the United States provides its share of NATO headquarters and support forces and the necessary U.S. headquarters and support forces.

Third, the U.S. must project crisis-response forces. In addition to forward presence, the ability to respond to regional crises is another of the four components mentioned in *National Military Strategy.* Although crisis-response forces usually come from the United States, forces stationed in Europe as forward presence forces are also available to be used as crisis-response forces in regions close to Europe, provided that they are not engaged in operations in Europe. The movement of a corps from Germany to Saudi Arabia to participate in the Gulf War is the model for forces assigned this role. These crisis-response forces from Europe could be employed unilaterally or as part of a NATO out-of-area force.

To fulfill the three roles, the Bush administration set future European force levels at 150,000. At this level, these forces are fully capable of performing all three of Dr. Snider's roles. A forward presence force of 150,000, which is almost half of the U.S. forces that were forward deployed during the Cold War, provides unimpeachable evidence of this nation's commitment to Europe. The force also fully meets all NATO force requirements. The corps is fully resourced with two full-strength heavy divisions and the full complement of corps support units. The air component consists of ten squadrons of combat fighters along with the necessary support. All together, this represents a formidable combat force, similar in size to the force deployed from Europe to the Gulf War, that is fully capable of performing the crisis-response role.

The Clinton administration, motivated by budgetary and political concerns, however, has talked of reducing the U.S. military presence in Europe below 150,000. If a force level of 150,000 provides a robust U.S. contribution to NATO, what is the smallest force that could perform satisfactorily? Dr. Snider argued that a force of approximately 75,000 would be just enough to fulfill the three NATO roles. To reach this size, the air component would have to be reduced from ten squadrons to six, with the excess squadrons returned to the United States but able to reinforce NATO on short notice. The bulk of the reduction would be accomplished by reducing the two army divisions to two forward-deployed brigades representing about one-third of the combat power of a division. The remaining divisional forces would be stationed in the United States, with sets of equipment prepositioned in Europe. The two division headquarters and the corps headquarters would maintain planning and liaison cells in Europe to work with the other elements of the multinational corps to which they are assigned. Modern simulation and communications technology will allow the headquarters in the United States to participate fully in NATO planning exercises without needing to relocate. Two other full-strength U.S. brigade-sized units would be assigned to the NATO reaction forces—one to the Immediate Reaction Force (a threefold increase in capability over the battalion now assigned) and one to the Rapid Reaction Corps. This force structure, backed up by reinforcing parent units in the United States with which the forward-deployed units would regularly exercise, would provide a creditable demonstration of U.S. commitment. Moreover, U.S. troops would be well represented in NATO's reaction forces—the first forces employed in any NATO missions—thus providing the United States with both leverage and visibility. The smaller force structure would have an impact on the crisis-response role because the forward presence brigades would have to join their parent divisions and other forces in the crisis area. This may be a significant disadvantage if movement time from the United States to the crisis area is greater than that from Europe. However, when the time required to assemble shipping and move the forces in Europe to the ports is considered, the advantage in terms of shorter movement time gained by stationing forces in Europe may be slight.

The optimal size of the U.S. forces that should remain in Europe lies somewhere between 75,000 and 150,000, probably closer to the latter.

It is important now for the United States to begin the detailed analysis, with input from the NATO staff, to determine a final structure. In performing this analysis, the military planners need to take into consideration the longer warning times and search for innovative ways to reduce forces without reducing capability. At the same time, the U.S. contribution should be designed, in part, to reflect those areas in which U.S. forces possess a unique capability or a technology lead, such as armed helicopters, intelligence-gathering platforms, airlift, and automation. However, it is also important that U.S. forces fulfill missions that keep them highly visible to the Europeans. Once a final structure is determined, it should be thoroughly explained to NATO's European members and implemented in a phased, deliberate manner. Every effort should be made to develop bipartisan support in Congress to prevent the annual debate over U.S. troop strength in Europe.

Conventional Arms Control

The CFE Treaty, the most ambitious conventional arms control treaty since World War II, entered into effect in July 1992 after having been ratified by the twenty-one original signatories and the Soviet successor states. The parties to the treaty now have until December 1995 to reach the new limits (also known as "entitlements") set by the treaty. As a part of this ratification, the Soviet successor states agreed among themselves, with some Western assistance, on the distribution of the entitlements formerly belonging to the Soviet Union.[13] As a result of the CFE Treaty, the former members of the Warsaw Pact will destroy over 33,000 treaty-limited weapons. This is in addition to approximately 100,000 other treaty-limited weapons that were either destroyed, converted, or removed from the CFE area prior to November 1990, when the baselines for the signatories were established. This latter figure includes over 58,000 treaty-limited weapons that were shipped beyond the Urals by the Soviets. Representatives of the former Soviet Union have committed to destroy or convert 16,000 of these weapons and to place another 29,500 in inactive storage, but this commitment is a political one and is not a legally binding part of the treaty.[14] The net reduction to NATO forces is negligible, totaling less than 100 weapons.

The breakup of the Warsaw Pact and the dissolution of the Soviet Union subsequent to the signing of the CFE Treaty in November 1990 has done more to reduce the risk of a major war than any arms control agreement. However, the impact of CFE is not insignificant. In addition to reducing absolute numbers of weapons, CFE entitlements among the Eastern European members of the Warsaw Pact have significantly reduced previous disparities among these states, which should improve stability and predictability in their military relationships.[15] Limits imposed on Russian forces west of the Urals eliminate the capability for a sudden attack against the West even if Russia were able to solve the many other problems currently plaguing its forces. Violation of treaty limits by a resurgent Russia could also provide warning, but this warning would vary significantly depending upon whether the equipment west of the Urals were available for rapid reinforcement. The verification measures in the CFE Treaty and the aerial verification agreed under the "Open Skies" agreement signed in March 1992 should improve the clarity surrounding military activities in Eastern and Central Europe and that part of the former Soviet Union west of the Urals.

Although the CFE Treaty has been ratified and has entered into force, the difficult task of destroying the excess treaty-limited weapons remains to be completed. In Russia, the CFE Treaty is highly unpopular among the military, which sees it as an agreement designed to create a balance between the Warsaw Pact and NATO. The Warsaw Pact is now gone but NATO remains, and the conventional balance has now shifted effectively to NATO. Moreover, given all their other problems, Russian military leaders have not placed CFE compliance too high on their list of priorities. Nevertheless, it is important for the United States and the other NATO members to press the former Warsaw Pact states to meet their treaty obligations and to include the equipment moved west of the Urals. Failure to comply with the treaty limits will have an adverse impact on stability in the region and respect for international obligations.

Given the ongoing implementation of CFE, what direction should the United States and NATO take in regards to future conventional arms control and further reductions? First, the United States and other NATO members must continue to coordinate their positions on conventional arms control to insure that NATO speaks with a single voice. NATO should continue to participate, under the aegis of the CSCE, in the CFE follow-on negotiations as a means to include personnel reductions and to clean up loose ends in the basic treaty. It is important to keep the Russians involved in the CFE process to address their legitimate concerns and to maintain pressure on them to complete the equipment destruction. Those members of the CSCE that did not sign the CFE Treaty should be integrated into the treaty with force reductions comparable to those made by the original parties. However, in spite of the success in achieving the first round of conventional arms reductions, pressure for further reductions, other than personnel reductions to match weapons reductions, should be avoided at this time. As Richard Betts argued:

> Arms control could make sense in the Cold War because the relevant alignments by which stable force ratios might be estimated seemed clear and durable. By the same token, limitations on individual nations' forces could be pernicious after the Cold War because there is no logical basis by which to determine the allowed ratios before new cleavages emerge and harden. Military balances that appear neutral under one pattern of alignment or lack of it can instantly become de stabilizing when countries start lining up in a different pattern.[16]

Moreover, attempts to gain further reductions at this time may only serve to convince the Russian General Staff and others that NATO is intent on achieving military hegemony at their expense. This, in turn, could lead to a slowing of the already agreed-upon reductions as the Russian General Staff attempts to reverse the earlier CFE agreements.

Nuclear Weapons in Europe

The numbers of nuclear weapons in the U.S. and formerly Soviet arsenals, both strategic and tactical, will continue to drop through the end of the decade, if presently agreed reductions continue. By 2003, the United States will retain 3,500 strategic nuclear warheads against 3,000 for the Russians and 300 to 400 each for the United Kingdom and France. All of the U.S. and Russian ground-launched tactical nuclear weapons have been removed from Europe, and the number of air-launched nuclear weapons will be reduced significantly. Although these reductions are phenomenal when compared to the many thousands of warheads in service at the height of the Cold War, it will be impossible to put the nuclear genie back in the bottle in the foreseeable future. The continued possibility of nuclear proliferation and the possession of nuclear weapons by nations such as China will ensure that. In the meantime, the U.S. nuclear commitment will continue to be required to support NATO Europe and to ensure that Germany does not feel the requirement to develop nuclear weapons itself. If the European Union is successful in creating a common European defense that combines and subsumes the U.K. and French national nuclear forces, then the United States may be able to finally withdraw the nuclear umbrella.

Conclusion

Europe stands today at a watershed between the old and the new. The Soviet Union and the Warsaw Pact are no more, and Europe is no longer divided. Eastern and Central Europe and the Soviet successor states are in transition to democracy, virtually all of them for the first time in their history. Although the threat of a major war has almost disappeared, the threat of instability is rising. Ethnic conflict and nationalism have reemerged in the East after having been suppressed for so long under communist governments. Yugoslavia has torn itself apart. Significant numbers of refugees have been created so far, with the possibility of more to come. Western Europe is in transition to a potentially new form of political integration beyond the traditional scope of the nation-state. Although this new European Union has the potential to become a superpower, its members have been reluctant so far to assert their power to decisively deal with the instabilities in Eastern Europe.

In spite of all the developments in Europe since 1989, when the Soviet Union began to visibly disintegrate, the United States retains the same vital interests in European security and stability that it had in 1947. Circumstances have changed, but the interests remain the same. In addition to a stable and secure Europe, the United States also requires a strong Europe, one that is willing and capable of sharing the burden of dealing with instabilities that effect their common interests outside of Europe. Although circumstances have changed, they have not yet reached the point where the United States can afford to completely withdraw from Europe. That day may not be far off, but it has not yet arrived. The United States must retain a leadership role to deal with the instabilities that threaten the security of the Eastern and Central European transition and that could threaten Western Europe if allowed to proceed unchecked. At the same time, the United States should work to strengthen the European security organizations with the goal of gradually reducing its role to one of a partner as European integration proceeds. The strongest and the most capable European security organization at this time is NATO, and this should be the central focus of U.S. efforts. Although it may later yield its primacy to other organizations, a strong NATO is essential during this transition to provide a structure for coordinating U.S. and European efforts to handle serious threats to instability. The CSCE and the WEU have potential, but they are currently capable of carrying only a small share of the load.

When the Soviet threat in Europe was real, the rationale for the U.S. role in Europe was clearly understood by most Americans. In the future, U.S. leaders will no longer have that luxury. Instead, they will be faced with a complex situation with the probability of high levels of frustration. Nevertheless, the United States cannot withdraw prematurely; its investment in Europe and its interests there are just too great. The only solution is for the U.S. leadership, both executive and congressional, to recognize this fact and restore a bipartisan approach to European policy and strategy. At the same time, this must be coupled with an effort that explains this policy to U.S. voters and gains their support for what will probably be a frustrating and, at times, demanding and dangerous relationship.

Notes

1. For the purpose of this chapter, *conflict prevention* refers to the use of nonviolent political means such as conciliation and mediation to resolve the sources of a conflict before it moves into a violent stage. *Peacekeeping* refers to the use of military forces to separate parties to a conflict once they have agreed to stop fighting and to accept peacekeeping forces. *Sanctions* are coercive measures that fall short of coming under the rubric of military operations (for example, an economic embargo or freezing of assets) that are designed to force one or more of the parties in a conflict to alter their behavior in some fashion, usually to cease fighting or to withdraw. *Peacemaking* is the ultimate sanction, in which outside military forces are introduced into the conflict to force one or both of the parties to cease their conflict.

2. Robert Gates, "Statement of the Director of Central Intelligence Before the Senate Armed Services Committee," (mimeographed, January 22, 1992), 4.

3. Jonathan Dean and Randall Watson Forsberg, "CFE and Beyond: The Future of Conventional Arms Control," *International Security* 17, no. 1 (1992): 112.

4. Stephen R. Covington, "NATO and Soviet Security reform," *The Washington Quarterly* 14, no. 1 (1991): 47–49.

5. "Into the Void: A Survey of the European Community," *The Economist*, July 11, 1992, p. 28.

6. The Defence Planning Committee of the North Atlantic Council, "Final Communiqué," Brussels, Belgium, May 27, 1992, paragraph 6.

7. Philip Zelikow, "The New Concert of Europe," *Survival* 34, no. 2 (1992): 19.

8. Michael Howard, "The Remaking of Europe," *Survival* 32, no. 2 (1990): 105.

9. The North Atlantic Council, "The Alliance's New Strategic Concept: Press Communiqué S-1(91)85," Rome, November 7, 1991.

10. The new NATO conventional force structure will consist of an Immediate Reaction Force (IRF), numbering about 5,000 troops, deployable anywhere in Europe within seventy-two hours; a Rapid Reaction Corps (RRC) of up to 100,000 multinational troops, headquartered in Germany and capable of being deployed to a crisis within six to ten days; and Main Defense Forces (MDF) of seven multinational corps to be deployed in the event of a high-intensity crisis.

11. *National Military Strategy of the United States* (Washington, D.C.: Government Printing Office, 1992), 8.

12. Don M. Snider, "Appendix A: Residual U.S. Military Forces in Europe," in David M. Abshire, Richard R. Burt, and R. James Woolsey, *The Atlantic Alliance Transformed* (Washington, D.C.: Center for Strategic and International Studies, 1992), 43–67.

13. *Entitlements* are the legally binding maximum future holdings in each weapon category (battle tanks, armored combat vehicles, heavy artillery, combat aircraft, and attack helicopters) allowed to each signatory nation and each of the Soviet successor states.

14. Dean and Forsberg, "CFE and Beyond," 86–88.

15. Ibid., 89.

16. Richard K. Betts, "Systems for Peace or Causes of War? Collective Security, Arms Control, and the New Europe," *International Security* 17, no. 1 (1992): 36.

12

U.S. Military Strategy in the Middle East

Edward B. Atkeson

The Middle East is a region of perennial political and military conflict into which the United States has seemingly been drawn ever deeper. During the era of communist ascendancy in Eastern Europe, the interests of the major powers became so intimately intertwined in the Middle East that it appeared for a while that conflict in the region might become a catalyst for a third world war. That threat has faded, but the region continues to labor under problems of great complexity, just as it remains one of the most heavily armed in the world. Military expenditures in the region in the last decade approached US$1 trillion.[1]

This chapter assesses the military strengths and policies of the principal Middle Eastern powers in the wake of the Gulf War and attempts to forecast how the alignment of power may shift in the latter part of the decade. It also identifies a number of implications for U.S. policy stemming from the forecast. This examination draws on a larger CSIS study that developed an objective methodology for projection of force potential calculations in the future.[2] Like the CSIS study, this review takes a broad geographic approach. Recognizing that a number of trends, such as the proliferation of long-range missiles and the rise of transnational Islamic fundamentalist groups, impact wide areas, this study includes both the subregions of the Persian Gulf and the Levant and the area of primary Arab-Israeli confrontation. The involvement of Syria, Egypt, and Israel in the Persian Gulf conflict of 1991 demonstrated a greater awareness on the part of the countries themselves of new factors and trends that have increased the interdependence of these two subregions.

Perceptions of Threat and Risk

At a high level of aggregation, a visitor to the Middle East may gain the impression that most of the people there yearn for change in the macro-regime under which they live and that they believe that foreign (Western) interests are largely responsible for their plight. The principal symptoms of this emotion are expressions of pan-Arabism, resentment of royal oil wealth, resentment of Zionism, and resentment of historical foreign-imposed borders and foreign influence. The suggestion is strong that most of the people are looking for radical changes in favor of greater autonomy, better distribution of wealth, and greater control of the lands they believe to be their national patrimony.

Conversely, there is a smaller group of more-privileged people who share a wariness about threats they perceive from radicals, revolutionaries, and terrorists. They include the royal houses of Kuwait, Saudi Arabia, and a number of the Persian Gulf sheikdoms and emirates, together with right-wing elements of the Israeli political spectrum. In Saudi Arabia, the view manifests itself largely in xenophobia. In Israel, a perception of continuing threat from hostile neighbors is mixed with a historical and religious sense of mission to seize and hold territories considered to have been designated for the Jewish people by divine authority.

From time to time, charismatic Arab leaders have come to prominence by making strong appeals to the dissatisfied masses and promises for fulfillment of their aspirations. Saddam Hussein attempted to play such a role, striking a responsive chord among many peoples, especially Palestinians, Jordanians, and Yemenis. The Ayatollah Ruhollah Khomeini and his fellow religious leaders in Iran have offered a different type of mass appeal, one based upon a return to Islamic fundamentalist principles. Nominally, Iranian objectives resemble those pursued in Saudi Arabia but with important differences. The Saudis maintain an absolute monarchy and strive for amicable relations with their principal trade partners in the West, whereas the Iranian fundamentalist movement is theocratically oriented, antiroyalist, anti-Zionist, and anti-West. It is also given to much offensive rhetoric.

At a lower level of aggregation, it is apparent that almost every state in the region perceives a threat of some sort from its neighbors. The Arab-Israeli dispute is only the most prominent threat to peace. Mutual antagonism, distrust, and wariness among the states is more the norm than the exception. Almost no scenario for conflict can be discounted, given the poisonous atmosphere under which the states exist.

Although terrorism and guerrilla warfare are endemic to the region, the greatest threats to long-term U.S. interests stem from international military conflict. This does not necessarily mean war between Israel and its Arab neighbors. As dangerous as that can be, one should bear in mind that of nineteen interstate conflicts in the region since 1947, Israel has been a party to less than a third.[3] This analysis focuses on the states that have substantial military potential or a strategic location with a view to assessing their relative strengths and weaknesses.

The calculus of military power is complex. Table 12.1 displays data on military forces and budgets. It also provides rough gauges of the principal states' degree of militarization in terms of ratios of military personnel to civilian populations and defense expenditures to gross domestic product.

As important as the figures in Table 12.1 may be, they can only reflect the broadest dimensions of the security programs of the various countries. For deeper insight into the military concepts and intent behind the figures, we must examine how the leaders of these countries perceive threats to their national security and their strategies and programs for dealing with them. The following analysis is based on interviews and discussions I have conducted with some forty government officials, military leaders, defense intellectuals, and U.S. diplomatic personnel in seven countries in the region, together with documentary research.

Israel

Most Israeli leaders recognize that the collapse of the Soviet Union and the defeat of Iraq have greatly reduced the magnitude of threats to their security. They believe, however, that this is a temporary situation and that matters could deteriorate in the latter part of the decade. They profess concern in the longer term about the large military forces of neighboring countries that could be brought to bear against them in another outbreak of fighting. Some Israeli leaders perceive the number of potential enemies to be increasing, rather than decreasing, as technology and political changes bring additional, more distant Moslem states into the circle of potential adversaries. They believe that long-range missiles and the proliferation of weapons of mass destruction in the Middle East bode ill for Israeli security and that Israel must constantly strive to maintain a qualitative edge and quantitative sufficiency to be able to defeat any combination of possible opponents.

The Israelis have no overt nuclear strategy. The 1981 Israeli raid on the Iraqi nuclear installation at Osirak revealed the limits of Israel's tolerance for regional competition. In June 1992, Major General Herzl Bodinger, commander of the Israeli Air Force (IAF), indicated that his government's position in that respect had not changed.[4]

Press revelations have placed the total Israeli nuclear inventory at about 300 weapons of various types.[5] Opinions differ regarding the purpose of such a large inventory. Prime Minister Yitzhak Rabin has stated that Israel should be prepared to inflict 100 times as much damage on any opponent as it might visit upon Israel.[6] Some analysts believe that there is a mindset among some Israelis that says, "If we are going to be destroyed, we

TABLE 12.1. Demographic and Economic Strength and Indices of Comparative Militarization of Selected Middle East States, 1992.

Country	Population (million)	Armed Forces (thousands)	Military/Civilian Ratio	GDP (billion US$)	Defense Budget (billion US$)	Defense/GDP Ratio
Egypt	55.2	430	1:128	40.9	2.5	.06
Iran	58.9	473	1:125	71.0	5.5[a]	.08
Iraq	18.4	382	1:48	20.0	–	–
Israel	5.1	176	1:29	64.7	7.4	.11
Jordan	4.5	101	1:45	4.7	.5	.11
Saudi Arabia	12.3 (native)	158[b]	1:78[b]	122	14.5	.12
Syria	13.9	408	1:34	15.8	1.2[c]	.09[c]

[a] Author's estimate.
[b] Includes active National Guard.
[c] May not include arms acquisitions.

Source: International Institute for Strategic Studies, The Military Balance 1993–1994 (London: Brassey's for IISS, 1993).

will take all our regional enemies with us."[7] More credible is the possibility that the Israeli stockpile was developed with deterrence of Soviet intervention in the region in mind. Whatever the case, potential opponents cannot disregard the possibility of more draconian intent.

In the area of high-technology conventional weapons, Israel is heavily dependent upon access to U.S. research and development programs. But this dependence does not extend to every case. Israel has a well-developed military-industrial base and can often adapt U.S. concepts to its peculiar circumstances before equivalent systems are available to U.S. forces. Its objective, of course, is to maintain technological superiority over all potential opponents.

Israeli planners believe they can count on a window of probable peace lasting three to six years during which they can prepare for another round of fighting. If a war occurs, they believe that it will be intense and of brief duration. They count on being on the defensive initially because the political leadership may not grant permission for preemptive strikes against developing threats for fear of international criticism.

The planners believe that missiles and unconventional warfare teams may be used by both sides to strike deep into the other's territory. Lieutenant General Ehud Barak, chief of staff of the Israeli Defense Forces (IDF), has cautioned, "We plan for a conventional war, but missiles are our biggest problem, and we should not discount the possibility of an Arab country getting a nuclear capability by the end of the decade."[8]

The planners believe that secret, high-technology weapons will be the key to "befuddlement" of the enemy. These are described as having the "ability to unhinge an enemy offensive at the very outset, within the very first few hours of engagement, and thereby completely upset its original plan."[9] The identity of such a weapon, or weapons, is a matter of some speculation. Whatever form the weapons may take, the achievement of a "befuddling" capability within the three- to six-year window of quiescence is considered essential, regardless of cost.

Also critical for this small country is high-quality intelligence. The Israelis have invested heavily in space technology. The current low-orbiting *Ofek* (Horizon) platform provides a telescope for periodic optical observation. They have also undertaken a more ambitious, half-billion-dollar program dubbed *Amos*. Carrying communications, imaging, and infrared (missile launch warning) packages into geosynchronous orbit, *Amos* will provide continuous coverage of the Middle East.[10]

Former Defense Minister Moshe Arens was enthusiastic about development of the Arrow antiballistic missile (ABM) system for engaging enemy missiles at extended ranges. The weapon might become operational by 1997. If the program is not successful, a fallback may be available. The United States is separately developing a Theater High Altitude Area Defense (THAAD) system, which could be ready around the same time. THAAD would intercept approaching missiles at still greater ranges and higher altitudes than Arrow, virtually eliminating ground damage on Israeli territory from warheads or other falling missile parts.[11]

The Israelis attach particular importance to their air force. Unlike the ground forces, the IAF is a highly professional service, with less reliance on reserves. Of some 700 combat aircraft, all but 100 are believed to be in active service. The total Israeli force potential of its air arm exceeds that of its closest competitor (Syria) by over 40 percent and almost matches that of all of the other Arab forces in this analysis combined.[12] The versatility of the IAF should also be borne in mind. Over 80 percent of Israeli combat aircraft are dual capable (air superiority and ground attack), whereas almost all the aircraft of its potential opponents are optimized for a single mission.

The combination of many of these factors, especially Israel's nuclear weapons monopoly, its access to U.S. research and technology, and its remarkable capability for adapting advanced technology to its own requirements, places Israel in a class by itself, distinct from the surrounding powers. Accordingly, there is no attempt in this review to make a detailed comparison of Israel's forces with those of its actual or potential opponents.

Egypt

Egyptian leaders identify three principal threats to their national security: a lack of regional strategic balance, stemming from the overwhelming preponderance of Israeli military power; a threat of encirclement by Islamic fundamentalists; and internal threats to domestic order. They express no sense of acute threat from Israel but argue that the magnitude of the imbalance between Israel and its neighbors in both the "post-conventional" high-technology and nuclear fields is an unnatural and unhealthy state of affairs. They believe the imbalance to be conducive to ill-considered actions on the part of the Jerusalem leadership, such as the 1982 invasion of Lebanon. Israeli superiority, they argue, tends to facilitate Israeli resort to force for dealing with many types of issues that could be settled by political means among nations entertaining greater respect for their neighbors. Indeed, they interpret the current Arab-Israeli peace negotiations as exactly the sort of discussions that should have been undertaken long ago but were impossible to initiate because of reckless attitudes among some officials in Jerusalem fostered by confidence in Israeli military prowess.

Cairo is also disturbed by the spread of Islamic fundamentalism to Sudan and Algeria. Although Egyptian spokespersons are not keen to discuss internal security problems in great detail, it is apparent that they recognize a vulnerability among the Egyptian people to the march of militant Islam. Extension of the movement to additional countries in the region could trigger reactions in Cairo of unforeseeable dimensions and ramifications.

Cairo looks primarily to the peace process sponsored by the United States and Russia for a solution to most of its difficulties with Israel.

Egyptian leaders are enthusiastic about the concept of a "new world order" and embrace the notion that the age of naked force is over. They are supportive of the arms control proposals made by President George Bush but believe that the large number of Israeli nuclear weapons is the greatest threat to the security of the Middle East and hence should be addressed first. They suggest, somewhat enigmatically, that if an international solution to this problem is not found, Egypt will have to find one on its own.

Egypt possesses a large, obsolescent military establishment. Fifty to 60 percent of the equipment is of Soviet design, much of it twenty or more years old. There is no apparent ambition for expanding the forces, but the Egyptians hope to modernize through gradual transition to Western equipment. The United States provides Egypt with an annual military subsidy of US$1.3 billion, the great bulk of which is used for procurement of U.S. matériel. This sum constitutes about 75 percent of the Egyptian defense budget and some 85 to 90 percent of its military procurement budget.[13] Under a coproduction agreement with the General Dynamics Corporation, Egypt will produce some 550 M-1A1 tanks, gradually assuming a larger share of the manufacturing task.[14]

Iran

Iran is in the grip of a massive arms buildup, but as Kamal Kharrazi, Iranian ambassador to the United Nations, has pointed out, much of it may be justified as prudential measures against a reoccurrence of the beating the country took at the hands of Saddam Hussein in the 1980s.[15] Iran has largely complied with the U.N.-mandated isolation of Iraq; notably, it has retained for its own use some 115 Iraqi combat aircraft flown to the country during the Gulf War to escape destruction by the coalition. Russia is supplying replacement parts, ammunition, and personnel training for many of these planes.[16]

Nevertheless, the government chooses to isolate itself from the peace process in the region. In December 1990, President Ali Rafsanjani called for the establishment of a pan-Islamic army for the annihilation of Israel.[17] In 1992, then director of the Central Intelligence Agency (CIA) Robert Gates identified Iran as a state "hostile to U.S. interests," saying, "Tehran is rebuilding its military strength not only to redress the military imbalance with Iraq, but also to increase its ability to influence and intimidate its gulf neighbors. . . . Its clerical leadership has not abandoned the goal of one day leading the Islamic world and reversing the global dominance of Western culture and technology."[18]

Estimates of Iranian defense spending vary widely. Gates has stated that procurement of foreign weapons will total US$10 billion for the period 1990 to 1994. Although some reports from Iranian émigré sources indicate that total defense spending reached as high as US$19 billion in 1991 and that the figure for 1992 would be US$14.5 billion, a more likely figure appears to be about US$5 to US$6 billion per year.[19]

At sea, Iran apparently seeks to gain control of the Strait of Hormuz.[20] It has contracted with the People's Republic of China (PRC) for delivery of a number of missile boats and with the CIS for two or three Kilo-class attack submarines. Iran already has some 9 to 18 CSS-N-2 Silkworm antiship missiles deployed at three coastal sites that, together with mines, could prove hazardous to ships entering the Persian Gulf. Furthermore, in 1992 Iran expelled all Arab residents of Abu Musa Island, a key territory of the United Arab Emirates (U.A.E.) just west of Hormuz, and has undertaken extensive amphibious exercises in the area. The weeklong exercise "Victory-3" in May 1992 depicted operations to prevent an opponent from entering the Persian Gulf.[21]

Of special significance in Tehran's rearmament program is the apparent intent to acquire 12 TU-22M Backfire bombers. These aircraft could enable Iran to strike any country within a 2,400-mile radius (unrefueled). A low-altitude attack approach to Israel would take no more than an hour from bases in western Iran.

Besides current foreign procurement, Iran's expansion of its arms production base is continuing apace. Tehran claims to seek self-sufficiency in the production of main battle tanks, ballistic missiles, and some types of aircraft by the year 2000. The number of persons employed in the defense industry is expected to expand by a third.[22]

Iran probably has active programs for the development of weapons of mass destruction in all major fields. President Rafsanjani stated in 1988, "We must fully equip ourselves with defensive and offensive chemical, biological and radioactive weapons."[23] Iran demonstrated a chemical warfare capability during the war with Iraq.

In early 1992, there were reports that international smuggling operations were transferring weapons-grade material and some complete nuclear weapons from former Soviet republics to the Middle East. At least two weapons were believed to have reached Iran in 1991. The CIA reportedly investigated the matter but was unable to substantiate the allegations.[24] Whatever the truth, U.S. intelligence does not estimate that Tehran will have a weapon of its own manufacture before 2000.[25]

Iraq

Saddam Hussein is alternatively viewed as a man desirous of raising Arab national consciousness, as leading the people to a destiny that he believes to be their birthright, and as a blatant opportunist and despot. He probably harbors concerns about a hostile Syrian neighbor to the west and a revanchist Iran to the east. For the time being, however, the threat of revisitation by the air offensive mounted by coalition forces must loom large in Iraqi calculations. Certainly, Iraqi leaders have been careful to avoid unnecessarily precipitating another such attack. After lengthy stalling, they have met U.N. minimal demands for cooperation in locating and destroying nuclear research and manufacturing facilities and missile weapons.

Whether, indeed, all facilities and equipment will be revealed cannot at present be determined.

In the opinion of Robert Gates, Iraq probably still has some 200 Scud missiles hidden in the country. In addition, there are reports that Iraq has taken advantage of its relationship with Jordan to sequester certain key matériel in that country and possibly to transship some to Sudan. This may include Scud missiles and nuclear or nuclear production materials.[26] Failing that, he estimated that it would take Iraq several years to restart its nuclear weapons program after the removal of international controls. Iraq might be able to pose either a chemical or a bacteriological threat much sooner.[27]

Iraq emerged from the 1991 war with substantial quantities of equipment intact. It still has more combat aircraft and tanks than Iran and probably as much artillery, and significant reconstruction has taken place at artillery and ammunition plants.[28] It is outclassed in the region only by Israel, Syria, and Egypt. Further, Iraq probably has sufficient manufacturing capability and expertise to maintain its forces for some time, but inevitably the forces will degrade as they are denied critical replacement parts.

The former defense minister, Major General Ali Hassan Al-Najid, has denied any intention to rebuild the armed forces to their previous levels. He told Baghdad's *Al-Thawra* newspaper in January 1992: "[The government decided to build] a small, but powerful, well-maintained and effective army. We have turned a page in determining the size of the army. . . . Iraq needs a strong, though small, army to fulfill two roles. One at the Arab level and to be used in response to an Arab resolution, and one at national level to protect Iraq's borders."[29]

It would seem from these remarks that Baghdad had learned from the Gulf War experience the relative values of quality and quantity in force development. Quantity may still be of value in internal security operations, but high-technology quality appears to be in the ascendancy on the conventional battlefield. If Major General Al-Najid was reporting government views accurately, we may expect a very different distribution of military investment in Baghdad when (and if) import restrictions are lifted.

Jordan

Jordan has ridden a roller coaster since the Gulf War. In the immediate aftermath, Jordan found itself with a hostile Israel to its west, a suspicious Syria to its north, and a Saudi Arabia to its east that was both suspicious and hostile. As one high-ranking Jordanian military official said, threats to Jordan's security originated from "360 degrees of the compass."[30] With time, however, tempers have cooled to such a degree that King Hussein has achieved an agreement for peace with Israel.

The Jordanian leadership insists that its position during the Gulf War was badly misunderstood abroad; Jordan, they assert, was not in sympathy with the Iraqi occupation of Kuwait but hoped, as a friend of both parties, that it could broker a settlement of the dispute that would avoid war and achieve the greatest good for the people of the region. In addition, Jordan has a large Palestinian population and therefore had a domestic constituency to speak for. The government takes pride in representing the people as well as ruling them; hence, the voice of Amman was a voice that echoed some of the more seductive notes of messianic appeal struck by Saddam Hussein.[31] A fundamental element of Jordan's strategy appears now to be the recovery of its erstwhile position in the good graces of the U.S. government.

Suspicions of lax Jordanian controls over transshipment of contraband goods to Iraq and rumors of Iraqi officers training in Jordan have continued to bedevil U.S.-Jordanian relations. King Hussein's gesture of meeting with Iraqi opposition leaders in London in early fall 1992 certainly signaled a determination on his part to close the gap.[32]

Other elements of Jordanian strategy for surviving its period of economic hardship include the reduction of the armed forces, the postponement of modernization plans, and the sale of excess equipment. If the kingdom proceeds with the austerity measures, the capabilities of the Royal Jordanian Armed Forces will become increasingly marginal in a region undergoing significant rearmament. The greatest threat to the country, and to Western interests in it, may not, however, be one of armed attack by a neighboring state. If the Jordanian military were to become sufficiently dispirited under the new circumstances, it might become vulnerable to initiatives from Baghdad promising aid and calling for closer relations. A Jordanian officer corps under Iraqi influence would be troublesome for regional peace.

Saudi Arabia

Saudi Arabia perceives itself to be virtually surrounded by hostile states. Jordanian and Yemeni support of Iraq during the Gulf War were seen as acts of treachery in Riyadh. Saudi suspicions ran high that had Iraq gone on to invade Saudi territory, both Jordan and Yemen would have joined in the attack to settle old scores dating back to the Ottoman period. To the east, Iran is viewed as a powerful potential foe.

The Saudis believe that their traditional practice of "rialpolitik" (the paying off of potential enemies with *rials*, the national currency) failed them in their most extreme test. Strapped for cash in the wake of the Gulf War anyway, they resolved to shift their strategy and seek deterrence of foreign attack primarily through heavy investment in arms rather than bribes. Their objective is the development of a credible deterrent force on the model of the coalition of armies that faced Iraq in October 1990, prior to the U.S. announcement of its intent to build a force capable of ousting the Iraqis from Kuwait.

Although there is little expectation that the Saudis will match the Desert Shield model, their plans are ambitious. They seek armed forces of

200,000 men (regular and national guard) by the year 2000. The ground forces would expand to 90,000 men and 7 divisions. Large orders are being placed abroad for armaments. In addition, they have contracted for construction of new airfields and for a high-technology air defense system to integrate existing forces and installations.[33]

Some analysts are skeptical that the native Saudi population base is large enough to sustain armed forces of 200,000. CIA estimates place the number of native-born, physically fit males between the ages of 15 and 49 in the year 2000 at 1.08 million.[34] A force of 200,000 would require a soldier-to-citizen ratio (counting only native-born Saudis) of 1:40, a figure lower than that of either Israel or Syria but higher than that of most countries of the region (see Table 12.1). Militarization of the populace on this scale would probably require conscription and could pose a disruptive factor in Saudi society. Nevertheless, the goal appears feasible, if distasteful. The Saudi government itself expresses confidence that it can be done by increasing recruitment quotas among the Bedouin tribes and by tapping the increasing pool of urban youths.[35]

Syria

Syrian leaders feel that the country is mired down in a wasteful arms race with Israel because Israel continues to hold Syrian territory. Large armed forces are necessary, they insist, to protect the country from further Israeli aggression and to maintain internal security. Without tight control, they argue, the country could slip into the Islamic fundamentalist orbit, which would thrust its social programs backward in time. If Israel would return the Golan Heights, Syria could turn its energies to commerce and industry and raise the standard of living of its people.[36] Syria cannot compete with Israel on a military plane without allies and the backing of a superpower. Accordingly, it looks to the peace negotiations for justice.

Barring a settlement with Israel, Syrian strategy is to wait for things to change, "even if it takes 100 years." Recovery of the Golan Heights is a matter of national honor, the leaders insist, and nothing can ever make them accept anything less than the entire area. They may suffer many reverses, but they are resolved to recover their territory.[37]

According to one report, President Hafez al-Assad has revised his strategy toward Israel. Rather than seeking "strategic parity," as the government claimed in the 1980s, the goal is now "strategic deterrence" to discourage Israeli attack. The strategy has three components: the upgrading of the armed forces with advanced military equipment; the development of a concept for "long and protracted conflict, unlike previous Arab-Israeli wars" in the event deterrence fails; and emphasis on "strategic depth" as a decisive factor in any large-scale conflict.[38]

As recently as 1992, informed U.S. observers in Damascus believed that the likelihood of another war in the region in the next ten years was higher than 50 percent. The peace discussions have probably attenuated that judgment. However, if a rightist leader were to come to power in Israel and to consolidate Israeli control of the occupied territories, the probability would approach certainty. The chance that the Syrians can be cowed into surrender is very low. Furthermore, the matter of nuclear warfare in the region must be taken seriously.

Reports of funds received by Syria from Kuwait and Saudi Arabia in 1991 for its part in the war with Iraq range from US$700 million to US$2.5 billion. It has been the intention of the Syrian government to spend the money largely on arms acquisitions. Reports have indicated that because of Russian insistence on cash payments, many orders have been placed in doubt, but if Damascus is unable to obtain what it wants from Russia, there are other suppliers to which it might turn.[39]

In the longer term, Syrian initiatives to develop its domestic missile industry could be more important than the purchases from abroad. Reportedly, Syria and Iran have undertaken a joint effort to construct a plant in Syria, with Iranian funding, for the production of Scud-C missiles. North Korea will provide technical support.[40] The project could substantially enhance Syria's capability for massed missile offensives.

Syria's major element of military strength is its large, active land force. Mostly deployed on the Damascus plain facing Israel, the army would require few relocations to mount a massive armored and missile attack on the Israeli-held Golan Heights. Some analysts believe that the Israelis might not receive more than twenty minutes to two hours warning.[41] Syrian artillery is trained and equipped to deliver massed fire and has recently been strengthened through the acquisition of modern Soviet self-propelled howitzers.[42] The Syrian air forces are heavily weighted for air defense but, together with air defense missile forces, they could provide strong cover for such an operation. If the air action could be adequately coordinated with massive missile and air attacks on Israeli airfields, reserve equipment parks, and command and control centers, the Syrians might calculate that such an offensive could score some initial successes.

Syria is a signatory of the Nuclear Non-Proliferation Treaty and thus far has shown no more than marginal proclivity for breaching the agreement. Although some believe that Damascus is seeking nuclear weapons, no observer has suggested that Syria has progressed beyond the research stage.[43] Syria's chemical warfare capability, which includes nerve agents, however, is well developed. As early as 1985, U.S. officials were quoted as saying the Syrians had "the most advanced chemical weapons capability in the Middle East."[44]

Trends in Military Potential

The foregoing discussion has provided an overview of the perceived threats to the security of the principal Middle Eastern states and the strategies and military programs being pursued to deal with those threats. The specific arms acquisition programs are summarized in Table 12.2.

TABLE 12.2. Major Equipment Items on Order by Middle Eastern States

Country	Combat Aircraft	Helicopters	Tanks	Armored Vehicles	Artillery	SAM[a]	SSM[b]
Saudi Arabia	146	102	465	110	—	14 Battery	—
Syria	72	—	700	—	250	?	174
Iran	350	—	500	—	—	2,000	320
Egypt	116	24	550	—	—	—	—
Iraq			—No arms orders on record				

[a] SAM—surface-to-air missles.
[b] SSM—surface-to-surface missiles.
Sources: "MEED Special Report: Defense," *Middle East Economic Digest,* April 26, 1991, pp. 9–16; Stephen Pearlstein, "Patriot Missile Deal Expected with Saudis," *Washington Post,* November 12, 1991, p. C1; Paul Betts and David White, "Saudi Bid for F-15s Shows US Hold over Arms Orders," *Financial Times,* November 6, 1991, p. 1; "Pentagon: No 'Cap' on F-15s for Saudis, but 98 is Enough," *Aerospace Daily,* November 8, 1991, p. 221; and Barbara Opall, "Saudis Explore Additional Buys of AWACS Planes," *Defense News,* September 7–13, 1992, p. 1.

The full impact of these acquisitions on the relative combat power potential of the various countries is a complex calculus. Although the countries are generally knowledgeable about the arms inventories and acquisition programs of their neighbors, interpretation of the intent and possible use of the equipment is more problematical. It must be borne in mind that arms alone do not confront one another; they are but observable elements in the compilation of forces. Nevertheless, when suitably evaluated according to their potential utility on the battlefield and aggregated, arms accumulations can be used to determine rough indices of force combat potential. In juxtaposition with corresponding indices of possible adversaries, the figures yield insights into relative force power. The Analytic Sciences Corporation model TASCFORM (Technique for Assessing Comparative Force Modernization) provides the medium for this analysis.[45]

Two techniques have been employed. In the first, "adjusted weapon system performance" coefficients contained in the model were used to determine aggregate "designated force potentials" (DFP) for the air and land forces of the countries under investigation. Current growth rates were determined from retrospective calculations from a 1991 data point.[46] Projections were then made assuming linear extension of the growth rates. In the second method, changes to the DFP based on anticipated acquisitions, together with certain assumptions regarding delivery dates, yielded vectors indicating likely upper and lower ranges of air and ground force potential in the latter years of the decade. The target year selected in this method was 1996. Some calculations required additional assumptions, first about equivalencies of equipment not indexed in the TASCFORM database and second about probabilities regarding order and shipment quantities in particular arms procurement packages.

These DFPs do not reflect qualitative aspects of a force that are not inherent in the matériel being counted. Leadership skills, integrative and coordinative factors, doctrine, training, and organizational matters are all neutral. Furthermore, the process makes no provision for weapons of mass destruction. Accordingly, it is not useful to address all countries as a single class. As noted above, Israel is a regional superpower and is not to be compared with other states of the region, which are primarily reliant for their military strength upon observable equipment indexed in the database. It should also be noted, however, that if current trends for proliferation of mass destruction weapons and long-range strike systems continue, the outlook could begin to change sometime after 2000.

Figure 12.1 depicts indices of both the present and future (1996) force potential of the major states in the region. From this chart, we quickly see that Iran is likely to undergo the greatest growth in force potential (from an index of roughly 13,000 to somewhere between 25,600 and 31,000). At the same time, Iraq, because of the U.N. arms embargo, appears likely to slip from its current index of over 27,000 to a lower figure—perhaps as low as 23,400. We can conclude that Iraq and Iran are likely to be far more evenly matched toward the close of the decade than they are now.

Designated Force Potential (DFP)

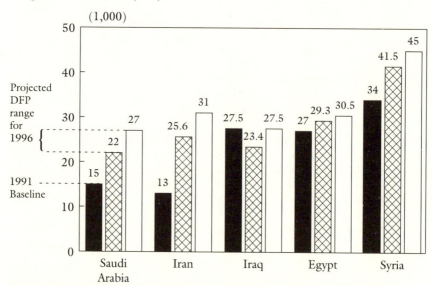

FIGURE 12.1. Middle East "Big Five" 1996: air-ground potential Note that Iraq's DFP projected for 1996 may fall below its current rating.
Source: Edward B. Atkeson, *A Dynamic Net Military Assessment of the Middle East,* Prepared for CSIS (Carlisle Barracks, Pa.: Strategic Studies Institute, U.S. Army War College, January 1993).

Not surprisingly, Iran's prospective growth is disturbing to the Saudis, and we see a corresponding effort on their part to keep abreast. Their programs, however, are not as broad as those of Iran, and the Saudis may actually be overtaken by their Persian competitors in conventional air-ground strength sometime around mid-decade. Nevertheless, Figure 12.1 would lead us to believe that Saudi Arabia may make good on its avowed intention to build a credible defense force against Iraq.

To the extent that they balance residual Iraqi power, both the Iranian and Saudi programs would appear to contribute to the stability of the region. It is not, however, Iran's air-ground combat potential that disturbs U.S. planners. As noted previously, it is the acquisition of submarines and long-range bombers that weighs most heavily in their calculations. These, as well as long-range missiles and, potentially, weapons of mass destruction, would appear most important to Israeli and Saudi planners, too.

This is not to say that the balance of conventional force is likely to diminish in importance at any particular point in the future. The world has lived with weapons of mass destruction in one form or another for a long time. Chemical and nuclear weapons are inventions of the twentieth century, but poisoned wells and salted fields predate biblical records. By and large, these more terrifying weapons have proven to be of greater political than military impact. Not only are they less predictable in their ramifications, but also fear of retaliation has probably played a significant part in deterring their use. Ecological weapons, such as the Iraqi ignition of Kuwaiti oil fields in 1991, often turn out to be primarily of economic importance.

Not among the "big five," and thus not depicted in Figure 12.1, are the Jordanian forces, which merit mention because of their strategic location, bordering Israel, Syria, Iraq, and Saudi Arabia. Although the region as a whole is expected to make significant strides in new armaments over the next few years, Jordan has no means of matching the pace. Without outside assistance, the kingdom is likely to become increasingly vulnerable to pressures from its neighbors—particularly Iraq. Jordan's pariah status since the Gulf War tended to isolate it from any prospect of regional assistance other than from Baghdad. Subsequent events indicate that Israel, in particular, has come to understand that this situation should not be allowed to remain for long.

Implications for U.S. Policy

The foregoing observations have important implications for U.S. policy in the Middle East. The most notable fall into the categories of arms control, security assistance, technology transfer, and U.S. force presence.

Arms Control

In this area, it is important to bear in mind that many aspects of U.S. experience in the field in Europe do not transfer well to the Middle East.

In Europe, there were two blocs and, for most practical purposes, only two major parties to reach agreement. The Middle East, as we have noted, is multipolar, and the polarities are constantly undergoing change. Clearly, a number of the states, or factions within them, have mutually exclusive agendas, particularly with regard to the order in which peace negotiations and arms controls should be addressed.

Some promise may lie in the need to address several problems at once. Arms control can neither await political settlement nor precede it. As Foreign Minister Esmat Abdel Meguid of Egypt remarked with regard to the chemical-nuclear, chicken-or-egg question, "Any progress on banning chemical weapons is tied to the conclusion of a parallel ban on nuclear arms." And as Geoffrey Kemp pointed out with respect to high-technology weapons, "High technology items cannot in the last resort be decoupled from the peace process."[47]

If the United States is to play a useful role in the stabilization and pacification of the region, it must emphasize that no one party can expect to be made completely secure unless all parties are secure. This means that the United States, and possibly other major powers, must be prepared to play a balancing role where imbalances cannot otherwise be eliminated. Most prominent in this area is the matter of nuclear weapons. If nuclear balance is to be achieved, either Israel must surrender its lead or some formula must be devised guaranteeing the other parties in the region a measure of protection against nuclear blackmail.

A fruitful path for investigation in this case may lie in the direction of a substantial reduction in the Israeli nuclear weapons inventory. If the quantity of weapons now held was based to any extent on deterrence of Soviet aggression, there should be an identifiable package that could be disposed of with minimal risk. If Jerusalem wished to temporarily retain a number of these weapons for bargaining purposes with other parties, it could probably still make a significant unilateral cut as a gesture of goodwill and for the good of the entire region.

A balance in conventional weaponry is highly important, but it is less cogent than the need to balance weapons of mass destruction because the ramifications of failure are less drastic. Like the nuclear issue, however, the question of conventional balance does not have to be solved through quantitative or qualitative equivalencies. Guarantees by outside powers may be applied to even the scales. And U.S. guarantees are likely to enjoy greater respect than those of most other powers or supranational organizations.

There is a third area of arms control concern. Certain elements in the "postconventional" realm that cannot be observed are of great importance in determining the true relative military power between states. These include advanced computer technologies and their applications. The matter is of special importance to the security of Israel, which depends heavily upon such systems for maintaining a margin of military superiority over its neighbors.

The United States needs to develop a thorough understanding of the impact of the new technologies as it shapes future arms control regimes. Certain types of reconnaissance, targeting, and weapons control systems may be substantially more important than the numbers of weapons that they support or control.

Security Assistance

Arms sales and grants are not necessarily antithetical to arms control. On the contrary, they can play a definite role in sustaining a balance conducive to peace. The possibility of Iranian acquisition of Backfire bombers, for example, would seem to increase the cogency of Saudi requests for additional fighter aircraft. The key lies in the proper allocation of weapons acquisition authorizations for the development of an overall regime for the region. This is most usefully determined through multilateral negotiations, possibly coupled with the extension of specific security guarantees where imbalances persist.

Another country that would seem to merit some enhancement is Jordan. The kingdom has paid for its identification with Baghdad during the Gulf War, but the price has been extraordinarily high. National revenues fell drastically in connection with the U.N. sanctions against Iraq. Virtually all support from the oil producers ceased, and Jordanian workers were expelled from their former jobs in the Persian Gulf area. If there is danger in the situation today, it would appear to stem more from a continuing Jordanian dependence upon Iraq than from a Jordanian threat to its neighbors. Accordingly, it would seem wise for the United States to play a larger role in stabilizing the position of the Hashemite house in Amman, in part through more extensive security and economic assistance.

The greatest problem in the security assistance and arms sales programs in the Middle East appears to lie in a lack of a coherent, overarching policy for guidance of U.S. program managers. Ideally, the U.S. government, including the legislative branch, would have an internally coordinated concept of specific objectives to apply in discussions among the principal weapons supplier and recipient nations. Although complete closure of such a document, with universal agreement among all parties, may be unrealistic, the process of discussing it might help to identify areas of principal difference and to improve understanding of others' concerns. It would also help the U.S. government to develop its own plan for arms allocations, either through the security assistance program or commercial sale.

Technology Transfer

The United States has agreements with many countries in the Middle East related to sales of military equipment of U.S. design. The closest association is with Israel, amounting to a substantial, if unmeasured, pillar of

Israel's security structure. Unfortunately, allegations have been made that Israel has abused its privileged position, casting some doubt on whether the relationship can continue to be as close as it has been in the past.

Israel is a manufacturer and worldwide exporter of quality military equipment. It is heavily dependent upon the approximately US$2 billion it earns through foreign sales of its arms to underpin its own weapons acquisitions and to support its industrial base. With a close and many-faceted relationship with U.S. research and development activities, the country has an awkward conflict of interest.

There is a clear need for a low-profile, comprehensive review of U.S.-Israeli technology connections, in all their many forms. The partnership is too important to permit a cloud to remain over the process, perhaps endangering benefits currently being realized by both sides. Ideally, such a review would be chartered and conducted on a bilateral basis to ensure that the investigation itself would not become a cause of further suspicion or distrust.

U.S. Force Presence

As has been previously noted, the United States has become a player in the Middle Eastern arena. It has committed a significant measure of its prestige to the quest for peace and has raised the expectations of all parties in the region about its determination to ensure the success of its efforts. Indeed, the United States can take considerable credit for the low level of violence currently prevailing in the region.

But it cannot be expected that a lasting peace can be established exclusively by diplomatic and political means. There are still too many disparate interests that might take advantage of opportunities for short-range gain by illegal means. The peace process will require time to develop and must be undergirded by substantial strength and staying power. A modest U.S. ground force presence in the region would provide a visible statement of U.S. interest and commitment to the achievement of its goals and lend credibility to the overall effort for peace. Apparently former Secretary of State James A. Baker III had these points in mind in August 1992 when he reportedly asked Israel and Syria about stationing U.S. troops on the Golan Heights.[48]

A U.S. force presence on the ground in the Middle East might be used to offset other types of commitments that have not proven useful in settling disputes. Particularly, it might prove reassuring to Israel if that country were to agree to sacrifice some of its territorial holdings in order to gain peace agreements with neighbors. Arabs and Israelis alike will want to ensure that there is no effort by the other side to take undue tactical advantage of any concessions that may be conceived in the peace negotiations. The Golan Heights, the Jordan Valley, and the Sinai Peninsula have all been suggested as possible areas of U.S. troop presence.

There are many ways in which a force presence might be undertaken. The various options could be addressed within the context of the current series of negotiations. Generally speaking, the United States should not station troops in significant numbers in the region on a permanent basis. More desirable would be the rotation of brigade-size organizations for extended exercise periods—perhaps for two to three months at a time. The units could be drawn from Europe, from the United States, or from both. Smaller formations, perhaps of battalion size, might be detached for shorter periods for training with different host country forces. Base areas for the support of such deployments could be designated in a number of different countries—the more, the better. Ideally, the bases would be operated by host government forces to minimize the appearance (and the implications) of a U.S. occupation of the area.

However such a presence is arranged, certain principles should be established to minimize the pitfalls that may be encountered. Some of these might be

- In view of cultural differences and sensitivities, contacts between U.S. troops and local traditional communities should be held to a minimum.
- U.S. troops should not be employed to interdict terrorist activities. Israeli troops are better trained and better psychologically attuned for this type of duty.
- U.S. troops should be deployed in areas between other national forces where all commanders agree to the allocation of space.
- U.S. forces should be deployed in sufficient strength to be capable of defending themselves against partisan groups that do not identify with the peace process.
- Adequate immediate close air support should be ensured.
- U.S. forces should be deployed where they have sufficient space to exercise their operational capabilities and can maintain their skills.
- Sufficient air or sea transport should be maintained in the vicinity of the troops so that they can be quickly relocated to deal with developing threats.
- Adequate provision should be made for rest and recuperation for the troops during their deployment.

A Final Word

The Arab-Israeli peace negotiations have been under way since October 31, 1991. Although substantial progress has been made, the future is translucent at best. Whatever the outcome, there is little assurance that the Middle East will be able to shake its reputation for strife. As has been noted, there are many disputes besides that between Arab and Israeli, and the likelihood remains that political issues, usually defined by the ruling elite, will remain dominant over the long-neglected economic problems that burden the majority. In any event, it would appear that many of the military factors discussed here will remain a principal area of focus.

Paradoxically, although these factors convey mixed messages to differing audiences, they could combine to facilitate the peace process. Israeli military superiority, for example, is reassuring to Tel Aviv and Jerusalem, but it is very disturbing to the Arabs. Threats of nuclear and long-range missile proliferation within the region, however, have the opposite effect. The most hopeful aspect is that these factors could converge to nudge the parties in the direction of political settlement, lest the downsides of each lead to a much more dangerous situation than now exists.

If the peace negotiations were to go into prolonged deadlock or otherwise fail, the world has had plentiful warning from knowledgeable observers that the military focus would be likely to shift increasingly toward proliferation of weapons of mass destruction and the means for their delivery—not only in "radical" states but in moderate ones as well. As an Egyptian defense intellectual commented to me, possibly with tongue in cheek, "Oh, I did not say that *we* would turn to nuclear weapons. I just said that everybody would."

Notes

1. U.S. Arms Control and Disarmament Agency, *World Military Expenditures and Arms Transfers 1989* (Washington, D.C.: Government Printing Office, 1990), table 1.

2. Edward B. Atkeson, *A Dynamic Net Military Assessment of the Middle East,* prepared for CSIS (Carlisle Barracks, Pa.: Strategic Studies Institute, U.S. Army War College, December 1992).

3. Anoushiravan Ehteshami, *Nuclearisation of the Middle East* (London: Brassey's, 1989), 57. Some of the conflicts listed by Ehteshami are not within this study's region of focus. Accordingly, they are not counted.

4. Benny Morris, "Nuclear Peril, Israel's Non-Issue," *New York Times,* June 23, 1992, p. 21.

5. "Israel Under Pressure Over Nuclear Policy," *Financial Times,* October 24, 1991, p. 4.

6. Yitzhak Rabin, remarks to the author, Tel Aviv, April 24, 1991.

7. Ehteshami, *Nuclearisation of the Middle East,* 57.

8. Robert Rudney, "GPALS Tempts Israel to Abandon Offensive Stance," *Armed Forces Journal International* (February 1992): 43.

9. U.S. military attaché, remarks to the author, Tel Aviv, February 3, 1992.

10. Yossi Melman, "Israel's Race Into Space," *Washington Post,* May 17, 1992, p. C4.

11. Barbara Opall, "U.S. Ponders Plan to Lure Israelis Away from Arrow," *Defense News,* August 31–September 6, 1992, p. 1.

12. International Institute of Strategic Studies (IISS), *The Military Balance 1991–1992* (London: Brassey's for IISS, 1991), 108–121.

13. Philip Finnegan, "Egypt Seeks Surplus Gear," *Defense News,* March 9, 1992, p. 1.

14. Christopher F. Foss, "Egypt's Winning Formula," *Jane's Defence Weekly,* December 14, 1991, p. 1181.

15. Andrew Borowiec, "Iranian Defends Arms Buildup, Cites Iraq Threat," *Washington Times*, February 20, 1992, p. A9.

16. Patrick Cockburn, "Russia Helps Iran Equip its Warplanes from Iraq," *Independent* (U.K.), January 13, 1992, p. 1.

17. David Dolan, *Holy War for the Promised Land* (London: Hodder & Stoughton, 1991), 219.

18. R. Jeffrey Smith, "Gates Warns of Iranian Arms Drive," *Washington Post*, March 28, 1992, p. A1.

19. The higher figures are quoted by Tony Banks and James Bruce, "Iran Builds Its Strength," *Jane's Defence Weekly*, February 1, 1992, p. 158. *The Egyptian Gazette*, January 29, 1992, provided "Western analysts" as its source of the US$5 billion figure. Nicholas Protonotarios, economic analyst for IISS, stated that the US$3.2 to US$3.8 billion that appears in IISS's *Military Balance 1991-1992* (105) covers only operations and maintenance costs—not procurement costs.

20. Rowan Scarborough, "China to Boost Iran's Navy," *Washington Times*, April 22, 1992, p. A1.

21. Youssef M. Ibrahim, "Iran is Said to Expel Arabs from Gulf Island," *New York Times*, April 16, 1992, p. A7, and *Foreign Broadcast Information Service— Near East and South Asia* (hereafter *FBIS-NES*) 92-085, May 1, 1992.

22. Banks and Bruce, "Iran Builds Its Strength," p. 158.

23. "Iran's Reach for a Nuclear Sword," *Boston Globe*, November 13, 1991, p. 18.

24. *The European*, May 3, 1992, cited in "Iran Got Soviet Nukes," *Washington Inquirer*, March 15, [*sic*] 1992, p. 1; "A Threat to All," *Jerusalem Post*, January 1, 1992, p. 8; *FBIS-NES* 92-085, May 1, 1992, p. 41; and Martin Sieff, "Kazakh Chief May Not Control Nuclear Arms," *Washington Times*, May 24, 1992, p. A13.

25. Smith, "Gates Warns of Iranian Arms Drive," p. A1.

26. "Jordan Storing Iraqi Nuclear Material," *Jewish Institute of National Security Affairs*, March 1992, p. 8, and Paul Reid, "Finishing Saddam," *Boston Globe*, February 18, 1992, p. 13.

27. Robert Gates interview, *Time*, April 20, 1992, p. 61.

28. "Iraq Has Scuds, Nuke Equipment, CIA's Gates Says," *Washington Times*, March 28, 1992, p. A6.

29. James Bruce, "How Saddam is Picking Up the Pieces a Year After 'Storm,' " *Jane's Defence Weekly*, February 22, 1992, p. 284.

30. General Ehsan Shrdom, chief of staff, Royal Jordanian Air Force, Amman, remarks to the author, January 19, 1992.

31. Comments by Jordanian officials to the author in Amman, January 18, 1992.

32. Elaine Sciolino, "Saddam Hussein Strengthens, US Says," *New York Times*, June 16, 1992, p. A3; "Yemen," *Middle East Reporter Weekly*, May 16, 1992, p. 9; and Shayam Bhatia, "King Hussein Shuns Iraq's Saddam, Further Isolating Him," *Washington Times*, October 6, 1992, p. A10.

33. Youssef M. Ibrahim, "Gulf Nations Said to be Committed to U.S. Alliance," *New York Times*, October 25, 1991, p. A9, and Barbara Starr, "Saudis Pause for Thought," *Jane's Defence Weekly*, December 14, 1992, p. 1175.

34. Cited in the U.S. Naval War College study, "Southwest Asia 2000: Force Structures for a New Century" (Strategy and Campaign Department, Center for Naval Warfare Studies, U.S. Naval War College, Newport, R.I., n.d.), 21-23.

35. Ibrahim, "Gulf Nations Said to Be Committed to US Alliance," p. A9.

36. General Mustafa T'lass, Syrian defense minister, remarks to the author, Damascus, January 20, 1992.

37. U.S. military attaché, remarks to the author, Damascus, January 19, 1992.

38. Yassin Rafaiya, *Ash Sharq Al Awsat* (London), cited in *Middle East Reporter,* May 30, 1992, p. 8.

39. Sid Balman, "Huge Russia-Syria Arms Deal Scrapped," United Press International, Executive News Service, November 5, 1992.

40. Associated Press Wire News, October 2, 1991.

41. Geoffrey Kemp, " 'Solving' the Proliferation Problem in the Middle East," in Aspen Strategy Group, *New Threats* (Lanham, Md.: University Press of America, Inc., 1990), 219.

42. Major General Uri Sagi, chief of IDF Intelligence Branch, in interview with Yed'iot Aharonot, translated and published in *FBIS-NES* 97-078, April 22, 1992, p. 34.

43. For example, see Aharon Levan, "Declawing the Nuclear Beast," *Jerusalem Post,* May 23, 1992, p. 7.

44. Tom Diaz, "Syria Said to Have Offered Chemical Weapons to Iran," *Washington Times,* December 9, 1985, p. A4.

45. The Analytic Sciences Corporation, "Technique for Assessing Comparative Force Modernization" (Arlington, Va., December 20, 1991).

46. The data point for this analysis is the 1991 arms inventories of the selected states as reflected in *The Military Balance 1991–1992,* modified where appropriate.

47. Kemp, " 'Solving' the Proliferation Problem," 203.

48. *Haaretz,* August 18, 1992, cited in "Top of the News," *Washington Times,* August 20, 1992, p. A2.

13

U.S. Military Strategy in East Asia: From Balancing to Bargaining

THOMAS L. MCNAUGHER

What should the United States do with the military forces it now deploys to East Asia?[1] The Bush administration wanted to leave them there for "deterrence purposes" and to assume whatever "potential regional role" might arise.[2] But it left unspecified who was to be deterred (besides North Korea) and what the most likely future role for U.S. forces might be. In fact, the U.S.-Japan security relationship is drifting now that the Soviet threat no longer gives these allies common military purpose. And although many Asians are worried about China's rising power, the United States seems to be more concerned with that country's arms exports and human rights policies than its potentially enormous strategic presence. U.S. forces continue to protect South Korea and Japan, but these seem more like Cold War holdovers than the basis for a long-term strategy toward the region as a whole.

In the background can be heard an array of voices questioning the need for a sustained U.S. military presence across the Pacific. Some are moved by domestic political pressure; U.S. legislators would rather close overseas bases than those at home. Others simply see no need for the United States to provide a regional police force; as one authority recently wrote, "Asian-Pacific dynamics should be unleashed to be dealt with by regional actors."[3] Meanwhile, U.S. defense budgets and forces are shrinking, while many in the region have begun to climb. The United States remains much more powerful than any state in East Asia, but the gap is narrowing and will probably continue to do so.

The sense of drift in U.S. military strategy toward East Asia is surprising, given the region's importance to the United States. It has fought three major wars in this region in the past half century, including both of the Cold War's major "hot" wars, in Korea and Vietnam. The United States has also acquired an enormous economic stake in the region; U.S. dependence on trade has increased, while East Asia has quietly moved into position as its leading regional trading partner (see Table 13.1). U.S. interests are clear: It needs sufficient *stability* in East Asia to encourage further economic growth, continued *access* to the region's markets and technology, and *security* for its investments and assets in the region. Why isn't the strategy equally clear?

One might argue that the region is already satisfying U.S. interests; East Asia's relative stability allows busy U.S. policymakers to grease squeakier wheels in places like Bosnia, the Persian Gulf, and the former Soviet republics. Yet "benign neglect," if that is what accounts for drift, is dangerously short-sighted. For one thing, relatively closed regional economies, notably Japan's, do not satisfy the U.S. interest in access. This gets plenty of attention from policymakers but none from military strategists, despite the fact that continued frustration on the trade front could undermine public support for continued U.S. military engagement, especially in the absence of a compelling threat. For another, the region's current stability masks ongoing changes in power relationships—the Soviet Union's collapse, China's gradual rise, and Japan's search for a wider security role—that could produce instability and conflict down the road.

The region's spectacular economic growth might be expected to promote stability and harmony, as increasingly wealthy states see little to be gained from war that cannot be gained by trade and much to be lost as well. East Asians certainly want to get on with business, and in key cases this has led them to overlook old conflicts in favor of cooperation, trade, and cross-investment. Yet these states are also converting their wealth into larger and more capable military forces in what one commentator has already dubbed "the next great arms race."[4] Regional governments are not counting much on the long-term stabilizing and pacifying effects often attributed to increasing economic interdependence.

TABLE 13.1. Distribution of U.S. Merchandise Trade
(billions of current US$)

	1970	1980	1990
Asia	19.65	140.47	327.40
EU	20.52	96.57	189.89
Western Hemisphere	32.54	152.80	295.04

Source: U.S. Department of Commerce, Bureau of the Census, *Statistical Abstract of the United States* (Washington, D.C.: Government Printing Office, 1980, 1991).

Neither should the United States. Although economic growth is changing East Asia's strategic character, the region remains marked by vast disparities in the distribution of power and power potential, and these, combined with its turbulent history and lack of regional integration, create the bases for conflict despite economic growth. Continued U.S. involvement and leadership will be crucial in helping the region bypass these sources of conflict—if that is possible—both because the U.S. is already enmeshed in East Asia's security structure and because it is the only conceivable balance for key regional powers, notably China. More important, although it may wind up balancing regional powers, the United States is better positioned than any other state to bargain for more cooperative organizations for regional security.

East Asia in a Century of Transition

The "fundamental problem of international relations in the contemporary era," Professor Robert Gilpin wrote, "is the problem of peaceful adjustment to the consequences of the uneven growth of power among states."[5] East Asia's pre–Cold War history certainly bears out this observation. It was an era of truly tectonic changes in regional power relationships. These changes were both caused by, but also caused, repeated wars.

Between 1840 and 1940, the region's largest, oldest, and most powerful state, China, slowly disintegrated under pressure from outsiders as well as the internal decay of its Ch'ing (Qing) dynasty. Britain began this process with the Opium Wars (1838–1842), in which its forces easily defeated China's to "open" the country to freer trade and wider penetration by European imperial powers. There followed other defeats at the hands of outsiders, plus massive internal unrest; the Taiping rebellion (1850–1864), for example, is thought to have cost over 20 million lives. Although the last Ch'ing emperor did not formally abdicate until 1911, the dynasty had by then long since lost its grip on much of the country and its surrounding vassal states. Not until the Communists won China's civil war in 1949 was the country to have coherent political leadership.

While China fell, Japan rose. Isolated under the Tokugawa after 1640, Japan was forcibly "opened" by U.S. Commodore Matthew C. Perry in 1853. With the Meiji Restoration in 1867, Japan chose to meet Western intruders by aping their industrialization; given Japan's lack of natural resources, industrialization almost inevitably forced it to ape Western imperialism as well in an effort to secure resources to fuel its booming economy. Japan thus roared onto the East Asian scene in a path scarred by war. It defeated China in 1894 to "free" Korea from Chinese suzerainty and then defeated Russia in 1904 and 1905 to further secure its hold on Korea, finally making both Korea and Formosa (Taiwan) colonies in 1910. As Britain's ally, Japan gained from World War I without firing a shot, collecting Germany's imperial possessions in the Far East, including its position in China. In 1931, Japan's army, acting on its own authority, invaded Manchuria to set up the state of Manchukuo, and in 1937, Japan invaded the rest of China, securing the coastal areas. In 1941, Japan turned its forces south toward Indochina and Indonesia's vital oil fields, but in attacking the United States to protect its increasingly long and exposed flank, it provoked World War II in the Pacific and brought disaster on itself.

Although China and Japan were the major characters in this drama, other states had crucial supporting roles. Russia did not really arrive in the Far East until 1860 and even then faced the daunting logistical problems of supporting forces that far from Moscow. The weakness of its position in the Far East and the iciness of its ports gave Russia powerful geostrategic interests in Korea, and this brought it into conflict first with China but above all with Japan. Although Japan decisively defeated Russia in 1905, this competition ended only in 1917, when revolution took Russia temporarily out of international action. Russia's (or rather, the Soviet Union's) late entry into the Pacific war, and especially its occupation of northern Korea near the end of World War II, are easily interpreted in historical terms—as is the latent hostility that marks Russo-Japanese relations even today.[6]

Despite its obvious access to the Pacific and the presence of U.S. traders in the Far East from colonial times, the United States was not a significant military power in the region until Japan's attack on Pearl Harbor. To be sure, it took the Philippines from Spain in 1898 and established bases there like a good imperial power. It maintained small forces in China as well. And it intervened diplomatically, sometimes crucially, in the region's conflicts, helping to bring the Russo-Japanese War to conclusion, for example. Finally, with its Washington Conference (1920–1923), the United States sought to control a budding naval arms race and to "internationalize" and thus stabilize the situation in China.[7] Yet when the Washington Conference system broke down and Japan's army charged into Manchuria and then China proper, it became painfully obvious that the United States had little interest in fielding military forces capable of competing with Japan in the western Pacific. Under these circumstances, U.S. bases in the Philippines were more liability than asset.[8]

Of the other imperial powers involved in the Far East in this era, the United Kingdom was far and away the most important. This stemmed partly from its position as the dominant imperial power in China. But it stemmed as well from the success of the Anglo-Japanese alliance (1902–1922) in calming Japan's increasing resentment of what its people perceived, rightly or wrongly, as racial slights by the Western states. Particularly galling to Japan were U.S. laws passed in 1924 that banned Japanese immigration. The Japanese also increasingly resented the Washington Conference naval treaty, which left their navy smaller than the United Kingdom's or France's. The Anglo-Japanese alliance tempered Japan's latent paranoia by making Japan an equal member of the imperialist "club." But the alliance was allowed to lapse in 1922, as the Washington Conference system took shape. When the latter system collapsed later in the decade, unfortunately, Japan was left completely alone to deal with perceived racial slights, its growing dependence on overseas resources, and its militaristic subculture.[9] Ultimately, Japan's military leaders took control and drove the country toward World War II and disaster.

East Asia in the Cold War

Japan's attack on Pearl Harbor brought the United States into a region that the Europeans, exhausted by World War I and the Depression, had vacated a decade earlier. Having defeated Japan, the United States stayed on to counter the Sino-Soviet threat, ultimately allying with its former enemy and maintaining a strong military posture in the region for the first peacetime period in its history. For forty years, East Asia was part of a global system of alliances and bilateral relationships designed to balance Soviet power.

That balance helped stabilize the region after a century of conflict. Scholars generally attribute the "long peace" of the Cold War to structural and military features of the Cold War system. A bipolar international system proved to be a relatively easy to manage in comparison to the complex bargaining that marked Europe's classical balance of power. And the presence of nuclear weapons substantially raised the risks of adventurism. Some add that the lack of interdependence between superpower blocs gave them less to argue about and hence fewer grounds for conflict.[10]

These arguments apply more to Europe than to Asia, which saw both the Korean and Vietnam Wars, innumerable internal and border conflicts, and a good deal of political fluidity, including China's momentous break with the Soviet Union. Still, East Asia was certainly more stable during the Cold War than it had been in the previous century, and this was due largely to the structural features noted above. The U.S. military overshadowed power disparities at the regional level, muting in particular the effects of China's growing power, which remained comparatively small. The Cold War also helped cement the U.S.-Japan relationship, which enveloped Japan's military power in a U.S. embrace. The presence of nuclear weapons deterred war among the great powers. The United States and China fought directly in the Korean War, for example, but as the Soviet Union and China developed nuclear arsenals, the Korean standoff acquired nuclear risks that gave the United States, the Soviet Union, and China increasingly powerful incentives to keep their respective Korean allies in check. Arguably, the U.S. nuclear arsenal also helped deter China from invading Taiwan.

Stability did not produce harmony, however. East Asia never sprouted the multilateral economic and security organizations that took root in Europe during the Cold War. Whereas in Europe, the United States confronted the Soviets through the Atlantic Alliance, in East Asia, it relied on "multiple bilateral" ties to allies like Japan, South Korea, and Taiwan. Whereas over the course of the Cold War, the Western European states became virtually a "security community"—a group of states among which war is no longer thinkable—in East Asia, memories of Japan's recent aggression, not to mention other lingering rivalries, hampered security cooperation.

The U.S.-Japan relationship did little to overcome regional bitterness toward and suspicion of Japan. To the contrary, in the wake of their defeat, the Japanese turned inward, focusing on economic development and resisting U.S. entreaties to contribute more forces to the anti-Soviet alliance. They also resisted apologizing for their behavior before and during the war. Perhaps because the Soviet threat was never as pressing in Northeast Asia as it was in Europe, the United States slowly relaxed its pressure on Japan to raise its defense spending; in Europe, by contrast, the sheer size of the Soviet threat forced NATO to face the issue of German rearmament in the 1950s. In Asia, the United States handled security, while Japan tended its economy.

Geographical differences hampered alliance formation. Although Western Europe confronted a coherent Soviet threat across the inter-German border that encouraged a unified military response, in Asia the threat was dispersed and disparate in form—the United States and Japan confronted primarily a Soviet naval threat emanating from the Sea of Okhostk, whereas South Korea confronted a ground force threat from North Korea. Given that these two countries were hardly on speaking terms, the U.S. developed separate command arrangements in each case.

In Southeast Asia, the threat was more dispersed still; Singapore worried mostly about the Soviet threat, while Indonesia worried more about China. In addition, security cooperation was hampered by geographical differences among potential allies—the Association of Southeast Asian Nations (ASEAN) includes Indonesia, the world's fourth largest state, and Singapore, among the world's smallest states. Differences like these did not prevent cooperation on issues like Cambodia, but they did make the ASEAN states relatively timid about formalizing security relationships among themselves, let alone with larger and more powerful Asian states such as Japan and China.[11]

East Asia in the Global Economy

Amidst the Cold War's relative stability and within the free-trade framework organized and supported by the United States, East Asian economies boomed in waves starting with Japan, moving next to the four "little dragons" (South Korea, Taiwan, Hong Kong, and Singapore), and moving most recently to China, Thailand, Malaysia, and Indonesia. With the exception of Japan, much of this growth was based on trade and the investment of international firms, making East Asia an active participant in the global economy. This raises the crucial question of whether, now that the Cold War is over, the sinews of economic interaction will encourage the same kind of stability that this region saw during the Cold War. Or will the end of the Cold War's overarching bipolar structure give rise to *dis*integrative forces likely to lead to conflict?[12]

Although the Cold War ended too recently to allow these questions to be answered definitively, a survey of the present situation suggests that optimism is unwarranted; this region remains relatively unintegrated *as a region*, while disparities of economic power create an underlying fear of domination.

The Most Global of Regions

Scholars generally agree that a crucial underlying cause of economic growth in East Asia was the emergence of strong states.[13] Japan was the first of these, and the states that followed often emulated Japan in protecting new industries. They remained much more open than Japan to foreign investment, but here, too, strong states played a role, both in attracting multinational firms and in negotiating shrewdly with them to extract the right kind of economic benefits.[14] Stability *within* states thus played an important role in spawning economic growth.

The role of stability *among* states in generating growth is less clear. On the one hand, growth occurred within the overarching stability of the Cold War and with the help of a relatively stable U.S.-sponsored free-trade regime. On the other hand, however, regional *in*stability clearly contributed to growth in key cases. Japan's initial burst of postwar economic growth was fueled by the need to produce supplies for U.N. forces in Korea. The Vietnam War provided an infusion of U.S. dollars and also an impetus for economic growth among Southeast Asian states. The evidence is mixed at best.

One point stands out, however; states in this region grew less by trading with each other than by trading with, and accepting investment from, the world in general and the United States in particular. Trade among the ASEAN states, for example, has rarely risen above 20 percent, considerably less than the trade these states enjoy with the United States. Japan trades far more with the United States than it does with the states of Southeast Asia. Although Japanese private investment and government aid to these states have been high, U.S. private investment in Southeast Asia has also been high. Intraregional trade in East Asia grew throughout the 1980s but no more than would have been expected, given the relatively fast growth of its states compared with other regions around the world. Trans-Pacific trade and investment links remained strong throughout the decade.[15]

Thus far, in short, East Asia's economic boom has not produced regional integration. These states are less interdependent with each other than with the globe and especially with the United States. If there is an emerging economic "regionalism," it is trans-Pacific and not specifically East Asian. To the extent that interdependence mutes conflict, one would not expect to find it working powerfully among the states of East Asia.

China's Quest for Stability

China's phenomenal economic growth over the past few years, combined
with relatively slow growth in Europe and the Western Hemisphere, has
produced an increase in intraregional trade in East Asia. In general, East
Asians are happy to reap the benefits of trade with and investment in
China. Yet they wonder what they will ultimately produce—an engine for
continuing growth or the region's next dominant power, potentially much
more powerful than even Japan?

For the time being, at any rate, it is clear that China's desire to grow,
which dates from Mao's death in 1976, has also made it, in the words of
Dwight H. Perkins, "a force for stability, except vis-à-vis Vietnam, and
perhaps, in a very different way, Taiwan. . . . The Chinese leadership's
desire for a peaceful environment in which to build a strong and prosperous nation has led to efforts to reduce tensions on the Korean peninsula
and elsewhere in Asia."[16]

What no one knows, alas, is whether China's encouraging attitude is
the product of interdependence or simply independence. Beijing recognizes that it has fallen behind its neighbors, especially the overseas Chinese
community. It thus has a powerful interest in tapping into their advanced
potential and in calming longstanding fears among Southeast Asian nations of their resident Chinese, who were seen in the early years of the
Cold War as fifth columns for advancing Beijing's revolutionary interests.
Chinese officials have been at pains to reassure neighbors that "China does
not, and will not, impose hegemony and power politics on others and
will not threaten or bully anyone."[17]

Evidently, these statements do not apply to Vietnam, however, against
which China has used naval power to secure disputed islands in the South
China Sea. Other Southeast Asian states also lay claim to some of these
islands and wonder whether China will not act more aggressively toward
them as its economy grows. After several years of relative decline, China's
defense budget has begun to rise, and part of the increase has gone to
purchase projection forces—long-range aircraft, refueling aircraft, and the
beginnings of a blue-water navy.[18] These activities leave Southeast Asians
wary of China's long-term intentions and help account for rising defense
budgets among these states. And even Japan has reportedly warned
Moscow not to upset the East Asian balance of power in its sales of arms
and arms production technologies to China.[19] The problem is less China's
intentions, which remain unclear, than the "objective" threat posed by
the expanding economy and interests of this huge, centrally located
country.

China's future is uncertain. Uneven economic growth and continuing
political inflexibility could produce disintegration. Or a capitalist, increasingly developed China could be too decentralized to wield economic and
military power aggressively. But another plausible future is one in which
China retains coherence as it exploits the full potential of its size and
resources. In that case, China would, over several decades, become the

region's dominant economy, in size if not in relative sophistication. This implies a China that is increasingly independent of its neighbors and armed with the potential to exercise the hegemonic control inherent in that situation. This need not imply military domination or even the ruthless exercise of power, any more than the relationship between the United States and Canada is marked by such features. But it does imply a historic shift from a U.S.-Japan–centered economy to one increasingly centered around China—the "uneven growth of power among states" that, as Robert Gilpin warned, has created conflict in the past.[20]

Japan, East Asia, and the United States

At the moment, questions about China's future apply to Japan's present; Japan is less interdependent with than independent of its neighbors. Japan's GNP is one or two orders of magnitude larger than those of its neighbors; even per capita GNP is three or more times higher than all save Singapore (see Table 13.2). Although Japanese imports from Pacific Rim states grew sharply over the 1980s, trade with Japan is far more valuable to these states than it is to Japan (see Table 13.3)—a point that grows considerably stronger if we remember that Japan depends substantially less on trade than any other East Asian state (see Table 13.4).

It is difficult to find evidence of Japanese efforts to use the power that flows from this one-sided situation for its own ends. Japanese policymakers are well aware of regional sensitivities to Japan's behavior and are reluctant to exercise available power lest it provoke a response that would run counter to Japan's regional interests. Tokyo also realizes that, again for historical reasons, its freedom of diplomatic and economic action in East Asia depends importantly on the health of its relationship with the United States.[21] Thus, history reinforces its interdependence with the United States as well as its reluctance to move outside the U.S. security embrace

TABLE 13.2. East Asian GNPs, 1991

	GNP (billions of US$)	GNP per capita (US$)
Japan	3,337	26,930
United States	5,620	22,240
China	425	370
Hong Kong	78	13,430
South Korea	274	6,330
Indonesia	111	610
Malaysia	46	2,520
Philippines	46	730
Singapore	40	14,210
Thailand	90	1,570

Source: World Bank, *World Development Report 1993: Investing in Health* (New York: Oxford University Press for the World Bank, 1993), 238–239.

TABLE 13.3. Relative Dependence on Trade, 1992

Japan's Trading Partners	Tradeᵃ with Japan as a Percent of the Trading Partner's Total Trade	Trade with Japan as a Percent of Japan's Total Trade
United States	15	26
China	13	5
South Korea	21	5
Hong Kong	12	4
Taiwan	20	5
Indonesia	32	3
Malaysia	19	3
Philippines	21	1
Singapore	13	3
Thailand	23	3
ASEAN	20	13

ᵃImports plus exports, merchandise trade.

Sources: International Monetary Fund, *Direction of Trade Statistics, June 1993* (Washington, D.C.: International Monetary Fund, 1993); and *Information Division, Coordination Council for North American Affairs*, "Economic Statistics of the Republic of China on Taiwan for the Year 1992," Washington, D.C., February 1993.

TABLE 13.4. Total Merchandise Trade as a Percent of GNP, 1991

United States	17
Japan	16
China	40
South Korea	50
Hong Kong	200
Taiwan	77
Indonesia	45
Malaysia	157
Philippines	50
Singapore	277
Thailand	70

Sources: International Monetary Fund, *Direction of Trade Statistics, June 1993* (Washington, D.C.: International Monetary Fund, 1993), 2–3; World Bank, *World Development Report 1993: Investing in Health* (New York: Oxford University Press for the World Bank, 1993), 238–239; International Monetary Fund, *International Financial Statistics, July 1993* (Washington, D.C.: International Monetary Fund, 1993), 62–63 [for Taiwan trade data]; and Council for Economic Planning and Development, Republic of China, *Taiwan Statistical Data Book 1992* (July 1992), 1 [for Taiwan 1991 GNP].

established during the Cold War. This means that the end of the Cold War does not eliminate the basis for the U.S.-Japan security relationship, at least from the Japanese side. But it also means that Japan's relative quiescence in East Asia may have less to do with economics than with history.

In truth, Japan's interdependence is with the United States, not its neighbors. This is hardly "balanced" interdependence, to be sure; it is marked by massive imbalances in trade and cross-investment that breed an especially divisive brand of frustration in the United States. And neither is the interdependence purely economic; security considerations still hold them together, although perhaps more weakly now that they no longer face the Soviet threat. Still, no interdependence is likely to be pure and balanced, and few that exist today are as complex and interwoven as the U.S.-Japan economic relationship, which thus remains a useful case study of the effects of interdependence.

What we find is a two-edged sword; interdependence is in this case a source of benefit but also a source of conflict. Unquestionably, for example, U.S.-Japanese trade benefits both societies, notwithstanding imbalances. Billions of dollars' worth of exports flowing in both directions add to each country's economic growth, its total employment, and the well-being of its consumers. But although trade is always beneficial in general, it is always painful in particular to those whose jobs, industries, and communities are threatened by foreign competition, and this makes it politically controversial.[22] And with largely similar exports, the United States and Japan are guaranteed to compete across a wide range of products, whatever the overall trade balance.[23]

Much of this trade involves technology-intensive products, as befits two technologically developed societies. But this adds a layer of controversy to the relationship, since high-technology industries are seen to have special national welfare and security benefits.[24] Unless or until the United States and Japan operate virtually as a unit, U.S. reliance on Japan for weapons components will remain controversial—a logic that applies to Europe as well. And the loss of market share in technology-intensive commercial sectors will probably always raise concern in some quarters about "de-industrialization" or a stunted "technology trajectory."[25] A more balanced relationship in the high-technology realm would unquestionably quiet these concerns but probably not eliminate them.

As with trade, U.S.-Japanese cross-investment generates benefits and strengths but also conflict. Without the willingness of foreign countries, Japan included, to finance its federal deficits, the United States could not have financed the consumption binge that began in the early 1980s and continues despite efforts to balance the federal budget. Cross-investment creates jobs and incomes and helps transfer technology. Each society acquires an interest in the other's economic success, and within each society new groups—workers at Japanese-owned factories in the United States, for example—join exporters in supporting free trade and sustained good relations. Overall, it becomes increasingly expensive and politically difficult to unravel the relationship; as Robert Jervis has written: "Direct foreign investment is greater [today] and . . . many firms, even if they are not formally multinational, have important international ties. It would be harder for states and firms to arrange for substitutes if conflict or war severed these financial ties than would be the case if it were only goods that were being exchanged."[26]

Yet cross-investment breeds resentment and irritation. This stems partly from the presence of "foreign" plants and managers on "home" territory but more importantly from the perception that investment creates political power. Whereas to some, Japan's U.S. investments give it an interest in the health of the U.S. economy, to others, they give Japan the means to "strangle the U.S. economy by cutting off investments or purchases of Treasury bonds."[27] In part, the acrimony of the latter position stems from Japan's marked reluctance to accept foreign investments nearly comparable to its own overseas investments, which can plausibly be seen as part of a strategy to take technology from the world without giving any back. But at some size, even more balanced cross-investment will create what each state's citizens may perceive as a disturbing degree of political cross-penetration.[28, 29]

Meanwhile, global financial transactions do, in fact, force nations to share control over such vital economic tools as interest rates, exchange rates, and money supply. Treasury Secretary Nicholas Brady attributed the 1987 U.S. stock market crash to a Japanese decision to dump U.S. government bonds—"a worry by the Japanese about U.S. currency."[30] But the problem is hardly confined to the U.S.-Japan relationship. Ten years ago, the French could blame Paris for high interest rates. In the recent crisis over Europe's "exchange rate mechanism" (ERM), they could blame Germany's central bank or more broadly the politics of German unification.

Interdependence thus creates grounds for conflict between states but also creates forces that encourage amicable resolution. The balance here is crucial but difficult to assess from the U.S.-Japan relationship, given its special economic and political features. Even Japan's harshest critics wish to avoid a break in the relationship; the issues are merely how aggressively the United States should pressure Japan for greater openness and which steps it should take to revitalize its own economy so as to compete with Japan more effectively.[31] Nonetheless, the sheer size and uniformly apprehensive tone of the literature on the U.S.-Japan relationship suggests that no one assumes ineluctable movement toward greater integration. Even those who are convinced that Japan is changing wonder if change will come quickly enough to avert a collision on trade and investment issues. The collision would be driven less by policymakers than by citizens in each country. Although even "Japan-bashers" regard it as undesirable, a competitive run-up of nationalisms in each country remains plausible.

Such a run-up is probably unavoidable, of course, if U.S. critics are right in suggesting that Japan is exploiting global trends—and perhaps a slumbering, consumption-happy United States—for its own ends.[32] This image of Japan is harder to sustain in the midst of its current recession; this is hardly the "machine" critics often suggest. Significantly, an upturn in Japan's economic fortunes will produce gains for the United States as well and will also actually reduce the U.S.-Japan trade imbalance, since a return of consumer confidence in Japan will lead to increasing imports of U.S. products. Both facts will undermine the image of U.S.-Japan economic competition as a zero-sum game.

Still, it is remarkably difficult to distinguish a Japan out for power from a Japan that is simply competing very successfully against a United States that suffers (but may slowly be recovering) from self-inflicted economic wounds. It is equally difficult to distinguish a United States that is being exploited from one that is having trouble adjusting to the inevitable erosion of the economic position it enjoyed after World War II. No one denies inequalities in Japan's economic relations. But for some, these spring from historical, cultural, and institutional sources that are slowly changing, whereas for others history and culture merely add depth and resilience to Japan's contemporary strategy.

The fact of inequality remains; for whatever reason, Japan has protected itself better than any other industrialized state from the inroads of globalizing trends while exploiting them to its own relative advantage. To some extent, Japan has moved in recent years toward greater openness, but less in response to economic forces than in response to outside pressure. Such interdependence as there is in the U.S.-Japan relationship, stemming from history as well as economic ties, gives the United States far more economic and political leverage over Japan than any other country. This suggests that if U.S. policymakers want to sustain and deepen the U.S.-Japan relationship, they have the policy tools to do so—so long as they remain engaged.

The Foundations of U.S. Military Strategy

In this brief survey of East Asia's past and present, I have suggested a continuing need for U.S. engagement if the United States wishes to promote stability and openness. Part of the reason arises out of the past; Japan's neighbors still eye it suspiciously, because of its economic power and obvious military potential. The U.S. allays these concerns by mediating between Japan and its neighbors. An abrupt end to the U.S.-Japan security relationship could create, in the words of former Singaporan Prime Minister Lee Kuan Yew, "a disastrously unstable state of affairs."[33]

The U.S.-Japan security relationship is grounded in the present as well as the past, however. In the absence of the U.S. nuclear umbrella, Japan and South Korea would both feel pressured to obtain nuclear weapons. Indeed, North Korea's purported nuclear program, combined with tests in May 1993 of a missile capable of reaching Japan, have already stirred the nuclear debate in Tokyo.[34] Such events could prompt a nuclear arms race involving China and Russia as well as Japan and Korea and would serve neither U.S. nor regional interests. As difficult as the relationship may be to manage, it makes more sense to sustain and deepen the U.S.-Japan partnership than it does to end it slowly.

Meanwhile, an important future U.S. role stems from the massive disparities in the distribution of power that mark this region's basic structure. Economic growth has clearly produced an interest in stability. But it also has produced both economic power and the wherewithal to create military power. In a region in which power and power potential are skewed heavily toward two nations—Japan and China—it simply is not clear that East Asia can achieve interdependence rather than a series of unhappy dependencies.

At the moment, Japan remains far and away the dominant economic power in the region, but for special reasons its power is already balanced by the United States. The more pressing concern is China, which could emerge, in the long run, as a global superpower as well as the dominant power in East Asia. A Chinese-dominated East Asia is not something the United States should automatically oppose; it may be an open region with which the United States can cooperate. But the transition from Japanese to Chinese hegemony could produce instability and conflict, as such transitions have done in the past. The steady emergence of a powerful China could renew suspicions around Southeast Asia of economically powerful Chinese minorities, another source of past conflict. Given China's size and potential, the United States stands as the only power capable of providing a regional balance should this country continue to grow.

Surely these conclusions constitute a powerful argument for long-term U.S. military as well as economic engagement in East Asia. In this way, the United States can balance local powers with the potential to vastly overshadow their regional neighbors, creating a structure of power likely to enhance the cooperative and stabilizing incentives imbedded in the region's burgeoning economic growth. Meanwhile, continuing U.S. engagement enhances the nation's ability to encourage greater economic openness, especially among the region's major powers, whether this be Japan or, in the long run, China. The most feasible and beneficial form of interdependence is one that spans the Pacific.

Such a strategy may engage the United States in balancing Chinese power, providing the region with a military balance it is unable to provide for itself. At worst, China and the United States may be pitted against each other, competing both militarily and economically. Yet within the overarching security framework created by its continuing engagement, the United States should seek to test arguments that economic growth and interdependence foster incentives to cooperate. Precisely because it is so powerful, the United States is better positioned than regional powers to encourage or coax China and its neighbors into cooperative engagement. How it does so will depend principally on its policies toward Japan and China, the region's major powers, and with Korea, the historical focus of their competition and thus perhaps a focal point for generating future cooperation.

The United States and Japan

The historical reasons for continuing the U.S.-Japan security relationship have to do with Japan's domestic politics as well as wariness between Japan and its neighbors. By assuring Japan's access to raw materials and by allowing the Japanese largely to avoid dealing seriously with their own military forces, U.S. policy has also buffered the Japanese from two central problems that drove them toward war in the 1930s. Although Japan maintains reasonably large and very sophisticated "self-defense" forces, they remain "legal but unconstitutional."[35] Because security politics in Japan have largely to do with the U.S.-Japan relationship rather than the government's relationship with its self-defense forces, the basic institutions of civil-military relations in Japan remain embryonic. A break in the relationship would thus force the Japanese to confront issues they have happily avoided for nearly half a century.

Although these historical rationales discourage an abrupt break in the U.S.-Japan relationship, they provide no guidance for the future. Should the United States support Japan's gradual emergence as a "normal" state, with military and diplomatic resources commensurate with its enormous economic clout? Or should the United States seek to bind itself and Japan more closely into a "corporate" whole that cooperates in the security area and perhaps in the economic realm as well?[36] And if the second option makes more sense, what is the strategic basis for the relationship now that the Soviet threat has disappeared?

The second option does indeed make more sense. Important strategic rationales for the U.S.-Japan security relationship did not disappear with the end of the Cold War. The first of these has to do with the continuing importance of the U.S. nuclear umbrella to Japan's security, as discussed earlier. Although during the Cold War, the issue of "extended deterrence" was debated in Europe more than in Asia, with the Cold War over, North Korea seems to be shifting the debate to Asia and especially to Japan. It remains to be seen whether Russia and China engage in nuclear arms control or the opposite; significantly, the Russians have already begun to express vague apprehensions about "the shift in power between them [and China] as a result of Chinese economic growth."[37] Former Secretary of State Henry Kissinger has stated categorically, for example, that "failure to resolve the North Korean nuclear threat in a clear-cut way will sooner or later lead to the nuclear armament of Japan."[38] But Japan's choices under such circumstances would presumably depend heavily on the state of the U.S.-Japan security relationship. Given that the historically accepted way of conveying nuclear assurances has involved stationing U.S. forces on the territory of states lying under its umbrella, a continuing U.S. military presence in Japan makes sense.

More generally, Japan remains bereft of natural resources and thus constantly worried, perhaps excessively, about access to overseas areas. An isolated Japan makes even less sense today than it did in 1930. Meanwhile, there is little historical or strategic logic to the argument that Japan can acquire security partners in East Asia, fashioning an Asian region set apart from the rest of the world. Until it is clear that we lie on the cusp of a revolution in world politics, the United States, rich in resources and endowed with a large and powerful navy, will remain Japan's logical strategic partner. (These same features still make the United States a formidable enemy, which is another reason for sustaining the relationship.)

The end of the Cold War and Japan's rising technical prowess create a new rationale for continuing U.S.-Japan cooperation. Shrinking defense budgets have already begun to erode the U.S. defense industrial base and will ultimately force it to seek partners in the development and production of new weapons. Having come abreast or even pulled ahead of the United States in several important technological areas and evidently having mastered production techniques at least partially applicable to defense, Japan would seem to be an obvious choice. With missiles posing one of the few real threats to Japan's physical integrity and with Japan's neighbors ever wary of Japan's procurement of "projection" forces, missile and air defense would seem to be especially fruitful fields for collaboration.

Overall, these arguments imply continuing inequality in the U.S.-Japan relationship. Indeed, the United States should scuttle its Cold War policy of pushing Japan to spend more on defense. This would do nothing to undermine Japan's security, which improved substantially with the demise of the Soviet threat. Meanwhile, deemphasizing the military side of the relationship would calm Japan's neighbors and leave open possibilities for arms control and cooperative security measures that would surely diminish if Japan began to acquire more arms. Finally, it makes no sense to push Japan to acquire more forces when the United States remains uncertain about the role of force in regional or world politics.

A relationship based on these premises will be no less controversial than the Cold War U.S.-Japan relationship, but the controversies will surround different issues. With their own defense burden declining, Americans have already grown less interested in the overall size of Japan's defense burden; burden sharing based on defense spending as a percent of GNP is no longer very relevant. With U.S. troops engaged in real fighting, rather than simply planning to fight a war too risky to begin, however, blood has replaced money as a sign of burden shared, as was evident during the Persian Gulf crisis when U.S. diplomats pressured Japan (unsuccessfully) to send people as well as money. To the extent that the burden-sharing debate has also shifted to trade, cooperative development of weapons will be seen as helping to advance Japan's technological prowess at U.S. expense.

Each of these sources of controversy in the United States will have its echo in Japan. Few Japanese will object to the overall inequality in the military relationship; the social and political bases of Japanese antimilitarism remain firmly in place.[39] For that very reason, however, the possibility of taking casualties in U.N. peacekeeping operations remains controversial. Meanwhile, if the FSX controversy is a guide, Japan's industries are likely to see U.S. efforts to collaborate in defense procurement as part of a strategy to prevent Japan from acquiring system integration skills in such U.S.-dominated fields as aerospace technology.

These controversial issues pose serious challenges to management of the relationship. Tokyo took a major step toward bringing the "blood-casualties" issue under control in 1992, with passage of the "PKO Bill" authorizing the government to send members of the Self-Defense Forces abroad as part of U.N. peacekeeping operations. Japanese engineers and police advisors participated in the U.N. Transitional Authority in Cambodia (UNTAC), and although the deaths of two Japanese advisors in Cambodia sparked controversy in Tokyo, Japan continued its participation. Japan has also sent a small group to Mozambique. Assuming that the United Nations continues to acquire serious missions like those in Somalia and Cambodia, continued Japanese participation will expose Japan to the blood risks of global security. In return, the United States must back Japan's membership on the U.N. Security Council, a position it has supported, though not actively, since 1972.[40]

Collaborative procurement of weapons will be more difficult to manage. But then virtually *all* collaborative projects are controversial, since they involve national pride and military organizations wedded firmly to differing doctrines. U.S.–West German tank collaboration in the 1960s, for example, ended in failure as each country turned to developing its own tank. Collaborative development of the Tornado aircraft, involving the United Kingdom, Spain, West Germany, and Italy, produced a good aircraft but not without controversy. So long as Japan remains relatively closed to foreign trade and investment, however, U.S.-Japan weapons collaboration will have an additional layer of controversy surrounding questions of technology transfer and the distribution of responsibilities with individual projects.

In the end, the future of the relationship comes back to economics. A substantially more open Japanese economy would take much of the tension out of U.S.-Japan relations. Alliance problems would remain, but they would be no more than alliance problems, typical of all such relationships. Clearly, however, the argument that Japan must change is another argument for continued U.S. engagement, not only because a degree of U.S. leverage flows from the role it plays in Japan's security but also because U.S. pressure on Japan's trade has been a major source of such change as there has been in Japan's trade patterns.

The United States and China

Whether a rich China will be a domineering China or a democratic and cooperative China remains to be seen; U.S. policy must hedge against both possibilities while trying to coax China toward the latter situation. Some argue that the United States has little leverage over Beijing and ought to isolate the country or perhaps even destabilize its government.[41]

Such policies are unworkable; East Asians see too much to be gained by bringing China into the regional economy and thus won't support the strategy. The policy is also unwise; given its size and location, even a weak China, alienated and with no stake in the regional economy, could retaliate by fostering instability that threatens the absolute gains of its neighbors. Overall, a policy of isolating the largest country in the world would seem to be absurd on its face.

Thus, the only workable strategy is to balance Chinese power, assuming it continues to grow. The United States should assume, until events prove otherwise, that in the long run, Chinese military *and* economic power cannot be contained within East Asia alone. There is a need for external balance on both scales, and the United States is far and away the optimum external balancer. Accumulating evidence about the role of force and the nature of interdependence might change this assessment. So could events in China itself; the country could begin to disintegrate, or economic development could impose a degree of decentralization on China that reduces its ability to wield either military or economic power coherently. But it would be risky to act on concrete assumptions in either of these areas until we know more about China's future.

Significantly, the way to balance China's economic power is to integrate it firmly into the global economy. This means more U.S. and European investment in China, more U.S. and European trade with China, and more cooperation with China in global economic undertakings. All of these policies are in conflict with the prevailing desire to use economic sanctions to punish China's human rights and arms sales policies. Public pressure in the United States may ultimately deprive its policymakers of any freedom on these issues, especially if political dissent were to produce another display of official repression like the violence at Tiananmen Square in 1989. Until that occurs, however, focusing U.S. responses to China's conduct narrowly in those areas where undesirable behavior occurs is preferable to across-the-board sanctions like revoking China's most-favored-nation trade status.

Through Korea to a Regional Security Dialogue

More important than China's arms *sales* are its arms *purchases* and *deployments*. The United States has little leverage over these issues. Moreover, given China's central location and many common borders, efforts to limit its arms purchases and deployments would have to be regional and multipolar in nature, taking into account, at the very least, the major powers of Northeast Asia.[42] Generating agreement among this diverse group would be daunting even in the absence of East Asia's underlying animosities and suspicions. With them, it would seem to be nearly impossible.

There are some grounds for optimism. Japan's constitution is itself a form of arms control, as was its decision to hold defense spending to less than 1 percent of GNP. Russia is anxious for naval arms control, largely to consolidate and formalize its otherwise weak position in the region. China and Russia have resolved many of the border issues that almost took them to war in 1969 and have even agreed in principal to create a "safety zone" on either side of the border in which neither country would deploy forces.[43] Finally, movement toward a Korean accommodation will require arms reductions on the peninsula.

The prospects for cooperation depend crucially on continuing U.S. military engagement. A healthy U.S.-Japan security relationship will mute Japan's security concerns, whereas a deteriorating relationship would probably kill Japan's interest in arms control. More important, by balancing China's power, the United States would reduce the returns that Beijing attaches to increased military spending, in effect amplifying the stabilizing effects of economic growth by muting the power effects. Finally, continued engagement would give the United States two ways to interest China in arms control—the promise of some control over U.S. deployments and operations and the implicit threat that a unilateral reduction in U.S. force levels might unleash Japanese arms expenditures.

Arguably, the basis for a broadening regional security dialogue is already in place, centered on the Korean Peninsula.[44] Progress toward a Korean accommodation began in 1988 but has been choppy at best and has come to a virtual standstill as the United States and North Korea bicker about the latter's purported nuclear weapons program. As of this writing, the future of the accommodation process and the possibility for further inspections of North Korea's nuclear facilities remain in doubt.

On the good side, however, such progress as there has been on the Korean Peninsula has resulted from an informal multilateral process. Economic pressure on North Korea began with the Soviet Union's decision to reduce its aid to Pyongyang and to begin charging market prices for resources, especially oil. The U.S. decision in the fall of 1991 to withdraw nuclear weapons from the Korean Peninsula encouraged Pyongyang to agree to give up its own purported nuclear ambitions, albeit its genuine interest in doing so remains to be seen. And the promise of investment and reparations payments from Japan, as well as the United States and South Korea, are major inducements to North Korean openness. The discussions surrounding a Korean accommodation were initially orchestrated by South Korea, via its "northern strategy," in which Seoul has used economic leverage to attract China and Russia. Thus, the discussions have taken the form of "multiple-bilateral" talks. But the absence of a multilateral forum should not obscure the presence of a loosely coordinated multilateral approach to the Korean problem.

This should not be surprising. In the past, Korea's poor location made it a pawn in the games of the larger powers around it. In particular, it became the focus of Sino-Japanese and then Russo-Japanese competition in the last quarter of the nineteenth century.[45] Korea's location still draws the attention of those powers and now the United States as well. All have an obvious interest in avoiding war on the peninsula, which would inevitably involve the United States and China as well as the two Koreas. All are anxious to bring North Korea's nuclear program under international control, although they disagree on the means by which this can be brought about.

More broadly, all have an interest in the evolving shape of a Korean accommodation. This stems in part from the disruptive potential of a unified Korea. Acutely conscious of Korea's historical vulnerability to its powerful neighbors, the leaders of a unified Korea could try to play them against one another—a tactic that depends on and could exacerbate differences among the surrounding powers. An independent Korea, surrounded by nuclear states and a near-nuclear Japan, might also seek to acquire nuclear weapons, a move that would pressure Japan to reconsider its longstanding nuclear aversion—with destabilizing consequences for Japan and the rest of Asia. Alternatively, a unified Korea could seek nuclear as well as conventional protection from a nearby larger power. But this would force it to choose between the United States and China (and perhaps Russia in the distant future), a move that could upset the rejected power.

Indeed, from this perspective, some of Korea's neighbors might actually prefer a divided Korea, provided they can defuse the military confrontation and control Pyongyang's nuclear ambitions. Many Japanese see a unified Korea as a potent economic rival and possible military threat. Beijing seems more comfortable than Tokyo with the economic implications of unification, since a unified Korea could help China develop its own economy. Whether Beijing would be similarly comfortable with the strategic implications of unification, however, is likely to depend on Korea's security choices and China's relations with its neighbors. Presumably Moscow holds similar views.

Neighbors' efforts to stall or at least control Korean unification would implicitly reopen the historical regional competition over Korea—hence, neighbors' choices are as potentially disruptive as those of a unified Korea. If the Koreas were to merge slowly—Seoul's preference, given the enormous cost of coping with the collapse of North Korea—neighbors would have plenty of time to meddle in the politics of one or the other Korea for their own political ends. Some may even try to stymie unification. If, as seems more likely, the Koreas are unified by the collapse of North Korea, the resulting unified country would be weak and thus vulnerable to economic and military pressure.

Whether it happens quickly or slowly, Korean unification is clearly a regional security issue, potentially a very divisive one. Yet precisely because of its divisive potential, the unification process might provide leverage for launching and expanding a broader regional security dialogue leading, hopefully, to a new and more cooperative future for the region. Clearly U.S. strategy is crucial; the United States provides the stabilizing framework within which the dialogue can proceed, its forces are major bargaining chips in any emerging arms control scheme, and U.S. diplomacy mediates between Japan and suspicious neighbors.

A good place to start is where the Korean accommodation is now stalled—the nuclear issue. Advocates have argued for some time that making Korea a nuclear-free zone (NFZ) would relieve Pyongyang's—and perhaps also a unified Korea's—incentives to acquire nuclear weapons. At the moment, such an agreement might also restart the accommodation process. Even if Pyongyang believes that U.S. nuclear weapons have been removed from Korea, after all, it knows that the United States can return them quickly or simply fire nuclear-tipped cruise missiles from submarines. A U.S. guarantee not to use nuclear weapons in Korea would reassure Pyongyang while not endangering South Korea, since sophisticated conventional weapons now handle what were once nuclear missions. The United States can take such a step, however, only if Moscow and Beijing make the same guarantee. Given Japan's nuclear capability and Korea's suspicions about it, Japan should also sign the agreement.

An NFZ agreement would explicitly recognize the link between Korean and Northeast Asian security. It would be signed by all four major regional powers (the United States, China, Russia, and Japan) plus the two Koreas, and the concluding ceremony would bring these parties together and call attention to their related security roles and interests. If it takes up the NFZ idea, the United States should push to make it a matter of regional discussions.

The same logic would apply to almost any further movement toward a Korean accommodation. Following the completion of an NFZ agreement, for example, the Koreas should seek to broaden the modest set of confidence-building measures—a nonaggression pact and an agreement to notify each other of impending military exercises—signed at the end of 1991. They could seek to back both country's forces away from the demilitarized zone (DMZ), for example, and ultimately to reduce force levels.

To the extent that the Koreas alone took such steps, however, they would be increasing their sense of security with respect to one another at the cost of *decreasing* their sense of security with respect to at least some neighbors—notably China, whose defense budget is rising. Thus, such measures should also extend to Korea's neighbors. In particular, China should be asked to thin army deployments near its border with Korea. Reducing Chinese forces along a border it shares with Russia, however, would raise Sino-Russian security concerns. And Pyongyang, China, and Russia would probably be reluctant to reduce their forces without commensurate cuts in, or at least some control over the deployment of, U.S. and Japanese forces. Talks focused initially on forces deployed to the Korean Peninsula thus could easily move into the broad area of regional arms control.

The United States avoided such agreements during the Cold War, arguing, among other things, that it would only negotiate from a position of strength. It is now strong, but it is destined to get relatively weaker in the years ahead, as its defense budget and force posture shrink (albeit from a very high plateau) while some in the region rise. It makes sense to contain the decline of U.S. forces as a hedge against the failure of steps toward regional arms control. But it makes no less sense to be willing to trade the U.S. presence, or the operational tempo of U.S. forces, for verifiable agreements that reduce or curb emerging threats. It would be tragic indeed if the United States allows its forces to shrink without at least trying to obtain commensurate constraints on the offensive capabilities and deployments of other regional states.

Conclusion

With the Cold War over, Asians and Europeans alike have wondered whether the United States would slowly retreat to its island bastion, as it did after World Wars I and II. Asians have also worried that it would grow even more Eurocentric, prodded not only by historical links to Europe but perhaps also by increasing frustration with Japanese trade and investment policies. Although long-term U.S. policy remains uncertain, for the moment, at least, the Clinton administration's internationalist orientation and, in particular, its embrace of East Asia is allaying both concerns. Although U.S. military strategy in East Asia has changed little from that pursued by the Bush administration, Clinton has clearly linked the issues of U.S. jobs and economic growth to continuing economic engagement with East Asia.

I have suggested in this chapter that continuing U.S. engagement makes even more sense from a security perspective than it does from the economic perspective. It is possible to imagine East Asia as an integrated regional economy. But nothing in the region's history, the underlying structure of its state system, or the status of its fledgling security institutions suggests that such a region would satisfy U.S. interests in stability or openness. In sharp contrast to Europe, power or the potential for it is distributed quite unevenly, creating hegemonic tendencies that the United States is best positioned to counter. Again in sharp contrast to Europe, East Asia's states remain deeply suspicious of each other, and regional institutions remain weak at best. Arguably, in the post–Cold War era, it is East Asia, far more than Europe, that needs a continuing U.S. security presence.

In the absence of real threats beyond North Korea, the size and structure of U.S. forces in the region are less important than the continuing presence of those already there. Their role is not so much to counter threats as it is to shape an environment conducive to U.S. interests. Threats may arise, the most likely military threat being China. But the Chinese threat will be many years in the making, and in the meantime, U.S. engagement gives it the opportunity to help East Asians shape a different kind of environment, one based on arms limitations rather than arms procurement. Whether or not the new environment requires the continued commitment of U.S. military forces, it will certainly require U.S. support to come into existence. In this sense, ironically, the best way for the United States to

ensure future reductions in the security burden it carries in East Asia is to stay deeply engaged now.

Notes

1. Asia is a huge place; it includes India, Pakistan, the smaller states of South Asia, the newly independent republics of central Asia, the states around the Persian Gulf (Southwest Asia), and East Asia, which stretches from Russia and Japan in the north through Indochina and Southeast Asia to Australia and New Zealand. This chapter focuses on the last of these groups—states in which U.S. economic interests run quite high and in which U.S. power has been exerted for many decades.

2. Department of Defense, *A Strategic Framework for the Asian Pacific Rim: Report to Congress 1992* (Washington, D.C.: Government Printing Office, 1992), 20.

3. Edward A. Olsen, "A New American Strategy in Asia?" *Asia Survey* 31, no. 12 (1991): 1153.

4. Michael Klare, "The Next Great Arms Race," *Foreign Affairs* 72, no. 3, (1993): 136–152.

5. Robert Gilpin, *War and Change in World Politics* (Cambridge: Cambridge University Press, 1981), 230.

6. See especially Donald S. Zagoria, "Russian Policy Toward Korea: A Historical and Geopolitical Analysis," in Robert A. Scalapino and Han Sung-joo, eds., *United States–Korea Relations* (Berkeley: Institute of East Asian Studies, University of California Press, 1986), 203–216.

7. On the Washington Conference treaties, see especially Robert Gordon Kaufman, *Arms Control During the Pre-Nuclear Era* (New York: Columbia University Press, 1990).

8. This point is well made by A. Whitney Griswold, *The Far Eastern Policy of the United States* (New Haven: Yale University Press, 1938), 125–132. On the size and status of U.S. forces in East Asia during this period, see Paul R. Schratz, "The Orient and U.S. Naval Strategy," and Roy K. Flint, "The United States Army on the Pacific Frontier, 1899–1939," both in Joe C. Dixon, ed., *The American Military and the Far East, Proceedings of the Ninth Military History Symposium, United States Air Force Academy, 1–3 October 1980* (Washington, D.C.: Government Printing Office, 1980).

9. From Germany's defeat in World War I, Japan's military elite took the lesson that modern war required states to control fully resources on which they depended. As a result, Michael A. Barnhart asserted, Japan's "impulse for security became, slowly, an impulse for empire, and it led directly to the Pacific War." See his *Japan Prepares for Total War: The Search for Economic Security, 1919–1941* (Ithaca, N.Y.: Cornell University Press, 1987), 9.

10. John Lewis Gaddis, "The Long Peace: Elements of Stability in the Postwar International System," *International Security* 10, no. 4 (1986): 99–142. See also Barry Buzan, "Economic Structure and International Security: The Limits of the Liberal Case," *International Organization* 38, no. 4 (1984): 597–624.

11. On the latter point, see Leszek Buszynski, "ASEAN Security Dilemmas," *Survival* 34, no. 4 (1992): 91–94.

12. As suggested by Kenneth N. Waltz, "The Emerging Structure of International Relations," *International Security* 18, no. 2 (1993): 44–79.

13. Dwight H. Perkins, *China: Asia's Next Economic Giant?* (Seattle: University of Washington Press, 1986), 15–17, and Peter L. Berger and Hsin-Huang Michael Hsiao, eds., *In Search of an East Asian Development Model* (New Brunswick, N.J.: Transaction Books, 1988), chapters 2 and 4.

14. Susan Strange, "States, Firms, and Diplomacy," *International Affairs* 68 no. 1: 1–15.

15. See Jeffrey Frankel, "Is Japan Creating a Yen Bloc in East Asia and the Pacific?" (Cambridge, Mass.: National Bureau of Economic Research, NBER Working Paper No. 4050, April 1992), 4.

16. Perkins, *China: Asia's Next Economic Giant?* 6; also Roy Hofheinz, Jr., and Kent E. Calder, *The Eastasia Edge* (New York: Basic Books, 1982).

17. The words of Foreign Minister Qian Qichen, quoted in Raphael Pura, "Beijing Pursues Good-Neighbor Image at ASEAN Meeting," *The Asian Wall Street Journal*, August 2, 1993, p. 4.

18. David A. Fulghum and Paul Proctor, "Chinese Coveting Offensive Triad," *Aviation Week and Space Technology*, September 21, 1992, pp. 20–21. For more general assessments of China's defense spending, see Gerald Segal, "As China Grows Strong," *International Affairs* 64, no. 2 (1988): 217–231, and David Shambaugh, "China's Security Policy in the post–Cold War Era," *Survival* (Summer 1992): 88–106. In fairness to China, defense budget increases have also gone toward purchasing the loyalty of the People's Liberation Army (PLA) in future domestic political crises and giving China's ground forces a mobile defense capability that does not threaten distant neighbors. See Nicholas D. Kristof, "China to Reward Army With 13% Increase in Military Budget," *New York Times,* March 22, 1992, p. A10. Moreover, China's defense budget remains substantially smaller than Japan's. See *The Military Balance 1990–1991* (London: Brassey's, 1990), and Timothy Hu, "Chinese Army: Fewer Men, More Arms," *The Nikkei Weekly,* February 1, 1992, p. 20.

19. Bin Yu, "Sino-Russian Military Relations: Implications for Asian-Pacific Security," *Asian Survey* 33, no. 3 (1993): 313.

20. See again Gilpin, *War and Change in World Politics,* 230.

21. A point well made by Michael J. Green, "Arms, Technology and Alliance: Japan's Search for Autonomous Defense Production, 1945–1993," Ph.D. diss., The Johns Hopkins School of Advanced International Studies, 1993. Joseph Nye, Jr., attributed similar views to Ezra Vogel. See the former's "Coping With Japan," *Foreign Policy,* no. 89 (Winter 1992): 101.

22. As I. M. Destler has pointed out, in this "political imbalance between those who benefit from trade protection and those who pay the costs" lies the political challenge to sustaining free trade. See his *American Trade Politics,* 2nd ed., (Washington, D.C.: Institute for International Economics, and New York: The Twentieth Century Fund, 1992), 4.

23. C. Fred Bergsten and Marcus Noland, *Reconcilable Differences? United States–Japan Economic Conflict* (Washington, D.C.: Institute for International Economics, 1993), 1.

24. See the arguments in Laura D'Andrea Tyson, *Who's Bashing Whom? Trade Conflict in High-Technology Industries* (Washington, D.C.: Institute for International Economics, 1992).

25. See, respectively, Robert Z. Lawrence, *Can America Compete?* (Washington, D.C.: The Brookings Institution, 1984), and Wayne Sandholtz et. al., *The Highest Stakes: The Economic Foundations of the Next Security System* (New York: Oxford University Press, 1992), 25–35.

26. Robert Jervis, "The Future of World Politics: Will It Resemble the Past?" *International Security* 16, no. 3 (1991/92): 49.

27. Samuel P. Huntington, "Why International Primacy Matters," *International Security* 17, no. 4 (1993): 79.

28. Joseph Nye, Jr., noted that there is four times as much Japanese direct investment in the United States as there is U.S. investment in Japan; "with only 1 per cent of its GNP produced by foreign firms, Japan diverges strikingly from other advanced economies" ("Coping with Japan," 105).

29. U.K. direct investment in the United States remains larger than Japanese direct investment, as does U.K. financing of the U.S. federal deficit. In both cases, however, Japan's holdings are more controversial. Differing political effects of these investments may result from imbalances in U.S.-Japan trade and investment. But they could also result from cultural and racial differences or historical animosities, in which case they would not lessen were the economic relationship more even.

30. Quoted in Huntington, "Why International Primacy Matters," 78.

31. See, for example, Huntington, certainly one of Japan's more strident critics: "Why International Primacy Matters," 81.

32. Strong arguments on this point can be found in Sandholtz et. al., *The Highest Stakes,* chapter 1, and Huntington, "Why International Primacy Matters," 25–29 and chapter 6.

33. Quoted in Michael Richardson, "Deep Concern over U.S.-Japan Relations," *Asia-Pacific Defence Reporter,* February–March 1992, p. 36.

34. See Selig Harrison, "A Yen for the Bomb," *The Washington Post,* October 31, 1993, pp. C1, C4.

35. For a discussion, see Masaru Tamamoto, "Trial of an Ideal: Japan's Debate Over the Gulf Crisis," *World Policy Journal* 8, no. 1 (1990): 89–106.

36. Depending on the answers to these two questions, a third might concern whether the United States should resist Japanese efforts to acquire more military and diplomatic power. Yet Tokyo seems unlikely to make such a choice willingly, no matter what its intentions in the economic sphere. Indeed, arguably a Japan bent on economic domination is more likely than those with more benign motives to want U.S. "cover" and to avoid military expenditures as long as possible. On Japan's likely security choices now that the Cold War is over, see Peter J. Katzenstein and Nobuo Okawara, "Japan's National Security: Structures, Norms, and Policies," *International Security* 17, no. 4, (1993): 84–118.

37. Roy Allison, "Russian Defence Planning: Military Doctrine and Force Structures," in Lars B. Wallin, ed., *Lectures and Contributions to East European Studies at FOA,* The Swedish National Defence Research Establishment, June 30, 1993, p. 7.

38. Henry Kissinger, "Why We Can't Withdraw From Asia," (op-ed), *The Washington Post,* June 15, 1993, pp. 3–4.

39. Thomas U. Berger, "From Sword to Chrysanthemum: Japan's Culture of Anti-militarism," *International Security* 17, no. 4 (1993): 119–150.

40. See the discussion in Nye, "Coping With Japan," 111; he argued that Brazil, Germany, India, Japan, and Nigeria would probably all be admitted to nonveto, permanent seats on the U.N. Security Council simultaneously.

41. See, for example, Roger W. Sullivan, "Discarding the China Card," *Foreign Policy* no. 86 (Spring 1992): 3–23.

42. India should also be included, at least at the nuclear level. Although Indian and Chinese conventional forces confront one another in several disputed territories along their common border—they fought each other in 1962 and came close

to fighting in 1988—the Himalayas provide a formidable natural barrier to conventional forces likely to confine such conflicts to disputed territory; large-scale invasion across these mountains is virtually out of the question. Thus, Sino-Indian conventional force issues are less pressing than nuclear ones.

43. "CIS, China End Talks on Border: Russia To Withdraw Troops," *Foreign Broadcast Information Service–Soviet Union* (*FBIS-SOV*) 92-234, December 4, 1992, p. 2.

44. The arguments in this section draw heavily on Thomas L. McNaugher, "Reforging Northeast Asia's Dagger? US Strategy and Korean Unification," *The Brookings Review* 11, no. 3 (1993): 12–17.

45. This was not Korea's first bad experience with neighbors, however. In 1592, one of Japan's Daimyos (Hideyoshi) invaded Korea, producing great destruction as he worked his way northward. Sensing danger on their flank, the Manchus, then in the process of establishing the Ch'ing dynasty in China, launched a counter invasion that drove the Japanese back to their home islands. The Ch'ing then established suzerainty over Korea, which they held until their dynasty disintegrated in the nineteenth century. See Hisahiko Okazaki, *A Grand Strategy for Japanese Defense* (New York: University Press of America, 1986), 13, and Jung-Hoon Lee, "Korean-Japanese Relations: The Past, Present and Future," *Korea Observer* 21 (1990): 159–160.

PART FOUR

Summing Up

14

Military Strategy for an Era of Transition

Martin van Creveld

The period from 1989 to 1992 has witnessed some of the most dramatic political upheavals since the end of World War II. The Warsaw Pact and the Soviet Union have disintegrated, leaving behind a Commonwealth of Independent States whose future is by no means assured. For good or ill, Germany has reunited, whereas NATO, which once represented the single most important linchpin in Western foreign and defense policy has been left searching for a mission that will justify its continued existence.

As might be expected in times of turmoil, there has been no shortage of analysts who are attempting to understand this process of change, trace it back to its origins, and forecast its results. At one time or another, it has been suggested that we may be entering some kind of new world order based on loose cooperation between the most important powers left on earth; that this world may in some sense be "postnuclear"; that the future will see less armed conflict and more economic competition among the giant blocs now forming in North America, Europe, and East Asia; that major war itself may soon follow slavery and the duel in heading for the dustbin of history; and even that history itself may be coming to an end.[1]

In this chapter, I shall leave economics and international politics alone as much as possible, focusing instead on the military side of the question. My thesis is that insofar as all of the ideas enumerated in the previous paragraph pertain to the future of armed conflict, they are either incorrect or, at best, one sided and incomplete. Large-scale, conventional interstate war may indeed be coming to an end; however, this is not at all the same as saying that war per se is also ending. On the contrary, as is shown by any number of examples from Northern Ireland to Yugoslavia, Somalia, Lebanon, Afghanistan, and Peru, "WARRE" in the elemental, Hobbesian sense—in which entire ethnic groups are sometimes slaughtered—is not only alive and well but about to enter an altogether new epoch.

I

Attempting to understand the development of war during the second half of the twentieth century, future historians will probably find themselves facing a curious paradox. On the one hand, the power to inflict destruction was developing by leaps and bounds. On the other hand, although bipolarity in power relationships has by no means been a rare phenomenon ever since the time of the Peloponnesian War, never before had most of the planet been divided between two superpowers, each subscribing to a vociferously opposing ideology and regarding the other—to quote President Reagan's well-known phrase—as "an evil empire."

Directly or by way of alliances, each of those powers occupied a continent and controlled the better part of a hemisphere. Each commanded the allegiance of several hundreds of millions of highly educated, capable people, to say nothing of productive resources entirely beyond the imagination of previous generations. Each, too, possessed such vast armed forces as to eclipse all the rest of the world's nations. This applied to their conventional armies as measured in the number of tanks, aircraft, and ships, but it was even more true in respect to nuclear forces on the one hand and strategic power projection capabilities on the other.

Though the superpowers' war-making preponderance was in part the product of sheer size, comparison with large but undeveloped countries such as China or India suggests that the role played by technological competition was probably even more important.[2] It goes without saying that people had always applied their inventive genius to war; however, the absence of a proper theoretical framework before the seventeenth century made progress in this respect, as well as others, slow, incidental, and almost accidental.[3]

The advent of the scientific and, later, the industrial revolution changed all that. Modern military research and development was partly an offshoot of civilian technology and partly, to quote Trotsky, the locomotive that pulled it forward. Originally, it was carried out mainly by individual tinkerers who acted on their own initiative and tried to sell their inventions to the powers that be; during the second half of the nineteenth century, it was institutionalized in the hands of giant firms such as Krupps in Germany, Vickers-Armstrong in the United Kingdom, Schneider-Creusot in France, and in the United States, Du Pont. After 1914, the industry came to be state directed, if not actually state owned. It gave birth to vast bureaucratic structures, capable of acting almost on demand and producing a steady stream of technological innovations.[4]

Developing modern weapon systems, particularly those that are large and complicated, often launches designers into altogether unknown realms of technological endeavor and can take many years. Since none could afford to fall behind, more and more the process was carried out continuously; as George Orwell and, before him, Erich Ludendorff had foreseen, war became peace and peace a form of (cold) war. As research expanded (and as scientists and research institutes everywhere jumped on the bandwagon), it embraced one field of knowledge after another until not even the brains of cats or the surface of the moon remained immune to the Pentagon's or the Kremlin's clutches. It was brought to such a pitch and waged with such intensity as to push even the largest powers to the verge of bankruptcy, if not beyond.[5]

Against this background of unprecedented war-making capabilities, future historians will note that both the size of interstate war and its importance—as measured by the extent to which the most important powers participated in it—were actually declining. There was no successor to World War II, with its armies numbering in the tens of millions—the Germans alone had almost 20 million men pass through their forces between 1939 and 1945—and the equally large number of casualties it produced. What is more, the two largest powers never put their economies on a true war footing. They never mobilized anything like their entire available personnel pool and never engaged each other in open hostilities. By some accounts, during forty-five years of intense competition, the hardheaded, rational men who led them never even came close to engaging each other.[6] Though there were many tense moments, particularly before the construction of the Berlin Wall in 1961, the superpowers' principal allies in the so-called Central Theater were almost equally immune. Only in Korea did a superpower fight a conventional war against one of its rival's close allies. And that war, it should be noted, took place in spite of the fact that the U.S. Joint Chiefs of Staff saw the region in question to be of no strategic relevance to them.[7]

It is true that the remaining states went to war more frequently and not seldom put their all into those conflicts. However, for the most part the belligerents were third- and even fourth-rate powers. By virtue of the small size of their population, low per capita gross national product, general backwardness, or all of these factors, their military forces tended to be small, outdated, and possessed of a limited strategic reach. They could not even come close to matching medium powers such as Germany or Japan if those had been willing to make the necessary effort, let alone stand in comparison with the superpowers.

The most important interstate clashes took place in a region stretching from western to eastern Asia that previous generations had known as the "rimlands." The Middle East saw the Arab-Israeli Wars of 1948 to 1949, 1956 (when the United Kingdom and France, both of them medium powers, also participated), 1967, 1973, and 1982 as well as the Iraq-Iran War of 1980 to 1988 and the Gulf War of 1991. South Asia saw five interstate wars, including three between India and Pakistan (1947, 1965, and 1971), one between India and China (1961), and a minor one between China and Vietnam. In 1955 and 1958, Communist Chinese and Taiwanese air and naval forces engaged each other on a considerable scale, though on both occasions a major war between the two countries was probably averted through U.S. threats to intervene. Finally, the British in

1982 fought and won a splendid little conventional war in the South Atlantic—a region so remote, thinly populated, and peripheral to their interests as to leave many people wondering why the war had to take place at all.

Otherwise put, the critical difference between the wars of 1648 to 1945 and those of 1945 to 1992 is the fact that, without exception, the latter were fought between, or at any rate against, third- and fourth-rate states. Almost by definition, the latter-day hostilities took place far away from the main centers of military-political power; whereas previously it had been a quite common occurrence for great capitals such as London, Paris, Moscow, Rome, Berlin, and Tokyo to be bombed from the air, attacked from the ground, besieged, and even occupied, after 1945 no war took place within hundreds of miles of the capital of a medium power and thousands of miles of either Moscow or Washington, D.C.

There are probably many reasons for this state of affairs, including not least sheer war-weariness among the populations that had borne the brunt of World Wars I and II. Still, experience after both 1648 (the end of the Thirty Years' War) and 1815 (the end of the Napoleonic ones) suggests that this kind of weariness seldom lasts for much longer than a generation, if that. Even if it does last, which some have argued was the case in Western civilization after 1918,[8] in all likelihood the result will merely be the rise of some leaders and some countries eager to take advantage of it. Almost certainly, our imaginary future historians will conclude that the long peace between the most important military powers that characterized the years from 1945 to 1992 can only be accounted for by a novel factor that was not previously present. That factor was nuclear weapons.

The fact that "atomic" bombs and their still more powerful successors were different and could not be used as other weapons could was not understood all at once. On the contrary, for forty years and on both sides of the Iron Curtain, immense financial and intellectual capital was spent looking for ways in which they might be used.[9] Many of the ideas, particularly those that suggested some kind of international agreement concerning limits on the size of weapons and the kinds of targets that might be hit, never got off the ground.[10] Others appear hair-raising in retrospect. Particularly during the 1970s, a new generation of miniature warheads and much more accurate delivery vehicles, known as MIRV (multiple independently targetable reentry vehicles) and cruise missiles, came into service. Faced by what was considered to be an overwhelming Soviet conventional advantage, U.S. strategists sought to exploit these technological advances. They talked about "selective options," "nuclear shots across the bow," "limited nuclear war," and "decapitation," the latter being equivalent to sending a small warhead through Mr. Leonid Brezhnev's Kremlin window in the hope that this would cause the Soviet Union to disintegrate.[11] All these were euphemisms for the first use of nuclear weapons in ways that would not lead to the destruction of the world, at any rate not automatically.

To judge by results—the fact that no nuclear weapons have been employed in war since Nagasaki and that the arsenals of the superpowers are even now being drastically reduced—these attempts have ended in failure. As some far-sighted critics had argued from the beginning,[12] nuclear weapons differed from all their predecessors in two crucial respects. First, previously every weapon could be countered or, if not countered, imitated and put to use against its original owner; however, in the case of nuclear weapons, half a century of intensive research has failed to discover a credible means of defense, and indeed such is the magnitude of the threat as to render the term *credible* itself almost meaningless.[13] Second, the fact that a defense was always available meant that previous armies had been able to guarantee their countries' safety by defeating the enemy's armed forces, occupying its country, and achieving something known as victory. Now, however, nuclear weapons and their delivery vehicles meant that it was possible for an army to win complete, even easy, victory and still find its own country instantly turned into a smoking, radiating desert. And indeed, the more complete the success achieved, the greater the danger that the enemy, pushed to anger and desperation, would in fact cause this to happen.

Nuclear weapons were originally limited to one of the superpowers and then to both. However, by 1964 they had spread to medium powers such as the United Kingdom, France, and China. All of them sought the bomb as a way of providing immunity against large-scale military attack of the kind to which they had been subjected before and during World War II,[14] and all of them have achieved that aim to the point that such an attack has become almost inconceivable. By the late 1960s, if not earlier, several other countries were in a position to acquire nuclear weapons if they wanted to, including not just long-established industrial powers such as Germany and Japan but also developing ones such as Brazil, Argentina, and India (in 1964, Jawaharlal Nehru announced his country could build the bomb in eighteen months).[15] In the end, all these countries decided not to go ahead with such plans or else to keep acquisition secret. By so doing, they showed that something fundamental had changed in the role that large-scale interstate war can play in international relations.

By 1965, several countries other than the large and medium powers possessed nuclear reactors, either such as had been given to them for peaceful purposes or else domestically developed. By 1970, it was becoming clear that given the political will and the decision to allocate resources, any country capable of building and maintaining large, powerful, modern conventional armed forces should also be capable of acquiring nuclear weapons. To judge by some actual cases, building nuclear weapons was in fact easier than bringing together the scientific, technological, and industrial infrastructure needed to produce many conventional ones.

For example, Israel, initially with French aid, started constructing its first nuclear reactor *cum* plutonium separation plant in the late 1950s. The reactor must have gone critical at some time between 1963 and 1965, and the first devices were probably assembled in 1968 and 1969.[16] Yet

Israel at that time was a small, poor, recently established country of less than two and a half million people. Although possessing some impressive institutes of advanced scientific learning, it engaged in very little R&D and was only beginning to build up a modern industrial infrastructure. Several more years were to pass before Israel could also produce its own tanks and fighter bombers; to this day, the engines for those fighter bombers (the Lavi, which has now been canceled) and those tanks continue to be imported from the United States.

A similar phenomenon was demonstrated by Pakistan, which by most standards is among the least-developed countries on earth, with a very large, backward, illiterate population and an abysmally low per capita GNP. As of 1992, almost twenty years had passed since a Pakistani engineer, Abdul Khader Khan, was able to steal uranium-enrichment centrifuge technology from a Dutch plant at Almelo; probably almost ten years had passed since Islamabad first acquired the wherewithal for building nuclear weapons.[17] Nevertheless, with the exception of short-range surface-to-surface missiles that were being tested in 1992, to this day Pakistan remains incapable of producing advanced conventional arms. Instead, it is dependent on China, which itself demonstrates the same phenomenon insofar as its arms industry remains comparatively backward almost three decades after having exploded its first nuclear device.

The question of whether nuclear weapons would cause regional balances to develop in the same way as the central theater—namely, in the direction of stalemate—has been the subject of prolonged debate among scholars.[18] Because the original members of the nuclear club wanted to keep their monopoly to themselves, this debate, especially as conducted by the U.S. "arms control" community, has not been free either of tendentiousness or of political considerations. Against all evidence, it was suggested that third-world leaders were less responsible and more prone to suicidal action than their first- and second-world counterparts; that arsenals consisting of a few small nuclear weapons were somehow less controllable and more dangerous to stability than those that consisted of multimegaton weapons numbering in the tens of thousands; and that, the danger of fallout and radiation notwithstanding, small countries whose territories are contiguous to each other and whose rivers often flow across each others' borders are more likely to resort to nuclear weapons than are superpowers located in separate hemispheres.

In practice, these fears have proved to be almost totally unfounded. In spite of countless international crises and some very scary personalities with fingers on the nuclear trigger, to date no regional nuclear states have gone to war against each other, much less challenged the world's most important powers to a nuclear showdown. On the contrary, there are indications that possession of nuclear weapons is compelling these states to follow the same political-military road in their relations with each other as was previously taken by the superpowers. For example, relations between India and Pakistan continue to be as bad as ever; however, they now have an agreement that requires each side to notify the other in advance of any large-scale maneuvers planned to take place near their common border. South and North Korea are talking about a mutual process of inspection and verification. And so it goes.

Moreover, and again following in the wake of earlier developments that took place among the most important powers, nuclear weapons have also acted as a deterrent against full-scale conventional war. The latter has been swept under the carpet, as it were. With one possible exception—Israel in 1973—no nuclear power has ever been subject to serious conventional military attack by such of its neighbors as were themselves nonnuclear, and even that attack turned out to be much less dangerous than it appeared then. Plenty of evidence exists to show that the Arab leadership at that time—Anwar Sadat and Hafez al-Assad—were well aware of the near certainty of nuclear weapons existing in Israel's hands.[19] Almost certainly, this awareness played a major role in dictating their decision to limit their offensive to a few square miles of Israeli-occupied territory.[20]

Since such nonnuclear powers as are still able to fight each other in earnest are by definition weak and technologically underdeveloped, the effect of proliferation was to push war itself into the nooks and crannies of the international system. This, of course, is not to say that nuclear war will definitely never take place. It is to say that nuclear weapons, so long as they are not used, appear to be causing large-scale interstate war of the kind that did so much to shape world history from 1648 to 1945 to be on its way out; if they *are* used, then almost certainly such war, the armed forces by which it is fought, and the political entities by which it is waged will already be out.

II

The approaching end of large-scale interstate war should not, however, be equated with the end of war as such. This is because war is rooted in human nature; Clausewitz and the whole of modern strategic thought to the contrary, it is best understood not as a means but as an end.[21] The political usefulness of war may be, and often has been, questioned by some of the greatest minds that ever lived.[22] However, its inherent power to fascinate is beyond doubt. As the billion people who are said to have watched CNN during the 1991 Gulf War showed, this fascination extends far beyond those whose interests are directly involved.

War is life written large; of all human activities, it is by far the most spectacular, the most intense, and the most exciting. More important still, it is the only one in which there are no rules, no artificial restrictions on the amount of force that may be used and the means that may be employed. It is for this reason that war has so often been seen as representing the supreme criterion of personal worth or, to speak with previous generations, the judgment of God. As history's greatest poets from Homer to Nietzsche knew, there is a sense in which war is the only activity that allows those who engage in it to be completely free, completely themselves, completely human. At bottom, the reason why there has always been war is neither international anarchy, nor economic competition, nor even the need to satisfy some mysterious psychological drives with fancy names derived from the Greek; but simply because men love to fight and women, those who are prepared to fight on their and their children's behalf.

As of the end of the twentieth century, nuclear weapons seem to be well on their way to creating a situation where, on pain of committing suicide, men are no longer able to fight each other in the name of the state. However, this does not at all mean that they will now be content to say farewell to arms; what it does mean is that they will look for, and most assuredly find, "political" entities of a different kind for which they *will* be able to fight. In fact, since 1945 perhaps three-quarters of all the wars waged on this planet have been fought not between states but between, or against, organizations that were not states. Among these, the most prominent were independent warlords, militias, guerrillas, and terrorists.

The wars fought by, or against, organizations other than internationally recognized territorial states are usually known as LICs, which stands for low-intensity conflicts. Originally introduced during the late 1960s, this term is misleading on two counts. First, some of the conflicts waged between states—for example, the one between India and Pakistan along their common Himalayan border—are equally slow-burning, sporadic, and interminable.[23] Second, many of these nonstate wars have been *much* more bloody than all but the very largest interstate ones.

For example, the wars that took place in and around the Persian Gulf between 1980 and 1988 and again during 1990 and 1991 were the largest and, particularly as regards the second, the most modern of the post-1945 world. Still, in the number of dead and wounded they did not even come close to such "low-intensity" conflicts as Biafra (1966–1969), Vietnam (1947–1975), Cambodia (1970–present), Afghanistan (1979–1988), and Somalia (1976–?). All of these claimed their victims in the millions; some even threatened to end in the physical elimination of entire peoples.

To select another instance, Israel is as well armed as any country and has fought far more than its fair share of wars. Yet the total number of Israeli dead in all those conflicts combined was only around 17,000, a figure that is now being eclipsed by the number of those killed in traffic accidents. This death toll has already been equaled, indeed probably exceeded, in several months of Yugoslav civil war between ill-organized, ill-trained, and ill-equipped militias that can hardly be told apart from each other, not even by themselves.

Wars, unlike games, should be judged not by some points system but by their political results. By this criterion, too, the term *low-intensity conflict* is entirely inappropriate. Other appellations, such as "brushfire war," "guerrilla war," and "terrorism" are even more misleading, in part because they were deliberately designed to conceal the fact that this kind of war has been far more significant than its larger brother. The facts, however, speak otherwise. During the decades since 1945, there has only been a single case when any state succeeded in moving an international border or creating a new one by means of interstate war—Israel in 1948 and

1949. Even if a few doubtful instances are included, for example, the creation of Bangladesh out of Pakistan's rib in 1971 or North Vietnam putting an end to the independent existence of South Vietnam in 1975, the number can still easily be counted on the fingers of one hand.

During the same period, dozens of so-called low-intensity conflicts have led to the liberation from colonial rule of entire continents. Many hundreds of millions of people have seen themselves transferred to the sovereignty of political entities that had no previous existence, all without a single large-scale conventional war between regular armed forces. The largest and most powerful empires that ever existed have been carved up and humiliated by LIC, and neither, contrary to the expectations of some, did this kind of thing come to an end when the last European colonies were set free in 1975. Even now, LIC is spreading from the third world into what used to be known as the second world including—besides the remains of Yugoslavia—Moldavia, Armenia, Tajikistan, Georgia, and so on. Nor, as visitors to London or Los Angeles (or the Twin Towers) will know, is there any reason to think that the so-called first world is necessarily immune.

Instead of *low-intensity conflict,* it might be better to employ a different term, *nontrinitarian war.* The term *trinitarian* is derived from Book I of Clausewitz's *On War.*[24] It stands for the kind of war that is waged by states on the basis of the "remarkable trinity" (*wunderliche Dreifältigkeit*) comprising the government, the army, and the people. As Clausewitz himself was well aware,[25] the type of political-military organization in which these elements are clearly separate from each other is a relatively new phenomenon; indeed, the word *state* itself only came to be used in anything like its present meaning during the second half of the sixteenth century.[26]

Although one can find some earlier parallels, especially in Hellenistic Greece and Imperial Rome, on the whole the state did not make its appearance before 1648 and then only in the 2 or 3 percent of the earth's surface comprising the European West from Gibraltar to the Vistula. Historically speaking, the vast majority of war-making political entities have not been states, and neither were they organized on trinitarian lines; hence, there is no a priori reason to assume that this will always be the case in the future, either. In fact, since 1945 the great majority of wars waged on this planet have been waged between, or at any rate against, organizations that were not states and did not have the trinitarian organization in the same form. Even at this moment in 1992, *every one* of the score or so of wars actually being fought is of the nontrinitarian kind.

In its modern form, nontrinitarian warfare is largely the upgrowth of World War II. For three centuries before 1939, it had been the custom, enshrined in international law, that wars ended when the enemy's armed forces had been beaten, part or all of its country had been occupied, and its government had signed a peace treaty. Now, however, both Germany and Japan found that there was more to war than defeating the opposition's armed forces; it was also necessary to keep down its population even if the country's government had formally surrendered. Although circumstances differed, in every country that had been overrun by the Axis Powers, resistance movements sprang up within a matter of months. Claiming to represent the people—even the right to replace the previous government—they were determined to carry on the fight forever, if necessary, and waged war with growing effectiveness.

Perhaps more remarkable still, the traditional view that war was only war insofar as it was waged under legitimate authority by combatants wearing uniforms and carrying arms openly began to be overturned. The resistance movements, instead of being condemned for breaking international law, were applauded and, as far as possible, assisted by the entire civilized world. This, in turn, reflected the idea—which had been taking hold in the Western world since 1918—that offensive war, occupation, and attempts at "subjugation" were not so much legitimate instruments of policy as criminal acts—acts that ordinary people had the right to resist even in the teeth of an agreement entered upon by their own lawful government.

Once the idea had established itself among "civilized" nations, it did not take long to spread to the colonial peoples, some of whom had, in fact, been mobilized to participate in the struggle against the Axis Powers. Having their masters' example in front of their eyes, they, too, saw themselves as the victims of aggressors who had come from outside and subjugated them without any right or reason. From Mao down, two generations of third-world ideologues and politicians proclaimed their right to use any means to resist imperialism and bring about national liberation— in other words, to wage war even though they did not own territories, have governments, or constitute states.

Thus, in the postwar world, modern states found their monopoly over war disputed by other organizations ranging from the Indochinese Vietcong to the Cypriot EOKA and from the Algerian FLN to the Lebanese Hizbollah. As this process took hold, they discovered—much to their consternation—that the most powerful weapons available to them were almost entirely useless. Already, the "tactical nuclear warfighters" of the late 1950s and early 1960s understood that the best, perhaps the only, way to cope with nuclear weapons is for the forces of both sides to come to close quarters with each other;[27] by so doing, they cannot be targeted by nuclear weapons for fear of causing massive casualties among friendly troops.

In other words, the real reason why nontrinitarian political entities can live and fight in the nuclear world is precisely because, unlike the state, they neither have nor require a distinct, large, continuous, impenetrable, territorial base. Looked upon in this way, these entities and the wars that they fight simply represent a sound tactician's response to nuclear weapons: If you cannot overcome your enemy by main force, seek a way to undermine it from beneath.

What is true of nuclear weapons is increasingly becoming true of conventional ones also. Fighting organizations that do not resemble modern armed forces, with their powerful, advanced firepower, do not stand a chance in the open, much less at sea or in the air. The logical response is to move armed conflict away from open spaces into complicated environments: either such as are natural—mountains, jungles, and swamps—or the even more complicated artificial ones presented by human populations—cities, villages, arteries of communication, and means of production.

As experience shows, the most important conventional weapons, such as fighter bombers, tanks, APCs (armored personnel carriers), artillery, and surface-to-surface missiles, do not function well in such environments. If unguided, they are too inaccurate, too indiscriminate, and too wasteful to inflict meaningful damage on an invisible enemy. If guided, their dependence on electronic sensors and computers usually means that targets appear in the form of blips on a screen; this makes them unable to distinguish friend from foe and both from innocent bystanders. Events since 1945 prove that nontrinitarian organizations—provided that the country is large enough and/or that asylum is available across the border—can carry on the armed struggle almost indefinitely. As they do so, they inflict casualties on the regular forces, usually breaking their political will and sometimes bringing them to the point of total disintegration.

Another advantage that modern nontrinitarian war-making organizations have over the regular forces, and one whose importance is becoming increasingly obvious, is the fact that they do not require heavy weapons and large quantities of mechanized transport. As a result, their logistical load—including various kinds of supply, maintenance, and administration—is cut by a factor of 90 percent or more. Of the commodities that constitute the remaining 10 percent, a great many can normally be found almost anywhere and taken away directly from the surrounding population by means of purchase, taxation, or requisitioning. Others are sufficiently simple to be manufactured on a clandestine or semiclandestine basis; such was the case in the border zone between Pakistan and Afghanistan, where primitive workshops turned out very large quantities of light arms and their ammunition. Any items, such as heavy weapons and their ammunition, that are not locally available are usually needed only on a surge basis and in relatively small quantities. They can be brought up under cover without requiring much in the way of heavy mechanized transport or extensive lines of communications of the kind that form the umbilical cords of modern conventional armed forces.

As the Americans discovered while dropping hundreds of thousands of tons of bombs on the Ho Chi Minh trail in Laos and Cambodia, a force that does not have lines of communications cannot be cut off from its bases. Living off the countryside implies that the usual distinctions between "front" and "rear" areas do not exist in the same form. Not being tied to fixed territorial bases that it must screen and protect, such a force cannot be outflanked, broken through, pushed back, or surrounded in any but the narrowest tactical sense. Like water that parts in front of a blow, in many ways it is beyond the reach of strategy as ordinarily understood—strategy, say, of the kind first formulated by Antoine Jomini in his *Traite de grande tactique*[28] and practiced by all great commanders from Napoleon Bonaparte at Ulm in 1805 all the way to Norman Schwarzkopf in the Persian Gulf in 1991.

Given the tremendous differences between trinitarian and nontrinitarian warfare, it is perhaps not surprising that the record of armed forces organized and trained for fighting the former in dealing with the latter has, with very few exceptions, been abysmal. For example, the Germans found themselves helpless against Tito's partisans during World War II. Since then, the British, the French, the Dutch, and the Portuguese each in turn tried to put down nontrinitarian warfare in their colonies and, with hardly any exception, ended up by throwing in the towel. Next, the Americans, seeking to take the place of the French, blundered their way into Vietnam; the resulting disaster is still haunting the national psyche to the point that, when future historians come to write the history of the U.S. decline as a world power, it is likely to warrant at least a footnote.

Neither was fate any kinder to the Israelis, albeit that they entered Lebanon with what was surely one of the best-equipped, best-motivated, and most-experienced armed forces of all time. Confronted by ill-organized and ill-armed militia—at the time, the heaviest PLO weapons consisted of a few World War II leftover tanks—the IDF only took one week to reach Beirut. However, in a nontrinitarian environment, reaching Beirut proved to be the beginning of the war rather than its end. Having floundered about for three years and taken 650 casualties in dead alone (four times as many as were killed in the highly successful 1956 Sinai Campaign), the Israelis were finally obliged to retreat without having achieved a single one of their objectives. As of 1992, the best that their Apache helicopter gunships and Merkava tanks were able to achieve against the various ill-organized militias active on their northern border was a draw.

The failure of Western armies to put down nontrinitarian movements has often been attributed to political constraints and humanitarian scruples that caused them to fight with one hand tied behind their backs. Whatever the truth of this explanation, it is not supposed to apply to the Soviets during their invasion of Afghanistan; yet they, too, fared no better when confronted by largely illiterate mujahideen. Unlike the Vietcong, who, though operating in a backward country, were led by the Communist Party and in this sense modern, the mujahideens' idea of politico-military organization was the tribe. They never even learned to cooperate with each other on a level above that of battalion.

And the forces of developed countries were not the only ones to fail. The Cubans in Angola were defeated by UNITA. The South Africans in Namibia finally gave way to FRELIMO. The Indians got their fingers burnt by the Sinhalese Tigers in Sri Lanka and are barely managing to hold on to Kashmir. The Vietnamese in Cambodia were driven out by the Khmer Rouge. The Pakistani Army is hardly able to cope with disorder in the Sindh, and the government of Mozambique has been forced to come to terms with the rebels. These cases represent only a few of the third-world countries that tried their hand at this game and, having got their fingers burnt, often found themselves in a worse situation than when they started.

III

As the supreme war-making instruments of all time, nuclear weapons and their delivery vehicles are the product of modern natural science. The origins of science in intellectual, social, and economic developments have often been told;[29] however, the connection between science and the modern state has been all but overlooked by historians who, writing in the nineteenth and twentieth centuries, took the latter for granted.

One connection between science and the state is suggested by the fact that, as Aristotle said, a certain modicum of protection is necessary if intellectual activity is to flourish. One of the principal differences between modern science and its predecessors, and one that is in large part responsible for its success, is its character as a large-scale, long-term, collective enterprise relying on the cooperation of many individuals. Like any such enterprise, but perhaps to a greater degree, it presumes both protection and long-term stability; among all the forms of political organization that have existed on this planet since ancient times, so far the state has been the only one capable of providing that stability and that protection. It was not by accident that the scientific method and the modern state originated at the same time and in the same place, that is, seventeenth-century Western Europe. From there it was that, proceeding pari passu, they spread to Eastern Europe, the more developed European colonies, and eventually all over the world.

An even deeper link between science and the modern, impersonal state is suggested by the notion of law as opposed to arbitrary decisions on the part of people or gods. A good case in point is the U.S. Constitution, which the Founding Fathers intended as "a machine that would go of itself";[30] science and the state are rooted in the assumption that nature, on the one hand, and political life, on the other, are (or should be) based on verifiable, impartial, and permanently operating laws rather than on vague custom or the whims of individuals.

The modern idea—which is far from self-evident—that nature and political life are both governed by "law" may also explain why the same people were sometimes active in both fields. For example, Francis Bacon, who, in his own words, "rang the bell" for modern science, was also one of the most important English lawyers of his generation and rose to become Lord Chancellor. William Harvey, who discovered the circulation of blood, explicitly compared the operation of the human body to that of a state and its government. Baruch Spinoza and Thomas Hobbes both sought to root their political theories in science, the one in geometry and the other in physics. And in his old age, Isaac Newton was put in charge of creating a stable state currency for England.

By way of final proof, to this day it is only where states are strong, well-developed, and capable of protecting their citizens—both externally and internally—that science exists and where, indeed, it is even conceivable. Places where states are weak, such as much of Asia, Africa, and Latin America, never had much to show by the way of science and technology, either; recently, this has also begun to apply to the ex-Soviet bloc where, in the absence of state funding, science appears to be disintegrating.[31] Without peace, as Thomas Hobbes put it, "there is no place for industry . . . no culture of the earth . . . nor use of commodities that may be imported by sea; . . . no account of time, no art, no letters, no society; . . . and the life of man [is] solitary, poor, nasty, brutish, and short."[32]

One of the state's primary characteristics, in which it differs from some previous political entities and which in large part is responsible for its stability, is its territorial nature and the fact that it has clearly defined borders separating it from other states. However, the factor that makes the state powerful in one way makes it vulnerable in another. By definition, any state whose population occupies an extensive and continuous territory can also be subjected to a nuclear holocaust—and indeed the more pronounced these characteristics, the more true this becomes. Looking back, it is almost certainly no accident that the only two nuclear weapons used up to the present were dropped on an enemy 1,500 miles from the nearest friendly base and several thousands of miles away from the U.S. homeland. Thus, the weapon that was the supreme product of the state in its capacity as a war-making organization at the same time went a very long way to putting an end to the state's ability to wage war.

I have suggested in this chapter that nuclear weapons are progressively making the states that have them unable to fight each other in earnest. This is true even if the number of weapons is quite small; even where delivery vehicles and C³I capabilities are relatively primitive; and even, as is the case both in the Middle East and in southern Asia, where proliferation is covert rather than overt. In consequence, those states are finding themselves deprived of their essential raison d'etre. In many places all over the third world, states have never succeeded in striking roots but, faced by much more persistent tribal societies, started falling apart almost as soon as they came into being. In other areas, including not least the democratic West, a growing number of people are coming to see them as "Cold Monsters" [Friedrich Nietzsche] whose sole reason for existence is to rob their citizens and regulate them to death.

Simultaneously, since World War II, the state's monopoly over legal violence—read, war—has been increasingly contested by entities that are not states. Not having a territorial basis, such organizations cannot be threatened with nuclear weapons; not being constructed on trinitarian lines with a clear differentiation between government, army, and people, they cannot be targeted by the majority of heavy conventional weapons. As of the end of the second millennium A.D., these entities are by far the most important, and effective, war-making organizations still left in our world. Either the state will succeed in putting an end to them or, without a shadow of doubt, they will put an end to it.

Notes

1. Probably the best single collection of these visions is presented in S. M. Lynn-Jones, ed., *The Cold War and After* (Cambridge, Mass.: MIT Press, 1990), with articles by J. L. Gaddis, J. Mueller, R. Jervis, C. Kaysen, J. Snyder, J. J. Mearsheimer, and S. Van Evera.

2. See most recently D. M. Snow, "High Technology and National Security: a Preliminary Assessment," *Armed Forces and Society* 17, no. 2 (1991): 243–258.

3. See Martin van Creveld, *Technology and War from 2000 B.C. to the Present* (New York: Free Press, 1989), chapter 15, for a discussion of the different nature of military-technological progress before and after 1815.

4. See William H. McNeill, *The Pursuit of Power: Technology, Armed Force and Society* (London: Weidenfeld & Nicolson, 1982).

5. The most famous argument that military competition results in economic bankruptcy was made by Paul M. Kennedy, *The Rise and Fall of the Great Powers: Economic Change and Military Conflict from 1500 to 2000* (New York: Vintage Books, 1987).

6. See McGeorge Bundy, *Danger and Survival: Choices About the Bomb in the First Fifty Years* (New York: Random House, 1988).

7. J. J. Muccio (U.S. Ambassador to South Korea), "Memorandum of Conversation at the Pentagon, May 10, 1950," *Foreign Relations of the United States* 7 (1950): 78–79.

8. See above all J. Mueller, *Retreat from Doomsday: The Obsolescence of Major War* (New York: Basic Books, 1989), and P. Fussel, *The Great War and Modern Memory* (New York: Oxford University Press, 1975).

9. See L. Freedman, *The Evolution of Nuclear Strategy* (New York: St. Martin's Press, 1981) for the most detailed account.

10. Henry Kissinger, *Nuclear Weapons and Foreign Policy* (New York: Harper and Row, 1957), 227–228.

11. On these weapons and the doctrines that were constructed around them, see *Report of Secretary of Defense James Schlesinger to the Congress on the FY 1975 Defense Budget* (Washington, D.C.: Government Printing Office, 1974); L. Etheridge Davis, *Limited Nuclear Options: Deterrence and the New American Doctrine,* Adelphi Paper no. 121 (London: IISS, 1976); and C. Gray, "Warfighting for Deterrence," *Journal of Strategic Studies* 7 (March 1984): 5–28.

12. For example, see Bernard Brodie, *The Absolute Weapon* (New York: Columbia University Press, 1946), 22–69.

13. In 1991, the Gulf War demonstrated how not even the most powerful and advanced air forces and air defenses ever assembled were able to locate all Iraqi launchers, let alone to prevent some Iraqi missiles from being fired and reaching their targets; yet the launchers were so primitive that they sometimes disintegrated while en route. See Thomas Postol, "Lessons of the Gulf War Experience with Patriot," *International Security* 16, no. 3 (1991): 119–171, for a thorough analysis of Patriot performance. An article in the *Washington Post* (June 25, 1992) even claimed that the coalition failed to destroy any of Saddam Hussein's mobile launchers.

14. In 1961, Mao Zedong told visiting French author Andre Malraux that "all I need are six bombs. Then nobody will dare touch me." Quoted in H. Gelber, *Nuclear Weapons and Chinese Policy,* Adelphi Paper no. 99 (London: IISS, 1973), 19.

15. See K. Subramanyam, *India and the Nuclear Challenge* (New Delhi: Lance International, 1986), 222.

16. The best evidence for this is the fact that the Israeli ambassador in Washington, Yitzhak Rabin, noted that the United States suddenly dropped its pressure on Israel not to proliferate; the Americans, it seemed, had concluded that the horse had already escaped the barn. See Yitzhak Rabin, *Pinkas Sherut [Memoirs]*, vol. I (Tel Aviv: Ma'ariv, 1978), 257–258.

17. For an account of the Almelo episode, see K. Subramanyam, *Nuclear Myths and Realities: India's Dilemma* (New Delhi: ABC Publishing House, 1981), appendix 1. For Pakistan's bomb program in general, see A. Kashok, *Pakistan's Nuclear Development* (London: Croom Helm, 1987), and ABC Publishing House, *Pakistan's Bomb: A Documentary Study* (New Delhi: ABC Publishing House, 1986).

18. For the dangers of nuclear proliferation, see, for example, L.A. Dunn, "The NPT and Future Global Security," in D. Dewitt, ed., *Nuclear Proliferation and Global Security* (New York: St. Martin's Press, 1987), 13–24; for the opposite opinion, see Kenneth N. Waltz, *The Spread of Nuclear Weapons: More May Be Better,* Adelphi Paper no. 171 (London: IISS, 1981).

19. As it happens, the first full-length book on Israel's nuclear arsenal was written in English by an Arab living in London: F. Jabber, *Israel and Nuclear Weapons: Present Options and Future Strategies* (London: Chatto & Windus, 1971). The volume was immediately translated into Arabic.

20. On this entire question, see Martin van Creveld, *Nuclear Proliferation and the Future of Conflict* (New York: Free Press, 1993).

21. See Martin van Creveld, *The Transformation of War* (New York: Free Press, 1991), chapter 6, for a more extended discussion of this argument.

22. For example, Immanuel Kant, *Perpetual Peace* (1796; reprint, New York: Garland, 1972), and Norman Angell, *The Great Illusion* (London: Heinemman, 1913).

23. See R. G. Wirsing, "The Siachen Glacier Dispute: Part I," *Strategic Studies* 10, no. 1 (1987): 49–66; "Part II," *Strategic Studies* 11, no.3 (1988): 75–94; and "Part III," *Strategic Studies* 12, no. 1 (1988): 38–54.

24. C. von Clausewitz, *On War,* ed. Michael Howard and Peter Paret (Princeton: Princeton University Press, 1976), 89.

25. Ibid., 586ff.

26. See N. Rubinstein, "Notes on the Word *Stato* in Florence before Machiavelli," in R.G. Rowe and Wallace K. Ferguson, eds., *Florilegium Historiale: Essays Presented to Wallace K. Ferguson* (Toronto: University of Toronto Press, 1971), 313–326.

27. See, for example, O. Heilbrunn, *Conventional Warfare in the Nuclear Age* (London: Allen & Unwin, 1965).

28. Originally published Paris, 1805.

29. The best short account is probably H. Butterwick, *The Origins of Modern Science* (New York: Free Press, 1975).

30. M.G. Kammen, *A Machine That Would Go of Itself: The Constitution in American Culture* (New York: Vintage Press, 1986), 17–19. The quotation itself is attributed to James Russel Lowell, 1988.

31. *Christian Science Monitor,* March 4, 1992, p. 1.

32. Thomas Hobbes, *Leviathan* (Oxford: Blackwell, 1946), 82–84.

About the Book
and Editors

Now that the initial patriotic euphoria over the spectacular "Desert Storm" campaign has settled down, people are looking for more sophisticated accounts of the war and what it can teach us for the future. The editors of this volume have assembled the world's foremost military authorities to reexamine the nature of warfare in the wake of the Persian Gulf War.

Not just a book for military specialists, *Turning Point* offers a broad perspective on the nature of warfare and its role in international politics. The chapters are all written in an engaging, jargon-free style by authors whose individual works have found wide general appeal. Furthermore, the authors offer significant elaborations upon their previous writings. For example, noted strategist Edward Luttwak offers a piece on his argument for an era of "geoeconomics," Joseph Nye expands on his notion of "soft power," Martin van Creveld refines the argument of his recent book *The Transformation of War,* and Thomas Schelling develops his analysis of nuclear weapons' strategic impact.

The book features a gripping account of the ground war from John Keegan, the air war from Eliot Cohen, and the "end game" from General John Cushman (including some criticism of Norman Schwartzkopf's planning). Covering a broad range of political-military subjects, from the development of U.S. military doctrine to the nature of combat in the Gulf and the future of security challenges in Europe and the Far East, these preeminent authors provide insightful analysis that makes *Turning Point* a superb source for everyone interested in U.S. foreign policy and strategy.

L. Benjamin Ederington was an analyst in the Political-Military Studies program at the Center for Strategic and International Studies (CSIS), Washington, D.C. **Michael J. Mazarr** is legislative assistant for foreign affairs and chief writer in the office of Dave McCurdy (D-OK). He is coauthor (with Don M. Snider and James A. Blackwell, Jr.) of several books, including *Desert Storm: The Gulf War and What We Learned* (Westview, 1993).

Index